THE WRONGFUL DISMISSAL HANDBOOK

THIRD EDITION

Ellen E. Mole
Marion J. Stendon

LexisNexis®
Butterworths

The Wrongful Dismissal Handbook, Third Edition
© LexisNexis Canada Inc. 2004
November 2004

All rights reserved. No part of this publication may be reproduced, stored in any material form (including photocopying or storing it in any medium by electronic means and whether or not transiently or incidentally to some other use of this publication) without the written permission of the copyright holder except in accordance with the provisions of the Copyright Act. Applications for the copyright holder's written permission to reproduce any part of this publication should be addressed to the publisher.

Warning: The doing of an unauthorized act in relation to a copyrighted work may result in both a civil claim for damages and criminal prosecution.

Members of the LexisNexis Group worldwide

Canada	LexisNexis Canada Inc, 123 Commerce Valley Drive East, Suite 700, MARKHAM, Ontario
Argentina	Abeledo Perrot, Jurisprudencia Argentina and Depalma, BUENOS AIRES
Australia	Butterworths, a Division of Reed International Books Australia Pty Ltd, CHATSWOOD, New South Wales
Austria	ARD Betriebsdienst and Verlag Orac, VIENNA
Chile	Publitecsa and Conosur Ltda, SANTIAGO DE CHILE
Czech Republic	Orac sro, PRAGUE
France	Éditions du Juris-Classeur SA, PARIS
Hong Kong	Butterworths Asia (Hong Kong), HONG KONG
Hungary	Hvg Orac, BUDAPEST
India	Butterworths India, NEW DELHI
Ireland	Butterworths (Ireland) Ltd, DUBLIN
Italy	Giuffré, MILAN
Malaysia	Malayan Law Journal Sdn Bhd, KUALA LUMPUR
New Zealand	Butterworths of New Zealand, WELLINGTON
Poland	Wydawnictwa Prawnicze PWN, WARSAW
Singapore	Butterworths Asia, SINGAPORE
South Africa	Butterworth Publishers (Pty) Ltd, DURBAN
Switzerland	Stämpfli Verlag AG, BERNE
United Kingdom	Butterworths Tolley, a Division of Reed Elsevier (UK), LONDON, WC2A
USA	LexisNexis, DAYTON, Ohio

Library and Archives Canada Cataloguing in Publication

Mole, Ellen E.
    The wrongful dismissal handbook/Ellen E. Mole, Marion J. Stendon. — 3rd ed.

Includes index.
ISBN 0-433-44006-6

    1. Employees—Dismissal of—Law and legislation—Canada. I. Stendon, Marion J. II. Title.

KE3262.M65 2004   344.7101'2596   C2004-905665-4
KF3471.M65 2004

Printed and bound in Canada.

ABOUT THE AUTHORS

Ellen E. Mole, B.A., LL.B.

Ellen Mole is a legal writer, arbitrator and mediator, specializing in employment and labour law. She is a former Vice Chair of the Ontario Public Service Labour Relations Tribunal, and a former Vice Chair of the Workers Compensation Appeals Tribunal. Ms. Mole has written extensively on various topics in employment and labour law for both legal practitioners and human resource professionals. Some of her publications are *Wrongful Dismissal Practice Manual* and *Employment Contracts: An Employer's Guide*, published by LexisNexis Canada Inc.

Marion J. Stendon, B.Comm., LL.B.

Marion Stendon is an arbitrator and mediator, and has been a consultant to a number of owner-operated businesses and public companies active in the Canadian and American stock exchanges. Ms. Stendon has also been a long-time contributing editor for the *Wrongful Dismissal Practice Manual*, published by LexisNexis Canada Inc.

PREFACE

When the first edition of this book was published back in 1990, the *Wrongful Dismissal Practice Manual*, on which it was loosely based, had grown to enormous proportions due to an explosion in case law during the 1980s. Our goal at that time was to present the basics of wrongful dismissal law in a streamlined version, without the distraction of case references and footnotes to obscure the principles. Our belief was that this outline of the law would be useful for a number of readers, including lawyers seeking a quick reference before conducting further research, and non-legal professionals and business people wishing for an introduction to wrongful dismissal principles.

Not much about our goals, or the reason for *The Wrongful Dismissal Handbook*, has changed since then. What has changed with this third edition, however, is our approach to streamlining. Rather than a text-heavy discussion of the law, we have tried to state principles as plainly as possible, and follow them up with real-life examples taken from the voluminous case law now available. We have eliminated some legalistic areas that appear in *The Wrongful Dismissal Practice Manual*, in order to focus on the topics that are most useful and practical in everyday business and legal situations. And, we have formatted the information in a style that facilitates finding the relevant information as swiftly as possible. The result, we feel, is our most user-friendly, streamlined, quick-reference publication yet. We hope you will agree.

Readers wishing for more depth, and for the case law citations to go with the text, are referred to the *Wrongful Dismissal Practice Manual*, which contains all the information in *The Wrongful Dismissal Handbook*, plus much more. Those wishing for further information on notice periods should also see the *Wrongful Dismissal Notice Searcher*, an interactive electronic product to help determine the appropriate range of notice in a particular case, based on reported case law in similar scenarios.

Although a third edition in name, this book felt a lot like a brand-new work, and certainly required the same number of hours to produce. We would like to thank our families, Neil and Anne McGillivray, and the Tamazand crew, for their patience and support during the long writing process. We would also like to thank our numerous contacts at LexisNexis Canada for their faith in us and in this project, as well as their technical assistance in helping to make it a reality.

Ellen E. Mole
Marion J. Stendon
August, 2004

TABLE OF CONTENTS

Page

About the Authors iii
Preface v

PART A: WRONGFUL DISMISSAL FUNDAMENTALS

Chapter A-1: General Principles of Wrongful Dismissal Law 1

A-1.1   The Common Law Principle 1
A-1.2   The Quebec Principle 2
A-1.3   Exclusions from the General Principle 3
A-1.4   Illegal Contracts 3

Chapter A-2: Employment Status and Types of Employment Contract 5

A-2.1   Employment Status and Types of Employment Contract 5
A-2.2   At-Will or At-Pleasure Employment 6
A-2.3   Indefinite Employment 7
A-2.4   Definite-Term Employment 8
A-2.5   Examples of Definite-Term Employment 10
A-2.6   Termination of Definite-Term Contracts 11
A-2.7   Series of Seasonal or Other Definite-Term Contracts 12

Chapter A-3: Probationary Employment 15

A-3.1   Types of Probationary Employment 15
A-3.2   Existence of Probationary Period 15
A-3.3   Termination of Probationary Employees 18
A-3.4   Disciplinary Probation 20

Chapter A-4: Dismissal Rights of Specific Types of Workers 21

A-4.1   Crown, Public and Municipal Employees 21
A-4.2   Employees Governed by Statute 23
A-4.3   Shareholders, Directors and Partners 25
A-4.4   Managers 25
A-4.5   Salespersons and Sales Agents 27
A-4.6   Casual, Temporary, Assignment, Seasonal and Part-Time Workers 28
A-4.7   Agents, Independent Contractors and Other Non-Employees 30
A-4.8   Other Workers 31

Chapter A-5: Identifying the Employer 33

A-5.1   Purpose of Determining the Employer 33

A-5.2	Sale or Transfer of Business	33
A-5.3	Related Entities	34
A-5.4	Liability of Corporate Directors and Shareholders	36
A-5.5	Unincorporated Associations and Partnerships	37
A-5.6	Receivers and Trustees	37
A-5.7	Other Individuals	38

PART B: TERMINATION OF EMPLOYMENT

Chapter B-1: Termination of Employment: General Principles 41

B-1.1	General Principles	41
B-1.2	Express Termination under By-Law, Contract or Statute	42
B-1.3	Express Termination at Common Law	42
B-1.4	Effective Date of Termination Notice	46
B-1.5	Layoffs, Suspensions and Similar Actions	48

Chapter B-2: Change of Employer 51

B-2.1	Common Law vs. Statute	51
B-2.2	General Principles	52
B-2.3	Novation or Assignment of Contract	52
B-2.4	Effect on Service Length	53
B-2.5	Sale of a Business	54
B-2.6	Transfer to a Related Company	55
B-2.7	Winding up, Receivership, Bankruptcy, Financial Restructuring	56

Chapter B-3: Frustration of the Employment Contract 59

B-3.1	General Principles	59
B-3.2	Self-induced Frustration	60
B-3.3	Illness and Disability	60
B-3.4	Labour Disputes	62

Chapter B-4: Resignation 63

B-4.1	Resignation: General Principles	63
B-4.2	Threats to Resign and Words Amounting to Resignation	64
B-4.3	Conduct Amounting to Resignation	66
B-4.4	Involuntary Resignation	68
B-4.5	Resignation Following Constructive Dismissal	69
B-4.6	Lack of Requisite Mental Capacity	70
B-4.7	Consequences of Resignation	70

Chapter B-5: Repudiation by Employee 73

B-5.1	General Principles	73
B-5.2	Work Refusals	74
B-5.3	Absence from Work	75
B-5.4	Inability to Attend Work	75

B-5.5 Legal Dispute with Employer 76

PART C: CONSTRUCTIVE DISMISSAL

Chapter C-1: Constructive Dismissal: General Principles 79

C-1.1 Constructive Dismissal: General Principles............................. 79
C-1.2 Unilateral, Fundamental Change.. 80
C-1.3 Establishing Constructive Dismissal.. 82
C-1.4 Exceptions.. 84
C-1.5 Duty to Mitigate in Constructive Dismissal Situations............. 85
C-1.6 Condonation 85

Chapter C-2: Change in Remuneration... 89

C-2.1 Change in Pay or Manner of Payment 89
      C-2.1.1 Pay 89
      C-2.1.2 Overtime 91
      C-2.1.3 Commissions 91
      C-2.1.4 Layoffs... 92
      C-2.1.5 Method of Payment 92
C-2.2 Change in Bonus or Other Profit Sharing 92
C-2.3 Change in Benefits... 93
C-2.4 Change in Method of Computing Remuneration 94

Chapter C-3: Change in Job Content, Job Status or Working Conditions 97

C-3.1 General Principles.. 97
C-3.2 Change in Job Duties 98
C-3.3 Demotion.. 100
C-3.4 Reassignment Without Demotion 102
C-3.5 Downward Change in Status.. 103
C-3.6 Change in Job Title or Reporting Level 104
C-3.7 Change in Employment Status 105
C-3.8 Change in Working Conditions.. 106

Chapter C-4: Other Constructive Dismissal Situations 109

C-4.1 Contractual Changes 109
C-4.2 Humiliating Treatment or Harassment................................... 110
C-4.3 Unfair Dealings by Employer 111
C-4.4 Discipline, Suspensions, Layoffs... 113
      C-4.4.1 Discipline and Suspensions 113
      C-4.4.2 Layoffs... 113
C-4.5 Geographical Transfers.. 114
C-4.6 Retirement.. 116
C-4.7 Compulsory Resignation.. 117
C-4.8 Pay in Lieu of Notice 118

PART D: DISMISSAL FOR JUST CAUSE

Chapter D-1: Just Cause: General Principles 119

- D-1.1 Summary Dismissal 119
- D-1.2 Single Instance of Misconduct 121
- D-1.3 Repeated Minor Misconduct 122
- D-1.4 Significance of Written Rules 122
- D-1.5 Timing of Misconduct 123
- D-1.6 Onus of Proof and Pleadings 123

Chapter D-2: Duty to Warn and Duty of Fairness 125

- D-2.1 Duty to Warn 125
- D-2.2 Content of Warning 126
- D-2.3 Duty to Warn in Good Faith 128
- D-2.4 Duty of Fairness 128
- D-2.5 Procedural Fairness and Natural Justice 129

Chapter D-3: Condonation of Misconduct 113

- D-3.1 General Principles 133
- D-3.2 Effect of Warnings 135
- D-3.3 Behaviour Constituting Condonation 136
- D-3.4 Dismissal with Notice, Pay or a Non-Cause Explanation 137
- D-3.5 Revival of Past Misconduct 138

Chapter D-4: Unacceptable Performance 139

- D-4.1 General Principles 139
- D-4.2 Performance Standards 140
- D-4.3 Single Incident 141
- D-4.4 Chronic Performance Problems 142
- D-4.5 Probationary Periods and Assistance Programs 143
- D-4.6 Written Contract 143

Chapter D-5: Dishonesty 145

- D-5.1 General Principles 145
- D-5.2 Dishonesty: Prejudicial Conduct 147
- D-5.3 Dishonesty: Revelation of Character 148
- D-5.4 Financial Improprieties 150
- D-5.5 Lies and Failure to Tell the Truth 151
- D-5.6 Professional Qualifications and Résumé Disclosure 152

Chapter D-6: Conflicts of Interest and Abuse of Authority 155

- D-6.1 Conflicts of Interest: General Principles 155
- D-6.2 Fiduciary Duties and Corporate Opportunities 156
- D-6.3 Sales Agents 157
- D-6.4 Competing with the Employer 157
- D-6.5 Moonlighting and Outside Business Interests 158

D-6.6	Favouring Personal Interests	159
D-6.7	Dealings with Family Members or Friends	161
D-6.8	Dealings with Employer's Customers or Suppliers	162
D-6.9	Dealings with Other Employees or Shareholders	163
D-6.10	Improper Use, Disclosure or Non-Disclosure of Information	164
D-6.11	Abuse of Authority	165

Chapter D-7: Disobedience and Disloyalty 167

D-7.1	Disobedience Generally	167
D-7.2	Neglect of Duty or Refusal to Perform Duties	170
D-7.3	Breach of Rules	171
D-7.4	Insolence and Insubordination	173
	D-7.4.1 General Principles	173
	D-7.4.2 Examples	175
D-7.5	Disloyalty	177

Chapter D-8: Workplace Conflicts and Harassment 179

D-8.1	Personality and Workplace Conflicts: General Principles	179
D-8.2	Workplace Conflicts: Managerial Standards	181
D-8.3	Sexual and Other Harassment	182
D-8.4	Age and Other Discrimination	184
D-8.5	Personal Appearance and Habits	185
D-8.6	Customer Relations	185

Chapter D-9: Attendance and Substance Abuse 189

D-9.1	Absence From Work Generally	189
D-9.2	Absence Due to Illness	191
	D-9.2.1 General Principles	191
	D-9.2.2 Mental Illness	193
	D-9.2.3 Failure to Return to Work; Malingering	193
D-9.3	Vacations	194
D-9.4	Lateness	195
D-9.5	Substance Abuse	197

Chapter D-10: Off-the-Job Conduct and Other Just Cause Situations 199

D-10.1	General Principles	199
D-10.2	Sexual Conduct	200
D-10.3	Criminal Conduct	201
D-10.4	Redundancy, Economic Problems, Company Reorganization, Strikes	202
D-10.5	Driving of Company Vehicle; Loss of Driver's Licence	203

PART E: OTHER DEFENCES TO A WRONGFUL DISMISSAL ACTION

Chapter E-1: Collective Agreement, Arbitration or Appeal Procedures 205

E-1.1	Existence of Collective Agreement..	205
E-1.2	Existence of Arbitration or Appeal Procedure	207
	E-1.2.1 General Principles...	207
	E-1.2.2 Statutory Procedure	208
	E-1.2.3 Contractual Procedure	209

Chapter E-2: Issue Estoppel: Previous or Concurrent Actions 211

E-2.1	Issue Estoppel Generally...	211
E-2.2	Employment Standards Rulings..	212
E-2.3	Employment Insurance (EI) Rulings...	214
E-2.4	Human Rights Complaints	214
E-2.5	Other Adjudications	215
E-2.6	Previous Civil Action..	216

Chapter E-3: Settlements and Delays 217

E-3.1	Settlements..	217
E-3.2	Accord and Satisfaction	218
E-3.3	Releases...	220
E-3.4	Delay and Limitation Periods	222

Chapter E-4: Written Employment Contracts 223

E-4.1	Written Contracts: General Principles	223
E-4.2	Parol Evidence Rule..	224
E-4.3	Matters of Form	225
E-4.4	Failure to Enter into Written Contract	226

Chapter E-5: Standard Form Contracts, Employers' Policies and Other Documents 229

E-5.1	Standard Form Contracts	229
E-5.2	Employers' Policies	229
E-5.3	Application Forms	233
E-5.4	Offers of Employment	234
E-5.5	Other Documents	235

Chapter E-6: Express Termination Provisions 239

E-6.1	Expiry and Extension of Fixed-Term Contracts	239
E-6.2	Effect of Promotions or Lapse of Time....................................	240
E-6.3	Severance Clauses vs. Termination Clauses	241
E-6.4	Termination Agreements...	242

PART F: NOTICE

Chapter F-1: Reasonable Notice: General Principles 245

F-1.1 The Parties' Obligations 245
F-1.2 Purpose of Notice Period 246
F-1.3 Time For Assessing Reasonable Notice 246
F-1.4 Factors Affecting Reasonable Notice 247
F-1.5 Effect of Parties' Expectations 248
F-1.6 Minimums, Maximums and Formulas 251
F-1.7 Who Decides the Notice Period: Employer, Judge or Appeal Court? 252

Chapter F-2: Reasonable Notice Factors: Character of the Employment 255

F-2.1 Significance of Job Character 255
F-2.2 Job Status 256
F-2.3 Degree of Specialization 258
F-2.4 Nature of Job 258
F-2.5 Nature of Industry and Employer 259
F-2.6 Where Job Precarious 260
F-2.7 Time of Assessing Job Status 261

Chapter F-3: Reasonable Notice Factors: Age and Service Length 263

F-3.1 Age 263
F-3.2 Service Length 265
F-3.3 Calculating Service Length 267
    F-3.3.1 Interruption in Service 267
    F-3.3.2 Change of Employment Status 268
    F-3.3.3 Change in Employer 269
F-3.4 Enticement by Employer 270

Chapter F-4: Reasonable Notice Factors: Availability of a New Job 273

F-4.1 Training, Qualifications and Experience 273
F-4.2 Job Characteristics 274
F-4.3 Personal Characteristics 275
F-4.4 Geographic Location 278
F-4.5 Economic Climate 278
F-4.6 Employer's Financial Problems 279
F-4.7 Proving Job Availability 280

Chapter F-5: Effect of Parties' Conduct on Reasonable Notice 283

F-5.1 Assurance of Job Security 283
F-5.2 Manner of Dismissal 284
F-5.3 Employer's Bad Faith 286

xiv TABLE OF CONTENTS

F-5.4 Employee's Near Cause 289
F-5.5 Employee's Merits 289

PART G: DAMAGES

Chapter G-1: Damages: General Principles 291

G-1.1 General Principles 291
G-1.2 Damages for Benefits 293
G-1.3 Time From Which Damages Run 294
G-1.4 Time at Which Damages End 295
G-1.5 Early Termination of Fixed-Term Contracts 296
G-1.6 Contractual Notice Provisions 298

Chapter G-2: Salary, Wages and Allowances 299

G-2.1 General Principles 299
G-2.2 Salary and Wages 300
G-2.3 Rate of Pay 300
G-2.4 Raises During Notice Period 301
G-2.5 Overtime Pay 303
G-2.6 Other Remuneration 304

Chapter G-3: Commission and Bonuses 307

G-3.1 Contractual Entitlement to Commissions 307
G-3.2 Evidence Commissions Would Have Been Earned 309
G-3.3 Calculating Damages for Commissions 310
G-3.4 Deductions from Commission Damages 311
G-3.5 Bonuses Generally 312
G-3.6 Bonus Entitlement 314
G-3.7 Calculating Damages for Bonuses 316

Chapter G-4: Profit Sharing and Stock Options 319

G-4.1 Profit-Sharing Plans 319
G-4.2 Stock Options and Stock Purchase Plans 320

Chapter G-5: Insured Benefits, Sick Leave and Disability Benefits 325

G-5.1 Damages for Insured Benefits Generally 325
G-5.2 Amount of Damages 326
G-5.3 Medical and Dental Insurance 327
G-5.4 Life Insurance 328
G-5.5 Sick Leave 329
G-5.6 Disability Benefits 330

Chapter G-6: Employment Insurance and Pension Benefits 333

G-6.1 Employment Insurance 333
G-6.2 Canada Pension Plan 334

G-6.3	Registered Retirement Savings Plans (RRSPs)	334
G-6.4	Private Pension Plans	335
	G-6.4.1 Entitlement to Damages	335
	G-6.4.2 Calculation of Damages	337
	G-6.4.3 Effect of Retirement	338
	G-6.4.4 Other Pension Issues	339

Chapter G-7: Automobile Benefits, Vacations, Statutory Holiday Pay and Other Benefits 341

G-7.1	Car Allowance	341
G-7.2	Company Vehicles	342
G-7.3	Other Automobile Benefits	344
G-7.4	Vacations	344
G-7.5	Statutory Holiday Pay	346
G-7.6	Living Allowances and Housing Benefits	347
G-7.7	Professional and Membership Fees and Club Dues	349
G-7.8	Loans and Discounts	349
G-7.9	Other Benefits	350

Chapter G-8: Job Search Expenses, Moving Expenses and Costs of Mitigation 353

G-8.1	Costs of the New Job Search	353
G-8.2	Moving Expenses	355
G-8.3	Mitigation Expenses	358

Chapter G-9: Aggravated and Punitive Damages 361

G-9.1	General Principles	361
G-9.2	Mental Distress Damages	363
G-9.3	Damages for Loss of Reputation or Opportunity	366
G-9.4	Punitive Damages	367

Chapter G-10: Other Damages and Remedies 371

G-10.1	Other Damages and Remedies Generally	371
G-10.2	Losses in Reliance on Employment	371
G-10.3	Loss of Seniority	372
G-10.4	Lost Opportunities	373
G-10.5	Post-dismissal Financial Decisions	373
G-10.6	Income Tax Consequences	373
G-10.7	Cost of Professional Advice	374
G-10.8	Compensation for Proprietary Information	375
G-10.9	Damages for Spouses	375
G-10.10	Reinstatement	376
G-10.11	Other Specific Performance	377

Chapter G-11: Deductions From the Damage Award 381

| G-11.1 | Deductions from Damages Generally | 381 |

xvi   TABLE OF CONTENTS

G-11.2   Notice, Severance Pay and Termination Pay 381
G-11.3   Benefits 383
G-11.4   Future Contingencies 385
G-11.5   Other Deductions 387

PART H: MITIGATION OF DAMAGES

Chapter H-1: Mitigation of Damages 389

H-1.1   The Duty to Mitigate 389
H-1.2   Fixed-Term Contracts and Contractual Notice Periods 391
H-1.3   Effect of Failure to Mitigate 392

Chapter H-2: Reasonable Mitigation Efforts 395

H-2.1   Standard of Reasonableness 395
H-2.2   Timing of Job Search Efforts 396
H-2.3   Quality of Job Search Efforts 398
H-2.4   Effect of Refusing Assistance 400

Chapter H-3: Career Changes and Relocating 401

H-3.1   Similar or Dissimilar Job 401
H-3.2   Retraining 403
H-3.3   Relocating 404
H-3.4   Starting a Business 406

Chapter H-4: Rejecting an Offer and Other Failures to Mitigate ... 409

H-4.1   Offer from New Employer 409
H-4.2   Offer from Dismissing Employer 411
H-4.3   Offer of Working Notice 413
H-4.4   Other Offers 414
H-4.5   Other Failures to Mitigate 415

Chapter H-5: Deduction of Earnings in Mitigation 417

H-5.1   Mitigation Earnings Generally 417
H-5.2   Higher-Paying New Job 420
H-5.3   Different Type of Job 421
H-5.4   Employee's Own Business 421
H-5.5   Business Expenses 423
H-5.6   Mitigation Expenses 424

Appendices

Appendix 1: Statutory Termination Notice Provisions 427
Appendix 2: Related Actions that are Commonly Joined with
       Wrongful Dismissal Actions 431
Appendix 3: Precedents 437
Appendix 4: Reasonable Notice Charts 443

Index 501

Chapter A-1

GENERAL PRINCIPLES OF WRONGFUL DISMISSAL LAW

TABLE OF CONTENTS

A-1.1 The Common Law Principle
A-1.2 The Quebec Principle
A-1.3 Exclusions from the General Principle
A-1.4 Illegal Contracts

A-1.1 THE COMMON LAW PRINCIPLE

Creation of common law — Wrongful dismissal law, in all of Canada except Quebec, is largely a creation of the judge-made common law that developed in relation to masters and servants. Nowadays, the terms are "employer" and "employee", but the principles remain the same.

Matter of contract — The relationship between those rendering service and those receiving it is regarded as a matter of contract, whether written or not. A written contract is not usually required, unless the parties have agreed to a fixed-term hiring for more than one year.

Express vs. implied terms — An express contractual term is one that is actually written down or that is clearly discussed and agreed to between the parties. An implied term is one that was not directly discussed, but on which it can be assumed the parties would have agreed if it had been raised directly. Most contracts, whether written or not, contain both express and implied terms.

Implied terms — Where there is no express term to the contrary, certain terms are implied into an employment contract by the common law. Specifically, the law implies a right to be dismissed only upon being given reasonable notice, unless just cause exists for immediate dismissal.

Essential components of law — The essential components of wrongful dismissal law are:

- It applies automatically to employees, and may also apply to those in other employment-like relationships, such as sales agents or independent contractors.

- It does not apply to employees whose rights are otherwise defined, such as those whose employment is governed by statute or a collective agreement.
- It applies to employees hired under indefinite contracts, that is, with no fixed time for the end of employment.
- It applies to termination of employment, as defined by the judge-made common law.
- An employer can dismiss an employee without notice or pay if the employee gives the employer just cause for dismissal, or if the employee otherwise repudiates the contract.
- It applies only if there is no clear agreement limiting notice or other rights upon dismissal.
- It requires the employer to give the employee reasonable advance notice of dismissal if there is no just cause for dismissal.
- If reasonable advance notice is not given, it requires the employer to pay damages in place of the notice that should have been given.

Each of these components is discussed in detail within this book.

Effect of statutes — Employment or labour standards statutes throughout Canada also provide for termination notice. However, these laws generally do not infringe on employees' greater common-law rights, except in the case of some Quebec employees whose rights may be limited by statute. Thus, an employer must meet the common-law requirement, even if it has already met the statutory requirement and even if the common-law requirement is much higher than the statutory requirement.

A-1.2 THE QUEBEC PRINCIPLE

Reasonable notice required — While the Quebec law of dismissal is partly regulated by the Quebec *Civil Code* and Quebec's *Labour Standards Act*, much of it has been left to the interpretation of the courts. In reality, Quebec's law is similar to that in the rest of Canada. An employee terminated without just cause must be given reasonable notice or pay instead of notice.

Considerations similar — Where reasonable notice is assessed by the courts, the factors are similar to those considered by common-law courts, and include the employee's age, length of service, the status of his position, and the time required to find a new job.

A-1.3 EXCLUSIONS FROM THE GENERAL PRINCIPLE

Exclusions — Certain classes of workers are not treated as falling within the wrongful dismissal doctrine, even though they are clearly employees. These include employees covered by a collective agreement; workers whose employment is created or affected by a specific statute; and workers with a statutory right to arbitration or another dismissal remedy. In most provinces, this includes Crown and some municipal employees; teachers; police officers; and firefighters.

Office holders' rights — Certain employees, including office holders and those whose contracts have a statutory or public flavour, may have additional rights to fairness or a hearing upon termination. An office holder usually has more autonomy in his or her duties than a regular employee. Usually, only statutory office holders such as police officers and ministers are entitled to the doctrine of procedural fairness, which includes a right to be told the reason for dismissal and a chance to respond. An office holder may also be entitled to seek reinstatement, or a declaration that the dismissal was null and void due to it being carried out improperly.

Employees with limited rights — Employees who may have different or limited rights upon dismissal include probationary employees dismissed within the probationary period (see Chapter A-5, "Identifying the Employer"), and those hired for a definite or fixed term of employment (see Chapter A-2, "Employment Status and Types of Employment Contract").

A-1.4 ILLEGAL CONTRACTS

Courts will not enforce — Courts will hesitate to enforce contracts that are unlawful. Some of the contracts that have not been enforced under the rule against illegal contracts include:

- A contract whose terms had been rescinded by statute; the employee was entitled to his common-law rights instead.
- A contract with a federal civil servant made without statutory authority.
- A junior stock trading clerk was not entitled to enforce an agreement giving him a share of commissions on business he brought in, as this was prohibited by the *Securities Act* (Ont.) and the stock exchange by-laws.
- An agreement that provided for an employee to repay part of her training costs if she left her employment within three years. The agreement penalized her even if she gave the resignation notice

required by the employment standards law, and therefore it breached the law's minimum standards.

Minor illegalities — In cases of minor illegalities, the courts may assist employees. For example, where a contract was not approved by by-law as required by statute, but the employer had affirmed the contract by assuring the employee that its terms remained in force, the contract was upheld.

Chapter A-2

EMPLOYMENT STATUS AND TYPES OF EMPLOYMENT CONTRACT

TABLE OF CONTENTS

A-2.1   Employment Status and Types of Employment Contract
A-2.2   At-Will or At-Pleasure Employment
A-2.3   Indefinite Employment
A-2.4   Definite-Term Employment
A-2.5   Examples of Definite-Term Employment
A-2.6   Termination of Definite-Term Contracts
A-2.7   Series of Seasonal or Other Definite-Term Contracts

A-2.1 EMPLOYMENT STATUS AND TYPES OF EMPLOYMENT CONTRACT

Employees automatically entitled to implied terms — A worker in an "employment relationship" is automatically entitled to the implied terms regarding wrongful dismissal, unless his or her contract's express terms state otherwise.

Tests for employment relationship — Historically, the courts have looked at a number of factors when deciding who is an employee and who is an agent or independent contractor. The courts will examine the parties' entire relationship. The factors considered by the courts include:

- The employer's control over the worker includes hiring, payment of wages, control over the method of doing the work, and the right to suspend or dismiss the worker.
- Who owns the tools used to perform the work?
- Who has a chance of profit or risk of loss from the work?
- Whether the worker is an integral part of the business.
- Whether the worker is economically dependent on the alleged employer.
- Whether the worker has been asked to provide services, or to provide a specified result.
- How the parties have labelled their relationship.

- Payroll practices, such as deduction of statutory deductions at source and payment of benefits.

Broad range of employees — If control and other factors indicate an employment relationship, the worker's employee status will not be changed by the fact that remuneration is by the job, by commission, from a third party, or paid out to a third party such as a personal corporation or a spouse. Part-time, temporary and seasonal workers may also be entitled to reasonable notice, depending on the circumstances. See the discussion in Chapter A-4, "Dismissal Rights of Specific Types of Workers".

Employment status no longer definitive — Modern courts have accepted that even workers who are not "employees" in the strict legal sense may be entitled to reasonable notice of dismissal. However, those who are not employees will have to prove their entitlement to notice, based on the express or implied terms of their agreement. Workers in an "intermediate category" between employees and true independent contractors or agents will generally be entitled to some reasonable notice, although it may not always be as much notice as would be granted to an employee. Those who are strictly agents or independent contractors may or may not be entitled to notice of termination.

Three types of hirings — For those who are employees, there are three types of hirings or employment contracts, whether written or unwritten. These are:

- At-will or at-pleasure employment.
- Indefinite employment.
- Definite-term employment.

Affects dismissal rights — Indefinite employment with the implied right to reasonable notice of dismissal is the norm. Those hired under at-will or definite-term contracts may have limited dismissal rights.

A-2.2 AT-WILL OR AT-PLEASURE EMPLOYMENT

Definition — Those employed at the employer's will or pleasure can be dismissed at any time, without notice or cause. Thus, they generally will not be entitled to sue for wrongful dismissal. They may still be entitled to procedural fairness in dismissal, including the right to be given an explanation or a hearing before being dismissed.

Rare in Canada — This type of employment is now rare in Canada, although it was common up to the early 1900s. It is still common in the United States, and this can give rise to conflict-of-laws arguments for employees who have worked both in the United States and in Canada for the same employer.

Consider all circumstances — To determine whether an employee is employed at pleasure, it is necessary to consider all the circumstances of the hiring and the employment contract. In general, at-will employment must be specifically agreed to between the parties, and will not usually be implied into an employment relationship. Where an employee is appointed for a fixed term, this contradicts at-will employment. An employee does not become employed at will just because the employment continues beyond age 65.

Examples of at-will employment — At-will employment still applies in some cases:

- Certain Crown employees, public employees and municipal employees, as specified by statute.
- Where there is an industry custom of at-will employment, such as in the case of some commissioned salespeople.
- Some agents and independent contractors.

A-2.3 INDEFINITE EMPLOYMENT

Definition — In indefinite employment, an employee is hired for a job which the parties assume will continue as long as the relationship is satisfactory to both of them, rather than for a specified or definite term. This is often referred to as "permanent" employment, although it is not necessarily permanent in the sense that it will last for the duration of the employee's working life.

Presumption of indefinite employment — When no specific job length has been agreed to by the employer and employee, the employment is presumed to be for an indefinite period.

Changing indefinite employment — Once an employee is hired indefinitely, any change to the term of hiring must be very clear, and must be agreed to by both parties. The fact that an employer has imposed certain terms and conditions of employment for a set time period will not create a definite-term hiring for that period, unless both parties specifically agree to a definite term of employment. An employer's policy manual providing for one-year contracts did not apply where an employee was not aware of the policy manual and was told that her hiring would be indefinite and permanent, subject only to termination for misconduct. Similarly, where parties have agreed to an indefinite hiring, or where nothing was said about a fixed term at the time of hiring, the adoption of fixed-term contracts as a payroll device will not limit the employment to a fixed-term hiring.

Dismissal rights of indefinite vs. definite-term employees — An employee hired for an indefinite term is entitled to be dismissed only for just cause or with reasonable notice, unless the individual contract of employment states otherwise. An employee hired under a definite term who is dismissed before the end of the agreed term, however, will be entitled to damages until the end of the term. An employee dismissed at the end of a fixed-term contract usually is not entitled to any notice or damages.

Guaranteed term within indefinite hiring — It is also possible to have an indefinite hiring that is guaranteed for a certain period, for example one or two years. A dismissal within the guaranteed period may then be treated like termination of a definite-term contract. A probationary period for a specific time may in some cases be treated as a guaranteed period within an indefinite hiring. However, a temporary assignment does not necessarily create a definite hiring for the expected length of the assignment.

A-2.4 DEFINITE-TERM EMPLOYMENT

Definition — Contracts for a definite or fixed term exist where the limited nature of the employment has been agreed to by both employer and employee, usually right from the time of hiring. If there is no clear agreement to a definite term, indefinite employment will be presumed.

Affects damages — An employee dismissed before the end of a fixed term is entitled to damages for breach of contract rather than damages for reasonable notice. This usually requires payment to the end of the term, which may be a longer or shorter time than the reasonable notice period. **Common types of definite terms** — A definite-term contract may exist for a fixed time period; for the length of a specified task or event; or until the employee reaches a certain age or reaches retirement.

Question of fact — The existence of a definite-term contract is a question of fact, and will be based both on the words used and the reasonableness of the parties' assumptions from those words. One party's assumption will not generally create a fixed-term contract unless it is communicated to the other party or is based on representations made by the other party.

Effect of expectations — A definite term will not be implied just because an employer mentions a possibility or an expectation that the job will continue for a certain length of time. For instance, an employer who told a prospective employee that it had long-term contracts to supply a third party did not create a contract to employ the employee for the entire length of those third-party contracts. But where an employer creates an expectation of employment for a certain time period and there are other contractual terms supporting that expectation, a court may find that a fixed-term contract existed.

Mutual commitment — Where an employee is asked to make a commitment to stay in a job for a certain length of time, it may be reasonable to assume the commitment is mutual and the employer has agreed to continue employment for that length of time. However, this will depend on the facts. A general discussion of the employer's preference for a long-term commitment will not necessarily create a binding fixed-term contract.

Effect of benefits or conditions — Where the employee alleges a definite-term hiring and the employer claims that it merely guaranteed salary for a certain time, a judge may look at the surrounding circumstances to see if they support the existence of a definite-term hiring. In one case, publication of an incentive pay scale for a several year period did not create an obligation to employ the employee until the end of the pay scale was reached. A transfer with certain financial conditions for the first two years did not create a two-year fixed term of employment. However, where an employee was promised a bonus if she remained with the employer until a certain date, the court found that a fixed term was created.

Formal requirements — Fixed-term contracts are often put in writing, although they may also be created orally some jurisdictions have a Statute of Frauds that requires contracts for a term of more than one year to be in writing in order to be enforceable. A fixed term may be limited to a maximum length. For example, Ontario's *Employers and Employees Act*, R.S.O. 1990, c. E.12, forbids employment contracts more than nine years long. This, however, does not apply to a written contract with an indefinite term that has lasted for more than nine years. Regulations to the Ontario *Employment Standards Act, 2000* also limit contracts for a definite task to a period of one year.

Employment beyond end of term — Continuing employment beyond the agreed to term will create an indefinite contract of employment, which then can be terminated only by giving reasonable notice, unless there is a clear intention to the contrary. In the alternative, renewal for an equal fixed term may be found, depending on the parties' intention.

Termination clause within fixed-term contract — Where a contract provides for employment for a fixed term, but also allows termination with a set amount of notice, which term takes precedence? The result depends on the parties' intentions, as well as how clear the contract language is. Results in the case law have gone both ways.

A-2.5 EXAMPLES OF DEFINITE-TERM EMPLOYMENT

Term defined by time or date — A definite term is often defined by the length of time or the date on which it will end. There must be enough information to know clearly when the contract will end.

Termination of business — Giving an employee notice that the business will cease or his position will end on a particular date does not necessarily mean the employer has agreed to employ the employee until that date. Whether or not that is the case will depend on the circumstances.

Term defined by project or event — A contractual term can also be set for the length of a particular project or event. Some examples include:

- The duration of a special event such as Expo 86.
- The retention by the employer of a contract with a third party.
- The uncertain but short term required by a receiver to wind up the company's affairs.
- A project engineer hired to supervise a project reasonably assumed that the job was to continue for the duration of the project. He was entitled to damages to the end of the project when he was wrongfully dismissed before the project ended.

Expectations of project length — An expectation that a project would last a certain amount of time did not create a fixed-term contract for that length of time where it was clear the hiring was for the duration of the project only. Where employment was guaranteed for the length of a project "to the extent allowed by government authorization", the employee could be dismissed when funding was cut back, even though full funding was later reinstated; the contract was not for a fixed term. On the other hand, an advertisement that represented a job as being for one year was said to create a fixed-term contract because the employer did not make the impermanence of government funding clear. Where an employee was hired for a specific project until "at least" a certain date, his employment was guaranteed even when the project ended earlier than that date.

Special considerations for project employment — While the usual rule is that an employee under a fixed-term hiring is entitled to damages for the entire unexpired term of the contract, this has been applied differently in some cases of project-based employment. In one case, where employment for the duration of a project was agreed to, and the employer could have told the employee the date on which employment would end but did not, the employee was held to be entitled to reasonable notice. In another case, the fact that the employee had agreed to a temporary job was said to be an important factor in setting notice, and both the formal and informal notice of the project's end were taken into account.

Employment until certain age — Definite hirings can exist which agree to employ people until they reach a certain age or until they reach their retirement date. However, guaranteed employment until retirement is rare and these agreements must be explicit. Discussions at the time of hiring about an employee's desire for job security until retirement, or of what would happen if the employee retired in a certain year, have not been found to create a fixed term of employment until retirement. A discussion with an employee after hiring, in which the employee stated a desire to retire in three years, did not create a three-year definite hiring. The fact that a long-term employee in his late 50s agreed to stay on after a change in the business's ownership did not create a fixed-term contract to employ him until age 65.

Explicit agreement required — Using the words "permanent employment" or referring to the company's policy of hiring long-term employees did not guarantee employment until retirement, and merely meant "indefinite hiring". The existence of a pension plan does not guarantee employment until retirement age, even in the case of a long-service employee. Where an employee was asked to give his commitment to remain until he retired, this did not create a corresponding obligation on the employer's part to continue to employ him until retirement, where the employee was only 44 years old at the time. In one case, an agreement that the 40-year-old employee "would have a job as long as he wanted it" was found not to be an agreement to employ him until age 65. However, in another case, an employer agreed that an employee could stay as long as she wanted unless the employer had just cause for dismissal. This created a contract which could only be terminated for just cause, whether it was regarded as a fixed-term or indefinite contract.

A-2.6 TERMINATION OF DEFINITE-TERM CONTRACTS

End of contract — By accepting a contract for a definite term, an employee has accepted termination of his employment at the end of the contract, without reasonable notice. The cessation of employment upon the expiry of the term or the happening of the specified event does not normally amount to a dismissal or give rise to any employer liability. Since the parties agreed to employment under certain conditions and those conditions have been fulfilled, there has been no breach of the contract.

Exceptions — Nonrenewal of a contract may involve a duty of fairness in a few, rare cases. In one case, a change by an employer which made it impossible to comply with an automatic renewal clause in a term contract was found to be a breach of contract. The employee was entitled to damages as if the contract had been renewed. Note that where there has been seasonal employment or a series of fixed-term contracts over a period of time, additional rights may accrue, as discussed later in this chapter.

Termination before end of term — The termination or breach of a limited-term contract *before* the end of its term involves the same issues as dismissal from an indefinite contract. Generally, any right to terminate before the end of the term must be clearly stated or must exist by statute. Constructive dismissal during the term of a fixed-term contract will be treated as a breach of contract, the same as in an indefinite hiring.

Damages for early termination — Damages for early termination of a definite-term contract generally are based on the compensation due under the remainder of the fixed contractual term.

Termination for just cause — Whether a fixed-term contract can be terminated for just cause, without liability for damages, is somewhat unclear, unless the contract specifically gives the employer that right. In one case, an employee who breached an implied term of faithful service was found to have repudiated the contract; as a result, he was not entitled to receive payment for the balance of the term. In another case, involving a sports contract, custom was held to establish a right to terminate before the end of the term.

A-2.7 SERIES OF SEASONAL OR OTHER DEFINITE-TERM CONTRACTS

Seasonal employment — Usually, a definite-term hiring has been upheld in cases of seasonal employment. In instances where there was no commitment on either side that employees would return next season and the return rate historically was about 50 per cent, no obligation to rehire was created.

Intention of permanence — Sometimes an employee is hired seasonally over many seasons. In some of these cases, judges have ruled that an indefinite or permanent employment relationship was intended, and that the employee is entitled to reasonable notice of dismissal. A hiring for a seasonal occupation such as fishing, that is intended to continue from year to year, may be an indefinite employment rather than a definite-term employment. A seasonal employee who had returned each spring for 30 years was held to have become a permanent employee entitled to notice of dismissal.

Series of term contracts — A series of term contracts renewed from year to year usually does not create a permanent or indefinite hiring. Courts have generally upheld this principle even where there has been a series of short-term contracts.

Examples — Definite-term contracts, without liability for reasonable notice, were upheld where:

- A teacher was continuously employed for a year under a series of identical short-term contracts, with a new one being signed just as the old one was about to expire. The employer was under no obligation to consider the teacher for further employment after expiry of the last contract, as that was the central purpose of the series of limited-term contracts.
- A contract provided for substantial pay in lieu of notice if terminated during its term. The employer was still entitled to not renew it without liability.
- The employee had an "expectation" or "understanding" that a contract would be renewed. The employer was entitled to not renew it where the expectation had never been translated into a contractual condition and the understanding was always subject to the employer receiving funding.
- An employee was hired for 12 separate projects over nine years, with termination in between each project. She had not acquired any collateral rights to be hired for the next project or to receive termination notice.

Long-term continuous employment — Sometimes an indefinite hiring may be created if there are other indications of permanence along with a long series of fixed-term contracts. For example, one employee who was hired for a specific project was frequently promoted and his service length increased to a total of six years. He was found to have become an indefinite employee. In another case, a 26-year employee, who had been employed on a series of one-year contracts that were not always signed or witnessed and who had been assured of a long-term relationship, had become an indefinite employee.

Chapter A-3

PROBATIONARY EMPLOYMENT

TABLE OF CONTENTS

A-3.1   Types of Probationary Employment
A-3.2   Existence of Probationary Period
A-3.3   Termination of Probationary Employees
A-3.4   Disciplinary Probation

A-3.1 TYPES OF PROBATIONARY EMPLOYMENT

Two types — Probationary employment is commonly used in two very different situations. The first is an initial "trial period" at the beginning of employment, during which the parties' termination obligations are lessened, in case the new relationship does not work out. The second is a disciplinary tool, similar to a final warning or a final chance to improve performance. The parties' legal rights may be quite different depending on which type of probation is in question. In this discussion, "probation" will be used to refer to an initial probationary period, while the other type will be referred to as "disciplinary probation".

A-3.2 EXISTENCE OF PROBATIONARY PERIOD

Express agreement required — The existence of a probationary period is a question of fact in each case. Since it takes away an employee's usual rights, a probationary period must be agreed to expressly. It cannot be implied into a relationship without a strong indication that it was mutually understood. Where the parties disagree about whether probation was agreed to, courts will judge each situation on the parties' credibility and the reasonableness of the assumptions they drew.

Agreement required before starting work — A probationary period must be agreed to before employment begins, and cannot be unilaterally imposed once the employee has started on the job (except in the case of disciplinary probation periods, discussed below under Section A-3.4). Imposing a probationary period upon an employee after he or she has started on the job may be treated as a constructive dismissal. It is not sufficient to say that the employee would have taken the job anyway, had the probationary period been brought to his attention beforehand.

Statutory probation — An employment standards law that allows dismissal without notice of employees with less than a certain amount of service does not create a probationary period at common law. Certain types of employees possess statutorily imposed probationary periods and may be affected by special provisions as to their right to notice or to a hearing. These include police officers, teachers, and provincial and federal civil servants. However, these employees have special status due to the statutes covering their employment, and they may not be entitled to bring a wrongful dismissal action under the common law in any event. See Chapter A-4, "Dismissal Rights of Specific Types of Workers".

Specific term needed — Specific terms must be used in obtaining an employee's agreement to a probationary period. A probationary period was not created by:

- Giving an employee a handbook upon hiring which provided for a 90-day probationary period, especially since the employer did not evaluate the employee within 90 days as required by the policy.
- A three-month waiting period for participation in a benefits plan.
- An initial six-month review and postponement of a possible promotion until that time, since probation was never expressly mentioned.

Agreement not found — No probationary period was found where:

- The employee had worked part-time for the employer in the past. Since the employer already knew she would be suitable, the court said there was no need for a probationary period.
- It was clear that the employee would never have taken the job if he had known it was probationary.

Agreement found — Probationary periods were upheld where:

- The employer had a policy of probation for all new employees, and the employee had avoided making commitments in the area. Also, the employer had refused other demands made by the employee, and likely would have refused to change its policy on probation.
- The employee had to undergo extensive training and pass exams at the beginning of his employment. This was said to make the employment more probationary than permanent.
- An employer said that he would "try the employee out".
- The parties had agreed to probation, although their agreement had not been put into writing.
- The letter offering employment contained many qualifying phrases, including a reference to a three- to six-month period of learning after

which, subject to performance, the employee would become sales manager.

Details in dispute — In some cases, the parties agree that probation was intended but disagree as to the details of the probationary period. Courts sometimes decide the matter on the basis of credibility and reasonableness, but they are also likely to hold any uncertainty against the employer, as it is up to the employer to make the details clear. For instance:

- In one case, the issue was whether the probationary period commenced when the employee first started working for the employer on a volunteer, part-time basis, or whether it started five weeks later when she began regular full-time employment. The judge ruled that it started on the later date, since it made sense that the employer could not properly assess her performance until she was performing the job's regular duties during the regular hours.
- An offer letter provided for a six-month probationary period, but the later-signed application form provided for a three-month extendable probationary period. The judge ruled that a six-month fixed probationary period was created, with no right of extension. However, since the employer had extended the probation within the initial six months, and the employee had accepted that change, the employee was still probationary when dismissed six and a half months after starting work.

Assurances can undermine — Where an employee is assured that probation is a mere formality, the employer may lose its right to dismiss without notice or just cause within the probationary period.

Extension of probation — Any extension of the probationary period also must be express. Extensions were not valid where:

- An employee became ill during probation and was unable to return to work before the probation ended, but the employer assured her throughout the illness that her job would still be available. She had become a permanent employee and could not be dismissed as a probationary employee upon her return to work.
- An employer did not tell an employee it was extending his probation until after it had expired, and it had already given him indications his performance was acceptable by voluntarily paying him bonuses.
- The extension did not start until after the probation had expired, and was never communicated to the employee.

Effect of acquiescence — An employee who continues working after a probation period has been extended is deemed to have agreed to the extension, since it is assumed that if he did not agree he would have been dismissed before the original probation expired. The employee must object to a unilateral extension, rather than lulling the employer into a false sense of security and allowing the employer to give up its right to terminate during the probation.

Extension found — Extensions have been upheld where:

- An employee had agreed to extend his probationary period until his evaluation could be completed. He was properly dismissed without notice once the negative evaluation was received.
- A contract stated that progressing beyond the probationary stage required "mutual agreement", and there had never been mutual agreement.

Expiration of probation — Where an employer allows the probationary period to expire and confirms the employee's permanent status, any dissatisfactions the employer had during the probation will no longer be enough to dismiss the employee without notice. The employer will have to show full just cause at law, or else will be liable for reasonable notice or damages.

A-3.3 TERMINATION OF PROBATIONARY EMPLOYEES

Right to reduce notice — Many employers believe they have the right to dismiss a probationary employee at will, without any obligation to give notice. But the case law does not support this. What the case law *does* support is a right to dismiss a probationary employee with reduced notice — which in some cases may be no notice — but only where certain conditions are met. Employers who wish to retain the power to dismiss at will during the probationary period can specify this in a written agreement. Another option is to provide for termination with a short amount of notice, for any reason, during the probation.

Conditions for reducing notice — In order to rely on the probationary period, the dismissal must occur: (1) in good faith; (2) in a non-discriminatory manner; and (3) for an actual failure to fulfill the requirements of the job.

Requirement for "just cause" — Some judges have described this standard as applying the principle of fairness to probationary employees. Other courts, including the Newfoundland Court of Appeal, have said this amounts to a requirement for just cause. Those courts usually have also accepted that the standard of cause is lower for a probationary employee; for example, a finding that the employee is unsuitable for the job can amount to just cause in the case of a probationary employee. Some courts say that just cause is required, but the fact of probation will shorten the notice period.

Majority view — Most courts take the view that it is not necessary to establish actual cause; it is enough to determine that an employee is unsuitable, as long as the employee is given a reasonable chance to show his suitability, and the decision is based on an honest, fair and reasonable assessment. The assessment may include not only job skills and performance, but also character, judgment, compatibility, reliability and the employee's future prospects.

Proper training required — A probationary employee must be given proper training before performance is evaluated. If proper training has not been given, a failure to meet expected standards will not count against the employee. The employee must be given a reasonable opportunity to demonstrate his or her suitability. This may include an obligation to assess the employee on all the normal tasks of the job.

Expected standard — An employee must be told the standard he is expected to meet. An employer's failure to properly evaluate the employee and provide feedback was held to be bad faith in one case.

Duty to warn — It may be unfair to dismiss a probationary employee for performance concerns without first discussing them with the employee and giving him a chance to improve, particularly if there was a chance of a misunderstanding.

Failure to follow procedure — An employer who had a procedure in its employer's handbook for disciplining probationary employees, but did not follow it, could not rely on the probation to reduce dismissal notice.

Objective reasons — An objective assessment is required, based on fair, reasonable and tangible factors rather than personal impressions. It was acceptable to dismiss an employee who did not work well with others in one case, but not in another case, where the employer made a subjective decision that the employee was not compatible. An employee was not properly dismissed for failing to be charismatic and exceptional, as these were intangible impressions.

Performance-related reason — The courts will not deprive a probationary employee of the right to at least some notice where he is dismissed for a reason unrelated to his performance, such as a reorganization, the employer's poor financial circumstances, or the fact that a more suitable candidate was found.

Timing of dismissal — Most courts agree that an employer who has fairly and reasonably determined that an employee is unsuitable may dismiss the employee immediately, without waiting until the end of the probationary period.

Employer must rely on probation — An employer must rely on a probationary period or the employee's unsuitability at the time of termination. If it does not, it may have waived the right to dismiss without notice (or with reduced notice).

Improper dismissal — Where a probationary employee has not been properly dismissed as described above, some judges have awarded reduced notice based on the employee's probationary status, but others have awarded full reasonable notice. Sometimes, judges have awarded the employee pay for the entire remaining portion of the probationary period.

Collective agreement — Normally an employee covered by a collective agreement is not entitled to sue in the courts for wrongful dismissal. This rule, however, has not always been applied to probationary employees with no recourse to the grievance procedure in the collective agreement. See Chapter E-1, "Collective Agreement, Arbitration or Appeal Procedures".

A-3.4 DISCIPLINARY PROBATION

Right to impose — The imposition of disciplinary probation may be treated as a unilateral change amounting to constructive dismissal, unless there is just cause for the change. See Chapter C-3, "Change in Job Content, Job Status or Working Conditions".

Full period to show improvement — A permanent employee who accepts the imposition of disciplinary probation, rather than treating it as a constructive dismissal, must be given the full period to show improvement. In fact, some judges have said a disciplinary probation period is more like a warning, and should be treated like a case involving just cause.

Good faith, etc. — Once a disciplinary probation period is established, the same requirements for good faith and objectivity apply as in other instances of probation. An employee cannot be dismissed for reasons unrelated to performance.

Timing of probation — Depending on the situation, a disciplinary probationary period will not necessarily begin immediately. The employer should be very specific about when the period starts, how long it will last, and what specific requirements must be met.

Chapter A-4

DISMISSAL RIGHTS OF SPECIFIC TYPES OF WORKERS

TABLE OF CONTENTS

A-4.1   Crown, Public and Municipal Employees
A-4.2   Employees Governed by Statute
A-4.3   Shareholders, Directors and Partners
A-4.4   Managers
A-4.5   Salespersons and Sales Agents
A-4.6   Casual, Temporary, Assignment, Seasonal and Part-Time Workers
A-4.7   Agents, Independent Contractors and Other Non-Employees
A-4.8   Other Workers

A-4.1 CROWN, PUBLIC AND MUNICIPAL EMPLOYEES

Presumption against at-will employment — In the past, Crown and municipal employees often held office at the pleasure of the employer, and could be dismissed without cause or notice. This is no longer true for most civil servants, other than a narrow range of exceptions such as judges, ministers of the Crown and others who fulfill constitutionally defined state roles. Some public employees' employment contracts are limited by statutory guidelines, but otherwise, the ordinary law of contract applies.

Statutory limitation — Statutes governing municipal law have historically provided that municipal officers hold office at the pleasure of council, with the result that officers have been subject to removal at any time without cause or notice in council's absolute, arbitrary discretion. In Saskatchewan, *The Rural Municipality Act*, R.S.S. 1978, c. R-26 even provides that *all* employees are employed at the pleasure of council, with the result that these employees are not entitled to reasonable notice. These employees may nevertheless be able to sue for other damages, such as wages and benefits owing up to the time of termination, damages for unlawful termination, and punitive damages.

Rebuttals of at-will employment — Modern courts tend to look for any indication rebutting the right to fire at will, even where the right to dismiss at pleasure is created by statute. For example, sufficient rebuttals have included:

- A contractual provision that an employee could not be fired due to illness.
- A fixed-term contract or appointment.
- Acceptance of an employee's resignation as of a future date; the council was bound to continue her employment until that time.
- Any provision providing for termination for cause or with notice in the absence of cause.
- Non-compliance with a statute's exact terms, such as a requirement for appointment by the Lieutenant Governor at pleasure.

Narrow interpretation of statutes — Where officers are employed at pleasure, courts have tended to restrict the view of who is an officer. Only persons who exercise powers which are necessarily the acts of the municipality, and who have real responsibility to perform the vital duties of the corporation, are officers. Those whose position is not created by statute, by-law or town council resolution, and who do not report to council, are not officers and are entitled to the usual common-law rights. The courts interpret statutory exclusions narrowly, and will find employees entitled to their common-law rights whenever possible.

Statutory protection of officers — Section 74(5) of New Brunswick's *Municipalities Act* provided that officers could be terminated only for retirement, death, resignation or cause. A municipal solicitor was found not to be an officer for purposes of this statute, especially since he was a second staff solicitor and not "the" city solicitor.

Statutory limit on notice — Some statutes impose a mandatory limit on termination notice for municipal employees. Where a statute provided for only one month's notice of dismissal, "subject to any contract to the contrary", it was said there was an oral or implied right to reasonable notice in the absence of just cause, which overcame the statutory provision. Similarly, an employee appointed indefinitely was entitled to reasonable notice if terminated without just cause, despite a statutory provision for only one month's notice.

Saskatchewan statute — In Saskatchewan, the *Crown Employment Contracts Act* overrides the terms of any employment contracts providing for termination payments, and requires that employees' rights be determined on the basis of common-law principles. It has been held that the *Act* applies only to written contracts, and does not take away the right to common-law damages for reasonable notice. In addition, it may not bar other damage claims based on mental distress, loss of reputation, punitive damages or tort damages.

Grievance schemes — Note that many Crown, public and municipal employees are given a statutory grievance scheme or are covered by a collective agreement. So their common-law rights are either no longer very important or are no longer available. See Chapter E-1, "Collective Agreement, Arbitration or Appeal Procedures".

Abolition or discontinuance of position — Some statutes permit permanent layoffs where a position has been abolished or the function discontinued. An assignment or contracting out of duties has been held to fall within this wording; however, a change in job title and some duties was not abolition of a position in another case.

Statutory dismissal procedure — Some statutes or by-laws provide for a hearing or other specific termination procedure. In one such case the employee did not complain at the time of the failure to accord him the specified hearing. It was held he was not entitled in his wrongful dismissal action to challenge the employer's jurisdiction to dismiss him, as it was no longer possible to restore his position to him. His remedy was limited to reasonable notice. A statute that provided for a review procedure was held not to limit a municipal secretary's right to sue for wrongful dismissal, since the procedure was not stated to be mandatory.

Right to procedural fairness — Where the right to dismiss with pleasure remains, the Supreme Court of Canada has stated that employees employed at will may still be entitled to procedural fairness upon dismissal. In fact, in one case it was held that a civil servant is owed a generalized duty of fairness in all dealings relating to employment, including promotions. But another case held that there is no such duty. See Chapter D-2, "Duty to Warn and Duty of Fairness".

A-4.2 EMPLOYEES GOVERNED BY STATUTE

Employees affected — Many workers' employment is controlled, at least in part, by statute. In most provinces, this category includes teachers, policemen, and firemen, who may have special rights in case of dismissal. Doctors who work at university-affiliated hospitals may also be affected. The governing statute should be consulted in all such cases.

Common statutory terms — Several cases have dealt with transfers which normally would have been treated as constructive dismissals. In these cases, since the employer had a statutory right to classify or to transfer, the employer's actions were not unjust. Some statutes provide for employees to hold office at pleasure; see Chapter A-2, "Employment

Status and Types of Employment Contract". Some statutes provide for employment security when positions become redundant.

Statutory dismissal procedure; duty of fairness — Many statutes specify a procedure that must be followed to dismiss an employee. Where the procedure is not strictly followed, the termination may be quashed by the courts, although the employer may still be able to attempt a second termination. Where a public element or statutory flavour is involved, an employee also may be entitled to procedural fairness upon dismissal or upon nonrenewal of a contract. See Chapter D-2, "Duty to Warn and Duty of Fairness".

Judicial review — Where an employer exercises its statutory authority, the employee's remedy may lie in an action for judicial review rather than wrongful dismissal.

Collective agreement — Many employees governed by statute are also covered by collective agreements, which will also affect their common-law rights upon dismissal. See Chapter E-1, Collective Agreement, Arbitration or Appeal Procedures".

Reinstatement vs. wrongful dismissal — Some statutes provide different or additional remedies, such as a right to reinstatement if unjustly dismissed. An employee who has exercised a statutory right to seek reinstatement, and who has been reinstated, is not entitled to sue for wrongful dismissal. An employee who elected to proceed on the basis of wrongful dismissal was not entitled to then seek reinstatement or damages on the basis of reinstatement.

Failure to follow procedure — An employee who has not exercised a right to seek reinstatement, but instead has accepted the dismissal and sought new employment, should not be awarded damages for the employer's failure to follow the proper dismissal procedure. His only remedy is damages for reasonable notice.

Job abolished by statute — Where a government body was abolished by statute, an appointee to the board was found to have no remedy for the breach of his contract. The statute had made performance of his contract impossible. But in another case, a government appointee was still entitled to notice of dismissal, even though the government had abolished the board to which he was appointed. While the government was free to restructure, it could not unilaterally affect the appointee's rights stemming from his contract of employment.

A-4.3 SHAREHOLDERS, DIRECTORS AND PARTNERS

Shareholders — The fact that an employee is also a shareholder has no bearing on his or her entitlement to sue for wrongful dismissal. This is so even where there is a written shareholder agreement, unless the agreement specifically deals with the issue of dismissal from employment.

Oppression remedy — An oppression remedy under business corporations law has been said not to apply to a wrongful dismissal claim where an applicant's interests as a shareholder were not indivisibly intertwined with his employment. However, it was said to be possible that an oppression remedy application and a wrongful dismissal action might be consolidated.

Directors vs. director-employees — Whether or not a director is also an employee depends on the contract and the facts; a director is not automatically an employee. Directors' remuneration is a gratuity which cannot be sued for. Where an employee was also an unpaid director, his removal as director but not as an employee was not a wrongful dismissal, and was not compensable.

Director-employees — A director who performed significant functions as an employee, for separate remuneration, and can show that the services were separate from the director's function, may still be entitled to damages for wrongful dismissal. This will be especially likely where the person started as an employee and was later made a director in addition to continuing the employment duties.

Partners — It is possible that the law as applied to director-employees could be applied to partners who also serve in an employee capacity. For example, an "incorporated partnership" was treated like an employment relationship in one case. The test for distinguishing between partners and employees is broadly stated as the right to participate in the profits, as opposed to the right to receive a fixed salary.

A-4.4 MANAGERS

Employees or independent contractors? — Sometimes managers' or professionals' employment status may be in question due to the independence of their functions and/or the decision-making nature of their duties. In these cases, courts look at the control exercised by the alleged employer, the risk of profit and loss, and the worker's integration into the business operation, along with the other tests of employment status discussed in Chapter A-2, "Employment Status and Types of Employment Contract".

Examples of Managers — Managers have been found to be employees, independent contractors and intermediate workers in various cases:

- District managers of a newspaper company were responsible under a contract for distributing newspapers to and collecting the price from the carriers. The contract required the distributors to work exclusively for the company and the company closely controlled the earnings of each distributor. They were employees.
- A property manager was an employee because of the kind and extent of the work performed and his integral part in the business.
- A joint venture franchise manager was an employee despite the terms of the franchise agreement, which was found to be ambiguous. The company owned the store and stock, and the manager was subject to the company's policies, was regularly monitored, was required to work long hours and could not engage in other work without the company's consent.
- A milk store manager was an employee under the terms of an employment standards statute, on the basis of the four fold test.
- A farm manager was subject to minimal control, invoiced for services, shared in profits but not in the risk of a loss, and had a written contract calling him an independent contractor. He was not an employee despite being an integral part of the organization. His status was found to be of the intermediary type.

Examples of Professionals — As with managers, professionals have been found to be employees, independent contractors and intermediate workers:

- A doctor practised his specialty from a hospital, where he was given office space, support staff and a stipend in return for administrative duties. He had no outside office and his income came from fees charged to patients. He was an employee because he administered a department which was an integral part of the hospital's facilities, and the hospital controlled the unit's policies and staff and owned its equipment.
- A junior lawyer who received a percentage of his billings was an employee, even though the senior lawyer had ceased making employee deductions from his pay. He received a regular salary rather than a draw, he had no cheque-signing authority, and the senior lawyer paid his expenses and retained final control of client services.
- An associate in a professional association who retained his own billings from clients and paid a percentage to a management company to cover expenses was not an employee.
- A pharmacist who managed a pharmacy and was paid a monthly draw against sales without statutory deductions was a worker of intermediate status between an employee and an independent contractor, based on organizational factors.

A-4.5 SALESPERSONS AND SALES AGENTS

Employee or independent contractor? — Again, the question is whether a sales agent is operating on his own behalf, on behalf of the "employer", or in an intermediate capacity, based on the employment status tests set out in Chapter A-2, "Employment Status and Types of Employment Contract".

Examples of employees — Salespersons and sales agents have been found to be employees in the following cases:

- Where the work was exclusive, work hours were set and control was maintained over daily activities in the form of mandatory reports or meetings, salespersons were employees, even though the actual sales were accomplished through their own direction and skills.
- Salespersons were paid on commission with advance draws, worked exclusively for the company and were provided with automobiles and uniforms, and were the sole source of the company's income.
- A sales manager employed under a sales agent's contract providing for immediate termination was nevertheless an employee in his capacity as sales manager, as he was subject to the company's control and was an integral part of the organization.
- A non-exclusive salesman was still found to be an employee, because he was supplied a list of customers, was subject to the company's policies and discipline, was expected to supply reports, and spent about 75 per cent of his time in generating a third of the company's sales.
- Where there was some control plus payment of benefits and government statutory contributions and the salesman was issued T-4 slips, he was an employee even though his standard form contract described him as an independent contractor.
- A salesman who had his remuneration changed from straight commission to a salary plus small commission and payment of benefits and expenses, changed from an independent contractor to an employee at the time of the change.

Examples of independent contractors — Where the work is not exclusive, there are no set work hours or sales quotas, and perhaps not even a specified sales territory, salespersons may not be regarded as employees since there is no control over when, where or how they work:

- A "freelance marketing consultant" who received commissions on sales and whose activities were mostly under her own control was an independent agent, not an employee. She was not entitled to notice of termination, as there was no evidence of any such intent by the parties.
- A real estate sales agent was an independent contractor who was not entitled to notice, even though he worked exclusively for the principal

and was called the marketing manager, because he had his own company, hired his own staff, and the principal retained control of the building process and acceptance of purchase offers.

Examples of intermediate status — Where the work was not exclusive and the salesman regarded himself as self-employed, but there was some supervision and control over his activities and he was not carrying on the business for himself, he was found to be of intermediate status and still entitled to reasonable notice of dismissal. So were:

- An exclusive distributor of a company's products who had agreed not to take on other new lines, and whose work for the company amounted to 75–90 per cent of his total business. He was entitled to reasonable notice because the terms of the distributorship indicated a long-term relationship.
- A sales agent who worked exclusively for a company and built up a substantial network for it. She was entitled to reasonable notice even though her contract described her as an independent contractor.

A-4.6 CASUAL, TEMPORARY, ASSIGNMENT, SEASONAL AND PART-TIME WORKERS

Casual, temporary, project, assignment employees — One case has stated that casual employees are a third category of employees without the rights and benefits of regular or permanent employees; thus a casual employee was not entitled to reinstatement. Where casual, temporary, project or assignment employment has become regular, is exclusive or is closely regulated by the employer, the employee may be entitled to some notice of dismissal, perhaps even full reasonable notice. For example:

- A casual worker who provided visiting nurse services on a case-by-case basis for nine years was not an employee entitled to notice of termination, since the employer had a discretion whether to offer her work or not and she had a discretion whether to accept offered work.
- An employee who had worked for a contractor and then performed the same job directly for the employer was a regular employee, not a casual worker.
- An employee hired for a specific task but for an indefinite time was entitled to reasonable notice of termination, although on a reduced basis. An assignment employee employed for more than one year but less than five years was said to be entitled to one-third to one-half of the notice for a permanent employee.
- A project employee who remained on the employer's job roster for possible future re-hiring, but who was passed by for an important project, was not entitled to reasonable notice or damages. She was not a

dependent contractor and the employer had done nothing that could be construed as a dismissal.
- A worker assigned by a third party employer as a casual employee with the provincial government who continued in the position for 10 years without a break, during which the third party employer changed two times, was entitled to reasonable notice of dismissal due to the number of years she was employed.
- A temporary worker who was led to expect at least one year's employment was entitled to reasonable notice when dismissed within that year.
- A temporary employee who was supposed to work for six months but who ended up working for more than two years, in several positions, was entitled to some notice of termination from the employment agency, although not as much as if the employment had been permanent.
- An apartment building manager who was offered interim employment by the building's new owner was not entitled to reasonable notice, since he had finished the projects for which he was hired, and since the mention of future employment was conditional and the condition was never fulfilled.

Change of status — Temporary and casual employees who have had their status changed after long periods of permanent full-time employment are still entitled to reasonable notice of termination.

Seasonal employees — The dismissal rights of seasonal employees who are not rehired in the next year depend on whether there was a commitment made to recall the employee, on the number of years the seasonal employment continued, and on the express or implied understanding between the parties as to future employment. Where the hiring was intended to continue from year to year, or a definite pattern of recall is shown over several years, a seasonal employee may be entitled to reasonable notice of dismissal. However, where there was no commitment to return on either side and the recall rate was about 50 per cent, there was no obligation to rehire even where the employee had been rehired for several years.

Dismissal during season — Where a seasonal employee has already started work for the season, dismissal will raise the same issues as dismissal of a regular indefinite or fixed-term employee, depending on the circumstances.

Part-time workers — Part-time workers generally have the same rights as full-time workers. However, a few judges have treated part-time employees as being entitled to less reasonable notice than full-time employees; see Chapter F-2, "Reasonable Notice Factors: Character of the Employment".

A-4.7 AGENTS, INDEPENDENT CONTRACTORS AND OTHER NON-EMPLOYEES

Status less important than in past — The distinction between employees, independent contractors, agents or intermediates has become much less important, since developments in the law have given workers in employment-like relationships the same dismissal rights as full employees.

Factors in determining entitlement to notice — Factors which are important in deciding who is entitled to reasonable notice of dismissal in the absence of just cause are indicated in *Carter v. Bell & Sons (Canada) Ltd.*, [1936] O.R. 290 at 297 (C.A.):

> There are many cases of an intermediate nature where the relationship of master and servant does not exist but where an agreement to terminate the arrangement upon reasonable notice may be implied. This is, I think, such a case. The mode of remuneration points to a mercantile agency pure and simple, but the duties to be performed indicate a relationship of a more permanent character. The choice of sub-agents and their training, the recommendation of them to the company for appointment, the supervision of these men when appointed, all point to this more permanent relationship. The fact that the plaintiff was entering a new territory as representative of the defendant and was endeavouring to create a market for the defendant's products and that to their knowledge he was taking his wife and children with him to the West indicate a relationship that could not be terminated at will by either party.

Examples where notice required — The same principles have been applied in cases of agents, independent and dependent contractors, and other intermediate status workers. For example:

- An acknowledged independent contractor who was an integral part of the business was found to be in a relationship of the intermediary type, and was still entitled to reasonable notice of dismissal.
- An associate dentist was not an employee, but the relationship was found to carry an implied obligation by both parties to give reasonable notice of termination.
- The fact that a worker was paid through his personal services corporation was said to make the relationship one of intermediate status in one case, but he was awarded the same damages based on reasonable notice as if he had been a regular employee.
- A courier whose hours, rates and procedures were controlled and whose expenses were paid was an employee because of the extent of the control, even though he supplied his own vehicle, did not have statutory deductions made from his pay, and had a standard-form contract describing him as a "contractor".

- A consultant was entitled to notice even though his contract referred to him as an independent contractor, because he was required to devote his full time to the project; his contract could not be assigned; he used the company's equipment and had no risk of loss or chance of profit apart from his salary; and he was subject to the company's control over his hours of work, travel and actions.

Examples where no notice required — Nevertheless, some workers have been denied notice of dismissal, including:

- An independent contractor who was not integrated into the employer's business objectives, and who was not expected to work exclusively for the employer.
- A newspaper delivery person who did not have statutory deductions made, and who filed her income tax returns as an independent contractor.
- A volunteer who had been elected, and whose activities were not controlled by an organization.
- A bailiff hired through his own personal corporation and who worked independently, who had a chance of profit but no risk of loss, but was integrated into the organization's business and paid benefits as an employee. He was found to be an agent at will who was not entitled to notice of dismissal.
- Real estate agents who felt free to terminate their own "employment" summarily. The relationship was more like that of principal and commission-sales agent than master and servant; it was said that the parties must have intended that either party could terminate at will, without reasonable notice.

Right to dismiss for cause — While courts have extended the right to reasonable notice to some non-employees, they may be less willing to give the "employer" the right to terminate for just cause without notice. However, at least one judge has said that relationships of an intermediate nature would also be subject to summary termination for just cause.

Office holders — Usually, an office holder is entitled to be told why he or she is being dismissed and have an opportunity to reply, and he or she may also seek reinstatement if dismissed improperly. See Chapter A-1, "General Principles of Wrongful Dismissal Law" under A-1.3 "Exclusions from the General Principle".

A-4.8 OTHER WORKERS

Elected officials — An elected union business representative was an employee, because the union had control over how he carried out his function and also had the power of dismissal. However, the elected editor of a university newspaper was a volunteer and was not entitled to notice of termination; the university had not selected him, did not assign him specific tasks or direct and supervise his activities, and could not discipline or dismiss him.

Personal services corporations — Most employees who provide their services and are paid through a personal services corporation or management company have still been awarded reasonable notice, as the essence of the relationship is employment. In some cases, though, the use of the corporation has been regarded as evidence of a non-employment relationship.

Ministers — Results have varied in cases involving religious ministers:

- A minister who was retained by his congregation but received salary and benefits from the parent church was an employee of the church, not the congregation.
- A captain in the Salvation Army was said to be the holder of an ecclesiastical office, not an employee, and he therefore could be dismissed without cause or notice.
- In another case, the issue between a minister and his church was said to be a matter not of employment, but of status beyond "mere employment".

Secondment, leave of absence — An employee on secondment continued to be an employee of his original employer, both because he was referred to in the secondment agreement as an "employee" and because the very meaning of "secondment" is "a temporary transfer". Employees on leaves of absence also have been found to remain employees.

Termination of job-sharing arrangement — An employer is not obliged to continue making a job-sharing arrangement available to an employee when the other job-sharer quits. Barring an express contractual term to the contrary, it has been held that the employer is entitled to terminate the ongoing employee's employment.

Prisoners — A prisoner who was employed within the prison was not barred from having his wrongful dismissal claim proceed to trial, since it was possible that he could prove rights as an employee, separate and apart from his status as a prisoner.

Employees of foreign government — Employees of a foreign government will not be entitled to notice or damages if the *State Immunity Act* applies.

Chapter A-5

IDENTIFYING THE EMPLOYER

TABLE OF CONTENTS

A-5.1   Purpose of Determining the Employer
A-5.2   Sale or Transfer of Business
A-5.3   Related Entities
A-5.4   Liability of Corporate Directors and Shareholders
A-5.5   Unincorporated Associations and Partnerships
A-5.6   Receivers and Trustees
A-5.7   Other Individuals

A-5.1 PURPOSE OF DETERMINING THE EMPLOYER

Multiple possible employers — Usually, the employer's identity is obvious and there is only one choice. In some cases, however, there may be more than one entity or person who could be regarded as the employer. Determining who is the employer can be complicated where there has been a sale of a business or where several related corporations are involved. In a number of situations, courts have found that there can be more than one "employer" for the purposes of wrongful dismissal liability.

Individual liability — In other cases, an employee wishes to sue both a business entity and one or more individuals. Generally, this can only be done if they can be regarded as the employers, or if there is a legal basis other than wrongful dismissal for imposing personal liability.

A-5.2 SALE OR TRANSFER OF BUSINESS

Issues — Two issues can arise where there is a sale or other transfer of a business:

(1)   has there been a dismissal? and
(2)   if yes, who is legally responsible for giving reasonable notice or damages?

There are three possible ways to assess liability:

(1) the old employer remains liable;
(2) the new employer is liable; or
(3) the old and new employers are jointly liable.

Old employer liable — The old employer generally will be liable if the employees do not work for the new employer. For instance, one old employer sold its business with an agreement that the new employer would employ the business's employees. However, the new employer and the employees were not able to negotiate terms of employment. Even though the employees provided services on a temporary basis while trying to negotiate new contracts, the old employer remained liable to them for wrongful dismissal.

New employer liable — Where the employees have become employed by the new employer, the new employer may be held liable for their later dismissal, with full credit given for past service with the old employer. Continuity of service is required by many employment standards statutes in Canada. Also, if the new employer has agreed to assume the old employer's obligations as part of the transfer, the new employer usually will be held liable to the employees.

Both employers liable — Where an employee is terminated shortly after the sale or transfer of business, and within the notice period that should have been given by the old employer if he had been terminated at the time of the transfer, both the old and new employers have been held liable. The employers generally are found to be "jointly and severally liable," meaning that either one can be held fully liable to the employee, but that one can seek indemnity for half the amount from the other employer.

A-5.3 RELATED ENTITIES

Who, in substance, is employer? — Where related parties, related companies or subsidiaries are involved, liability as between them will depend on the parties' treatment of the relationship, the employee's expectations and the reasonableness of those expectations. The question to be asked is "who, in substance, is the employer?"

Employee must accept any change — An employee must consent to a transfer of employment liability from one employer to another, although consent may be assumed from the circumstances. An employee is entitled to choose the employer that he is promising to serve. For example, a person who was hired by individuals but was paid for 21 years by a corporation owned by the individuals was found to be an employee of the individuals and not of the company. There was no evidence that she had accepted the change of employer.

Possible multiple employers — In some cases, one entity or the other is found to be liable to the employee while the other is not found liable. In a number of cases, however, entities have been found to be so linked that liability cannot be limited to just one. Liability in these cases tends to be imposed on a joint and several basis.

Services provided to more than one entity — Where an employee actually performs services for several related companies, he may be entitled to treat them jointly as his employer. This is especially the case when other factors support joint responsibility for the employment; for example, where a restrictive covenant was requested for the benefit of all of the companies.

Rebutting presumption — However, this presumption may not apply where the companies are unrelated. For example, where an employee performed services for a company under his contract with another company, he was not an employee of the first company and his action against it was dismissed. Furthermore, providing services for several related companies may not entitle the employee to treat them all as the employer where it was always clear that only one of the companies was regarded as the employer, or where it was clear that one of them was not regarded as the employer.

Payroll practices and common control — Where a subsidiary is technically the employer, but the hiring, paying and terminating are performed by the parent company, both companies may be liable. But in other cases, payroll practices have not been enough to create liability as an employer. For example:

- A company which issued paycheques and provided management services was not liable, because an individual was shown as the employer in the notice of termination and Record of Employment, and the company had never done anything to indicate it was the employer.
- Where an employee had first worked for a parent company and then had been transferred to a subsidiary, the subsidiary was solely liable as his employer, despite his dealings with the parent company throughout his employment and the close relationship between the companies. He had been paid and supervised by the subsidiary and it had been treated by the parties as his employer, so there was no justification for "lifting the corporate veil".
- An employee who worked for a subsidiary was not entitled to damages against the parent company simply because he received stock options in the parent company's stock as a benefit of his employment with the subsidiary.

Absence of payroll practices — The fact that one of several companies has not been shown as an employer on official documents or paycheques may be significant.

Employment standards — A company may be liable for termination pay under an employment standards law where it is "related" within the meaning of the legislation. Employees can also be entitled to treat their service for related companies as cumulative, both for employment standards and common-law purposes, as discussed in Chapter F-3, "Reasonable Notice Factors: Age and Service Length".

A-5.4 LIABILITY OF CORPORATE DIRECTORS AND SHAREHOLDERS

Piercing corporate veil — Generally, courts will not pierce the corporate veil to impose liability on a corporate employer's controlling mind, be it director or shareholder. However, in several cases, courts have found joint liability or have awarded punitive damages, against directors or shareholders personally. This has been done where it was proven that they, and not the corporation, were the true employer, or where they were the mind and actor carrying out the corporate employer's actions and their actions deserved censure. There also may be situations where a corporate employer and its controlling mind are both liable.

Other causes of action — Individual liability may also be imposed where another cause of action exists, such as a claim for inducing breach of contract. Courts have also awarded damages in cases of fraud or acting without authority.

Statutory liability of directors — Corporate directors may be personally liable under statute for certain amounts related to dismissal. Some provinces' corporation statutes exclude a civil action until the statutory remedy is pursued, while others do not.

Directors' liability for wages — A number of corporations statutes impose personal liability on directors for up to six months' wages. In some cases, these have been interpreted to include liability for termination pay or wrongful dismissal damages over and above the employment standards minimum. But in other cases, it has been said that damages are not a debt payable for services to the corporation and therefore directors are not personally liable for wrongful dismissal damages.

Directors' liability for other amounts — Directors have generally not been held liable for severance pay and termination pay under a company policy or for bonuses. However, directors have been held personally liable for vacation pay in several cases. Directors were also found personally liable for expenses incurred by an employee while on assignment, as the expenses resulted from the performance of work for the employer and were therefore a corporate debt.

Priority of payment — Even though a corporate director may not be personally liable to an employee, the finding of liability against the corporate employer may include a ruling that the judgment is to be in priority over any monies owed to owners, whether directors or otherwise.

A-5.5 UNINCORPORATED ASSOCIATIONS AND PARTNERSHIPS

Who to sue? — The courts' treatment of unincorporated associations as employers has varied. In one case, an employee was held to be entitled to sue the only member known to him at the time of his dismissal. An employee of an unincorporated group was allowed to sue the municipality that was responsible for his employment with the group. Some jurisdictions have special rules for suing unincorporated associations.

Suing unions — Unions are common examples of unincorporated associations acting as employers. In Ontario, it may not be possible to sue a union employer because of the *Rights of Labour Act*, R.S.O. 1990, c. R.33. However, some cases have allowed union employees to sue key individual members of a union.

Partnership — A partner in a law firm was held jointly and severally liable with the firm for the wrongful dismissal of an employee who had worked for the particular partner for many years and in several different firms.

A-5.6 RECEIVERS AND TRUSTEES

Involuntary assignment in bankruptcy — Statutory severance pay, termination pay and vacation pay as well as wrongful dismissal damages, may be a provable claim against a bankrupt employer's estate where termination resulted from the bankruptcy itself.

Voluntary assignment — However, it has been held that any voluntary assignment represents a termination by the employer. This gives rise to a provable claim for severance because the employer had a choice whether to make the assignment.

Receivers' liability — A receiver will not generally be liable for statutory severance pay, termination pay or wrongful dismissal damages, but may be liable to pay statutory vacation pay on the employer's behalf. It is up to the receiver to make clear to the employees that he or she will not be personally liable. If the receiver does not do so, he or she can be liable for notice or pay in lieu of notice based on the length of service with the receiver. Under some circumstances and under some statutes, a receiver may be treated as a successor employer and may be liable for statutory termination pay on the basis of service both before and after the receivership.

A-5.7 OTHER INDIVIDUALS

Acting within authority — A dismissed employee often feels wronged by the person who carried out the act of firing, particularly if dismissal was handled in an insensitive manner. Generally, an officer or employee will not be personally liable when he acts within his authority on behalf of the corporation or in the best interests of the corporation. There is no liability in the absence of an independent tort such as defamation, conspiracy, inducing breach of contract, personal fraud, misrepresentation or voluntary assumption of liability.

Bad faith — The protection for an individual officer or employee may depend on his or her *bona fides* or good faith. There will be no protection from liability for individual directors, officers or employees who engage in conduct which furthers their personal interests or where their conduct exhibits a separate identity or interest from that of the corporation. However, an action against a former co-worker due to the co-worker's mistreatment of the plaintiff, which allegedly forced the plaintiff to retire, was dismissed with costs, on the basis that bad faith alone was not enough to create liability where an employee was acting within the scope of his authority.

Denial of costs — Where a superior has been particularly cold and callous in carrying out a dismissal, costs may be denied when the action against the superior is dismissed.

Interference with contractual relationship — Some individuals have been sued for the tort of intentional interference with contractual relationships. This requires proof of:

(1) intent to injure;
(2) interference by illegal means; and
(3) economic loss.

More often than not, these claims have not succeeded.

Action against replacement employee — An action against an employee's successor for the amount of an incentive bonus paid to the successor rather than the dismissed employee was inappropriate. The employee's only remedy in such a case would be against the employer; the successor did not hold the payment in trust for the employee.

Government liability — The fact that an employee was hired under a government-funded training program did not give a cause of action against the government, as it was not a guarantor of the employment. Nor did an employee have an action against the government when his employment had, by statute, been transferred from the province to a local health board not owned or controlled by the province.

Action against insurer — Where an employee became disabled during the notice period and sued for disability benefits, the employer was the proper defendant not the related insurance company that provided the payments under the group benefits plan. An employer that failed to give working notice of dismissal, which would have extended an employee's group life insurance coverage, was liable for the amount of the benefit to which the employee's widow would have been entitled where the employee died within the extended coverage period but was no longer covered because of the dismissal. An insurer was a proper party where the issue related to when employment was terminated, and until what date the employee remained covered under a group insurance plan.

Chapter B-1

TERMINATION OF EMPLOYMENT: GENERAL PRINCIPLES

TABLE OF CONTENTS

B-1.1   General Principles
B-1.2   Express Termination Under By-Law, Contract or Statute
B-1.3   Express Termination at Common Law
B-1.4   Effective Date of Termination Notice
B-1.5   Layoffs, Suspensions and Similar Actions

B-1.1 GENERAL PRINCIPLES

Termination of contract — An employment contract can be terminated by a specific, anticipated event, such as expiry of a limited term, or it can arise from a repudiation by the employee or by the employer. The effect of a termination, including whether it is a wrongful dismissal or not, will depend on the terms of the contract and on the existence of just cause or any of the other possible defences available to an employer.

Wrongful termination — The fact that a termination or dismissal has occurred does not in itself make it wrongful. A termination is wrongful only if it is brought about without following the express and implied terms of the contract.

Repudiation by employee — Repudiation by the employee can take the form of resignation without proper notice, resignation contrary to the terms of the contract or of giving the employer just cause for firing. An employee who repudiates the employment relationship without justification will not have an action for wrongful dismissal.

Repudiation by employer — Repudiation by the employer can occur when an employer fires an employee without having just cause, without giving reasonable notice or by paying the employee in lieu of notice. It can also occur if an employer does not comply with a significant, specific term of the contract.

Breach of contract — A wrongful dismissal action is merely a specific type of action for breach of contract. The issue of whether a breach of an employment contract has occurred is similar to the question of breach in any other contract situation. The question can sometimes be complicated by the ongoing nature of the relationship but the general principle is the same: has the party refused to perform his bargain, and is this refusal serious enough to indicate a repudiation or an intention to abandon the contract, thereby also freeing the other party from the contract?

Constructive dismissal — Termination or repudiation by the employer can occur when an employer unilaterally imposes a fundamental change in the contract's terms. This may be so even where the employer had no intention to dispense with the employee's services. This is called a "constructive" dismissal.

Question of fact — In each case, whether a wrongful dismissal has occurred is a question of fact, which depends on the nature of the relationship between the parties as well as the express and implied terms of their contract.

B-1.2 EXPRESS TERMINATION UNDER BY-LAW, CONTRACT OR STATUTE

Lack of compliance — The effect of a dismissal that violates the terms of the employer's own by-laws or contracts is in dispute. Several cases have held that these dismissals are valid but that they will be treated as wrongful, regardless of the circumstances. In other cases, the dismissals have been held to be null and void. In still others, the dismissals have been valid and not wrongful.

Permissive language — The fact that legislation says termination "may" be effected in a certain way does not mean it is invalid if not done in that way, since the wording is permissive, not mandatory.

Statutory requirement — One employer who failed to give written notice of the reasons for dismissal, as required by a statute, was not allowed to defend a wrongful dismissal action on the ground of just cause.

B-1.3 EXPRESS TERMINATION AT COMMON LAW

Termination notice — Where notice is not received until the day it takes effect, the termination is without notice. Termination without the required notice, but with some notice, will still be wrongful, although damages will be reduced by the amount of notice given. The start of the notice period is usually the time from which damages run, as discussed in Chapter G-1, "Damages: General Principles".

Form of notice — At common law, a dismissal need not be in writing. Delivery of written notice after earlier oral notice will not necessarily change the date on which the notice period begins. The only formal requirement seems to be that the dismissal must be a proper expression of the employer's decision in the matter.

Technical mistakes — The employer's actual intention will govern, regardless of how that intention is expressed. Where the intent to dismiss is clear, a mere typographical error or technical mistake in a dismissal letter — even use of the wrong corporate letterhead — has been overlooked; the dismissals have still been valid.

Notice must be received — For notice of dismissal to be effective, it must be received by the employee. For example, where a letter was given to an employee's friend to deliver to him, but the letter was never delivered and the employee did not know about the dismissal, he had not been dismissed. In another case, an employee who missed a meeting announcing a plant closure was not dismissed until he received a letter advising him officially that he would lose his job.

"Magic words" — No particular words are necessary to create a dismissal, nor is the use of precise, formal language required, as long as a reasonable person would clearly understand from the words used that employment will end as of a certain point.

Examples — no use of express words — In the following cases, terminations were effective despite the lack of specific words such as "fired":

- An employee was forced to take a holiday and told to clear his things out of the workplace. Especially given the context of an ongoing dispute, these were clear signs of dismissal.
- An employer told an employee, "You're through — you're finished." There was no mention of a layoff or possible recall.
- An employer offered a severance package in a "with prejudice" meeting.
- A letter setting out three options by way of a severance package.
- An employee whose boss was authorized to negotiate a separation package with him, and whose assistant was appointed to take over his duties "effective immediately" was terminated. The fact that a relocation consultant was in the next room waiting to go over a financial offer with him was a further sign that he was dismissed.
- An employee was told in writing that his employment would end if he did not return to work by a certain date. He was dismissed even though the letter also stated that he had to submit medical information by that date. The request for medical information did not imply an intention to grant a medical leave, given the clear words of the termination.

Clear and unambiguous — Termination must be clear and unambiguous to be effective. It is helpful to include a specific date upon which employment will end. No clear, unambiguous intent to dismiss was found where:

- Nothing more was done after a municipal council adopted a recommenddation for an employee's dismissal but also adopted a recommendation that another job be found for him. The statement was too contradictory to be an effective dismissal.
- There had been discussions with the employer's Human Resources representative but it was unclear whether the employee was advised that he would lose his job.
- The notice was clear and unequivocal on its face, but the past practice was to purport to terminate employment but then continue it, and new employment was in fact offered to the employee before the termination date.
- An employer gave notice that employment was being put on a month-to-month basis, but did not say that employment would end.
- An employee understood the employer's statement to be merely a suggestion that he would be happier elsewhere, not that his employment was being terminated.

Ongoing negotiations — Where ongoing negotiations or ambiguity prevent an employee from being certain of his status, notice of impending dismissal may not be effective notice at law. For example, notice was not effective where:

- An employee had been given notice but was continually assured of the employer's intention to find another job for her.
- Notice of termination was conditional, because it left the impression that it was only effective if a job offer from the employer did not materialize.
- An employee was told his position would end at a certain future date but he was urged to discuss other opportunities within the company.

Belief must be reasonable — An employee's belief that another job will be found for him must be reasonable. Once an employee knows that his employment will likely end as of a certain date, the fact that there are ongoing negotiations will not postpone the start of the notice period.

Words said in anger — Angry words will not constitute dismissal, even where the employee thinks he has been dismissed, unless the words clearly show intent to end the employment relationship. For example, there was no dismissal where:

- A vice-president, under the influence of alcohol, fired an employee but withdrew the firing the next day, and the employee's continued job was confirmed by the vice-president's boss.

- A manager sent an employee home after discovering the employer's goods in the employee's bag, saying, "I will call you. I will have to think about this." Afterward, he phoned to say that the employee was expected at his next shift.

Test is objective — In considering whether a conversation has amounted to a dismissal, the test is what a reasonable man would understand from the words used, in the context of the particular industry and the particular workplace, and in all of the surrounding circumstances.

Employee's perception only one factor — An employee's personal characteristics and conduct may be important in deciding whether a dismissal has occurred. For example, where a loyal employee told others, including his spouse and doctor, that he had been fired, his belief was evidence of what had occurred. An employee's perception is not the only criterion however, and must be tempered with an objective view of the circumstances.

Warnings not effective — Specific information, particularly a proposed termination date, is usually needed. A warning about the chance of dismissal does not amount to notice of termination; nor is a preceding layoff or demotion. Similarly, notice is not implied by knowledge of the employer's poor financial condition, planned reorganization or layoffs, possible sale of the business, possible salary reductions or discussions about an employee's need to upgrade his or her computer skills.

Notice with indeterminate date — In some cases, long forewarning to an employee that his job would end, with no specific termination date, has been found to amount to formal notice of dismissal. So has a termination notice that included no date but was quickly followed up by notice of the termination date. In other cases, however, this "informal" notice did not amount to termination notice so as to be deducted from damages, although it was said to be an important factor in setting reasonable notice. Even where an employee quit and was rehired with the understanding that the employment might not last long, she was still entitled to full reasonable notice when dismissed.

Examples of effective notice — Effective notice of dismissal was given where:

- An employee was told he was being given six months' working notice of dismissal.
- An employee received a proposal to "phase him out" over several months.
- An employee was told that he would be kept on only until he found another job.
- An employee was notified that his position would be eliminated in six months' time.

- An employee whose contract required written notice of termination was given a paycheque with "termination" written on it, where the employee clearly knew he was being dismissed.
- An employee was told he would be terminated on a certain date unless the company's economic situation improved.
- An employee received notice that he would either be offered a position with the employer's parent company or with a new company.
- An employee received a letter "accepting his resignation" as of a certain date, even though the employer later offered to let him stay on until he was replaced.
- An employee was told he was terminated, with the timing and terms to be discussed. He knew at that point that his leaving was inevitable. An employee in a similar situation, whose proposal for a leaving date was not answered, left work on the date he had proposed. He had not resigned.
- An employee had been given notice and the employer had begun negotiating a severance package. The employer could not change its mind and require the employee to transfer into a new job and work through the notice period.
- An employee who, upon the sale of a business, prepared records of employment for each employee and had the records placed in their files. She could not argue she did not have notice of her own termination.

B-1.4 EFFECTIVE DATE OF TERMINATION NOTICE

General principle — The date on which a termination takes effect is important in calculating damages, because it is the date from which the damages period begins to run. Generally, a dismissal is effective on the date when the employee is told his services are no longer required. The important date is the date when the employee receives the notice and not the date the employer sends it. For example, in a case where notice of termination was mailed to an employee but was not received until three weeks later the dismissal started from the time of receipt and not from the time of mailing.

Working notice — Giving working notice or termination pay does not generally delay the termination date. The termination is effective as soon as the employee is clearly told his services are no longer required. For example, where an employee was kept on the payroll for two extra months at her request, rather than receiving two months' vacation pay in a lump sum, she did not remain an employee and had not extended her termination date.

Effective date where working notice given — Where the employer has given adequate working notice or pay in lieu, and therefore has not repudiated the contract, the contract will continue until the working notice expires. The employer will still be entitled to rely on any just cause that may arise during that time. However, if inadequate notice was given, so that the employer had already repudiated the contract, the result may be different. In one case, an employee had been given six months' working notice of dismissal. Three months later, he was dismissed outright but the allegations of just cause were not accepted by the trial judge. Even though the later dismissal was wrongful, the judge ruled that the dismissal was effective as of the original notice date, giving credit for the three months' notice during which the employee had worked.

Changes during notice period — An employee whose working conditions are changed during the notice period may have a claim to constructive dismissal. Also, some employment standards laws freeze all terms and conditions during the notice period.

Constructive dismissal — Constructive dismissal cases are an exception to the general rule. Termination may not occur until the employee accepts that the agreement has been repudiated or until the employee's work ceases. For example:

- In one case, termination was effective on the day the employee received a letter setting out the conditions that he immediately treated as a fundamental breach.
- Where changes were proposed but not accepted by the employee, termination was effective as of the express termination date, not two months earlier when the changes were proposed.
- Termination was effective as of the date the employee knew negotiations for continued employment were unlikely to succeed and that his employment would likely end.

Disability or other leave — The case law is inconsistent where an employee is on disability or other leave when he or she receives termination notice. In some cases, the effective date of termination notice is the date notice was given; in others, it is the date the employee would have returned to work. For example:

- The effective date of termination, of one disabled employee who had been given no sign his job was in jeopardy, was the date his replacement was hired. He was not told until he was ready to return to work that there was no work for him.
- Where an employee was on sick leave, termination occurred when he was told of changes amounting to constructive dismissal, not when formal notice of termination was given a few weeks later.

- In one case, where notice was given in the middle of a maternity leave, it was effective immediately.
- Where an employee was told her employment would be terminated at the end of her maternity leave, but was then offered a temporary job that she refused, the employer could not require her to work in the new position for a period of working notice after the leave.
- Where an employee was told that changes amounting to constructive dismissal would begin when she returned from maternity leave, the judge ruled there was no termination until the leave had ended.
- After being given notice of termination, an employee was allowed to take a paid sabbatical for which he had previously qualified. His termination did not take effect until after the sabbatical, although the notice still took effect from the time given.

B-1.5 LAYOFFS, SUSPENSIONS AND SIMILAR ACTIONS

Layoff must be permitted — There is no automatic, implied contractual term that allows an employer to lay off an employee temporarily. Most statutes do not allow layoffs as a matter of course. In the absence of a contractual or statutory right, a purported layoff will be a wrongful dismissal. However, the termination may not be effective until the employee clearly indicates that he or she does not accept the layoff. See also Chapter C-4, "Other Constructive Dismissal Situations".

Permitted layoffs — Where layoffs are permitted by contract or by statute and the employer's intention is merely to lay off temporarily, there will be no dismissal. Indications of a temporary layoff include situations where the employee concurs in the layoff, the employee retains recall rights, or where the contract anticipates layoffs.

Termination vs. layoff — Where a cessation of employment is permanent and there is no intention to recall the employee or there is no assurance of the job resuming, a dismissal has occurred, regardless of whether it is called a termination, a layoff or a leave of absence. Suspension of payment for an indefinite period, without abolition of the position itself, may in some circumstances amount to dismissal. For example, termination was found where:

- An employee was given an N.S.F. cheque, told there was no more work, and told to look for another job.
- The employer had no intention of recalling an employee at the time of "layoff", and only recalled her later in an attempt to improve its defence to her wrongful dismissal action.

- A contradictory message was given as to whether the layoff was temporary or permanent, and recall occurred only because another employee resigned.
- A layoff was purportedly due to lack of work, when in fact there was no economic reason for the layoff and, rather than calling the employee back, the employer gave other employees overtime.

Onus is on employer — It has been said that the burden is on the employer to prove that it offered re-employment after a purported layoff. It is not the employee's duty to track down the employer to see if the employer has a job available.

Effective date of termination — The effective date of termination may depend on the employer's intentions and on when the employee was notified that the layoff was permanent.

- In one case, an employee was laid off and was not told it was permanent until eight months later. She was found to have been dismissed at the time of the layoff because the employer never had any intention of recalling her.
- In another case, termination was effective when formalized seven months after the layoff, it being presumed that there had been an intention to recall when layoff notice was given.
- An employee who was laid off for a month and then terminated without just cause was awarded pay for the time of the layoff plus reasonable notice from the time of the termination.

Effect of suspension — A suspension will not be a dismissal, constructive or otherwise, unless there is repudiation or an intention to no longer be bound by the contract. Where an employee is suspended, the employment relationship continues, and the employee cannot be terminated retroactively to the start of the suspension. See also Chapter C-4, "Other Constructive Dismissal Situations".

Termination during strike — Employees engaged in a lawful strike were not terminated by reason of the strike but, rather, by reason of the employer's decision to shut down its business operations. Thus, they were wrongfully dismissed.

Chapter B-2

CHANGE OF EMPLOYER

TABLE OF CONTENTS

B-2.1   Common Law vs. Statute
B-2.2   General Principles
B-2.3   Novation or Assignment of Contract
B-2.4   Effect on Service Length
B-2.5   Sale of a Business
B-2.6   Transfer to a Related Company
B-2.7   Winding up, Receivership, Bankruptcy, Financial Restructuring

B-2.1 COMMON LAW VS. STATUTE

Employment standards laws — Most employment standards laws now deal with change of employer situations, including sales of businesses and transfers between related entities. These can provide important protections for employees and limits on employers' rights in these situations.

Effect on common law — However, in the context of the common law of wrongful dismissal, these statutes usually do not affect the parties' rights. In the common law context, the question is simply whether the employer's actions have resulted in a termination of an employee's contract. If so, then the next question is whether the dismissal was justified, or whether it was wrongful.

Parallels between statute and common law — In many cases, the statutory provisions and common law rules are similar. For example, most statutes provide for service length to be continuous throughout any change of employer; the common law generally does, too. Note, however, that both the common law and statutes can change, and they will not always be in harmony with each other. Therefore, it is important to consider them separately. This chapter refers to the common law situation, unless stated otherwise.

B-2.2 GENERAL PRINCIPLES

Issues — Two issues can arise where there is a sale or other transfer of a business:

(1) has there been a dismissal? and
(2) if so, who is legally responsible for giving the dismissed employee notice or damages?

The issue of whether there has been a dismissal is discussed here. The issue of who is liable for a dismissal is discussed in Chapter A-5, "Identifying the Employer". For the sake of simplicity, the employing entity before the change will be called the "old" employer, and the employing entity after the change will be called the "new" employer.

Many situations — A change of employer can occur in a number of ways, including a corporate change such as a merger or splitting off a subsidiary; a transfer to a related company; a sale of business; and a receivership or bankruptcy situation.

General rule — A change in the employer's identity usually ends an employee's contract with the old employer, and begins a new contract with the new employer, unless there has been a novation or assignment of the employment contract, as discussed below. The old employer may be liable for wrongful dismissal, although an employee's damages may be offset by work with the new employer.

Duty to mitigate — Although a change of employer usually creates a new contract, it is doubtful that an employee can leave the job and sue for wrongful dismissal. The courts will look at the business realities of the situation. An employee who refuses to continue in the same job under the same conditions merely because the employer is different may have his action denied on the ground of failure to mitigate. See Chapter H-1, "Mitigation of Damages".

Implied term — An implied term that the employee will accept a similar job upon a merger of the employer has been found to exist in some cases.

B-2.3 NOVATION OR ASSIGNMENT OF CONTRACT

Assignment or novation — In modern situations, businesses frequently are transferred with the new owner making known to all employees, either directly or by implication, that their jobs will continue on the same terms. Although some judges have disagreed, most take the view that where an employee continues to work for the new employer, the new owner has assumed the employee's contract, including the dismissal obligations.

This may be the case even where there has been no definite act or agreement to assign. This can also be described as a novation of the contract. Thus, the old contract has not ended, but has continued with the new employer replacing the old employer. This has implications for liability if the new employment does not continue, as well as for expectations or entitlements created under the old employer.

Factors to be considered — Novation requires the following:

(1) the new employer must assume complete liability for the employment contract;
(2) the employee must accept the new employer as principal debtor and not as agent or guarantor for the old employer;
(3) the employee must accept the new contract in full satisfaction and substitution for the old contract; and
(4) the new contract must be made with the consent of all the parties.

Where an employee was not told that he would not receive credit for his service with his predecessor employers, no novation occurred and he was entitled to notice based on his full term of service.

Time to decide whether to accept novation — An employee need not make an instant decision as to whether to accept the new employment. Generally, an employee will be entitled to a reasonable time to decide, under all the circumstances. In one case, where employees had not been told of the change in ownership, they were given the entire notice period in which to decide; but in most cases, a shorter period will be sufficient. See Chapter C-1, "Constructive Dismissal: General Principles" for a discussion of condonation and what is a reasonable time to decide.

Forced resignation — Even if an employee submits a resignation to the old employer, there may be no termination where the employee then continues with the new employer. This is especially likely where an employee's resignation and immediate hiring by the new employer is a staged event with the employee having no opportunity to make a free, informed decision.

B-2.4 EFFECT ON SERVICE LENGTH

Where ownership changes — Where ownership of a business has changed, there is a presumption that the employees' service will be treated as continuous. Thus, employees usually are credited with their full service under both owners for the purposes of wrongful dismissal notice. See also Chapter F-3, "Reasonable Notice Factors: Age and Service Length".

Circumstances showing otherwise — The circumstances may indicate that service is not continuous and a new relationship has been created. If so, the old employer may remain liable to the employee for dismissal. For example, a sale was said to create a constructive dismissal where the employee clearly did not accept the change and was reasonable in refusing to work for the new owner; the old employer remained liable for his damages. In another case, where an employee was told she could apply for a job with the new employer, she was also treated as having been dismissed.

Vendor's promise to terminate relationship — The new employer may avoid assuming long-term contracts where the old employer agrees to terminate all employment relationships. For example:

- One employee was told by his boss of 15 years that his employment had terminated, and he was paid statutory severance pay. The next day, the new owner offered the employee essentially the same job. When he was dismissed by the new employer after two months, he was entitled only to reasonable notice on the basis of being a two-month employee, not a 15-year employee.
- Where an employer was purchased by another corporation and there was no representation that the employees were employed by the purchaser, the purchaser was not liable for their wrongful dismissal.

Agreement between employers — In one case, the old and new employers agreed on a three-month probationary period for all employees, for the purpose of apportioning liability between them. It was held that an employee's rights against the new employer were not affected when he was terminated some five years later. He was entitled to be treated as a long-service employee.

Statutory service length — Many Canadian employment standards laws define service as being continuous where the business is sold or otherwise changes hands. However, the fact that a statute gives protection does not affect employees' rights under the common law. It has been held that New Brunswick's employment standards legislation does not impose continuous employment where a business is leased rather than bought.

B-2.5 SALE OF A BUSINESS

General principles — A sale of a business is the most common example of a change of employer, and the principles above apply to the sale of business situations. Results can vary, depending on the circumstances, as shown by the following examples:

- Where an employee continued in his old job for a week under the new ownership, the new owner had impliedly offered him that job. A later offer for a lesser job was a constructive dismissal. A clause in the

agreement of purchase and sale allowing the purchaser to reassign job duties did not permit the new owner to demote the employee.
- In one case, an employee stayed on with a new employer who had promised that his terms would remain the same. He did not respond to a letter offering the job with reduced dismissal notice. The new employer could not rely on the reduced notice provisions. The fact that the employee continued to report to work was not considered acceptance where the offer letter included an express acceptance provision and the employer never followed up.
- Where an employee provided services on a "without prejudice" basis while the parties negotiated a new employment contract, the new owner never became the employer. It could end the services without liability when the parties did not reach an agreement.

New employer's policies — Where there is an assignment or novation, the new employer's policies usually will govern the employee. This is not always so, however:

- In one case, a novation was held to have taken place as to only part of a contract, and the employees were entitled to sick leave in accordance with the old employer's policy. The new employer could not unilaterally change the policy.
- A new employer tried to impose retirement at age 65 on an employee who was 64 years old when the business was sold. The old employer had a policy of retirement at 65, but the new employer did not. The court held that the old employer's policy did not apply, because the new employer had told the employee he did not have to retire at age 65. The old policy would have governed had the new employer not waived it.

B-2.6 TRANSFER TO A RELATED COMPANY

Effect of transfer — The transfer of an employee to a subsidiary or related company can be a dismissal by the old employer, depending on the terms of the contract. The employee may be required to accept the change in order to mitigate his damages. However, the old employer will remain liable for any part of the damages not mitigated or the new employer may become liable for notice based on the length of service with both.

Test for statutory entitlement — Employees have succeeded in employment standards applications against related companies where the following tests were met:

(1) two or more business entities were involved in the form of a corporation or other arrangement;
(2) the activities of the business entities were related;

(3) the employee worked for one of the corporations during the period of time for which the benefits are claimed or the violation took place; and
(4) the intent or effect of the arrangement must have been to defeat, either directly or indirectly, the true intent and purpose of the Act.

In one case, there was a close functional interdependence between two companies. One company supervised, co-signed cheques, procured a line of credit, handled all financial matters and was involved with the personnel and operational matters of the other company. The adjudicator decided that the employee could claim statutory benefits against the supervising company when the other one went bankrupt. This was upheld by a reviewing court.

B-2.7 WINDING UP, RECEIVERSHIP, BANKRUPTCY, FINANCIAL RESTRUCTURING

Windup or dissolution of employer — Where an employer voluntarily dissolves or shuts down its operations, it will be liable to its employees for wrongful dismissal.

Appointment of receiver — The appointment of a receiver, whether under a debenture or by a court, has been held to terminate the employees' contracts of employment. Continued service after the appointment is rendered under a new contract with the receiver or with the purchaser. While a receiver must pay termination pay or give notice based on service with the receiver, it is not liable for statutory or common-law pay in lieu of notice for the dismissal caused by the receiver's appointment. This remains the original employer's liability, even though it may not have the funds to honour it.

Assignment in bankruptcy — An assignment in bankruptcy operates as a dismissal from employment, and the employee will have a claim for damages against the bankrupt estate through the trustee. An employee who agreed to a fixed-term employment contract in the context of a potential bankruptcy was still entitled to damages.

Petition into bankruptcy — Historically, it has been held that a petition into bankruptcy terminates all employees' employment, but they do not become entitled to damages for wrongful dismissal. Presumably this is because the termination is not voluntary to the employer.

Statutory pay on bankruptcy — Employees who continue to work, first for the trustee operating the business and then for the purchaser, may lose their rights to statutory termination and severance pay from the bankrupt employer.

Bankruptcy after dismissal — An employer who declares bankruptcy after dismissing an employee is not entitled to reduce the amount of notice or pay in lieu of notice that it owes to the employee. That amount is fixed as of the time of dismissal, and the employee remains entitled to payment for the full notice period.

Chapter B-3

FRUSTRATION OF THE EMPLOYMENT CONTRACT

TABLE OF CONTENTS

B-3.1   General Principles
B-3.2   Self-induced Frustration
B-3.3   Illness and Disability
B-3.4   Labour Disputes

B-3.1 GENERAL PRINCIPLES

Doctrine of frustration — Where a contract becomes impossible to perform through no fault of either party, the contract is terminated without liability. The contract is said to have been "frustrated".

Impossibility — Performance must actually be impossible, not just more onerous or less profitable than expected. For example, loss of work causing financial consequences for the employer is not enough to frustrate the employees' contracts and deprive them of their right to reasonable notice of dismissal.

Unforeseen and without fault — The frustrating events must have been unforeseen, or at least they must have occurred through no fault of either party. There must be no alternative to dismissal, such as modifying the job or finding the employee an alternative job.

Examples of frustration — The most common situations involving frustration claims arise in the context of employee illness or of labour disputes that effectively shut down an employer. Other examples include:

- A fire that destroyed an employer's business frustrated the contracts of all employees, even one employee who was kept on for a short time after the fire to deal with the insurance claims.
- The contract of a nursing director who had his registered nurse status revoked had been frustrated because the professional status was essential for the job.

Objective test — The test for frustration is objective and depends on the existence of facts amounting to frustration, not on the subjective beliefs of either party.

After-acquired knowledge — Some cases have allowed an employer or an employee to use facts that came to light after termination when deciding whether or not the contract was frustrated. Other cases have refused to take after-acquired information into account, and have judged the situation on the facts known at the time of termination.

B-3.2 SELF-INDUCED FRUSTRATION

Self-induced frustration — Self-induced frustration does not excuse non-performance of a contract. Where the frustrating event was caused by the employer, it cannot use frustration as a defence to a wrongful dismissal claim. If an employer has agreed to do something that can only happen under certain circumstances, it has a duty not to do anything to change the circumstances and make performance impossible. It must have used its best efforts to ensure that the frustrating event does not occur.

Examples of self-induced frustration — Self-induced frustration was found and the employer was therefore liable to pay damages in lieu of reasonable notice where:

- An employer's illness led to his retirement and the termination of his employee. The employer's eventual retirement must have been in the parties' contemplation, and therefore was foreseeable, so it could not be considered a frustrating event.
- Statutory abolishment of a board caused the termination of a board appointee. The same directing minds responsible for the appointment were also responsible for the termination. The breach could have been remedied by appointing the employee to the successor board.

Example where no self-induced frustration — In another situation involving a government appointment, the government was held liable only for the time between the employee's firing and the actual passage of the statute abolishing the employing entity.

B-3.3 ILLNESS AND DISABILITY

Nature and length of illness, prognosis — Both temporary and permanent illnesses have been alleged to frustrate employment contracts. The most important factors in deciding whether an illness is a frustrating event are the nature and expected length of the illness, and the prospect of recovery. The greater the degree of incapacity that exists, the longer the period of illness will last and the greater the likelihood that it will continue, the more likely it is that the illness has frustrated the contract.

Nature and length of employment — The nature and length of employment are also important factors to consider. A key employee's contract may become frustrated more quickly than a non-essential employee's contract.

Temporary illness — Temporary illness will not often frustrate a contract. In one case where an employee was terminated before either party knew his disability was permanent, the contract was still held to be frustrated and there was no wrongful dismissal. This finding, however, may have been influenced by the fact that he later did become permanently disabled.

Partial disability — The contract of one worker who became permanently unable to lift was found to be frustrated, even though he could perform the rest of his job, had performed the job on a temporary basis while still on sick leave, and the employer could have easily accommodated his disability. Usually, however, a job duty would have to be essential before an inability to perform it would lead to a finding of frustration.

Sick leave or disability benefits — The right to receive sick leave or disability benefits is important, as the period of leave or benefits may postpone the time of frustration. The fact that the employee's duties were handled by others on a part-time basis, and that the employee had not been replaced by a permanent employee, may also be factors to consider. A finding of frustration is unlikely where the employer has a statutory duty to not discriminate against an employee receiving workers' compensation, and a duty to accommodate the injured employee's needs. Similarly, a statutory right to refuse unsafe work defeated a frustration claim in one unusual case.

Examples where frustration found — Frustration was found where:
- A key employee was suffering from a prolonged illness of indeterminate length, given her key position and the employer's urgent need to fill the position before its upcoming busy season.
- A key confidential employee had already been off work for a year and it was not known when she would be able to return.

Examples where no frustration found — Frustration was not found where:
- An employee was unable to work due to temporary illness of an uncertain length, as she was entitled to sick leave and there was no sign

the contract would be impossible to perform after the sick leave expired.
- A non-key employee had been off work for only 10 months at the time of termination, and it was not yet known whether his work-related injury would be permanent.
- An employee had previously taken two long-term disability leaves and had returned to work.
- No steps were taken to determine the anticipated length of the temporary absence, and the employee had been told his job was not in jeopardy.

B-3.4 LABOUR DISPUTES

Shutdown due to strike — The first Canadian case to apply the frustration doctrine in an employment context involved a case where the employer promised to hire the plaintiffs if they would withdraw from a union. The resulting union actions caused such a disturbance that the police were unable to control it, and the employer was forced to give in and operate its shop under the union. Since the contract was based on the existence of an independent shop, it was held to have been frustrated, and the plaintiffs were not entitled to damages. More recently, an unresolvable union strike, which led to a decision to shut down the company, was held to frustrate the contract of a non-unionized employee. However, the employee was awarded damages for the seven weeks of the strike before the employer decided to shut down.

No frustration from shutdown due to strike — The defence of frustration following a strike has not always been upheld. For example, no frustration was found where:

- Only part of the employer's workforce was on strike. The employer could have made other arrangements to cover the duties of the striking employees.
- The business shut-down was a foreseeable consequence of the employer's negotiations with the unionized employees. The court also noted that the strike was short and was not a critical event at the point when the employer decided to shut down; the strike was not the sole reason for the shut-down; the parties were not incapable of performing their contractual obligations; and the employer could have provided for the possibility of a strike in the parties' written contracts.
- A strike that led to a decision to shut down the company was not sufficient to avoid statutory duties to pay termination and severance pay, since it was the company's liquidation that caused the termination and not the strike itself. The statutory amounts were simply a result of the choice to shut down the business.

Chapter B-4

RESIGNATION

TABLE OF CONTENTS

B-4.1   Resignation: General Principles
B-4.2   Threats to Resign and Words Amounting to Resignation
B-4.3   Conduct Amounting to Resignation
B-4.4   Involuntary Resignation
B-4.5   Resignation Following Constructive Dismissal
B-4.6   Lack of Requisite Mental Capacity
B-4.7   Consequences of Resignation

B-4.1 RESIGNATION: GENERAL PRINCIPLES

Resignation must be voluntary — To be effective, a resignation must be made freely and voluntarily. A court is entitled to look at the substance of the termination, not just its form. An employee who voluntarily resigns will not have a cause of action against the employer for his dismissal, since he has chosen to end the contract himself.

Clear and unequivocal — A resignation must be clear and unequivocal. The actual words used are not important if a clear impression is left that the employee has quit. A resignation can be implied by an employee's actions, in the absence of words. Note that in these cases, the resignation may be quite similar to a repudiation, as discussed in Chapter B-5, "Repudiation by Employee".

Test — The test for deciding whether an employee's words or actions amount to a resignation is objective: what would a reasonable person understand from the statement or actions in all the circumstances? This is the same test applied when considering whether an employer's words amount to a firing. While the test is objective, consideration should also be given to the employee's personal characteristics and mental state.

True reflection of intent — A resignation must be a true reflection of the employee's intention. A resignation made without the required mental capacity, or made in the heat of anger, may not be valid. For example, resignations were not valid where:

- An employee told several people he was quitting, including the Chairman of the Board, handed over his responsibilities to his assistant, left work, and did not communicate with the employer for two weeks. The directors met almost immediately and accepted his resignation without hearing from him. The judge ruled that the directors had acted hastily and should have waited until tempers cooled and they had heard from the employee.
- An employee and his employer exchanged heated words and the employee quit in the midst of the argument. The employer was found to have seized the opportunity to be rid of the employee despite 24 years of good, faithful and loyal service, without having made an effort to address the employee's concerns or make sure they were understood.

Indication of true intention — A resignation given in the heat of the moment was valid where it was followed up with a written resignation mailed the next day.

Onus is on employee — The onus is on the employee to prove he or she was dismissed and did not voluntarily resign.

B-4.2 THREATS TO RESIGN AND WORDS AMOUNTING TO RESIGNATION

Threat to resign — Where an employee's words invite dismissal, or where an employee threatens resignation if his demands are not met, the employer may be entitled to accept the resignation. Note, however, that a conditional resignation may not entitle the employer to accept it, as discussed below.

Request to be let go — Termination after a request to be let go may represent resignation, especially if the request follows a decision by the employee to leave the job.

Conditional resignation — A conditional resignation, i.e. one contingent on another event either happening or not happening, may not be binding. For example:

- Where an employee submitted her resignation to try to force the employer to address her grievances, she had not truly resigned, given the employer's practice not to accept a resignation without discussing it with the employee again after 24 to 48 hours. Her conditional resignation had been triggered by the turmoil created by the employer, and the employer had not acted reasonably in accepting it.
- An employee upset about complaints, who said he would resign if forced to attend a meeting that day to address the complaints, had not resigned where within a day or two he said he wanted the weekend to

think about it. It was held that his offer to resign was conditional or that it had been revoked before acceptance was communicated to him.

Hypothetical statement — A hypothetical statement, or an expression of opinion about the wisdom of resigning, may or may not amount to a resignation. A lawyer's letter stating that the employee had concluded "it would be appropriate to sever relations at this time" was held to be a resignation. The following examples, however, did not amount to a resignation:

- An employee who said he might as well resign if the employer would not be more reasonable, as he had no actual intention to resign when he said those words.
- A statement that an employee would resign if it were in the company's best interest.
- A discussion about the possibility of the employee resigning.
- An employee who asked, "What do you want — my resignation?" This was considered merely a rhetorical question.
- An employee expressed his view that he had been constructively dismissed and stated that he would continue in the new position while he sought another job.
- An employee who said that the matter would be settled in court.
- An employee stated that if the employer would not abide by the contract, he could not continue to work there. This was held to have been a statement about his future options.
- An employee mentioned he was having financial difficulties when he had trouble collecting money due from his employer.
- An employee said that he "would be resigning". He was held to have resigned only when the employer accepted "the necessary forms" it had requested the employee to send in.
- An employee who stated his intent to retire at some future time, without stating a date, had not resigned, and was entitled to change his mind.

Expressions of dissatisfaction — Expressions of dissatisfaction do not necessarily amount to resignation. For example:

- A memo written by an employee to protest an on-going dispute, in which he said he would seek other work, was found to be an expression of dissatisfaction, not an "open-ended resignation" entitling the employer to replace the employee.
- An employee's invitation to negotiate termination terms did not amount to a resignation.
- An employee who complained he "couldn't handle it any longer" after a gruelling road trip had not resigned.
- An employee who took a confrontational approach in response to performance criticisms had not resigned by claiming constructive

dismissal. However, the employer was justified in terminating him, as his conduct had destroyed the employment relationship.

B-4.3 CONDUCT AMOUNTING TO RESIGNATION

Resignation vs. repudiation — Occasionally, it may be unclear whether a resignation has taken place, or even whether an employee has repudiated the contract. Sometimes conduct without an express resignation can still act as a repudiation to the contract. See Chapter B-5, "Repudiation by Employee".

Types of conduct amounting to resignation — Behaviour that is commonly carried out upon resignation or dismissal may indicate an intent to resign. This can include behaviour such as clearing out one's personal effects; turning in employer property such as keys; asking for a paycheque that is not due, or asking for severance pay; and leaving or not attending work. The behaviour must always be assessed in the context of the employee's situation.

Examples of resignation based on conduct — Resignation was found where:

- An employee asked for all money owing to him, including "holdback pay", before leaving the province for a vacation.
- An employee left on vacation after being refused permission to go on vacation and being warned that he would be taken to have resigned if he left.
- An employee, upset with his remuneration package, did not attend an important sales meeting after being told he was expected to.
- A letter stated that the employee had not quit but was on an indefinite sick leave, but no date of expected return was given.
- An employee asked for her final paycheque after receiving no answer to her query whether she was dismissed; the employer's silence was not equivalent to a dismissal.

Examples where no resignation based on conduct — No resignation was found where:

- An employee who was in charge of the business returned his keys upon being suddenly hospitalized for an illness which was expected to be lengthy.
- An employee was absent from work due to illness during a period of working notice.
- An employee left the office after a disagreement and returned to find the locks changed.

- An employee refused to report for a work assignment that she had already told the employer had aggravated an injury, but she later apologized.
- After a dispute with staff and the board of directors, an employee suggested he take a leave of absence to allow the situation to cool off.
- An employee told her employer it could have her resignation if it wanted it and then failed to return to work after 24 hours. Her employer's decision to give her 24 hours to reconsider had not been communicated to her.
- An employee asked for a transfer and was refused. He expressly said he was not quitting and the employer was wrong to assume he would move away anyway.
- An employee asked for a new position without making it clear he was not resigning.
- An employee failed to apply for a new position with a newly amalgamated employer, despite being invited to do so.
- A shareholder/employee sold his shares, but had never agreed to suggestions that he retire when he sold his shares. His forced retirement was a dismissal, not a resignation.

Refusal to return to work — A refusal to return to work may amount to a resignation. It may also constitute repudiation, as discussed in Chapter B-5, "Repudiation by Employee". A deemed resignation clause in a contract, which stated that an unauthorized absence lasting 10 days would be taken as a resignation, might have barred an employee's claim if it had been clear that the clause applied to the employee.

Examples — resignation by absence from work — Resignation was found where:

- An employee asked for a severance package and letter of recommendation and was told by his supervisor, who did not have the power to fire him, that he could either resign immediately, resign later, or be fired. He took the position that he had been fired, despite the company's assurances to the contrary. His refusal to return to work amounted to a resignation.
- An employee refused to return to work and submitted a letter requesting either a severance package or to negotiate terms under which he would stay.
- An employee refused to respond to a performance review, refused to return after a disciplinary suspension and asked for a termination letter despite being assured that he had not been dismissed.

Examples — no resignation due to absence from work — Resignation was not found where:

- An employee was told he was being dismissed, with the date and terms to be negotiated, and left his employment on the date he had proposed, after he had received no response from the employer.
- An employee cleared out his desk and immediately took a vacation, when he had been told he was being removed from his position and he was awaiting details of a proposed new position.
- An employee removed his personal effects and did not return to work, after giving the employer a letter stating his view that his contract had been breached. He asked for either a reconciliation or his contractual termination pay, and it was found that he had not resigned because he had left the possibility of a reconciliation open.

B-4.4 INVOLUNTARY RESIGNATION

Voluntary vs. involuntary resignation — A demand by the employer for a resignation, or a choice between resigning or being fired, is the same as a dismissal, because the employee has no real choice whether to continue in the job. An invitation or a request to resign may amount to a dismissal. The effect of words such as "If you don't like it, there's the door" will depend on the employee's understanding of the words in the context of the job and the industry. A forced retirement may amount to constructive dismissal, as discussed in Chapter C-4, "Other Constructive Dismissal Situations".

Duress — A resignation obtained under coercion or duress will not bar a wrongful dismissal action. How much duress is needed to invalidate a resignation is a question of fact.

Severance pay — The fact that an employee accepted severance pay will not make an involuntary resignation valid.

Examples of voluntary resignation — The following resignations were deemed to be voluntary:

- An employee resigned in the face of continual performance complaints. The employer was entitled to bring justifiable complaints to his attention.
- An employee who refused to return to work after a disciplinary suspension, despite the employer's efforts to ensure a harmonious return, had resigned.
- An employee resigned in response to the suggestion of his boss (who was also a friend), after further instances of misconduct for which he had been warned. There was no intention to dismiss him if he did not resign, there was no pressure, and the employee had negotiated the details of his leaving over a two-day period.

- An employee, who was also a major shareholder, agreed to resign as part of a refinancing deal which he negotiated himself. The pressure to resign came from the marketplace and not from the employer.

Examples of involuntary resignation — Resignations of the following employees were invalid due to duress:

- An employee resigned rather than be transferred out of province. This finding may have been influenced by the fact that the employee would have been entitled to treat the forced transfer as a constructive dismissal, although in another case involving a potential constructive dismissal, the resignation was found to be voluntary. See Chapter C-4, "Other Constructive Dismissal Situations".
- An innocent employee was aggressively interrogated after money disappeared from his store, and resigned because he feared for his career when the investigator would not listen to him.
- An employee resigned following an unfounded allegation of theft which was brought forth in an attempt to goad him into quitting.

B-4.5 RESIGNATION FOLLOWING CONSTRUCTIVE DISMISSAL

General principle — A resignation in response to a constructive dismissal will not bar an employee's action.

Constructive dismissal must exist — The employer's actions must amount to constructive dismissal before a seeming resignation will be ignored. Resignations will be treated as voluntary where employees choose to resign rather than accept a change that does not amount to constructive dismissal. Employees, who resign because they believe they have lost the employer's trust, or because they did not get a requested raise, or because they feel discriminated against, will be found to have resigned voluntarily unless they can prove that they were constructively dismissed.

Allegations of constructive dismissal — An employee who aggressively alleges constructive dismissal without justification may give the employer cause for dismissal. However, an employee's justified objection to a unilateral change does not amount to a resignation.

Hard bargaining — An employee's "dogged determination" to secure a raise, along with challenging the terms and conditions of his employment during negotiations, did not amount to a resignation.

B-4.6 LACK OF REQUISITE MENTAL CAPACITY

General principle — An employee's resignation will be invalid if he or she lacked the required mental capacity at the time the resignation was given. Usually, this will require evidence of mental illness and/or a lack of understanding of his or her actions. Note that "temporary insanity" due to the heat of anger may invalidate a resignation, as discussed earlier in this chapter.

Examples where resignation binding — Attempts to withdraw a resignation for lack of mental capacity did not succeed where:

- Medical evidence was not contemporaneous and there was other evidence that the employee understood his actions.
- An employee's resignation was accepted to save her the embarrassment of dismissal for cause, and where there was no evidence her misconduct was caused by her mental illness.
- The employer had no knowledge of the employee's mental illness. The court said that even if the employer had that knowledge, there was no duty on it to not allow the employee to resign.

B-4.7 CONSEQUENCES OF RESIGNATION

General principle — An employee is obligated to give reasonable notice of his intention to resign. Failure to do so is a breach of contract, although not a breach of a fiduciary duty.

Employer's options on receiving resignation — Where an employee gives reasonable notice of intent to resign, the offer must be accepted as offered or it will not bind the employee. The employer has the right to accept or reject the employee's offer to work out the notice period, but once accepted, termination before expiry of that period will be a wrongful dismissal.

Employer not obligated to accept — A court refused to grant a declaration that an employer was required to accept a resignation. Doing so would have allowed the employee to profit from his own wrong by entitling him to severance benefits upon resignation, rather than being dismissed for just cause.

Resignation during notice period — An employee who resigns during a period of working notice of dismissal may or may not be entitled to further payment. For example:

- An employee who resigned during a period of working notice was not entitled to further compensation, except for one month's pay that had

already been offered by the employer. The requirement that he work through the notice period was reasonable.
- Another employee who resigned during a period of working notice was found not to have repudiated his contract. The employee was still entitled to damages.

Where improper notice given — An employee who quits his or her employment without proper notice to the employer may not be entitled to claim unpaid amounts such as a bonus, even on a *quantum meruit* basis. An employee who resigns without proper notice may also be subject to a claim for damages by the employer.

Resignation following employer misrepresentation — Where employees voluntarily retired based on an offer of benefits that turned out to be wrong, they were awarded damages equal to the offer they had accepted or, in the alternative, damages for misrepresentation.

Changes in employment after resignation — An employee who voluntarily resigned after 30 years of service was unable to receive the benefit of an early retirement incentive plan announced one month later. The employer had not made any representation or misrepresentation that induced him to retire early.

Entitlement to disability payments — The cases on entitlement to disability payments vary and seem to depend on what the employer knew at the time the employee resigned. For example:
- The estate of an employee who resigned voluntarily was not entitled to collect disability benefits on his behalf, even if it could establish that he had suffered from dementia at the time of his resignation. The employer had no knowledge of the employee's impairment, and it was not clear that he would have been entitled to disability benefits at the time of his resignation.
- In another case, it was held that an employer had a duty to provide an employee with long-term disability benefits despite her resignation, as it had failed in its duty to explain the benefits plan to her when she resigned.

Return to work following resignation — Where an employee who has resigned returns to work, the employer must be clear on whether the return is a continuation of the old contract, or a new arrangement. In one case, an employee who would otherwise have been deemed to have resigned was induced to return to work temporarily, with the promise of a letter of reference. No end point was established and the temporary nature of the arrangement was not confirmed. It was held that the return was an affirmation of the original employment contract, and the employer lost the right to assert it was a new contract.

Chapter B-5

REPUDIATION BY EMPLOYEE

TABLE OF CONTENTS

B-5.1   General Principles
B-5.2   Work Refusals
B-5.3   Absence from Work
B-5.4   Inability to Attend Work
B-5.5   Legal Dispute with Employer

B-5.1 GENERAL PRINCIPLES

Repudiation — Repudiation consists of actions by the employee that are incompatible with a continued employment relationship. Repudiation by the employee without resigning is analogous to constructive dismissal of the employer. It ends the employment relationship and disentitles the employee to further payment.

Employer must act — If the employer chooses to treat the breach as just cause, the employer is justified in dismissing the employee. But if nothing is done, the employer will be said to have condoned the employee's breach and will lose the right to dismiss, as discussed in Chapter D-3, "Condonation of Misconduct".

Examples of repudiation — Repudiation by an employee has included:
- A demand for higher pay.
- A refusal to continue working in a particular manner.
- A refusal to continue working with a particular co-worker.
- A refusal to accept a reasonable reassignment.
- A refusal to comply with a safety requirement or discuss alternatives with the employer.
- A resignation from a university, when a university affiliation was required for an accompanying hospital appointment.

Reasonable excuse — An employee's repudiation will not justify termination if there is a reasonable excuse for it. For instance, an employee who reasonably refused to take a required medical exam had not repudiated her employment.

Context important — An employee on leave of absence who angrily refused to return could not be taken to have repudiated her contract, since her words were said in anger and her employer knew she was suffering from emotional illness.

B-5.2 WORK REFUSALS

Refusal to report to work — In general, a refusal to report for work will amount to repudiation, unless the employer has already constructively dismissed the employee or the employee's contrary intentions are clear.

Refusal to accept work assignment — A refusal to accept a reasonable work assignment by the employer may lead to a finding of repudiation. For example:

- An employee refused to report to work or to inform the employer of his intentions.
- An employee angrily walked off the job after a confrontation and failed to contact the employer.
- An employee asked for a letter of termination at the end of a disciplinary suspension, and refused to return to work, although the employer assured him he was not fired.
- An employee left the job after a disagreement and later accepted severance pay.
- An employee refused to return from a layoff without certain guarantees.
- An employee refused to report for a new assignment made at the employee's request.
- An employee refused to accept a transfer that was the natural result of a retraining program accepted by the employee.

Examples where no repudiation — No repudiation was found where:

- An employee was unfit to return to work, even though the employer believed she was fit.
- An employee refused a work assignment because she had already told the employer it was aggravating her injury, and where she later apologized.
- An employee said he would resign if forced to attend a meeting, but later said he wanted to think about what to do and then affirmed his willingness to perform his contract.
- An employee suggested he take a leave of absence after a dispute. He was not renouncing his contract, but merely trying to allow things to cool off.
- An employee refused to accept a transfer imposed by the employer, even though she had initially agreed to it. The employee had not lost her right to sue for constructive dismissal.

- An employee refused an improper, unauthorized order.
- An employee refused to work through a dismissal notice period, but it was not reasonable to expect the employee to continue working.

B-5.3 ABSENCE FROM WORK

Unauthorized absence — An unauthorized absence from work may in some cases amount to a repudiation or resignation. See Chapter B-4, "Resignation", and see also Chapter D-9, "Attendance and Substance Abuse".

Authorized absence — An absence with the employer's consent, or with the employer's knowledge in the case of a personal crisis, is not repudiation or cause for dismissal. For example:

- An employee who left work suddenly due to poor health, but who made it clear he was taking a temporary leave of absence for medical reasons, had not abandoned his job.
- An employee who was absent for most of the period of working notice, due to illness, had not repudiated his contract.

Failure to return after illness — Failure to report for duty after illness, when capable of doing so, was a repudiation. An employee who was absent and failed to communicate with her employer, however, had not repudiated her contract where the employer knew she was still receiving medical benefits.

B-5.4 INABILITY TO ATTEND WORK

Failure to return after layoff — An employee who is unable to return to work after an authorized layoff may have repudiated his contract. For example, repudiation occurred where:

- An employee was unavailable to return to work from a layoff when recalled because he was serving a jail sentence.
- Employees accepted other employment while on a temporary layoff.

Accepting conflicting work — Repudiation can occur if an employee accepts employment that conflicts with and leaves him unable to fulfill his job commitments. For example, it was repudiation where:

- Employees accepted other employment before actually receiving notice of termination.
- An employee bound by a definite-term contract accepted other employment during the term of his contract. In so doing he had accepted the contract's termination.

Seeking new work — Repudiation did not occur where an employee sought a new job in response to termination rumours, since the employee would not have left his job voluntarily and would not have started at the new job until he was fired from the old one. Similarly, an employee who was required to be a shareholder in order to be employed did not repudiate his contract when he offered his shares for sale but did not actually sell them.

Acceptance of constructive dismissal — Constructive dismissal is a repudiation of the employment contract by the employer. An employee who accepts a new job after being constructively dismissed has neither repudiated his contract nor resigned. See also Chapter B-4, "Resignation", and Chapter C-1, "Constructive Dismissal: General Principles".

B-5.5 LEGAL DISPUTE WITH EMPLOYER

Duty to bargain in good faith — An employee who had no desire to reach an agreement about his continued employment after the sale of a business was held to have breached his duty to bargain in good faith, and to have repudiated his employment contract. An employee's inferior bargaining position relative to her employer did not entitle her to repudiate the contract.

Refusal to sign release or agree to settlement — An employee who was given working notice of termination did not repudiate his employment by refusing to sign a release. His immediate termination was a wrongful dismissal, as there was no cause based on his refusal to agree to the employer's proposed settlement of the matter.

Refusal to work through notice period — Repudiation was not found where it would be unreasonable to expect an employee to work through the notice period. However, if there is no acrimony or humiliation to the employee, the employee may be required to work through the notice period, as discussed in Chapter H-4, "Rejecting an Offer and Other Failures to Mitigate".

Suing employer — An employee who files a statement of claim while still working for the employer, or who leaves work and sues during the notice period, may have repudiated the contract by acting inconsistently within the employment relationship. There will be a repudiation if the statement of claim states that the employee has elected to treat the contract as at an end due to the employer's constructive dismissal. In one case, an employee sued for inadequate notice while completing the notice period she had been given. Even though the employer was found to have given inadequate notice and to have already repudiated the contract, her repudiation by suing resulted in her losing her entitlement to payment for the time between the start of her suit and the end of the inadequate notice period.

No repudiation by suing — In other cases, however, it has been held that suing while still employed does not repudiate the employment relationship, even in the case of a management employee. For example, there was no repudiation or resignation where:

- A letter stated that the employee had been constructively dismissed and the employee had reluctantly asked for a severance package.
- A statement of claim and pleadings were filed, where the employee's intention was to continue working through the notice period that had been given.

Chapter C-1

CONSTRUCTIVE DISMISSAL: GENERAL PRINCIPLES

TABLE OF CONTENTS

C-1.1   Constructive Dismissal: General Principles
C-1.2   Unilateral, Fundamental Change
C-1.3   Establishing Constructive Dismissal
C-1.4   Exceptions
C-1.5   Duty to Mitigate in Constructive Dismissal Situations
C-1.6   Condonation

C-1.1   CONSTRUCTIVE DISMISSAL: GENERAL PRINCIPLES

No right to impose change — Neither party to a contract of employment has the right to change a significant term of the contract without the other party's consent. Of course, the employee is seldom in a position to unilaterally change the terms of the contract; employers, however, frequently try to do so. Unless the employee accepts the change, the employer will have repudiated the contract and constructively dismissed the employee. The employer has no right to force an employee to accept the change, quit or take a severance package. The employer's refusal to abide by its original agreement ends the contract and the employee is entitled to receive damages. As in any other wrongful dismissal case, the employee is entitled to pay in lieu of reasonable notice.

Employee's options — The proposed change amounts to an offer of new terms, which the employee is free to accept or reject. If the employee accepts the change, or condones it by continuing in the employment on the new terms without complaint, the new terms become part of the employment contract. If the employee refuses to accept the change and the employer imposes it anyway, the employee may treat the change as a breach of contract, i.e. constructive dismissal, and sue for damages. An employee cannot accept the changes he likes while insisting on some of the old terms; the employee must accept or reject them all.

Resignation triggers right to sue — An employee who is forced to resign rather than accept a fundamental change has been constructively dismissed and is not barred from suing. The right to sue arises upon the resignation, not upon the employee's complaints about the changes or threats to resign.

Past acceptance — The fact that an employee accepted a fundamental change in the past does not give an employer the right to impose another fundamental change. The employee is still entitled to decide whether to treat the new change as a constructive dismissal.

Contract — The parties may expressly agree by contract to permit changes that would, but for their agreement, amount to constructive dismissal. Even where a contract allows reassignment, however, there may be a duty to exercise the term reasonably.

Reasonable time to decide — An employee must decide within a reasonable time whether to accept the change or to treat the contract as at an end. An employee who does not decide within a reasonable time may be said to have condoned the change.

Circumstances important — Where there has been no humiliation, undue pressure or other conduct that would make continued employment untenable, an employee may have to accept some changes. This is especially true where the changes are dictated by financial necessity or the employee's own performance, or where they would not become substantial for some time. Refusal may be justified if the relationship is sufficiently frayed by the proposed change that a reasonable person would not think the employee could work in harmony with the employer or the other employees, or where the good faith is gone from the relationship. See also Chapter H-4, "Rejecting an Offer and Other Failures to Mitigate", and Chapter C-4, "Other Constructive Dismissal Situations", for more on humiliating treatment.

No repudiation where notice is given — A fundamental change will not be a wrongful breach of contract where reasonable notice of the change has been given.

C-1.2 UNILATERAL, FUNDAMENTAL CHANGE

Change must be fundamental — Whether a change in terms amounts to a repudiation of the contract depends on the seriousness of the breach. The change must be fundamental, severe, serious, unilateral and substantial, and imposed without reasonable notice to the employee.

Single change — Deliberate breach of a single term of a contract may amount to a repudiation of the whole bargain if the provision is important, such as a significant change to pay or job functions.

Minor changes — Changes that are not fundamental may be imposed without consequence. Changes not found to amount to constructive dismissal include:

- A change of title, where accompanied by the same pay and work on a bigger, more important project.
- Assignment to a different office, where this was temporary or reasonable.
- Removal from an unpaid position which carried prestige and authority, but which did not affect the employee's paid position.
- A partial or minor decrease in status caused by the employee's request for a transfer.
- A dispute as to one or several minor provisions in an elaborate contract, or even a refusal to act upon what was later held to be the proper interpretation of those provisions.

Multiple changes — Where a number of elements are changed, there is a greater chance of finding constructive dismissal. Changes that have amounted to constructive dismissal include:

- A reduction in responsibility, along with a change in status and in actual functions.
- A change of title and responsibilities along with the assignment of a smaller office.
- A relocation, change in duties and change in working conditions.
- A refusal to respond to requests for information on an employee's status, when she was continually moved around to different locations and desks.
- A reduction in responsibility along with the elimination of a significant bonus.
- Assignment to a smaller office, along with reduced duties and a frozen salary.
- A request that a manager return to the bargaining unit, with lower pay and different work conditions that would not give him the flexibility he needed to care for his ill wife.
- Return of an employee to a job held much earlier in the employment.
- A change in job classification accompanied by a salary freeze, since the employee would not be entitled to his accustomed merit increases for several years.
- Changes to an employee's duties and perquisites, little by little, including changing his authority by adding positions above his, and finally changing the name of his position.

Incorporation into new job description — In one case, a number of changes were made gradually, and then were incorporated into a new job description. In that case, it was held that there had been no constructive dismissal, presumably because the changes had been accepted or condoned as they occurred.

Repudiation without changing specific term — Usually, a specific term must be changed to support a claim of constructive dismissal. Occasionally, though, constructive dismissal can exist even where no specific term has been breached. For example, where an employer's conduct demonstrates an intention to no longer be bound by the contract (i.e. a repudiation of the entire employment relationship), the employee may have been constructively dismissed even though no specific term of the contract has been changed. Another example is where the employer's treatment of the employee makes continued employment intolerable.

Anticipatory breaches — A fundamental breach can be present or anticipatory (in the future). Both present and anticipatory breaches are actionable.

Warning vs. anticipatory breach — Generally, notice of impending changes has been found to be a fundamental breach and not merely a warning of changes to come. In some cases, however, warnings of pending changes have not amounted to anticipatory breaches:

- Advising an employee of a change expected to take place in three to five years was held not to be an anticipatory breach, but merely a warning of future changes.
- An employee who requested a transfer, knowing the new position would likely involve shift work, had condoned the change to shift work, either by accepting the transfer or by doing nothing when he learned of the shift work a year and a half beforehand.
- Constructive dismissal was found where the employer claimed that it merely intended to give notice of impending changes prior to an imminent reorganization, and that the employee's refusal to return to work was a resignation. The employee's assistant had been appointed to take over his duties "effective immediately", and a relocation consultant was standing by in the next room to review the financial offer made to him.

C-1.3 ESTABLISHING CONSTRUCTIVE DISMISSAL

Objective question of fact — The question of whether a constructive dismissal has occurred is a question of fact. The answer depends on the nature of the relationship between the parties, as well as the express and implied terms of their contract. Where the employee has held a number of positions, the most current contract is the one to consider. Whether or not a fundamental breach has occurred must be judged objectively and reasonably, not just based on the employee's perceptions. It will be judged, however, only on the facts within the employee's knowledge.

Onus — The onus is on the employee to prove that a fundamental breach has occurred.

Factors to consider — The question of repudiation depends on the character of the contract, the number and weight of the wrongful acts or assertions, the intention indicated by those acts or words, the deliberation or otherwise with which they are committed, the cumulative effect of the employer's actions, and the general circumstances of the case, including whether just cause for dismissal exists. Good faith is also a factor to consider. A court should look at all the circumstances, including the reason for the change.

Manner of imposing change — The manner of imposing the change is usually not relevant to the issue of whether constructive dismissal exists. However, some judges have said that the manner of imposing a change is a relevant consideration.

Failure to manage change — The atmosphere surrounding a change can affect whether or not it is treated as fundamental. Even where a change would not otherwise be fundamental, there may be constructive dismissal where the employer fails to manage the change properly. This was the case where an employer failed to manage the introduction of a new computer system.

Intention — The employer's intention may not be relevant, as an employer can be guilty of constructive dismissal even if its motives are benign. The employer's intention may be taken into account in the following situations:

Accidental breach. In these cases, there may be no repudiation of the contract.

Anticipatory breach. The employer's intention may be considered in deciding whether an anticipatory breach occurred or the employee was merely given a warning of future changes.

Change based on a reasonable business decision. In this case, while there may have been constructive dismissal, the employee may have a duty to mitigate damages.

Examples — no intention to dismiss — There was no constructive dismissal where:

- An employee received no answer when she asked a meeting room full of people whether she was dismissed. Given the highly charged atmosphere, their silence could not be taken as a dismissal.
- Long-term disability payments started. The employer had provided six months' sick pay out of its own pocket and also paid the premiums for long-term disability insurance, and the employee still had some expectation of returning to his old job.

Constructive dismissal vs. termination — Constructive dismissal rather than termination occurred where:

- An employee was told her job was eliminated and her requests for clarification of her status were met with vague assurances.
- An employee had been transferred from Britain and was then asked to move to a different position. When he refused, he was asked for his office key and was told the employer was looking into the cost of moving him back home. This was found to be a constructive dismissal, despite the employer's argument that the employee could still have accepted the offered position.

C-1.4 EXCEPTIONS

When fundamental change is not constructive dismissal — In some situations, fundamental changes can be made without liability for constructive dismissal. These include:

At-will employees. The prerogative to dismiss at pleasure may protect an employer from constructive dismissal claims. However, at-will employment is now extremely rare.

Just cause. In the same way that just cause gives an employer the right to end an employee's contract, it can also give an employer the right to unilaterally change it, including changes that would otherwise amount to constructive dismissal. For instance, where there is just cause for dismissal, a demotion that would otherwise be considered constructive dismissal might be justified.

Existence of agreement. Parties may specifically contract with regard to constructive dismissal. They may define what actions will amount to constructive dismissal or, by defining what changes may not be made (e.g., that the department would not suffer further downsizing and would remain "high profile"), may impliedly agree that those changes would amount to constructive dismissal. They may also agree to reassignments at the employer's discretion, in which case constructive dismissal could not be claimed. However, a general clause requiring the employee to perform such duties as assigned by the employer may not entitle the employer to impose a fundamental change. And even where a contract allows reassignment there may be a duty to exercise the right reasonably.

Implied probationary period. Where an employee has been promoted, there may be an implied probationary period or an implied agreement that the employee can be demoted for inadequate performance in the new job.

Just cause following constructive dismissal — Where an employee has been constructively dismissed but, before the notice period begins, gives just cause for dismissal, the just cause will pre-empt his claim for constructive dismissal.

C-1.5 DUTY TO MITIGATE IN CONSTRUCTIVE DISMISSAL SITUATIONS

Unreasonable to refuse change — In some cases of constructive dismisssal, it may be unreasonable for the employee to refuse the alternate job. A refusal may lead a court to conclude that, while the change amounted to constructive dismissal, the employee has failed to mitigate his or her damages. See also Chapter H-4, "Rejecting an Offer and Other Failures to Mitigate".

Is continued relationship possible? — The question is whether the employee acted reasonably in refusing the new job. If there has been humiliation, loss of respect or other behaviour which makes a continued relationship impossible, the employee may be reasonable in refusing the job.

Example — Where a lumber industry manager refused a different job at the same pay, in circumstances where the industry was very depressed and other managers had agreed to accept new responsibilities, he had failed to mitigate and his claim for damages was denied. The change was not humiliating to the employee on an objective basis, and his chances of employment elsewhere were very low.

C-1.6 CONDONATION

Condonation — An employee must decide within a reasonable time whether to accept a change or to treat the contract as at an end. An employee who accepts the change will have condoned it, and the changed term will then govern his employment.

Express or implied condonation — Condonation can result from the employee's express consent, or from consent implied when the employee takes no action and continues to work without complaint. Even if the employee neither accepts the change nor leaves, he or she may be said to have condoned the change and will lose his or her cause of action.

Condonation requires knowledge of the change — Of course, there can be no condonation without knowledge of the change. For example, there was no condonation where:

- An employer unilaterally changed the standard form trade record sheet on which the employment contract and commission arrangement were based, but did not draw the changes to the employee's attention.
- An employer gradually eroded an employee's authority, status and pay, but constantly reassured him and never told him that the reorganization was permanent. The employee did not condone the situation by continuing in his job when his constructive dismissal became obvious.
- An employer discussed with an employee that the job might be changed when the employee returned from sick leave, but did not confirm the changes.

No condonation where no choice — An employer will not be able to argue that an employee condoned the change where the employee chose between two alternatives the employer imposed, each amounting to constructive dismissal.

No condonation where employer's offer considered — Mere consideration of an offer does not amount to condonation. An employee who attempts to clarify and negotiate the changes has not condoned them.

Working under protest — If an employee continues in his job but does so under protest while trying to resolve the dispute, his action for constructive dismissal may not be barred. For example, there was no condonation where:

- An employee continued under protest for nearly two years.
- An employee protested a decrease in his pay, stayed on while his pay was supplemented, but quit when the supplement was stopped.
- An employee filed a human rights complaint in response to her demotion. By filing the complaint, she had shown she did not accept the change; her wrongful dismissal action was not barred by the fact that she continued in the new job while she pursued the complaint.

No condonation if mitigating — An employee who continues in a new job due to the duty to mitigate his damages may not have condoned the change, even if the employee does not expressly claim constructive dismissal while working in the new job. An employee who stays on the job to enhance his prospects of finding a new job may still be able to bring an action for constructive dismissal for the balance of the notice period. See also Chapter H-1, "Mitigation of Damages".

Circumstances important — In considering whether an employee's actions amount to condonation, it is important to consider all the circumstances. For example, there was no condonation where:

- An employee continued in a job for five months after changes were imposed but she was alone in the country and knew nothing of her rights or prospects for re-employment.
- An employee accepted a change in status on certain conditions, which subsequently were not met.

Inferior bargaining position, finances, etc., no excuse — An employee who condones a change will not be able to argue that his bargaining position was weaker or that he was forced by financial circumstances to accept the change. Nor can an employee claim that he was waiting for a new contract where it is clear that one would not be forthcoming.

Reasonable time to decide — An employee who has accepted a change in terms may be entitled to a reasonable time in which to decide whether to continue in the new situation. The length of time depends on the facts and, to some extent, on the length of previous service.

Employee may have to wait — In fact, an employee may need to wait a reasonable amount of time to see if proposed changes materialize, or if their effect is truly fundamental. For example, where an employee made a claim three weeks after a takeover which resulted in his employer becoming a private company, it was found to be too soon to know whether his job would have changed significantly.

Limits on reasonable time — Staying in the new position up to the end of the reasonable notice period may not amount to condonation; but this is not always reasonable. An employee cannot stay indefinitely until the employer terminates the contract and then claim that constructive dismissal occurred in the past.

Examples of limits on reasonable time — Cases in which employees were found to have condoned a fundamental change, and were therefore unsuccessful in claiming constructive dismissal, include:

- An employee who did nothing for almost six months.
- An employee who willingly accepted a transfer without undue pressure from his employer, even though he changed his mind and claimed constructive dismissal after only one day on the job.

Examples of reasonable time — There was no condonation despite a lapse of time where:

- The employee was constructively dismissed by the imposition of a probationary period plus a salary cut, but he worked through the probation in an attempt to change the employer's mind.

- An employee was dismissed before the end of a condoned probation period. He was entitled to the entire period in which to have a chance of showing his capability. See also Chapter A-3, "Probationary Employment".
- An employee had accepted a demotion but then quit after three months, upon realizing the vast inferiority of the new position.
- An employee remained on the job for five months deciding whether to accept or to reject the new terms, given that there was no comparable job immediately available to him.
- An employee who had returned from sick leave and was depressed waited two months before claiming constructive dismissal.

Chapter C-2

CHANGE IN REMUNERATION

TABLE OF CONTENTS

C-2.1 Change in Pay or Manner of Payment
       C-2.1.1 Pay
       C-2.1.2 Overtime
       C-2.1.3 Commissions
       C-2.1.4 Layoffs
       C-2.1.5 Method of Payment
C-2.2 Change in Bonus or Other Profit Sharing
C-2.3 Change in Benefits
C-2.4 Change in Method of Computing Remuneration

C-2.1 CHANGE IN PAY OR MANNER OF PAYMENT

C-2.1.1 Pay

Reduction in pay or failure to pay — Remuneration goes to the root of the employment contract. A unilateral reduction in salary without proper cause has been held to be constructive dismissal, as has the refusal to pay amounts owing under the employment contract. As in other situations, the change must be fundamental to amount to constructive dismissal. Examples of constructive dismissal following a change in pay include:

- An employee's hours were cut, and therefore the employee's pay was cut in half.
- An employee whose employer said he could no longer afford to pay him and who then took over some of his functions.
- A reduction in pay, even though agreed to by the employee, where the agreement was not kept by the employer.

Example — no constructive dismissal — There was no constructive dismissal where an employee's appointment required him to perform a certain duty "when required". The employer could decide he would no longer be required to perform that duty, even though this caused a fifty per cent reduction in his income.

Limit on earnings — Where the parties had agreed that the salary of a fire chief would be based on a percentage of a regular firefighter's salary as negotiated from time to time, and the employer imposed a limit on the fire chief's salary, the employer had breached the contract and constructively dismissed the employee.

Minor changes in pay — A very minor change in pay may not amount to a fundamental change. For example, a decrease of less than $300 a year or three per cent of total income. An $8,000 reduction in a bonus, however, combined with other changes, was substantial.

Failure to hold annual review — Where an employee's salary was subject to an annual review, there was no constructive dismissal where the employer decided to offer bonuses instead of salary increases.

Failure to increase or renegotiate — Failure to grant a requested salary increase does not, on its own, amount to constructive dismissal. However, an employee who accepted a promotion with the expectation of a salary increase was constructively dismissed by the employer's refusal to increase his salary, as the employer had known of the expectation. A refusal to renegotiate compensation, as required by contract, was also a constructive dismissal. There was no constructive dismissal, however, where a change in pay was proposed during salary negotiations and the employer refused to put the proposal in writing.

Salary reduction when job changed — Constructive dismissal has been found where there was:

- A salary reduction for an employee who had initiated a change in his job description but had not discussed a salary change. He was impliedly entitled to the same salary.
- A job change with no assurance that earnings would not also be changed.

Salary freeze, red-circling or job reclassification — A salary freeze, red-circling or reclassification may be a constructive dismissal, where:

- An employee had always received merit increases in the past.
- The employee's earning potential, position and status were affected by a reduction in the employee's salary grade and a salary freeze until the mid-point of the grade caught up with the employee's pay.
- A job reclassification reduced the employee's entitlement to future increases and benefit entitlement, even though there was no immediate effect on salary.

Salary freeze, etc. — no constructive dismissal — However, some cases have found no constructive dismissal in similar circumstances. No constructive dismissal was found where:

- An employee assumed that his salary would be red-circled, but in fact, it was not.

- A salary freeze was part of an ongoing effort to deal with documented performance problems.

Pay reduction during probationary period — In one case, an employee was put on probation and his pay was substantially reduced due to concerns about the quality of his work. The employer's actions were held to amount to constructive dismissal and the employee was awarded damages at his former rate of pay. The court found his work was not sufficiently poor to constitute just cause for dismissal.

C-2.1.2 Overtime

Elimination of overtime pay — Changing entitlements regarding overtime and overtime pay may be a fundamental breach resulting in constructive dismissal. Constructive dismissal was found where:

- An employee's right to be paid for overtime work was eliminated, significant amounts were involved and the employer's offer of increased salary did not offset the employee's loss.
- An employee's previous entitlement to a week's vacation in return for attending meetings after hours was changed to require that he attend at least 22 meetings before being entitled to the vacation time.
- An employee's right to overtime pay was eliminated but not the duty to work overtime, where the employee had specifically bargained for overtime pay and substantial amounts were involved.

Elimination of overtime — Eliminating overtime itself may be constructive dismissal if the opportunity to work overtime is a right. But an employee was not entitled to pay for lost overtime where overtime had always been subject to review and approval by the employee's supervisor. See also Section C-3.8, "Change in Working Conditions".

C-2.1.3 Commissions

Failure to earn expected commissions — The fact that one employee did not earn as much in commissions as he had been led to expect was not a constructive dismissal. There had been no negligent misrepresentations and the employee, as an experienced salesman, should have known that sales projections are often optimistic. However, a demotion leading to the potential for significantly lower commissions than had been earned in the past was considered wrongful dismissal. See also Section C-2.4, "Change in Method of Computing Remuneration", below.

C-2.1.4 Layoffs

Layoff without pay — A short, temporary layoff is not necessarily a repudiation of the employment contract, and therefore not necessarily a constructive dismissal. However, constructive dismissal was found where:

- An employee was indefinitely suspended without pay and was essentially permanently laid off.
- An employee was temporarily laid off, but there was no implied term in his contract permitting layoffs.

C-2.1.5 Method of Payment

Change in payment method — There was an implied contractual term in one case, based on long past practice, to pay employees by cheque rather than by direct bank deposit. Where this term was fundamental to the employee, it could not be unilaterally changed by the employer and the employer was directed to pay the employee by cheque. In another case, however, the routine removal of a sick employee from an autopay system was permitted.

C-2.2 CHANGE IN BONUS OR OTHER PROFIT SHARING

Change in bonus payments — As with salary and commission changes, where the pay difference is small, refusal to pay the full amount of a bonus may not be a fundamental breach. Where the difference is substantial, however, a finding of constructive dismissal is more likely.

Examples — constructive dismissal — Constructive dismissal has been found where:

- An employee's participation in a bonus plan was terminated without offsetting compensation changes.
- A bonus plan, which would likely have resulted in substantial payment, was eliminated.
- An employer refused to pay any part of an agreed-to bonus.
- An employer unilaterally placed a cap on a previously unlimited bonus.
- An employee was paid a bonus at a fraction of the level given previously, while the bonus levels of other employees was maintained.
- A previously fixed bonus was made discretionary.
- A bonus was reduced by 15 per cent.
- An employer introduced a special compensation program which stated that an employee who resigned or was dismissed for cause before receipt of the annual payment would receive nothing.

Examples — no constructive dismissal — There was no constructive dismissal where:

- The pay difference received was $4,500 out of total compensation of $100,000.
- A profit-sharing plan was eliminated but the employee was paid a discretionary bonus instead that was greater than his entitlement under the plan.
- A reorganization decreased an employee's chance to earn a bonus, but the bonus had never been guaranteed and the employer had taken steps to ensure some bonus money would be available.
- An RRSP contribution was eliminated and vacation entitlement decreased, reducing total compensation by six to eight per cent, as these were collateral benefits that traditionally had depended on the employer's fortunes at the time.

C-2.3 CHANGE IN BENEFITS

New policies — Imposing policies that take away or limit entrenched benefits has been found to amount to constructive dismissal in a number of cases.

Change in benefits — A decrease in benefits has been found to be constructive dismissal where:

- A seasonal worker's entitlement to benefits was eliminated. The worker had been employed for many seasons with benefits and had been told at the start of the season that he would have them.
- A guaranteed level of benefits was lost through a change to straight commission, since this was bound to be a major concern to an employee with a young family.
- An employer refused to pay a professional membership fee that had been paid in the past. The refusal, along with a number of other changes in the employee's job, was found to be a symptom of the employee's reduced position.

Significant value — The elimination of just one benefit can be constructive dismissal where the employer should have known it was of significant value to the employee. For example:

- The free use of a company car was taken away.
- A company car and expense allowance were eliminated, base salary reduced and title changed.
- An employer refused to pay for car insurance even though it was a contractually-agreed benefit.
- A special expatriate allowance was no longer paid when a United States citizen employed in Canada became a Canadian citizen. The

allowance, which in effect raised the employee's salary by about five per cent, was a term of the employment contract which could not be unilaterally changed by the employer.
- A policy was adopted limiting compensatory vacation time.
- Share options provided for in an employee's contract were denied to him.
- An employer failed to provide the severance package to which an employee was contractually entitled.

Single change — no constructive dismissal — Examples of single changes that were not constructive dismissal include:

- Giving an employee a smaller company car.
- Failure to pay sick pay, in one case. While the sick pay was held to be owing, failure to pay it was not so fundamental as to be constructive dismissal.

Multiple changes — Although a finding of constructive dismissal is more likely where there have been multiple changes, the changes added together must still be fundamental. There was no constructive dismissal where:

- Multiple changes were made to an expense policy. They were ruled not to be fundamental, as they were part of a dynamic policy and were not part of contractual entitlement.
- Details of the benefits had not been forthcoming. The employee was promised comparable benefits on a restructuring. It was held that he should have relied on the promise made and had a duty to accept the new position to mitigate his loss, even without having received details of the benefits.

Frequent flyer points, etc. — The cases conflict on whether changing the rules for personal use of points earned through employment, such as travel miles, amounts to a constructive dismissal. Where personal use of the points had become an integral part of the employee's contractual benefits, there was constructive dismissal where an employer eliminated personal use of frequent flyer travel points. However, there was no constructive dismissal where the right to use the points was not a contractual entitlement.

C-2.4 CHANGE IN METHOD OF COMPUTING REMUNERATION

General principles — A change in the method of computing an employee's compensation can amount to constructive dismissal, unless there is an implied term based on past conduct that payment arrangements will be subject to renegotiation.

Salary to hourly rate or piecework — Constructive dismissal was found where there was:

- A change from salary to an hourly rate, where the rate was lower than the salary equivalent and the change also meant "no work, no pay", especially during the slow season.
- A change from a flat rate of pay to payment for piecework, where it was anticipated that the total annual pay would be significantly less or there was uncertainty about the employee's prospective minimum earnings.

Salary plus commission mix — In most cases a change from straight salary to lower salary plus commission, or from higher salary plus commissions to lower salary and higher commissions, is regarded as a fundamental change. This is usually so even where total compensation is expected to be the same, although there are some exceptions. This is said to be because base salary is guaranteed, but commissions are not. For example, constructive dismissal was found where there was a change:

- From salary plus commission to straight salary, which would result in a substantial decrease in income.
- From salary plus commission to straight commission, since it removed an employee's income security and raised long-term concerns even if total remuneration was the same over the short term.

Change of mix — no constructive dismissal — Some cases focus on total compensation rather than the calculation method. No constructive dismissal was found where there was:

- A change from salary plus commission to straight commission which would not decrease the employee's total income, where the employee was incapable of continuing in his former job.
- A reduction in commission rate offset by an incentive program that actually increased an employee's income.
- Change to a number of items which on the whole were beneficial to the employee, and he had accepted these benefits without complaint. He was not permitted to reject the less beneficial terms and insist on the previous arrangements.
- A change in sales positions to one with a higher base salary but uncertain commission potential, since the employee's commission earnings in the old job were not guaranteed either.

Manner of calculating commissions — An employer must make clear to an employee how it intends to calculate commissions. If the employer is not clear and the employee develops reasonable expectations based on the words used, the employer's imposition of its interpretation may be a constructive dismissal. Similarly, a change in calculation basis may create a constructive dismissal, where an employer changed the standard form trade record sheet, which substantially affected an employee's entitlement to commissions. However, there was no constructive dismissal where:

- There was no dispute about calculation, and the employee simply earned less than expected.
- A provision of the employer's policy manual was invoked and, as a result, an employee was denied commission on a sale.

Imposing reserve or surcharge — Constructive dismissal may or may not be found when the employer imposes a reserve or surcharge. For example:

- Constructive dismissal was found where the employer imposed a 10 per cent reserve for bad debts which was deducted from commissions earned.
- Constructive dismissal was not found where the employer imposed a surcharge on commissions to fund a new position to assist sales personnel.

Withholding commissions — The withholding of owed commissions without just cause may be a constructive dismissal where:

- An employer made a unilateral change limiting the conditions under which commission would be paid.
- An employer imposed a unilateral cap on an employee's previously unlimited bonus.

Change in territory or accounts — constructive dismissal — A change in territory or accounts might amount to constructive dismissal. For example, constructive dismissal was found where:

- A number of accounts that generated 35 per cent of an employee's income were removed.
- An employee was requested to include new business accounts in his forecast, thus eroding his potential to earn commission.

Change in territory or accounts — no constructive dismissal — No constructive dismissal was found where there was:

- A doubling in size of the sales territory, where it was accompanied by an increase in commission rate.
- A change in territory, where the employee's contract expressly allowed changes and where the change would not have a serious impact on the employee's earning potential.

Chapter C-3

CHANGE IN JOB CONTENT, JOB STATUS OR WORKING CONDITIONS

TABLE OF CONTENTS

C-3.1   General Principles
C-3.2   Change in Job Duties
C-3.3   Demotion
C-3.4   Reassignment Without Demotion
C-3.5   Downward Change in Status
C-3.6   Change in Job Title or Reporting Level
C-3.7   Change in Employment Status
C-3.8   Change in Working Conditions

C-3.1 GENERAL PRINCIPLES

Hirings under definite capacity — Imposing a different set of duties than those set out in a contract constitutes constructive dismissal. The court will not imply a term that duties may be changed where there is an express term setting out what the duties are. Several situations can give rise to a constructive dismissal claim: a change from one job to another, which may or may not include a demotion; a change in duties nominally within the same position; a change in job status; reduction to part-time work; imposition of probation; possibly even a promotion; and a change in working conditions.

Employer leeway — Some recent decisions have said that an employee's duties are not totally frozen when a job description is prepared, and an employer must be allowed reasonable leeway to reorganize, restructure and alter duties. This is especially the case where changes are necessary for the company's economic survival and where there is no objective element of humiliation or decrease in authority associated with the change. Even a demotion may be permitted in some cases, as discussed later in this chapter.

Express or implied agreement — Some employees may be found not to have been hired under a definite capacity; thus, their duties can be changed. In addition, an employee may be found to have expressly or impliedly agreed either that changes can be made, or that they will not be made. For example:

- An employer's right to make changes was limited where there was an implied term, based on past dealings, that the employee would be informed and consulted before fundamental changes were made to his duties.
- Where an employee is promoted, there may be an implied agreement that he can be returned to a position similar to his original job within a reasonable time if he does not perform well in the new position. In other words, a reasonable period of probation may be implied, and changing the employee's duties or status during this period might not amount to a fundamental breach.

Duty to inform — While employers must be free to reorganize and restructure, they must do so in ways that meet their obligations to employees. Refusing to give an employee information about his duties, status and authority level in a restructuring plan may be unreasonable. This may amount to constructive dismissal even in an emergency situation, although some vagueness may be reasonable in some situations. An employee may be entitled to refuse a proposed change where the employer does not give sufficient details of the change, especially about pay.

Duty of good faith and fairness — Lack of good faith or fairness on an employer's part may make a proposed change a constructive dismissal, especially where the employee has an express contract for a definite position.

C-3.2 CHANGE IN JOB DUTIES

General principle — Subject to the employer leeway mentioned above, asking an employee to perform functions other than the duties for which he or she was hired has often been found to constitute constructive dismissal. Constructive dismissal is more likely to be found where:

(1) the substituted duties are of a lower calibre or status, or require fewer skills, than the former duties; or
(2) the employee is not qualified or suited for the new duties.

Returning an employee to the original job after a brief reassignment, however, may not be constructive dismissal.

Examples of changed duties — constructive dismissal — Constructive dismissal was found where an employee was required to:

- Work in a gatehouse rather than as a yardman.
- File in a basement rather than fulfill other clerical duties in the main office.
- Perform physically heavy duties instead of lighter duties, where the employee's abilities were limited due to health problems.
- Lose two of five areas of responsibility, including the most significant one.

Appropriation or removal of duties — An employee was constructively dismissed where his duties were usurped by others and he was not allowed to perform his normal functions. A contract that requires a set period of working notice may include a duty on the employer to provide work during that time, and failure to do so may be a constructive dismissal.

Significant change in scope — Changing the scope of an employee's duties can amount to constructive dismissal. The mix of duties does not necessarily have to remain the same, though, and in each case it is a question of whether a substantial, fundamental change has been made. Constructive dismissal will likely be found where the employer removes a major portion of an employee's job duties or core functions. It is also likely if an employer removes a single duty that accounts for a major portion of an employee's income.

Minor change in scope — Constructive dismissal will not be found where the duties that are removed are minor or secondary. A mere change in proportion of duties that were always part of the job was not a constructive dismissal, particularly where this was due to an unusual, temporary situation rather than a permanent change.

Examples — constructive dismissal — Constructive dismissal has been found where:

- A sales manager's territory was reduced.
- A sales manager was asked to become a salesman in another territory.
- A teacher was restricted to teaching only a few subjects.
- An investment manager's investment funds were reduced by 50 per cent.
- An employee's supervisory duties were removed.
- Control over sales was removed from the employee's job, and with it control over the amount of his bonus.

Examples — no constructive dismissal — Constructive dismissal was not found due to:

- A minor change in duties due to a transfer to the same position in a different location.

- A reduction in a clerical employee's work on a particular project, where the clerk was to be assigned equivalent duties for the rest of her time.
- A change in a salesperson's products.
- A new job description reflecting changes that had already taken place gradually, and to which the employee had not objected.

Temporary or new assignments — Where an assignment is temporary, it is up to the employer to make this clear to the employee. An employee who is reassigned following a corporate reorganization must wait to see whether there have been any fundamental changes to the job. In one case, where there had not been any fundamental changes three weeks after a reorganization, a constructive dismissal claim failed.

Increase in duties — constructive dismissal — An increase in duties can be a constructive dismissal in some situations. Even a promotion that includes a salary increase can amount to constructive dismissal where it involves extra pressure and it was not wanted by the employee. For example, constructive dismissal has been found where:

- A newspaper editor was asked to do a reporter's work during a strike, in addition to his regular work.
- An apartment building rental manager was asked to perform superintendent's duties, including being on call 24 hours a day.
- A nanny was expected to take on the nursing care of two elderly boarders.
- A sales territory was increased and the change involved a new requirement to travel.

Increase in duties — no constructive dismissal — No constructive dismissal was found where:

- A sales territory was increased, along with an increased commission.
- A supervisor was asked to perform work alongside the two men he supervised, where his supervisory duties were not removed, the change was required for legitimate business reasons, and the supervisor's hiring letter had indicated he could be called upon to lend his talents in areas not normally associated with the position hired for.
- An employee took on many of her supervisor's responsibilities due to his illness, but was not officially given his title or salary. She did not have a claim when she reverted to her own duties and someone else was given the supervisor's job.

C-3.3 DEMOTION

General principle — A demotion is almost always regarded as a significant and fundamental change, i.e., constructive dismissal. Whether a demotion has taken place depends on whether there has been a downward change in pay or status. An employee's argument for constructive dismissal is stronger in a case of demotion than in a case of lateral transfer. The question of whether a reassignment involves a demotion is often an issue.

Express or implied term — In the absence of a specific contractual term, the right to demote depends on the circumstances. Some courts have found an implied agreement to accept reassignment in certain cases, but many have refused to hold an employee to an implied agreement where the change involves an actual demotion.

Just cause — Demotion will not be constructive dismissal if the employer would otherwise be able to dismiss the employee for just cause. Some judges may even imply a term that an employee will not be demoted unless there is cause.

Downward change in status — A job change may be regarded as a demotion where there is a downward change in status, with or without a corresponding salary change. Factors include a loss of responsibility, change in reporting status, change in job title, change in benefits or perquisites, as well as loss of pay. Many cases involve a combination of these factors. Lack of good faith or fairness may make a change more likely to be seen as a demotion.

Surrounding circumstances — At least one judge has said that all surrounding circumstances must be considered when assessing whether a demotion has occurred. Another case seemed to disagree, however, saying that the manner of effecting a change was not relevant to the issue of whether it was a demotion.

Minor changes — A minor change to one factor alone — for example, a minor loss of pay or prestige, or a minor change in duties — may not amount to a demotion. A change of title where accompanied by the same pay and work on a bigger, more important project was not a demotion in one case.

Office reassignment — No demotion and therefore no constructive dismissal was found where an employee was reasonably assigned to a smaller office, or where an employee was removed from a private office to which he had been temporarily assigned. Constructive dismissal was found, however, where:

- An employee was assigned to a smaller office, given reduced duties and a frozen salary.
- A secretary was continually moved around to different locations and furniture, and her requests for information on her status were refused.

C-3.4 REASSIGNMENT WITHOUT DEMOTION

General principles — A lateral transfer or reassignment to a different job altogether may or may not be regarded as a constructive dismissal. If there is no fundamental change in the terms of employment, and the reassignment is made in good faith for reasonable business purposes, the employee may have to accept it, even if some minor loss of prestige is involved. Where two positions are roughly equivalent, an employee may be required to accept a lateral transfer. This was the case even where the employee was concerned that the transfer would be stressful and would aggravate ongoing health issues. In other cases, however, constructive dismissal has been found even where there is no reduction in salary or status.

Agreement to reassignment — An employee will sometimes be found to have expressly or impliedly agreed to reassignments at the employer's discretion. In the absence of an express agreement, the parties' rights depend on the circumstances. An implied agreement to reassignment is more likely to be found where there is a history or expectation of accepting reassignments, or upon the employer's merger with another company, or where required by the employer's financial situation.

Express agreement — An employer may be able to impose a reassignment, even one involving demotion, where authorized by a governing statute or a contract. Even an agreement which expressly permits reassignments, however, does not give an employer the right to impose them unreasonably.

Right vs. obligation — The fact that a collective agreement allows an employee to return to the bargaining unit does not create an express obligation upon the employee to do so.

Custom — A custom of the trade may support an argument of implied right to reassign. Even in such situations, however, the courts are not always willing to force an employee to accept a demotion.

Examples — constructive dismissal — Constructive dismissal has been found where:

- An employee was told that another job would be found for him, without specific job details being provided, although this has not always been the case.
- A disciplinary transfer was made without proper grounds.
- An employee was forced to work in a different job temporarily, in order to work through a notice period.
- An employee was withdrawn from his duties until physically fit for the job, even though the employer knew the employee would never

recover. This was found to be a disguised dismissal, although in this instance it was not wrongful, since just cause existed.
- An employee was relieved of his duties and reassigned to other, unspecified duties.
- An employer failed to allow an employee to exercise his statutory right to appeal a suspension.

Examples — no constructive dismissal — No constructive dismissal was found where:

- An employee was removed from an unpaid position which carried prestige and authority, but this did not affect his paid position.
- There was a partial or minor diminution in an employee's status caused by complying with the employee's request for a transfer.
- A reorganization left most people with decreased responsibilities, but an employee's relative status was not affected even though he was performing fairly different functions.
- Supervisory duties were removed, but the employee knew that changes in job function were to be expected and the removal gave the employee more time to fulfill his other duties.

C-3.5 DOWNWARD CHANGE IN STATUS

General principle — Courts are more likely to find a fundamental change where there has been a downward change in status. A finding of constructive dismissal is especially likely where the worker's management or supervisory functions are removed, or if the employee is asked to report to his own former position or to return to a bargaining unit.

Objective standard — A downward change in status may have to be supported by evidence other than the employee's own subjective view of the change. A concern that the new job title may cause the employee loss of face among his family and friends in a small community may not be sufficient.

Return to job held previously — Workers who are asked to return to jobs they previously held are often, although not always, found to have been constructively dismissed. It may not be the case, for instance, where the new position was probationary.

Work with former subordinates — constructive dismissal — There may or may not be constructive dismissal where an employee is asked to work as a colleague among his or her former subordinates. Constructive dismissal has been found where:

- An employee was asked to accept a position of lower rank which was inappropriate for his or her background and training.

- An employee was asked to perform duties inconsistent with his or her position, such as asking an executive to perform secretarial duties, or asking a hockey coach to become a scout and thus harming his future potential as a coach.
- The department headed by an employee was downsized to a "mere rump" of its former self, entailing a loss of job status and prestige.
- An employee's training duties were removed and she was required to work in the kind of junior position for which she had formerly trained others.
- A mainstream supervisory employee was assigned to a job that had always been treated as a support position away from the company's mainstream, and that had been used in the past for those wishing less demanding work or recovering from serious illness.

Work with former subordinates — no constructive dismissal — There was no downward change in status where:

- A supervisor was asked to perform work alongside the two men he supervised, given that his supervisory duties were not removed, the change was required for legitimate business reasons, and his hiring letter stated he could be called upon to lend his talents in areas not normally associated with his position.
- An employee was relieved of responsibility for assigning files, allowing him to take on more of his own files.

C-3.6 CHANGE IN JOB TITLE OR REPORTING LEVEL

General principles — Reporting level is not the sole indication of a job's status. There may be no constructive dismissal where everything else about the job remains the same, or where the change is not fundamental. It is not a usual implied term that a junior employee will never be promoted over a senior employee.

Examples — constructive dismissal — Constructive dismissal was found where:

- A manager was required to report to a new person at a lower level of the hierarchy.
- A reorganization left an employee at the same level of salary and responsibility but raised the levels of his former colleagues and subordinates.
- A reorganization did not change the employee's title or functions, but resulted in the employee being placed in a subordinate position as the only department head required to report to a vice-president.
- An employee was transferred to a lesser job that also had less chance of promotion.

Examples — no constructive dismissal — Constructive dismissal was not found where:

- A reorganization decreased most people's responsibilities, but the plaintiff employee was left at the same relative status.
- An employee was told not to expect to be promoted if and when a more senior position were to be created.

Change in job title — A change in job title can sometimes indicate demotion, but it does not automatically do so. Constructive dismissal was not found where there was:

- A reduction in job title, but the employee had never been officially promoted to the higher title.
- A failure to give an employee a higher position in line with the duties he had been performing on a temporary basis, where the employee's official title, duties and pay had not been affected.

C-3.7 CHANGE IN EMPLOYMENT STATUS

Change in employment status — constructive dismissal — A change in legal employment status within the same job may amount to constructive dismissal, as was the case where:

- There was a change from permanent to temporary employee status.
- There was a reversion to the bargaining unit outside the terms of the collective agreement, resulting in a loss of seniority and loss of job.
- An established employee was put on probation, where his performance did not warrant it.
- An employee agreed to a probationary period but was dismissed before its end.
- An employee lost her permanent role and was required to float, and her requests for information on her status were refused.

Change in employment status — no constructive dismissal — There was no constructive dismissal where:

- An employee was not promoted, even though she had performed many of the job's duties on a temporary basis, as nothing about her official job had changed.
- A probationary period was extended, where the alternative would have been to terminate the employee sooner.

Leaves of absence — An employee with no express or implied right to a leave of absence cannot insist on being granted one. Nor can an employer arbitrarily impose one. Constructive dismissal was found where an unpaid leave of absence was imposed on an employee, with no guarantee of future work. A refusal to extend a leave of absence, where the employee had no contractual right to an extension, was not a constructive dismissal.

C-3.8 CHANGE IN WORKING CONDITIONS

General principle — A number of changes in working conditions may amount to constructive dismissal, including changes in work hours or schedules; location; and job requirements such as travel or independent work. Again, the test is whether the change is fundamental.

Work hours and schedule changes — constructive dismissal — Constructive dismissal has been found where:

- There was a reduction in an employee's hours of work, effectively reducing the employee to part-time status.
- An employee's job duties were reduced from 18 hours a week to three days a month, with a requirement that she perform other duties the rest of the time.
- A change was imposed in working hours, requiring Sunday work, Saturday work or night and weekend work for the first time.
- A change was imposed requiring night shift work where the employer knew this was a problem for the employee due to health concerns and where day shifts had been made a fundamental term of the contract. A change requiring night work was not a constructive dismissal in another situation.
- An employee was denied consecutive nights off.
- An employee was asked to rotate over more shifts or work different shifts.
- Employment was changed back to shift work and to membership in a bargaining unit from a salaried position with supervisory duties.
- Short notice was given of schedule changes.
- A specifically negotiated arrangement to work eight months and then take four months off was cancelled.
- A manager was returned to the bargaining unit and, in so doing, lost the flexibility in his work hours which he needed to care for his sick wife.
- A limit on extra vacation time to compensate for attending after-hours meetings was imposed although no limit had existed in the past.
- The hours of work were increased, along with other changes.
- An employee was asked to start 90 minutes earlier at a plant two and a half hours from home rather than at the usual location, 40 minutes from home.
- Large amounts of overtime work were required.
- The employer refused to pay for overtime, without reducing the employee's obligation to work a substantial amount of overtime.

Work hours and schedule changes — no constructive dismissal — No constructive dismissal was found where an employee requested a transfer that he knew might involve shift work. The requirement to work shifts was not a repudiation of his contract.

Location and job requirement changes — constructive dismissal — Constructive dismissal was found where:

- A department was downsized so dramatically as to make work conditions difficult.
- An employee was required to attend at the office most of the time, instead of leaving attendance at her discretion as originally agreed.
- An employee was required to travel one week out of four, when she had not had to travel before.
- The locks were changed on the employer's premises, restricting its bookkeeper's access, and her signing authority on the employer's bank accounts and credit card were removed.
- An employee's office, desk and telephone were removed, as was her name from the mailbox, message slot and telephone list.
- An employee was expected to work in a shack in the yard with no heat, no washroom and no access to secretarial staff, rather than in the main building.
- An employee was asked to work in the basement.
- An employee was asked to take on supervisory duties, rather than working independently.

Imposition of financial burden on employee — constructive dismissal — Constructive dismissal has been found where a financial burden was imposed on an employee. For example, where the employee was required to:

- Take an expensive course and pay for it himself.
- Take and pay for a training course at a cost that was large in relation to the employee's salary.
- Obtain a computer.
- Drive two and a half hours to work in his own car, without payment, when he had previously been provided a company vehicle and been paid for travel time from his base town.

Financial burden — no constructive dismissal — It was not constructive dismissal to require an employee to take an inexpensive course and to pay for only one-half of it.

Chapter C-4

OTHER CONSTRUCTIVE DISMISSAL SITUATIONS

TABLE OF CONTENTS

C-4.1   Contractual Changes
C-4.2   Humiliating Treatment or Harassment
C-4.3   Unfair Dealings by Employer
C-4.4   Discipline, Suspensions, Layoffs
        C-4.4.1 Discipline and Suspensions
        C-4.4.2 Layoffs
C-4.5   Geographical Transfers
C-4.6   Retirement
C-4.7   Compulsory Resignation
C-4.8   Pay in Lieu of Notice

C-4.1 CONTRACTUAL CHANGES

General principle — Imposing a different contractual term or refusing to comply with a term set out in a contract, constitutes constructive dismissal if the term is fundamental. For example, constructive dismissal has been found where there was:

- A policy requiring payment by direct bank deposit instead of by cheque.
- A failure to provide promised training and to conduct performance reviews.
- An attempt by an employer to replace an employment contract with one with substantially different terms.
- A requirement that an employee enter into a new employment contract permitting dismissal without cause.
- A contractual notice period imposed on an existing employment relationship.
- A termination of an employee for refusing to sign a release accepting the amount of working notice he had been given.
- A dispute about the terms of continuation of employment.
- A change in a by-law, making automatic renewal of an employment contract impossible, contrary to the terms of the contract.

C-4.2 HUMILIATING TREATMENT OR HARASSMENT

General principles — It is a fundamental implied term of employment that an employer treat an employee with civility, decency and respect. Continuous incidents of yelling and screaming, and repeated threats of termination, are examples of behaviour constituting constructive dismissal. Constructive dismissal may also be found where an employer:

- Undermined an employee's authority.
- Demeaned or otherwise humiliated the employee or damaged his or her morale.
- Harassed the employee or treated him or her abusively or unfairly.
- Discriminated against an employee or treated him or her blatantly differently from his or her co-workers.

Change in working relationship — Subjective feelings of anger and disappointment may not justify refusal of a proposed change that would not otherwise be fundamental. The fact that the relationship has deteriorated will not be enough to justify refusal where it would still be feasible for the employee to keep working for the employer. Refusal may be justified, though, if the relationship is so frayed by the proposed change that a reasonable person would not think the employee could work in harmony with the employer or the other employees, or where the good faith is gone from the relationship. See also Chapter C-1, "Constructive Dismissal: General Principles".

Sexual harassment — An employee who is dismissed or demoted for refusing to accept sexual harassment, or who is forced to resign due to being a victim of sexual harassment, may have been constructively dismissed.

Test for humiliating treatment — The test is whether the employer's conduct is such that a reasonable person should not be expected to remain in the job. The situation must be viewed objectively, although the employee's age, career goals and personal situation may be taken into account. The manner of making a change may be relevant where there is a hostile or embarrassing atmosphere surrounding the change.

Bad faith — Humiliating treatment can lead to a finding of bad faith dismissal, which can affect length of notice. See Chapter F-5, "Effect of Parties' Conduct on Reasonable Notice".

Humiliating treatment — constructive dismissal — Examples of humiliating treatment amounting to constructive dismissal include:

- Removing a bookkeeper's signing authority on the employer's bank accounts and credit card, changing the locks and restricting access to the premises outside of business hours.

- Giving an employee menial tasks to do, including reorganizing office supplies, cleaning the lunchroom, etc., or expecting her to sit around for hours waiting for something to do.
- Discussing unfounded performance complaints with the employee's crew members.
- Lying to an employee and giving a number of his functions to a subordinate.
- Proposing unreasonable severance arrangements and engaging in unjustified criticisms and accusations of misconduct during settlement negotiations.

Humiliating treatment — no constructive dismissal — There was no constructive dismissal where:

- An employer provided more input, closer supervision or stricter work rules. An increase in reporting requirements within an existing hierarchy is not a constructive dismissal. Responsibilities and authority are not diminished merely by such changes.
- An employee was told her junior colleague would likely be promoted instead of herself.
- Duties were redistributed in a reorganization and an employee who performed extra duties for years did not receive an increased title.
- An employee was asked to work with employees he had previously supervised, where the importance of the lower job had increased due to business factors at the time.
- A supervisor was asked to work beside the two people he supervised, where he retained his supervisory functions. The change was required for economic reasons, and his hiring letter had stated that he could be required to perform other functions.

C-4.3 UNFAIR DEALINGS BY EMPLOYER

General principles — As with humiliating treatment, unfair dealings by an employer can amount to constructive dismissal in some cases. They can also lead to a finding of bad faith, which can affect the employee's length of reasonable notice, as discussed in Chapter F-5, "Effect of Parties' Conduct on Reasonable Notice".

Allegations of theft or fraud — Unfounded allegations of theft against an employee may amount to constructive dismissal. However, an employer may be entitled to conduct an investigation and to call in the police without its actions constituting a fundamental breach, as long as its actions were fair and reasonable in the circumstances.

Unfair dealings — constructive dismissal — Examples of unfair dealings amounting to constructive dismissal include:

- A threat to fire an employee without cause, due to a personality conflict.
- Assault by an employer.
- Removal of most of an employee's duties, interference with her performance of the rest of her duties, refusal to sign her paycheque, and locking her out of the office.
- Unjustly calling a senior employee a thief, demanding his keys, locking him out of the office, and demanding that he sign an insulting and unfair confession.
- Making it impossible for an employee to perform his job, then giving him a choice between termination or a demotion.
- Persisting in an investigation and withholding information from an employee without having any evidence he was guilty of theft.
- Purposely keeping an employee in the dark, reducing his authority, impairing his ability to carry out his job and keeping him on edge by sudden changes without notice.
- Refusing to communicate instructions to a manager, particularly where orders had been given that action not be taken without the employer's authorization.
- Defrauding an exclusive sales agent of commissions.
- Transferring an employee from Britain and then failing to provide training, demanding that he change jobs or be fired, and refusing to pay his costs to return to Britain.
- Having an employee's co-workers testify before the employer's whole board with no opportunity for the employee to respond. This was found to offend the principle of natural justice, and the employee had been undermined before her co-workers and the community to the point that her continued employment was no longer possible.

Unfair dealings — no constructive dismissal — There was no unfair employer dealings where:

- An employer reported an employee to American immigration authorities after he refused a transfer and was terminated, as this was required by law.
- An employer refused to co-operate with an officer's financial strategies for the company.
- An employer failed to adequately respond to an employee's complaint of disparaging remarks and sexual harassment. The failure was not so fundamental that it indicated the employer no longer wished to be bound by the employment relationship, and the employee had the option to refer the matter to more senior management.

C-4.4 DISCIPLINE, SUSPENSIONS, LAYOFFS

C-4.4.1 Discipline and Suspensions

Disciplinary suspensions — No constructive dismissal has been found following suspensions where:

- The suspensions were with pay pending the investigation of alleged improprieties.
- The employer tried to ensure the employee's harmonious return to work following a disciplinary suspension but he refused to co-operate.
- The employee agreed to the suspension without pay pending the outcome of a criminal trial, and took no action.

Other disciplinary measures — Similarly, no constructive dismissal has been found where:

- Discipline was imposed in the form of a harsh written report and written warning, even where the report was unfairly investigated.
- An employee was put on performance review because the employer was said to have the right to do that if the employer deemed it appropriate.
- An employee was required to take a management training course after a disciplinary meeting.
- Probation and other disciplinary measures were imposed, as the employer had just cause for dismissal.

Unjustified discipline — Constructive dismissal has been found where discipline was not justified. For example:

- An employee was transferred for unjustified disciplinary reasons.
- Employees were given letters of reprimand and a suspension.
- An employee was placed on probation without identifying the improper behaviour.
- Allegations were made against an employee which were vague, short on specifics, unverified and unjustified, without a statement of expectations and a chance for the employee to respond, so that his position was intolerable.

C-4.4.2 Layoffs

Term permitting layoffs? — A layoff will be a dismissal unless the employment contract contains an express or implied term permitting layoffs. No implied term was found where there was a 32-year history without layoffs. On the other hand, where there was a history of short layoffs, they were permitted. See also Chapter B-1, "Termination of Employment: General Principles".

Returning to work is condonation — An employee who returns to work after a layoff will be deemed to have accepted it, i.e., condoned the layoff, and will lose any right to treat it as constructive dismissal.

Onus — The employer has the onus of proving an implied term permitting temporary layoffs.

Layoffs — constructive dismissal — Constructive dismissal was found where there was:

- A "layoff" and suspension of an employee's pay for the balance of his contract.
- A layoff for a reason not recognized as just cause under the employee's written contract.
- A layoff for no reason and no indication as to when or if the employee would be recalled.
- A layoff which resulted in another employee filling the employee's position and the employee being called back to a different, undefined position.
- Failure to recall a seasonal worker, where there had been a definite pattern of recall.

C-4.5 GEOGRAPHICAL TRANSFERS

Implied terms — Whether or not an employee will be forced to accept a relocation depends on the express or implied terms of the contract. These cases often turn on implied terms. Some cases have found an implied right to transfer, as long as the circumstances are reasonable; in other words, the employee does not have the right to refuse reasonable transfers. Others have found an implied term that an employee will not be transferred, so that even a relocation not involving a reassignment, or involving a promotion, may be a constructive dismissal.

Multiple changes — A relocation added to other changes may be more likely to amount to constructive dismissal. Since many transfers also involve job reassignments, the factors discussed in Chapter C-3, "Change in Job Content, Job Status or Working Conditions" will also be important.

Test reasonableness — Courts will consider the reasonableness of the proposed transfer in the circumstances of the case. One case has said that the overwhelming consideration is the employer's convenience, with only some regard to the employee's convenience. Others have held that personal considerations, such as the cost of housing or of an employee's educational preferences for his children, may justify an employee's refusal to transfer. For example:

- A transfer that was essentially disciplinary was a constructive dismissal, even though there were no other substantive changes, where the discipline was not justified.
- An employee who would suffer no loss of pay, benefits or status, and whose moving costs would be paid by the employer, unreasonably refused to transfer from Toronto to Calgary when his existing job was eliminated.
- One case held that an employer must give notice of a proposed transfer and allow an employee adequate time in which to make a decision. One day's notice was not adequate.

Employer's financial situation — The employer's financial need to reorganize may justify a transfer in some cases. In one case where an employer was relocating its entire operation for financial reasons, had given the employee some notice, and had offered to pay his moving expenses (although exact details were not provided), there was no constructive dismissal. The employer had acted reasonably, and the employee was not entitled to a job for life in the place of his choosing.

Failure to mitigate — Where ownership of an employer changes and the employee's contract terminates, the employee may not be entitled to rely on an implied term in refusing to relocate with the new employer, as this may be a failure to mitigate.

Multi-location employers — Several cases have shown sympathy for the multi-location employer. These cases have found an implied term in the contract that an employee will accept reasonable transfers not involving a demotion or undue hardship. As one judge stated, "I fail to see how large national or international corporations can operate effectively without such an implied term in their contracts of employment" (*Durrant v. Westeel-Rosco Ltd.* (1978), 7 B.C.L.R. 14 at 20 (S.C.)). Factors which seem to be important in persuading a court that such an implied term does or does not exist are:

- The employer's size, number of branches, area of operation, home base and number of employees.
- The importance of transfers within the employer's business structure, i.e., whether transfers are a way of life.
- The employee's job history with the employer, including the acceptance of previous transfers.
- The level at which the employee is employed.
- The absence of undue hardship to the employee and the existence of good faith on the employer's part.

Examples — constructive dismissal — Geographical transfers amounted to constructive dismissal where:

- The employee discussed his or her preference for a certain location when hired.
- The employee was a long-time resident of a location when hired.
- The employee's spouse could not relocate for employment reasons.
- The transfer would require a long commute on poor roads.
- The employer persistently refused to accommodate an employee's requests for re-transfer, after the employer originally transferred at the employer's behest.

Examples — no constructive dismissal — No constructive dismissal was found where:

- An employee who accepted the employer's retraining plan upon elimination of his job was held to have impliedly accepted a transfer at the end of his retraining. It was unreasonable for him to expect to stay in the same location given the nature of the industry and the nature of the job.
- An international salesman who traveled three weeks out of four refused a six-month transfer overseas. Given the amount he travelled, the nature of his position, the temporary nature of the assignment, and the employer's financial circumstances, the offered job was reasonable and was not a constructive dismissal. The employee's personal circumstances, including his forthcoming marriage, did not entitle him to refuse the transfer.
- A store manager refused a transfer just because he would be the manager of a smaller store with slightly different duties, where he had an express contractual term that he would accept transfers unless he had a legitimate reason to refuse.

Constructive dismissal after move — Where an employee was transferred from Britain to Canada at the employer's expense, then constructively dismissed, it was held that the employer should have paid his return moving costs and continued his salary if it expected him to report to work in Britain.

C-4.6 RETIREMENT

Forced retirement — Where retirement is forced upon a person without actual or implied consent, it is a coerced resignation and a constructive dismissal. The attainment of a certain age is not just cause. See also Chapter D-8, "Off-the-Job Conduct and Other Just Cause Situations".

Imposition of mandatory retirement age — Imposition of a mandatory retirement policy is constructive dismissal requiring reasonable notice where retirement at age 65 is not a term of employment when the employee is hired.

Retirement offer — An offer of early retirement made without coercion was not a dismissal, constructive or otherwise.

Forced retirement — constructive dismissal — Constructive dismissal has been found in forced retirement situations when:

- A policy of mandatory retirement at age 65 was imposed when it was not a term of employment when the employee was hired.
- An employee was forced to retire when he turned 65, although the company had no mandatory retirement policy and the employee never said he planned to retire at 65.
- A retirement date was forced upon an employee who had said he would retire at some indefinite future time. He was free to change his mind until he had set a retirement date.
- An employer had recently adopted a mandatory retirement policy; damages were not limited to the 14 months remaining until the dismissed employee's 65th birthday.

C-4.7 COMPULSORY RESIGNATION

General principle — A coerced resignation amounts to a constructive dismissal. See also Chapter B-4, "Resignation".

Forced resignation examples — constructive dismissal — Constructive dismissal has been found where:

- An employer "accepted the resignation" of an employee who had protested a change in his job. The employee had no intention of resigning.
- Employers attempted to treat employees as having resigned who said they would be willing to quit on certain conditions, or that they "would be resigning".
- An employer let a valuable employee resign without attempting to dissuade her or transfer her. The employer had initiated significant changes to her job and showed no flexibility when she had more trouble than most with the changes.
- An employee was advised that she must apply for a job with the re-organized employer.

Forced resignation examples — no constructive dismissal — No constructive dismissal was found where:

- An employee negotiated a buy-out of the company himself, which required him to resign.
- An employee refused to return to work after being told to return to work and assured he had not been dismissed.

C-4.8 PAY IN LIEU OF NOTICE

General principle — Requiring a dismissed employee to accept pay in lieu of notice rather than allowing the employee to work through the contractual notice period may or may not be a repudiation of the employment contract. This finding mainly affects damages.

Examples — constructive dismissal — Constructive dismissal has been found where:

- An employee had already been given notice of termination and was negotiating her severance. She could not later be forced to work out her notice period in a different job. She had not properly been given working notice, and she could not be forced to accept the temporary job in mitigation under the circumstances.
- An employee was offered the wrong severance package, based on the terms of his employment.

Voluntary offer of severance package — Merely asking an employee if he or she might be interested in a voluntary severance package does not amount to constructive dismissal.

Wrongful dismissal despite adequate notice — An employer who had pledged to avoid capricious firings was contractually bound by this promise, and had breached it by dismissing an employee without a true explanation, even though the employee had been given reasonable notice.

Chapter D-1

JUST CAUSE: GENERAL PRINCIPLES

TABLE OF CONTENTS

D-1.1   Summary Dismissal
D-1.2   Single Instance of Misconduct
D-1.3   Repeated Minor Misconduct
D-1.4   Significance of Written Rules
D-1.5   Timing of Misconduct
D-1.6   Onus of Proof and Pleadings

D-1.1 SUMMARY DISMISSAL

Just cause is exception — As a rule, an employee is entitled to reasonable notice of termination of his contract. The exception to the rule occurs when just cause exists. When just cause exists, the employer is entitled to dismiss the employee immediately or "summarily". This means that no notice or pay in lieu of notice is required. Amounts earned before dismissal, including salary and commissions, must still be paid.

Fundamental breach — The conduct of the employee amounting to just cause constitutes a breach of the employee's fundamental obligations to the employer and a repudiation of the contract. This is what gives the employer the right to put the contract to an end. If just cause exists, there is no right to "some" notice, even in the case of long-service employees.

Employer's remedies — Normally, dismissal for cause is an employer's only remedy for poor performance, incompetence or misconduct. However, in a few cases where the employer has suffered financial loss due to the employee's conduct or performance, the employer may have an action in damages against the employee. See Appendix 2, "Related Actions that are Commonly Joined with Wrongful Dismissal Actions".

Degree of misconduct for summary dismissal — Dismissal will be justified in response to conduct that is inconsistent with the employee's express or implied conditions of service, including the implied term of faithful service. The general rule has been stated as follows:

> If an employee has been guilty of serious misconduct, habitual neglect of duty, incompetence, conduct incompatible with his duties, or prejudicial to the employer's business, or if he has been guilty of wilful disobedience

to the employer's orders in a matter of substance, the law recognizes the employer's right summarily to dismiss the delinquent employee. (from the dissenting reasons of Schroeder, J.A. in *R. v. Arthurs; Ex parte Port Arthur Shipbuilding Co.*, [1967] 2 O.R. 49 at 55 (C.A.), whose reasons were affirmed in (*sub nom. Port Arthur Shipbuilding Co. v. Arthurs et al.*) (1968), [1969] S.C.R. 85.).

Narrow interpretation — A few cases have looked at just cause more narrowly; they have said that summary dismissal requires misconduct which interferes with and prejudices the safe and proper conduct of the business.

Breach must be fundamental — Given that dismissal for just cause is an exception to the employee's usual rights, it is clear that summary dismissal can be utilized only for serious misconduct or breaches of a fundamental kind. This is also true under the Quebec Civil Code, where immediate termination is only permitted for a serious reason. The decision to terminate must not be taken lightly. The fact that the employer made a good business decision, such as a decision to change its management style, does not give it the right to terminate without notice.

Objective test, onus — The question of whether misconduct is serious enough to justify dismissal will be a question of fact to be assessed individually in each case. The seriousness of the misconduct is to be judged objectively, although some cases have stated that the employer's subjective view of the conduct is a factor to be considered. An employer alleging just cause must prove, on a balance of probabilities, that the misconduct justifies dismissal.

Standard may differ — The degree of misconduct required to justify dismissal may differ from employee to employee. Less stringent standards may apply to a probationary employee. The standard may be greater than usual for a long-term employee or one employed at a more senior level. Behaviour that might not justify dismissal of a lower-level employee might justify dismissal of a supervisor or an employee in a position of trust or authority.

Entire context — The entire context of the employee's actions must be considered, including the employee's history, background and years of service. Past good conduct and the cause of the misconduct should be considered, particularly where the misconduct is out of character.

Right to dismiss — It is clear that if just cause for dismissal exists, the employer cannot be faulted for choosing to dismiss rather than imposing lesser discipline. A court cannot substitute its view as to appropriate discipline, even if it thinks a lesser penalty would have been appropriate. The proper issue for a judge is whether or not the employee has disregarded an essential condition of his service, not what penalty was appropriate.

Express agreement — An employer's right to dismiss for just cause may be limited where a written contract deals with termination for cause, or deals with termination without dealing with just cause. See Chapter E-4, "Written Employment Contracts".

Employment standards legislation — "Just cause" under employment standards laws is similar to "just cause" at common law, but is not always identical. Where the issue of cause has already been determined under a statute, issue estoppel may bar a court from considering it again. See Chapter E-2, "Issue Estoppel: Previous or Concurrent Actions".

Financial loss — A financial loss need not be shown to prove just cause. Nor will the existence of a financial loss prove just cause in itself.

Condonation — An employer cannot rely on just cause if the misconduct has been condoned, as discussed in Chapter D-3, "Condonation of Misconduct".

D-1.2 SINGLE INSTANCE OF MISCONDUCT

General principles — An employer is not entitled to seize upon a minor instance of misconduct in order to avoid the duty to give reasonable notice. Often a single incident will not be enough to create just cause, particularly if the conduct is provoked or aggravated by the employer, or if the employee was not wholly responsible for the problem.

When single incident sufficient — A single incident of misconduct or disobedience must be wilful, deliberate and show gross incompetence to justify dismissal without a prior warning. The need to warn is discussed in Chapter D-2, "Duty to Warn and Duty of Fairness".

Examples — single incident was cause — In exceptional circumstances, a single act of misconduct can justify summary dismissal. For example, cause may exist if the conduct is:

- Extremely harmful to the employer or puts the employer at great risk of harm.
- Likely to have future negative consequences.
- Clearly against the employer's rules.
- Serious and incompatible with the employee's duties.
- Significantly dishonest, deceitful or revealing an immoral character, causing a complete failure of trust in the employee.

In addition, just cause may exist based on a single incident if:

- It would be appropriate to dismiss an employee to avoid the type of message that would be sent if there were no dismissal.
- The employee denies the behaviour and there is no remorse.
- It would be difficult for the employee, because of his position, to fulfill his duties after the incident.

D-1.3 REPEATED MINOR MISCONDUCT

General principle — The cumulative effect of many minor instances of misconduct can also justify dismissal in some cases. To amount to just cause, the series of events must cause the parties' business relationship to deteriorate, or it must make it impossible for the employee to properly perform his or her duties and conduct the employer's business.

Misconduct must be serious — The pattern of conduct must be serious enough to show repudiation of the employment contract. Courts tend to be wary where repeated minor misconduct is relied on to prove cause, since some inadequacies and errors can be found in almost any employee's record.

Warnings may be necessary — An employer may need to show that it has warned an employee after incidents of minor misconduct. Otherwise, the employer may be taken to have condoned the misconduct.

D-1.4 SIGNIFICANCE OF WRITTEN RULES

General principle — A breach of an employer's rules may give just cause for dismissal, even if the same conduct would not have been just cause in the absence of the rule. Perhaps this is because existence of a rule shows that certain conduct is a fundamental term of the contract. The more contractual the rule appears to be, based on format and conduct, the more likely it seems to be that it will be enforced.

Example — A dismissal was justified where an assistant store manager breached a policy prohibiting him from buying distressed product from the company while on duty. He had signed three written acknowledgements of the policy while he was in a rush to receive his paycheque. He then denied knowing about the policy, saying he had not paid attention and had tuned out a warning from a cashier who reminded him it was against policy. A judge ruled that the assistant store manager was appropriately dismissed for failing to read and understand company policies which he was expected to know and enforce.

D-1.5 TIMING OF MISCONDUCT

After-acquired knowledge — An employer is entitled to dismiss an employee upon learning of conduct that amounts to just cause, even if it occurred much earlier, without the employer's knowledge. At the trial of an action, an employer can rely on any just cause which existed, even if its existence was not known to the employer at the time of discharge.

Settlement or offer of settlement — If the employer discovers the just cause after the employee has already accepted an offer of severance pay, the employer may not be able to revoke the bargain. However, if the employee does not accept the offer, the employer can rely on the cause. The only requirement is that the employer did not know about the misconduct before making the settlement offer. If the employer had previous knowledge of the misconduct, a settlement offer would amount to condonation of the misconduct.

Limits — At least one judge has expressed reservations about the use of after-acquired knowledge, pointing out that it should be carefully scrutinized for accuracy and good faith. If the employer has deliberately avoided finding out whether just cause exists, it may be taken to have condoned the misconduct. Another case has held that an employer cannot rely on after-acquired knowledge where it is alleging just cause due to revelation of character.

Misconduct after dismissal — Generally speaking, misconduct that occurs after dismissal is not just cause and cannot be relied upon. It is only conduct occurring during the course of employment that can be taken into account. Misconduct occurring after the employer has given notice of dismissal, but before the actual termination, may still justify immediate dismissal, at least where the employer has given reasonable notice, and therefore has not already breached the contract itself.

D-1.6 ONUS OF PROOF AND PLEADINGS

Onus on employer — The onus of proving just cause is on the employer. Self-serving evidence, such as a performance appraisal finally given to the employee after termination, may be rejected. The onus will not be satisfied if there are many possible explanations of what occurred and the employer cannot prove that the employee was responsible for the complained-of actions.

Standard of proof — Most judges say that the usual civil standard of proof on a balance of probabilities applies where just cause is alleged, even where criminal or dishonest conduct is alleged. Other judges, however, have suggested the need for "cogent evidence", "compelling evidence", a "preponderance of evidence" or proof "beyond the balance of probabilities" where dishonest conduct is alleged.

Criminal activity alleged — One judge has said that the evidence "requires a degree of probability commensurate with the occasion", while others have simply said that a standard of proof higher than the usual balance of probabilities is required. The fact that an employee was acquitted on criminal charges has been ruled irrelevant to the civil issue of wrongful dismissal.

Pleadings — Specific pleadings (allegations in a civil action) are important where just cause is alleged. Some judges may not allow an employer to rely on misconduct that is not pleaded. Pleadings of just cause, however, should only be made in good faith and with some justification; otherwise, they may lead to extra damages against the employer.

Chapter D-2

DUTY TO WARN AND DUTY OF FAIRNESS

TABLE OF CONTENTS

D-2.1　Duty to Warn
D-2.2　Content of Warning
D-2.3　Duty to Warn in Good Faith
D-2.4　Duty of Fairness
D-2.5　Procedural Fairness and Natural Justice

D-2.1　DUTY TO WARN

General principle — Where an employer relies on a gradual deterioration in performance, or the accumulation of many minor failings, the employer may have a duty to warn the employee and give him or her time to improve. A warning is especially necessary where: a substandard performance has been occurring for some time; an employee has had nothing but positive performance reviews in the past; or the employee has been asked to perform new functions in which he or she has no experience. Where a warning is required, the lack of one may contribute to a finding of no just cause.

No warning required — There may be no duty to warn where:

- A triggering incident itself amounts to just cause.
- There is serious misconduct or prejudice to the employer's business.
- A serious risk to health and safety is involved.

No duty to warn of investigation — As an employer is entitled to investigate suspected misconduct, an employer does not need to warn an employee about an impending investigation.

Onus — The employer has the onus to prove that a clear warning was given, that it was understood by the employee, and that a reasonable opportunity to improve was given.

Warning to refute condonation — Even if behaviour would otherwise give just cause for dismissal, an employer may need to give a warning first if an employee is following what he thinks is the employer's policy;

or if the employee believes he has the employer's tacit approval to pursue a certain course of action; or if the behaviour has been condoned in the past. In fact, multiple warnings may be needed in these situations.

Employer policy — Where an employer has established a discipline policy which requires that warnings be given, there is an even stronger implication that an employee must be warned before dismissal. However, a progressive discipline policy may not need to be applied when the employee's conduct amounts to a fundamental breach of the contract.

Need for new warning — The employer may need to issue a new warning if circumstances have changed substantially. For example, warnings given by a previous manager who was himself a problem employee were discounted in one case after the manager was fired. The new manager had only been on the job one month and had not discussed the employee's problems or given him any warnings, so the dismissal was said to be without cause or warning.

Need for multiple warnings — More than one warning may be needed if so much time has passed since a previous warning for the employee to be considered rehabilitated, or if the employer did not act upon failure to improve after a prior warning. Two warnings were not sufficient where a long-term employee's behaviour had previously been condoned and even accommodated, and thus the employee had no way of knowing that failure to comply would lead to dismissal.

Form of warning — A written warning is a proper way for an employer to express its disapproval of an employee's conduct, whether or not the employee agrees with the employer's assessment. However, a warning may not need to be in writing to be effective. If oral, the warning should be made in sharp, clear and unmistakable tones, not in casual conversation, so that its seriousness is clear. The best practice is to provide ongoing instruction, guidance, advice, direction and constructive criticism, as well as to explain the importance of following departmental protocol and policies.

Risks of oral warning — A written warning is usually the best practice, because it can be viewed later on, by whichever party needs to review it. A failure to put the warning in writing may be evidence that no clear warning was ever given, as may a failure to note an alleged warning in the employee's personnel file.

D-2.2 CONTENT OF WARNING

General principle — Whether written or oral, to be effective a warning must be:

Clear, unequivocal and unambiguous. A warning will not be effective where the employee has received a mixed message, such as giving the warning at the same time as a promotion and raise. A warning should be ambiguous as to consequences, such as a statement that if performance did not improve, "major changes" might have to be made.

Specific. The employee must be able to understand what he or she has done wrong. A warning may not be effective if a reasonable person would see it as a mere expression of concern or displeasure, or a pep talk or exhortation to improve.

Serious and not an idle threat. For example, a standard paragraph threatening "discipline up to and including dismissal" that is used for all minor infractions may lose its impact and lack seriousness.

Unaccepting. Warnings have been ineffective where they showed condonation or indicated that the matter was closed; for example, a statement by a manager that he would not raise the matter again.

Performance warnings — Where performance is in issue, it may be necessary to state the standard that is expected and the actions needed to improve, and even to give the employee feedback on his or her efforts to improve. An employee who is told that he or she has a certain amount of time to show improvement will generally be entitled to that time, without earlier dismissal for cause based on the same problem or misconduct.

Need to clarify consequences — Whether it is necessary to state the consequences of failing to improve is in dispute. Some cases have said that it is not necessary, as long as the employee was aware of his problems and had been given a chance to correct them. It must be clear that the employee's job is in jeopardy, although it might not be necessary to use the word "fired". However, other cases have said that there is a duty to spell out the consequences of failing to improve, and to make sure the employee understands the significance of the warning. Failing to do so may make the warning ineffective. For example, a warning was ineffective where the employee was told his work would be closely monitored for three months, but he was not told his job was in jeopardy.

Language barrier — Whether or not there is a need to clarify consequences in all cases, it is especially important to spell out the consequences with an employee with a language barrier. Otherwise, the employee may argue that the warning was not effective because he or she did not understand its significance.

Reconciling warning with company policy — It is important to reconcile the content of the warning with company policy. For example, where the company policy provided for permitted absences where medically required, a warning was not effective where the employee was told that even such absences would be considered unacceptable.

D-2.3 DUTY TO WARN IN GOOD FAITH

Need for good faith — A warning must be given in good faith. There was no good faith, and no effective warning, where a warning was:

- A "charade" because the employer had already decided to fire the employee.
- Given the day before an employee's vacation, and the employee was dismissed upon her return. She had been given no chance to improve, and the timing showed the warning was not in good faith.
- Followed by public monitoring of the employee's performance and a barrage of written criticism. The judge found that this conduct was designed to build a case for dismissal rather than to improve the employee's performance, which showed an absence of good faith.

D-2.4 DUTY OF FAIRNESS

Generalized duty of good faith — Employers have a generalized duty to treat employees fairly throughout the employment relationship, in the sense of treating them with good faith. However, employees who are not office holders have no general right to procedural fairness or natural justice in the absence of a statute, collective agreement or individual employment contract. This means that they are not entitled to be given reasons for dismissal; to be given a formal or informal chance to give their side of the story before a decision is made; or to have representation pending a decision to dismiss.

Reason for dismissal — Although an employer may not be required to give a reason for dismissal, some judges have commented negatively on an employer's failure to give a reason at the time of dismissal, especially where it may indicate condonation. In some cases, refusal to give a reason may be taken as bad faith that will increase the employee's damages, as discussed in Chapter F-5, "Effect of Parties' Conduct on Reasonable Notice". New Brunswick's employment standards statute requires employers to give reasons in writing when dismissing employees for cause. However, this requirement may be satisfied by giving an explanation in broad terms or within a reasonable time after dismissal.

Change of reason — Where an employer does provide a reason at the time of dismissal, but later alleges a different reason, an argument may arise that the employer condoned any just cause that existed. Giving an employee a patently false reason for dismissal was a denial of procedural fairness in one case, and in another it led to a finding of capricious firing that affected costs.

Proper investigation — Even where procedural fairness is not required, an employer's investigation procedure must be considered in assessing allegations of just cause. A dismissal carried out hastily, without adequate investigation or the advice of superiors, or without following the employer's internal policy, may indicate that the allegations are unreliable. In one case, an employer's investigation was criticized for being cursory, incomplete and unbalanced because the complainant and a witness to the event were interviewed together.

Opportunity to explain — Even though it may not be a legal requirement to give an employee a chance to explain his or her side of things, as a practical matter, it is probably wise to do so. Many judges think this is required by the duty of fairness. Other judges have also commented negatively on the fact that no opportunity to explain was given to the employee.

Office holders — Office holders, such as police officers and others with a public or statutory flavour to their employment, are usually entitled to natural justice, or at least to procedural fairness, meaning a chance to defend themselves from allegations before a decision is made against them. Other employees may be entitled to be given reasons or a chance to explain, if required by a statute, collective agreement or individual employment contract.

Office held at pleasure — Even where an office holder holds the office at pleasure, meaning he or she can be dismissed for any reason without notice, it is now recognized that these employees still have a right to fairness. However, this does not give the employee the right to receive reasonable notice of dismissal. It merely provides some advance notice of a possible decision and the opportunity to thoroughly discuss the employer's complaint.

D-2.5 PROCEDURAL FAIRNESS AND NATURAL JUSTICE

Procedural fairness vs. natural justice — Under administrative law, there is a distinction between a right to procedural fairness and a right to "natural justice". Both require a right to be told the substance of a complaint and to be given a chance to respond before a decision is made. In the case of natural justice, this must be done in a more formal way, often in an almost trial-like setting. A right to natural justice will often include the right to representation by a lawyer or other spokesperson.

Right to be heard — The employee must be informed of the accusations against him, given a chance to respond, and a decision must be made in good faith, i.e. the employer must actually listen and fairly consider the employee's response. Additional requirements may also exist, such as a duty to provide particulars. The right to be heard includes the right to plead for leniency. In one case, a judge commented negatively on the fact that an employee was expected to respond to anonymous complaints.

Examples — procedural fairness duty met — The duty of procedural fairness was met where:

- An employee was given a chance to explain, even though the employer had already decided to terminate him unless he had a good explanation. Advance notice of the meeting was not required in these circumstances.
- An employer had conducted its own investigation and given the employee a chance to explain. The employer was not required to await the outcome of a criminal trial.
- The employee was told termination was being considered and was given every opportunity to discuss the situation. This met the hearing requirement necessary for procedural fairness.
- An employee was given a chance to respond when he was questioned by his peers; it was not necessary to give him a chance to answer to his superiors.
- An employer failed to provide counsel for an experienced executive who was accused of wrongdoing. The employee was given the choice to resign or to be fired. The employer was under no duty to do so.
- An employee was given notice of a meeting, particulars of the complaint, a chance to retain counsel and a chance to address the employer's board in person. A direct confrontation and the chance to cross-examine his accuser under oath were not required.

Examples — procedural fairness duty not met — The duty of fairness was not met where:

- An employee was never told the nature of the case against him. Giving him a chance to respond was meaningless in that situation.
- The employee was given a chance to explain but was neither shown the results of the employer's investigation, nor given time to get advice or consider his position.
- A chance to explain was not given. In that case, the employer's failure to await the outcome of a criminal trial was a denial of procedural fairness.

- The employee's co-workers testified privately and individually before the employer's whole board, but the employee was given no opportunity to reply.

Third-party decision — An employee, whose licence to work in an industry was revoked, was wrongfully dismissed when the licence was reinstated. The employer made no independent attempt to see if the employee was guilty of the allegations. The situation would have been different if the employer had attempted to show that whatever the outcome of the investigation, the employee's conduct was incompatible with continued employment, but the employer made no attempt to do so.

Lack of hearing not significant — The failure to provide an opportunity to explain may not always be significant. For example, there may be no consequences where:

- A termination is not for cause or is totally unrelated to the employee. For example, a legitimate reorganization of a business may lead to an employee's termination.
- The employee has admitted the breach.
- The employee has already informally learned the reasons for dismissal and has had a chance to respond.
- The person imposing discipline has direct knowledge of the incident.
- Serious allegations of misconduct are subsequently proved to be true.

Failure to comply with duty — Where there is a true duty to provide procedural fairness or natural justice, the failure to do so may lead to the termination being ruled null and void. In some cases, this can lead to reinstatement although that is rare. More often, a dismissal without a chance to explain may lead a court to increase the notice period due to bad faith; to award extra general damages for mental distress, defamation or punitive damages; or to award solicitor-and-client costs against the employer.

Chapter D-3

CONDONATION OF MISCONDUCT

TABLE OF CONTENTS

D-3.1   General Principles
D-3.2   Effect of Warnings
D-3.3   Behaviour Constituting Condonation
D-3.4   Effect of Dismissal with Notice, Pay or a Non-Cause Explanation
D-3.5   Revival of Past Misconduct

D-3.1 GENERAL PRINCIPLES

Condonation defined — Condonation occurs whenever an employer indicates to an employee that it is overlooking conduct which would have given just cause for dismissal. This can occur directly or indirectly through the employer's behaviour. The most common type of condonation is where the employer does nothing and simply continues to employ the employee. As the rule was stated in a leading case:

> When an employer becomes aware of misconduct on the part of his servant, sufficient to justify dismissal, he may adopt either of two courses. He may dismiss, or he may overlook the fault. But he cannot retain the servant in his employment, and afterwards at any distance of time turn him away. (*McIntyre v. Hockin* (1889), 16 O.A.C. 498 at 502 (C.A.).)

Standard of conduct — Where an employer commonly tolerates certain conduct from other employees, or allows a lax atmosphere, it may not be able to rely on that conduct as cause for dismissal of any one employee. The result will, however, depend on the seriousness of the conduct; for example, sexual harassment was not accepted by one judge, even where it was common in the workplace.

Employer's knowledge — Condonation only applies where the employer knows the full nature and extent of the misconduct. A failure to investigate or act upon suspicions is not condonation. For example, an employer had not condoned misconduct where it was aware of rumours but had no actual knowledge of misconduct. An employer that allowed some rule infractions did not condone infractions of which it was unaware.

Imputed knowledge — An employer's lack of knowledge must be reasonable. Where an employer received daily reports in which rule infractions would have been clear, but the employer never took the time to read the reports, it was deemed to have known of the rule infractions.

Relevant time — The relevant time for assessing whether an employer has condoned misconduct is the time when he learned of it, and not the time when the misconduct occurred. However, in one case an employee was warned about sexually harassing one woman and he then "cleaned up his act". The employer later learned he had harassed another woman before the warning. The judge ruled that since he had been warned and had improved, he could not be dismissed for just cause based on harassment of the second woman.

Employer has time to decide — An employer is entitled to a reasonable time to investigate and decide on the appropriate course of action. There was no condonation where:

- It took an employer six months to complete a difficult investigation.
- The employer took time to investigate and seek legal advice, even where the employee had been immediately reprimanded and had then heard nothing more for several weeks. The employer acted in a timely way once it had all the information and advice.
- An employer had given the employee a warning and a period of time to show improvement. It was entitled to wait until the end of that period before taking action, even though the employee misconducted himself again early in the period.
- There was a three-month delay in a complex situation.
- An employer waited a few weeks to allow the employee to complete an important task for which no replacement employee was immediately available.
- A decision to dismiss was not made until after an employee was fit to return to work.

Employer bound by supervisor's conduct — Once conduct has been condoned by a supervisor or other person in authority, the employer is bound, as long as the supervisor has not misconducted himself or acted outside his authority. For example, there was condonation where:

- A new president wished to dismiss an employee after the previous president had condoned the employee's misconduct.
- A business was purchased. The purchaser could not fire an employee for incompetence occurring before the purchase, because any such incompetence had been condoned by the previous owner's failure to deal with it.

In another case, an employee's two immediate superiors turned a blind eye to his misconduct. A judge said this did not act as condonation on the company's behalf, because the immediate superior had reported the misconduct, and the senior superior's actions were tainted by the fact that he received a personal benefit from the misconduct.

Onus of proof — The onus of proving condonation is on the employee.

D-3.2 EFFECT OF WARNINGS

No condonation where warnings given — No condonation has been found where an employee was warned about his behaviour, either through an indication of displeasure or an indication that the behaviour would not be acceptable in future. For example, there was no condonation where:

- An employee's performance was unsatisfactory for nine years, and he was retained in his job for three years after he was severely warned and advised to change positions. The employer had not condoned the employee's incompetence because improvement was requested repeatedly and the employee was warned his job was in jeopardy.
- Disciplinary action was taken in the form of a transfer.

Warning for behaviour condoned in past — Where a certain standard of performance or behaviour has been tolerated in the past, i.e., condoned, the employer must give a genuine warning before there will be just cause for dismissal. This warning may have to include very specific objectives and deadlines.

Condonation where behaviour corrected — Where an employee is warned to improve and does improve, and where the employer is silent thereafter, the employer cannot rely on the employee's past unsatisfactory performance as cause for dismissal.

Condonation where warnings not acted on — Where an employee had been repeatedly given warnings but no action was taken when the guidelines were not met, the poor performance had been condoned.

Warnings where minor misconduct repeated — In one case, an employer had spoken to an employee after each incident of minor misconduct, indicating it did not condone his behaviour. The employee was finally dismissed for just cause, based on the cumulative effect of the many minor incidents. The judge ruled that the employer could rely on the incidents when dismissing the employee due to their cumulative effect. However, depending on the circumstances, a highly specific warning may still be needed before an employer can dismiss for just cause based on cumulative instances of misconduct.

Discipline instead of warning — In one case, an employer who disciplined an employee for improper behaviour regarding travel arrangements, by denying him the right to attend a conference, was found to have lost the ability to dismiss the employee for cause.

D-3.3 BEHAVIOUR CONSTITUTING CONDONATION

Acts of commission or omission — An employer can condone misconduct or poor performance both by acts of commission (taking inappropriate action) and by acts of omission (failure to take action). The effect of an action or inaction will depend on the circumstances.

Examples — condonation — Misconduct was condoned where:

- Employees were retained for four and one-half months after the employer learned of their misconduct.
- An employer allowed an employee to remain at work for a month, then asked him to take a three-month leave of absence with the expectation that he would return to work.
- An employer tolerated an employee's frequent insubordination over a two-week period and did not assert its authority or reprimand the employee.
- An employee discussed with his boss the fact that he was having an affair with the wife of a co-worker, and his boss assured him his employment would not be affected.
- An employer laid off an employee to avoid paying her statutory termination pay, and she was left on layoff for over two months before being told she was not coming back. The employer had condoned any just cause that may have existed.
- An employer chastised an employee but then said the matter would go no further.
- The problem was never mentioned and the employee continued to receive good performance reviews.
- The employee was given a raise.
- The employer refused an offered resignation.
- A promotion was given without a warning about past poor behaviour.
- An employer entered into a second fixed-term contract with an employee. This was condonation of misconduct occurring during the first contract.
- A casual employee's status was changed by adding her to the permanent payroll.
- An employee thought to be responsible for cash shortages was moved to another position where cash would also be handled.
- An employee was offered the very same job under different contractual terms.

Examples — no condonation — There was no condonation where:

- An employee was promoted despite two previous demotions for disciplinary and performance problems. He had been warned that he was being given a final chance to prove himself.
- A change in status from part-time to full-time was based on seniority, not merit. It was not a promotion amounting to condonation of past poor performance.
- An offer was made to transfer an employee to a position that was a significant demotion.

Failure to discipline others — Where other employees were aware of one employee's misconduct, the employer's failure to discipline him was not a condonation of the misconduct.

Personality conflicts — An employer cannot complain about an employee's abrasive personality or generally disruptive behaviour where it has been obvious from the beginning but the employer took no action. Abuse of staff, even that resulting in assault, may not create just cause where the employee's behaviour has been condoned. Where a personality conflict caused performance problems, and the employer preferred to retain the person who had caused the conflict, it could not rely on the performance problems to justify dismissal of the other person.

D-3.4 DISMISSAL WITH NOTICE, PAY OR A NON-CAUSE EXPLANATION

Notice or pay in lieu — Some cases have held that dismissal of an employee with some notice or pay in lieu operates as condonation or as an estoppel to raising the issue of just cause. Many other cases, however, have denied that condonation or estoppel arise in these cases. In one case, condonation was found where an employer offered a severance package and the employee accepted. However, it was said that if the offer had not been accepted, the employer could later have asserted just cause.

Non-cause explanation — Dismissal with a non-cause explanation, or with laudatory reference letters, may amount to condonation of any cause for dismissal. As one judge stated, the law should not encourage people to say one thing when they mean another. In other cases, however, it has been said that an employer can give untrue reasons for dismissal as long as just cause really does exist. Another appeal court ruled that an employer need not state any reason for termination at the time.

Examples — no condonation where non-cause reason given — No condonation has been found where:

- The non-cause reason was made to help the employee get unemployment insurance benefits, although some other judges have disagreed.
- The employer offered to discuss a severance package but made it clear that it believed it had cause for the dismissal.
- An offer of pay in lieu of notice was made in a termination letter which was stated to be "without prejudice".
- The employer offered a long-standing employee a settlement if he resigned, but dismissed him for cause when he refused. The settlement offer and the fact that the employer offered him another job at a lower salary were held not to constitute condonation; the employer was merely showing consideration for a long-term employee.

D-3.5 REVIVAL OF PAST MISCONDUCT

New instance of misconduct — The case law does not agree whether or not past misconduct which has been condoned can be revived by a new instance of misconduct. One view states that any condonation is subject to a condition of future good conduct; but there are many cases which disagree with it. In any event, if the later misconduct is sufficiently serious to constitute cause in itself, the employer need not rely on the earlier misconduct.

Cumulative effect or pattern of misconduct — It has been held that the later act need not be of the same kind to entitle the employer to weigh the accumulated misconduct in determining whether just cause exists. Past misconduct may also be used for the purpose of proving that new misconduct is part of a habitual pattern.

Chapter D-4

UNACCEPTABLE PERFORMANCE

TABLE OF CONTENTS

D-4.1   General Principles
D-4.2   Performance Standards
D-4.3   Single Incident
D-4.4   Chronic Performance Problems
D-4.5   Probationary Periods and Assistance Programs
D-4.6   Written Contract

D-4.1 GENERAL PRINCIPLES

Just cause — An employer is not entitled to dismiss an employee for mere dissatisfaction with his or her work. For just cause to exist, there must be:

(1)   actual incompetence;
(2)   inability to carry out duties; or
(3)   substandard work which persists after a warning to improve.

The fact that an employee is not suitable does not make the employee incompetent.

Overall performance — Where overall performance is good, concerns about the manner in which the employee performs his job may not be cause for dismissal. Disorganization is not necessarily incompetence; nor are concerns with management style and deportment.

Long-term employee — The degree of incompetence or substandard work necessary to justify dismissal may be greater for a long-term employee. For example, a previously satisfactory long-term employee who could not perform in accordance with a new set of expectations could not be dismissed for just cause.

Blame must lie with employee — The employer must establish that the substandard performance is the employee's own fault and is not caused by the employer's unreasonable demands or its failure to provide proper training, instructions, support, supervision, materials and working conditions.

Employer's knowledge — An employer who knowingly hires an employee inexperienced in a particular area of work can not rely on incompetence as grounds for dismissal. An employer cannot complain about the lack of certain skills when they were not emphasized during the hiring process.

Labour relations standard — Several judges seem to have applied what is, in effect, a labour relations standard for dismissal due to poor performance. They have said that the employer must prove:

(1) the level of performance required;
(2) that the standard was told to the employee;
(3) that the employer gave suitable instruction and supervision to enable the employee to meet the standard;
(4) that the employee did not meet the standard; and
(5) that the employee was warned that failure to meet the standard would lead to dismissal.

Serious financial loss — A mere lack of profit will probably not be cause for dismissal. Responsibility for a serious financial loss may justify dismissal if a causal connection is established between the loss and the employee's incompetence. In one case, however, responsibility for a single large loss was not just cause where the long-term employee had simply made the wrong decision when faced with a unique problem.

Mental or other illness — Poor performance caused by mental or other illness may or may not be cause for dismissal. In one case, no just cause was found where an employee was physically incapable of proper performance.

Employment standards legislation — The standard of just cause under an employment standards statute is similar but may not be identical to the standard at common law. Statutory decisions should not be relied on in assessing common law rights, and vice versa.

Warning — Where a warning is required and has been issued, after the employee's performance improves, he or she cannot be dismissed for cause without a further warning.

D-4.2 PERFORMANCE STANDARDS

Objective, reasonable standard — For there to be cause for dismissal, an employee's performance must fall below an objective standard of performance. The employer's performance standard must be reasonable, fair and non-discriminatory. An employer may also have to prove that it has applied its standards equally to all employees before the dismissal of one employee will be just.

Acknowledging standards — The acknowledgment of the existence of performance standards does not amount to a covenant or representation on the part of the employee to meet those standards. For example:

- An employee who was asked to come up with a plan to increase profits was not dismissible for failing to stick to the plan, in the absence of warnings or specific, major failures.
- A corporate culture that treated standards as minimum targets did not have contractual force, and an employee could not be dismissed for just cause for failing to meet them.

Competency test — Where an objective standard was applied in the form of a competency test, and an employee failed a second test after receiving more training, her dismissal was justified.

Examples — no cause — Cause was not proven where:

- The employee failed merely to meet goals set by the employer, and incompetence was not shown. This is especially the case where the goals or the consequences of not meeting them have not been communicated to the employee.
- The results were average.
- 84 per cent of the set objectives were met.
- An employer changed its performance standards. In such a case, it may be necessary to prove that an employee agreed to the revised standards before there will be just cause for dismissal for a failure to meet them.
- The industry standard or the employer's standard had increased, while the employee's performance had not. To justify dismissal it was necessary to give adequate warnings and a reasonable time to improve.
- An employee failed to meet a target, but the dismissal was really motivated by other considerations that did not amount to just cause.
- There was a lack of marketing support from the employer.

D-4.3 SINGLE INCIDENT

General principle — An isolated failure to maintain perfection, a single mistake or incident showing poor judgment, or an accident generally will not justify dismissal without a warning. A few isolated instances of less than perfect performance similarly will not justify dismissal.

Gross incompetence — A single incident showing incompetence or a single incident of poor performance can justify dismissal without a prior warning if it shows gross incompetence or has serious consequences. Similarly, a complete failure to display skills which the employee claims to possess can justify dismissal without prior warning.

D-4.4 CHRONIC PERFORMANCE PROBLEMS

Chronic substandard performance — Where chronic substandard work is alleged, the employer has a duty to warn the employee of its concerns and the possible consequences, and allow the employee time to improve his performance. The number of warnings required and the amount of time to allow for improvement will depend on the facts of each case, including the severity and consequences of the employee's unacceptable performance. The employer may be required to set out clear objectives and deadlines for the employee.

Poor performance after warnings — Where employees have been given several clear warnings and ample chances to improve but still fail to improve, and their performance is objectively unacceptable, courts now seem more willing than in the past to uphold dismissal, especially where safety is involved.

Warning not necessary — A warning may not be necessary if the incompetency raises safety concerns, or if the behaviour complained of is so egregious as to justify summary dismissal.

Condonation — Courts are less likely to uphold dismissals for cause where the employee received mixed messages about his performance, or where the performance problems were overlooked by the employer for a long period of time. However, occasionally judges uphold dismissals despite the employer's inconsistency, as long as the employer has not conducted itself in such a way as to show a reasonable man that the standard was unimportant.

Examples — Poor performance after warnings — In one case, an employee's minimally acceptable performance — even though the employee was given three warnings within 18 months — was not just cause, given his seven and a half years of satisfactory service. Dismissal, however, has been justified where:

- A 35-year employee's performance was unacceptable throughout his nine years in a managerial position, since he had repeatedly been requested to improve and had been warned his job was in jeopardy.
- A manager was warned that he could be dismissed if his performance did not improve. He continued to receive negative performance reports over the next 10 months. A further warning before dismissal was not required.

D-4.5 PROBATIONARY PERIODS AND ASSISTANCE PROGRAMS

Initial probationary period — It is a matter of dispute whether a probationary employee can be dismissed only for the same standard of poor performance as a permanent employee, or whether a lower standard of performance applies. See Chapter A-3, "Probationary Employment".

"Disciplinary" probationary period — Once an employee is warned, he or she must be given sufficient time to correct the problem before the employer can take other action. If a probationary period is imposed in order to correct performance, it may be improper to dismiss the employee before the end of the probationary period.

Assistance program — If an employer provides an assistance program to help poor performers, it may be unable to dismiss an employee for poor performance unless the employee has been given the chance to use the program. However, the employer may not have to apply a progressive discipline policy if the employee's conduct amounts to a fundamental breach of the contract. An obligation to assess an employee's work may include an obligation to assign a full range of normal duties on which to be assessed.

D-4.6 WRITTEN CONTRACT

Contract silent — An employee with a written employment contract whose contract is silent about dismissal for poor performance can still be dismissed if the performance is so bad as to amount to a fundamental breach of the contract. Similarly, an employee, who repudiated a fixed-term contract by breaching its implied term of faithful service, could be dismissed for just cause even though the contract was silent on this point.

Contractual standards — Where a contract sets out specific performance requirements, an employer could not dismiss an employee for mere dissatisfaction with his or her performance.

Objective standard implied — A contract stating that an employee could be dismissed for "failure" to meet a certain sales level implied some fault on the employee's part. Where the failure was due to the economic climate, there was no just cause. However, a contract specifying that the employee perform "to the best of his ability" did not absolve him from dismissal for incompetence. See also Chapter E-4, "Written Employment Contracts".

Industry custom — A custom of releasing hockey players from their fixed-term contracts for poor performance prevailed over the fixed term.

Agreed subjective standard — An employer may be able to dismiss an employee for mere dissatisfaction with his or her performance where the employment contract contains words such as "in the opinion of the employer". They import a subjective standard which is enforceable unless there is bad motive, dishonesty or lack of good faith.

Chapter D-5

DISHONESTY

TABLE OF CONTENTS

D-5.1   General Principles
D-5.2   Dishonesty: Prejudicial Conduct
D-5.3   Dishonesty: Revelation of Character
D-5.4   Financial Improprieties
D-5.5   Lies and Failure to Tell the Truth
D-5.6   Professional Qualifications and Résumé Disclosure

D-5.1 GENERAL PRINCIPLES

Categories of just cause — There are two categories of cases involving dishonesty amounting to just cause:

(1) where the employee's dishonest conduct is seriously prejudicial to the employer's interests or reputation; and
(2) where the misconduct reveals such an untrustworthy character that the employer is not bound to continue the employee in a position of responsibility or trust.

Modern approach — Judges usually first consider whether the dishonesty has led to serious harm or potential harm, i.e., prejudice, to the employer. If not, judges then consider whether the dishonesty reveals such an untrustworthy character that the employer is justified in not continuing the employment. The two categories are not as important as they once were. In many recent cases, the same type of conduct has been found to justify dismissal under both categories.

Objective standard — If the conduct is not objectively dishonest, the employer may have to provide guidelines before an employee's actions will amount to just cause for dismissal.

Criminal conduct — Criminal conduct can justify dismissal in some cases whether or not it is work-related. Criminal conduct that is work related is discussed throughout this chapter. Non-work-related criminal conduct is discussed in Chapter D-10, "Off-the-Job Conduct and Other Just Cause Situations".

Misconduct must be employee's — The fact that someone in the employee's area or under the employee's supervision commits a dishonest act will not justify dismissal, if the employee is not personally guilty of dishonesty.

Intention needed — Proof of an intentional element seems to be required. Any explanation showing an innocent intention or a lack of personal gain may overcome the implication of just cause. Carelessness, negligence, poor judgment or mistake may not be enough to justify dismissal. For example:

- An employee's failure to ensure that proper income tax was deducted from his pay was not equivalent to stealing from the employer.
- Where an employee immediately offered to reimburse the employer for personal long distance phone calls when confronted, it was not reasonable for the employer to refuse reimbursement and then rely on her failure to pay for the calls as cause for dismissal. Apparently, her offer vitiated any dishonesty involved.

Uncharacteristic act — An uncharacteristic act performed at a time of great personal stress may not amount to just cause. For example, there was no cause where:

- An employee mistakenly mixed his own money with funds held in trust. He had made an error and had not committed a crime.
- A manager had a sick employee babysit his sick child, and then submitted a claim for sick pay for the sick employee. He had used poor judgment but had not done anything to warrant dismissal.
- An employee committed three improper financial acts while seriously depressed.

Following orders — An employee who knowingly engaged in dishonest behaviour will likely not be excused by the fact that he acted at the request of his supervisor. However, this is not always true. For example:

- In one case, an employee who falsified a government document, believing he was following the orders of his superiors, was not dismissed for just cause.
- In another case, dismissal was just where an employee knowingly participated in a tax fraud and kickback scheme set up by a managing partner. The involvement of her superior did not alter the fact that her conduct violated her employment contract.

Balance of proof — Higher proof of the dishonest action than on a balance of probabilities may be required to establish just cause.

Suspicion — Most judges have held that an employer must have proof that the employee has committed the dishonest act. A mere suspicion or rumour of dishonesty is not enough to warrant dismissal. Videotaped actions will not be conclusive if the employee has an honest explanation for them. If there is no other reasonable explanation, this may amount to proof. The employer must prove that the employee had no colour of right to do what he or she did.

Duty of fairness — As discussed in Chapter D-2, "Duty to Warn and Duty of Fairness", there is a debate about whether an employer must allow an employee a chance to explain. However, it will usually be prudent to do so, rather than, for example, relying solely on an anonymous tip, which has been found to be insufficient to prove just cause in several cases.

D-5.2 DISHONESTY: PREJUDICIAL CONDUCT

Seriously prejudicial conduct — To amount to just cause, the dishonest conduct must result in serious harm or potential harm to the employer. In one case, it was said that there was no just cause where any improprieties would have been at someone else's expense, not at the employer's expense, although this might be just cause based on revelation of character.

"Minor" dishonesty — Where dishonesty involves a trivial matter of no real consequence to the employer, or only a small amount of money is involved, some judges have found that the dishonesty is not serious enough to amount to just cause. Other judges, however, have found just cause even where the amount involved is small, especially where criminal conduct is involved. One court has gone so far as to say that dishonesty is always cause for dismissal because it is a breach of the condition of faithful service. It has also been held that a pattern of minor dishonesty or even one incident may reveal a character that makes continued employment untenable.

Examples — Examples of dishonest behaviour that were seriously prejudicial to the employer, justifying dismissal, include:
- Theft from the employer.
- Intentional misapplication of the employer's funds.
- Taking an unauthorized raise or advance on salary or bonus, or claiming unauthorized commissions.
- Taking salary and payment for statutory holidays to which the employee was not entitled.
- Falsifying expense accounts or personal credits, or knowingly approving them.
- Double-dipping expense account payments.

- Personal use of company credit cards, or putting personal expenses through the company, unless systematically repaid, authorized or condoned.
- The deposit of social club funds into the employee's personal bank account.
- Taking unauthorized breaks.
- Claiming or permitting unauthorized overtime payments.
- Falsely maintaining a disability claim even though capable of returning to work.
- Allowing subordinates to perform large amounts of personal work on the employer's time.
- Unjustified demands for payment of a large commission.
- Taking "kickbacks" or secret commissions, or charging a fee to third parties for services which the employee was bound to provide by his contract with the employer.
- Trading in the company's sample goods for the employee's own benefit.
- Purposely breaching store security rules or cash handling procedures.
- Authorizing loans in breach of rules, after warnings not to do so.
- Purposely misrepresenting products to clients or clients to the employer.
- Submitting fraudulent warranty claims to a third party, which could have jeopardized the employer's relationship with that party.
- Undercharging customers for the employer's goods.
- Purporting to appoint a master distributor for the employer's products and announcing it to the trade without telling the employer.
- Falsifying customers' signatures to service contracts even where there was no loss to the customers, because the employer's integrity was placed in question.
- Taking advantage of a resident of the employer's nursing home.
- Submitting a false incident report to protective service officers.

D-5.3 DISHONESTY: REVELATION OF CHARACTER

General principles — The standards for dismissing on the basis of revelation of character are unclear. At least one case has stated that a pattern of minor dishonesty may reveal a character that makes continued employment untenable. The conduct must be serious enough to conclude that the essential trust required of the employee is lacking.

Special requirement of trust — Judges are more likely to find that dishonesty amounts to just cause where the employee is a manager or where the employer's business depends on the honesty and integrity of its employees, such as where:

- The employee occupies a position of special trust or confidence.
- The employer's business requires the appearance of absolute integrity.

- The employee's position (e.g., an internal auditor) carries a vital responsibility.
- The credibility of the employer (e.g., a public institution) would be at issue if the employee's actions were to be made public.

After-acquired knowledge — Where an employer alleges just cause due to revelation of character, it may not be able to rely on after-acquired information, since the issue is what the employer knew at the time of dismissal.

Examples — Examples of dishonesty revealing an untrustworthy character have included:

- Exchanging personal goods with office goods and refusing to comply with the company's accounting procedures.
- Misappropriating the employer's property.
- Padding or cheating on an expense account or improperly charging personal expenses to the employer.
- Taking an unauthorized loan from company funds.
- Unauthorized approval of overdrafts and inaccurate reporting of their levels.
- Obtaining an employee loan improperly.
- Receiving a preferential employee interest rate on funds other than his own.
- Selling goods to a fellow employee at a discount without following proper procedures.
- Giving false receipts for sale of damaged goods.
- Allowing a person into a store after hours who stole company merchantdise.
- Acceptance of favours or secret commissions from a third party.
- Misappropriating promotional travel tickets for personal use.
- Improper financial dealings with customers or suppliers.
- Improperly enrolling members in order to pack a meeting with supporters.
- A comptroller who advised another employee to pay illegal bribes.
- Commission of perjury by a probationary policeman.
- Pretending to take a specially authorized trip which was never taken.
- Fraudulently altering the employee's own written contract of employment.
- Attempting to obtain or obtaining an unauthorized salary increase.
- A manager who forged a signature on a company report.
- Falsely accusing a supervisor of theft.
- Providing the employer with falsified personal information.
- Résumé fraud or other misrepresentations of qualifications.
- Cheating on a qualifying exam, where the position required the highest moral character.

- Refusal to answer the employer's questions regarding a suspicious incident.
- Interfering with the employer's investigation by threatening other employees.
- Lying to clients.
- Defrauding the employer's insurance company by claiming for a computer that was not stolen during a break-in at the employer's premises.
- Covering up a loss caused by an unauthorized trade and then failing to pass on a letter of complaint from a client.
- Failing to disclose behaviour which created a potential conflict of interest.
- Misrepresenting the position of a third party negotiating a contract with the employer and intentionally perpetuating it to avoid blame for loss of the project.
- Avoiding work on health grounds although treatment was available to allow the employee to work.
- Knowingly filing false tax returns on behalf of the employer's client.
- An internal audit manager for a public institution engaging in personal GST fraud.

D-5.4 FINANCIAL IMPROPRIETIES

General principle — Financial impropriety is merely a type of dishonesty and, again, dismissal will be justified if the misconduct is seriously prejudicial or reveals such an untrustworthy character that continued employment would not be feasible.

Expense account abuse — To be able to dismiss for abuse of a promotional or expense account, the guidelines for use must be clear, and a warning may be required. Even where dismissal is not justified, the employer may be entitled to reimbursement.

Examples — just cause — Just cause was found where:

- An employee opened a separate bank account for the employer without authority, using his home address and telling the bank he was a board member when he was not, and that he would be the sole signing officer when company policy required two. He channelled funds into the account to retire a debt of the employer which he had guaranteed, and was dismissed for cause even though he did not appropriate any funds for himself, as his conduct was deceptive, deceitful and breached his fiduciary duty to his employer.
- A supervisor told employees to charge 15 hours per week in overtime whether they worked it or not, and approved expense accounts

containing large discrepancies. Even though he did not personally gain anything, his deceitful conduct breached his position of trust.
- An employee made changes to payroll records of staff worth $467 to avoid the appearance of overtime, even though he did not benefit personally.
- An employee sold his company shares, despite an order not to do so, at a time that would leave the company open to insider trading charges.
- A credit manager mismanaged his personal finances. Just cause was found because his conduct could potentially have embarrassed the employer and his actions put both his judgment and reliability into question.

Examples — no just cause — No just cause was found where:

- An employee set up her own bank accounts to handle donations and research grants, in breach of the employer's policy, in order to have more flexibility in handling the money. She used all the money for legitimate purposes and accounted for all funds. Her activities had actually benefited the employer in most regards.
- An employee permitted his employer to pay the surcharge to his car insurance premium, which was higher than average due to his bad driving record. The excess payment was not caused by an intentional act of dishonesty.

D-5.5 LIES AND FAILURE TO TELL THE TRUTH

General principle — A person in a position of trust may have a duty to tell the truth, and a lie may be just cause for dismissal. For example, there was just cause for dismissal where an employee lied outright about a personal matter that was a legitimate concern of the employer.

Examples — no just cause — There was no just cause for:

- Non-disclosure of a matter that did not affect the employment contract in any way.
- A brief delay in disclosing an important matter, with no dishonest intent.
- A lie told by a foreman about a matter not justifying dismissal where, in the judge's opinion, it would not affect his ability to properly perform his job.

Intent to mislead — A failure to disclose information may not be blameworthy where there is no intent to mislead, where there is mere carelessness or negligence, or where there is no breach of fiduciary duty. Downplaying a situation may not be just cause, especially where the employer does not ask for specifics.

Motive to lie — The motive for lying seems to be significant. For example, there was no cause for dismissal where a lie was told:

- To save others from embarrassment and not for personal benefit.
- When an employee was taken by surprise in a hostile confrontation.
- As a result of an employee's fear when confronted with an accusation of wrongdoing, given that the employee immediately tried to tell the truth and apologize.

Lying when directly confronted — Depending on the circumstances, lying when directly confronted may or may not be just cause for dismissal. For example:

- Just cause was found in one case even though the behaviour prompting the questions would not have been cause in itself.
- In another case, lying when directly confronted was not held to be just cause, even though the lie was about a matter for which the employer was being sued.

Duty of frank disclosure — In some situations, there may be a positive duty of frank disclosure, and silence in such a situation may constitute a lie. Although one case has said that there is no duty to voluntarily disclose one's own wrongdoing, another has said there is no obligation to correct a new employer's misunderstandings about an employee's income, benefits and bonuses unless the employee made fraudulent statements about them.

D-5.6 PROFESSIONAL QUALIFICATIONS AND RÉSUMÉ DISCLOSURE

Failure to be qualified — A failure to have the required professional qualifications was not cause for dismissal where the employer knew that the employee did not have them when he was hired.

Exaggerating qualifications — The exaggeration of one's qualifications on a résumé can be grounds for dismissal. The employer is entitled to assume that the employee is qualified to do what the résumé states. However, unintentional omissions which have no impact on the job will not likely give just cause for dismissal. There was no misrepresentation when an employee advised an employer that he was qualified as a principal (which was true) but he never said that he had worked as one.

Cheating — Cheating on a qualifying exam was just cause where the job required a person of the highest moral character.

Loss of professional qualifications — In one case, a loss of professional qualifications, which meant that an employee could no longer legally perform the majority of his job functions, was just cause for dismissal. In another case, an employee who intended to leave the industry notified his supervisor that he would not be taking an exam to maintain his Investment Dealers Association registered representative status. His subsequent dismissal was wrongful.

Chapter D-6

CONFLICTS OF INTEREST AND ABUSE OF AUTHORITY

TABLE OF CONTENTS

D-6.1 Conflicts of Interest: General Principles
D-6.2 Fiduciary Duties and Corporate Opportunities
D-6.3 Sales Agents
D-6.4 Competing with the Employer
D-6.5 Moonlighting and Outside Business Interests
D-6.6 Favouring Personal Interests
D-6.7 Dealings with Family Members or Friends
D-6.8 Dealings with Employer's Customers or Suppliers
D-6.9 Dealings with Other Employees or Shareholders
D-6.10 Improper Use, Disclosure or Non-Disclosure of Information
D-6.11 Abuse of Authority

D-6.1 CONFLICTS OF INTEREST: GENERAL PRINCIPLES

Duty of fidelity — An employee owes a duty to his employer to guard the employer's interests and to not acquire any benefit or profit from the employment other than the one agreed to with the employer. An employee must avoid conflicts of interest — that is, putting his own interests ahead of the employer's interests. This includes a duty to be faithful and honest in dealings with the employer, to not use special information obtained in the course of employment for his own purpose or contrary to the employer's interests, and to faithfully devote his time and attentions to the employer's business. Note that in some cases such conduct is regarded as disloyalty, as discussed in Chapter D-7, "Disobedience and Disloyalty".

Duty to disclose conflict — An employee has a duty to promptly disclose a conflict of interest. However, a brief delay in disclosure may not be just cause, particularly if there was no dishonest intent.

Conflict must exist — To be actionable, a real conflict may need to be proven. For example, a senior employee who told another employee that he was setting up a competing business was wrongfully dismissed where there was no evidence that he had ever intended to do so. His intention was to set up a "sting" operation against the other employee, even though he had not told his employer this.

Standard for dismissal — Most judges take the attitude that conflicts of interest justify dismissal regardless of the degree of conflict or competition. However, others have said that it depends on the degree of interference with the employer's interest and the nature of the employment. Bad faith or disloyalty may be required by some judges.

Employee defences — An employee's lapses may not justify dismissal where they are unintentional, minor, due to an error in judgment, or an isolated occurrence in a long and unblemished career. For example, conflicts of interest were excused where:

- An employee had explanations for sums received from a contractor that showed at most poor judgment or slight dishonesty.
- An employee kept a promotional gift, but the employer had no policy regarding such gifts and industry practices varied.
- An employee earned commissions from a distributor for servicing an account that the distributor supplied directly, which, in turn, reduced the amount of commission paid to his employer. The commission was at the discretion of the distributor and was not secret; if the employer had complained, it would have lost the account. The employee was the owner's son-in-law and, but for the breakdown of his marriage, there would have been no complaint. Even if receipt of the commission was secret and improper, it would have been seen as an isolated occurrence in a long and unblemished career.

Condonation — The principle of condonation applies equally to conflicts of interest. For example, an employee could not be dismissed for spending too much time on his own business without a warning. His business involvement was known to the employer when he was hired and he was not expected to work full-time for the employer.

D-6.2 FIDUCIARY DUTIES AND CORPORATE OPPORTUNITIES

General principle — Fiduciary employees have a higher duty to not appropriate opportunities for themselves that the employer would have accepted. Generally, fiduciary employees must have real power or control over the employer's business. The rule tends to be narrowly applied, with the result that no cause was found where:

- An employee brought a business opportunity to his employer, and continued to negotiate on it after the employer said they would share

the profits, even though he failed to keep the employer informed about the negotiations.
- Employees pursued an opportunity for their own benefit after their employer rejected it.
- An employee referred an opportunity to a company for which he was a director, after rejecting it as being unsuitable for his employer.
- A long-term employee appropriated a business opportunity for himself on the eve of his departure from his present employment.

D-6.3 SALES AGENTS

General principle — An agent has a duty not to acquire any benefit or profit from the agency other than the one agreed to with the principal. For example, an agent who bought the principal's goods on his own account and resold them at a profit was justly terminated.

Competing lines — The addition of a competing line may be a conflict of interest amounting to just cause. An isolated breach of a rule may not justify termination, however, when it is done in the employer's best interests in order to keep a client happy. Where an agent represented lines that were non-competing at the time, and the employer later added lines that put the agent into a conflict situation, the employer could not force the agent to give up his other lines. In this case, the employer had forced the agent into conflict.

Non-competing lines — Involvement with a non-competing line may be a conflict of interest where the employer has a known policy that its salesmen will not represent other products.

Right of refusal — A sales agent who granted her principal a right of first refusal on non-competing products was not dismissed for cause for failing to honour the agreement in three cases. The orders were minor and there was no evidence that the principal would have taken over the orders if it had been informed of them, so there was no proof of prejudice.

Secret or unauthorized discounts — Giving secret or unauthorized discounts to customers may be grounds for dismissal. However, there were no grounds for termination where the practice of giving discounts was well known to others within the employer's organization and was within the employee's authority.

D-6.4 COMPETING WITH THE EMPLOYER

Direct competition — Competing with an employer is a conflict of interest justifying dismissal in most cases.

Planning to compete — just cause — There is a special conflict where an employee planning to start his own business makes plans during work hours, tries to hire away the employer's staff, threatens to harm the employer's business, or approaches the employer's clients.

Planning to compete — no just cause — While some judges say an employer can dismiss an employee upon learning of his plans to open a competing business, others say the employee must be beyond the thinking stage and into active planning before just cause will be found. For example, just cause was not found where:

- An employee expressed some dissatisfaction with his employment to a competitor who had approached him with a job offer.
- An employee merely inquired into other opportunities, without further involvement.
- There were unsubstantiated rumours that the employee planned to join a competitor, which the employee specifically denied.

Duty of departing employees — There is no implied duty not to compete with an employer after termination. However, the departing employee must not take or use confidential information in doing so. There may also be a duty to be honest about one's plans.

Duty of independent contractor — In one case, an independent contractor was not found at fault for submitting a tender in competition with the organization to which she was providing services, because her arrangement with the employer was not exclusive.

D-6.5 MOONLIGHTING AND OUTSIDE BUSINESS INTERESTS

Moonlighting — Moonlighting (performing the same work as is done for the employer, but doing it outside the employee's normal working hours) may be just cause where it competes with the employer. This may be the case where the employee:

- Does work for a customer of the employer.
- Undercuts the employer's price.
- Uses goods or equipment obtained through the employer.

Acceptable moonlighting — Moonlighting has been found acceptable where the work was:

- Minor.
- Done for people with whom the employee had pre-existing relationships.
- Done for people who were not customers of the employer.

- Done for people who made it clear that they would not give the business to the employer in any event.

Outside business interests — senior managers — A senior manager may have a duty to use all his energy and ability for the benefit of the employer. Developing a business opportunity outside of the employer's business may constitute just cause for dismissal, even where there is no competition and the employer has not suffered an actual loss.

Outside business interests — non-managers — For non-managers, running a business or working for one which is not directly competitive with the employer's is not a conflict of interest, as long as it does not interfere with the employment. This is especially so if:

- The extra dealings would enhance the employer's business.
- It was not anticipated that the employee would devote his full time and attention to the employer's business.
- It was a reasonable way for the employee to protect himself in the face of a downturn in the employer's business.

Incompatibility — A conflict of interest justifying dismissal can exist where, although not competitive, the employee's involvement in outside activities is incompatible with his employment or leaves him unable to meet his duties to the employer. However, no just cause was found where an employee accepted an appointment to a commission whose principles were opposed by the employer, as the employer's embarrassment would not conflict with the employee's functions. Involvement with a non-profit group was held not to be a conflict of interest in several cases, even where the employee did similar work for the group and for the employer, or obtained goods for the group through the employer.

D-6.6 FAVOURING PERSONAL INTERESTS

General principle — Putting one's personal interests, especially financial interests, ahead of the employer's interests can give just cause in some cases, especially if the employer's interests are prejudiced. For example, dismissal was for cause where:

- An employee sold shares in the employer just before negative financial results were to be made public, and thereby left the employer open to insider trading charges.
- An employee threatened to walk out on urgent duties unless he was immediately paid an outstanding expense claim.
- An executive whose job required him to be a role model made personal use of company credit cards.

- An employee mismanaged his personal financial affairs and put his employer into a potentially embarrassing position.
- An executive participated in insurance fraud following a break-in at the employer's premises, which could have harmed the company's reputation and resulted in loss of insurance coverage.
- The manager of internal audit for a public institution organized a scheme to avoid paying GST on the purchase of a new car.
- A plant manager rented out the employer's warehouse space to his own company, with payments made by a third party.
- An employee secretly paid a rent subsidy from the employer's funds to a company in which he had an interest.
- A prison superintendent used a trust fund of which he was trustee for his own purposes, to acquire goods he was not entitled to acquire at a price below normal retail price.
- A manager bought large quantities of merchandise on behalf of the employer from a company in which he had an interest, without disclosing his interest.
- An executive of an employer that was going out of business, sold the employer's product and paid only the original cost back to the employer, while misdescribing the sales under a sales reporting system.

Examples — no just cause — There was no just cause where:

- An employee's own company was a customer of the employer, but she did not buy goods at a discount and the two companies did not compete for the same customers.
- An employee rented personally owned equipment to the employer. Even though the transaction was a bad deal for the company, there was no intentional imprudence or impropriety and the arrangement was not unreasonable at the time.

Right to negotiate employment terms — There was no cause for dismisssal where a manager negotiated a contract for himself with many generous terms. He had not breached his fiduciary duty to the company, as the contract had been openly negotiated with the company's principal officers and shareholders. Similarly, there was no just cause where an employee executed two employment contracts with the same employer, one standard and one a fealty contract with the employer's president. The second contract was signed at the president's urging and there was no evidence that the employee knew that it was improper.

Personal use of employer's tools — There was no just cause where an employee made minimal use of the employer's premises, supplies and staff for his own purposes, where he put in a great deal of extra time and his outside business involvement was known to the employer when he was hired.

D-6.7 DEALINGS WITH FAMILY MEMBERS OR FRIENDS

General principle — Conflicts between an employee's duties and the employee's relatives' or friends' activities may justify dismissal in some cases. Hiring a relative may also be a conflict of interest. For example, there was cause for dismissal where:

- A sales manager had crucial inside information on pricing, products and clients, and her husband started a competing business. The potential for conflict made her continued employment impossible.
- An employee provided large quantities of goods to a friend at wholesale prices, even though the employee received no personal benefit.
- A manager purchased goods for the employer from one relative, and sold the employer's goods to other relatives at wholesale prices and with unauthorized credit.
- An employee contracted with a family member, in breach of the employer's policy, even though the amount involved was only $500.
- A manager was told to help out a fledgling supplier, but his help went way beyond the point of reasonableness and included providing rent-free equipment, office space, and consulting services, for which he was paid.

Examples — no cause — There was no conflict giving rise to just cause where:

- An employee arranged a change to a contract that strengthened a third party's position, which might not have been in the best interest of the controlling shareholder. The employee had acted in good faith and for legitimate business reasons.
- An employee gave a contract to a person with whom he had had past personal dealings.
- A sales agent continued to associate with a former colleague who had joined another agency. She had not been disloyal, even when she had accepted some help from him with her sales activities.
- Employees met with friends or former co-workers who worked for a competitor.
- An employee took a business trip with a former co-worker who had recently been fired.
- An employee told a former employee about a drop in sales. It was a single incident of indiscretion that could not be used to the employer's detriment.
- An employee was a friend of one brother who sold his business to another brother as a result of a dispute. The purchasing brother's

concerns about the employee's loyalty were not grounds for dismissal, given that no visible animosity was shown.
- An employee's spouse had been dismissed for cause by the same employer.
- A father helped his sons to acquire and develop a business that benefited the employer's business.
- An employee awarded a subcontract to a company he owned with his son. In another case, though, a father's involvement in a son's competing business was unacceptable.
- A husband directed work to his wife's repair shop, where the employer had authorized the practice and there was a proper accounting.
- An employee provided inside information to his friend, an ex-employee who remained friendly with a number of employees. There was no proof that he had done anything more than accommodate a competitor to the normal degree.
- An employee discouraged other contractors from tendering for his employer's business so that the current contractor, a friend, could get the renewals. He did not benefit personally and no dishonesty or fraudulent intent was proven.

D-6.8 DEALINGS WITH EMPLOYER'S CUSTOMERS OR SUPPLIERS

General principle — Personal dealings with the employer's customers or suppliers can be a conflict of interest if the dealings would prejudice the employer's interests — in other words, if they would or might harm the employer's interests, profits, business, reputation or relationships. In some cases, this can apply to business dealings as well as personal relationships. Activities that were in conflict with an employee's duties and gave the employer just cause for dismissal have included:

- Accepting loans or gifts from the employer's clients.
- Engaging in business activities or financial dealings with or in competetion with the employer's customers.
- Accepting gifts or personal benefits from a company with whom the employer did business, thereby risking putting the employer into the company's debt.
- Giving a bad cheque to a customer.
- Filing false damage claims with suppliers.
- Bidding against the employer's customers for jobs, in breach of an express agreement.

Examples — no just cause — There was no just cause for dismissal where:

- An employee personally used a contractor who dealt with the employer. The employee paid for the services out of his own funds at the normal rates.
- An employee asked for tickets from an organization that had contacted the employer for free promotional products but then he refused to provide the free products when he did not get the tickets. This was found to be evidence of poor judgment but not just cause for dismissal.
- A sports editor for a local paper sought a part-time public relations job with a local hockey team that then became an advertising customer of the employer.
- An employee merely advised customers that she had received notice of termination.
- An employee sent Christmas cards to customers with whom she had a personal relationship, advising that her job had been eliminated without warning.
- An employee provided a supplier with a report which changed company policy regarding suppliers. It was not the employee's fault that the supplier raised a fuss.
- An employee bought discounted goods through a supplier. While it showed poor judgment, it was not just cause for dismissal because the employee had paid for everything obtained.

D-6.9 DEALINGS WITH OTHER EMPLOYEES OR SHAREHOLDERS

General duty — An employee cannot put his personal interests ahead of his employer's interests when dealing with other employees or with the employer's shareholders.

Manager's duty — A manager who prefers his own position to that of management's, or who takes the side of other employees against management in a dispute, is in a conflict of interest which may justify dismissal. See also Chapter D-7, "Disobedience and Disloyalty".

Examples — cause — An employer had cause for dismissal where:

- A manager attempted to protect himself by firing a subordinate with whom he was having an affair. He thereby placed the company in a position of having to defend a wrongful dismissal action.
- An employee misrepresented a situation to another employee merely to get revenge.
- An employee misrepresented his contacts in order to strike a deal with the other shareholders of the business.
- An employee criticized the employer to co-workers and customers. See also Chapter D-7, "Disobedience and Disloyalty".

Examples — no cause — The employer did not have cause for dismissal where:

- An employee championed a rival group that ultimately did not succeed in a takeover.
- An employee filed a lawsuit alleging constructive dismissal while continuing to work for the employer. Note, however, that in another case this was said to be inconsistent with the employment relationship. See Chapter B-5, "Repudiation by Employee".
- A manager rearranged employees' schedules so that they could babysit his sick child, and allowed an employee who called in sick to babysit for him and then submitted a sick pay claim for her. He had used poor judgment but did not deserve dismissal.

D-6.10 IMPROPER USE, DISCLOSURE OR NON-DISCLOSURE OF INFORMATION

Personnel and other employer records — Employees, who openly remove or copy information from their personnel files because they disagree with it or wish to protect themselves in the event of dismissal, have been found to have exercised poor judgment but not to have given just cause. The same is true for employees who have removed or copied confidential business documents to assist them in planned lawsuits or to protect themselves from possible lawsuits. Even where an employee paid another employee $50 to search their supervisor's desk on the sly, she was not dismissed for just cause because she did so after already being given notice of dismissal for other reasons.

Customer records — An employee dentist was entitled to remove his own patients' records. There was no restrictive covenant in the parties' agreement because he was not a fiduciary.

Failure to safeguard — Cases differ on whether failure to safeguard business information, particularly confidential information, may properly result in dismissal. Some say it may, but others say this does not constitute just cause, particularly where the breach is minor.

Threat to disclose, or disclosure of false or confidential information — A threat to disclose, or proven actual disclosure of, confidential or embarrassing information may be just cause. Spreading false information may also be just cause. For complaints to superiors, authorities, the public, the press or co-workers, see Chapter D-7, "Disobedience and Disloyalty".

Examples — disclosure — no cause — There was no cause despite the disclosure of employer information where:

- An employee provided information only once to a friend who was also a competitor of the employer. It was not repeated after a warning and there was an industry custom to share such information.
- A controller met once with a former employee socially and disclosed sales information that could not be used to the employer's detriment. The employee was found to have been indiscreet rather than disloyal or dishonest.
- An employee, whose job required that he co-ordinate with law enforcement agencies, gave the RCMP a briefing note that outlined two irregularities.
- An employee sought employment advice from a lawyer who was also the principal of one of the employer's competitors. There had been no breach of confidentiality.

Failure to disclose — An employer may have just cause for dismissal if an employee fails to disclose information that he or she had a duty to disclose. Such situations may destroy the essential trust necessary in the employment relationship. For example, a solicitor who failed to disclose information which he knew might affect the employer's willingness to hire him and his ability to perform the job had breached his duty of utmost good faith.

Examples — failure to disclose — no cause — There was no cause for failure to disclose:

- Information in which the employee thought the employer was not interested.
- A licensor's dissatisfaction with the employee.
- That the employee had conveyed his personal position to the Crown in a case in which the employer had an interest but was not a party.
- Knowledge of his superiors' misconduct to the company, although he had reported it to the superiors themselves.

D-6.11 ABUSE OF AUTHORITY

General principles — Employees, who believe that they are acting within the scope of their authority, may not be dismissed for just cause for exceeding that authority, at least not without a warning. Furthermore, employees may not be dismissed for exceeding their authority where the scope of that authority has never been set out for them.

Examples — just cause — There was just cause for dismissal for abuse of authority where:

- An employee used his employer's credit for personal purchases, even though the employee did not cause the employer any loss. However, where there was an established practice of using a company credit card

for personal expenses and reimbursing the employer, and where there was no dishonest intent, there was no just cause.
- An employee bought goods from stock as well as from suppliers and wholesalers. He kept his own records of the transactions, in breach of the company's procedure manual.
- An employee purported, without authority, to appoint a master distributor for the employer's products in an attempt to manipulate events for her own benefit, and announced this to the trade without telling her employer.

Examples — no just cause — There was no cause for dismissal where:

- A store manager did his personal shopping on Sundays while the store was closed, in breach of a store rule which he strictly enforced among other employees. His behaviour showed poor judgment, but he had paid for the goods and there was no dishonesty.
- An employee bought a display item from his employer at a discount without properly clearing the purchase with his supervisor in accordance with company policy.
- An employee granted an irate customer a $14 discount without authority.

Chapter D-7

DISOBEDIENCE AND DISLOYALTY

TABLE OF CONTENTS

D-7.1   Disobedience Generally
D-7.2   Neglect of or Refusal to Perform Duties
D-7.3   Breach of Rules
D-7.4   Insolence and Insubordination
         D-7.4.1 General Principles
         D-7.4.2 Examples
D-7.5   Disloyalty

D-7.1 DISOBEDIENCE GENERALLY

Different names, similar issues — Employment law deals with rebellious behaviour on the job and the refusal to accept the employer's authority under many names: disobedience, insolence, insubordination, abuse of authority, neglect of or refusal to perform duties and breach of rules. They are dealt with together here because all involve words, actions or inactions by subordinates that are considered improper by superiors. Often the same words or actions that are labelled in one way could easily be viewed as another, similar type of misconduct.

Single act — Usually, a single act of disobedience will not be enough to justify dismissal without a warning. To justify dismissal, a single act of disobedience must be wilful or deliberate, and not merely the result of an error in judgment. In addition, the act must be so serious as to show that the worker is repudiating one of the essential conditions of the contract, or it must be incompatible with the faithful discharge of his duties.

Passive rebellion — Usually, the employee must actively disobey an important order for just cause to exist. For example, there was no just cause for disobedience where:

- An employee was not enthusiastically co-operative but did not actually disobey any clear, specific orders or well-known policies or procedures.
- An employee disliked and avoided a certain task, but performed the task at a minimal level and had never been warned to increase the amount of time spent on the task.

Passive rebellion, where an employee does not directly refuse to obey orders but simply ignores them, could justify dismissal where it is ongoing and serious, or where it continues after warnings.

Requests must be reasonable — The employer's requests must be reasonable, and an employee will be entitled to refuse unreasonable requests unless:

- The employee has expressly agreed to be bound by a rule.
- The requests involve the manner of performing the job, which is within the employer's right to decide.
- The requirement is rationally related to efficient performance of the job.

Refusal must avoid insolence — Even where an employee refuses an unreasonable request, he must take care that his behaviour does not amount to insolence.

Clear, lawful instructions — Instructions must be clear and unambiguous before the failure to follow them can be held against an employee. An employee may refuse to participate in an unlawful or fraudulent scheme, or one in breach of his contract.

Contractual change — A refusal to accept a unilateral change of contractual terms, such as a change of position or job functions, change in geographical location, change in pay or reduction in hours, will not be just cause for dismissal if it amounts to a fundamental breach of the employment contract. See Part C, "Constructive Dismissal".

Repeated or combined disobedience — Less serious instances of disobedience can justify dismissal where they are frequent or combined with other misconduct, if the cumulative effect is serious. Dismissal without a warning may be justified if the cumulative behaviour prejudices the proper conduct of the business. If the overall effect is not serious, the employee must be warned and the misconduct repeated before dismissal will be justified.

Excuses for disobedience — Generally, dismissal will not be justified if:

- The direction, order or expectation being disobeyed is not clear and lawful.
- An employee honestly believes that he is acting within permissible limits or within the scope of his authority. This is especially the case if the employer has never spelled out the limits of his authority or if the employee has been given an undefined discretion.
- The employee has a reasonable excuse for disobedience, even a personal reason.

- An employer never meets with the employee to discuss expectations, there is no adequate job description or performance evaluations, or the employee is given no chance to adapt to the expectations.

Examples — no just cause — Dismissal for disobedience was not justified in these cases:

- A manager failed to accept a phone call from the president while the manager was embroiled in a crisis, where the refusal was a simple error in judgment and not insubordination.
- A journalist refused to disclose her sources even though the employer faced a libel action.
- A manager visited his office during his suspension pending investigation of alleged misconduct. The visit was not serious enough to amount to just cause.
- An employee refused to follow safety procedures once. A single instance was not serious enough to justify dismissal without a warning.

Examples — cause — The following were held to be serious acts of disobedience that justified dismissal:

- Refusal to attend an important meeting.
- Failing to attend work for a special event where staff attendance was mandatory.
- Refusal to change job assignments, followed by an ultimatum from the employee for a change in work conditions.
- Refusal to work assigned shift work, where shift work was within the contract's terms.
- An unauthorized absence from work; see Chapter D-9, "Attendance and Substance Abuse".
- Refusal to re-hire an employee dismissed contrary to instructions, or to demote someone with whom the employee was having an affair.
- Refusal of a minister to preach only accepted church doctrine.
- Hiring a person without the employer's approval, in breach of a direct order.
- Refusal to follow inventory control procedures designed to minimize theft, and other refusals to follow reasonable directions as to job duties or the manner of performance.
- Refusal or failure to follow important safety procedures.
- Failure to follow instructions with regard to credit or overdraft approvals.
- A deliberate attempt to obtain a salary increase after being told none would be given (although this may not always be just cause).
- Sale of shares in breach of an order, at a time when insider trading charges were possible.
- Failure to meet with the board of directors to deal with its concerns, despite being given three opportunities to do so.

D-7.2 NEGLECT OF DUTY OR REFUSAL TO PERFORM DUTIES

General principles — An employer is entitled to set job duties, procedures and rules as it sees fit, as long as they are legal and safe. It is not an employee's place to consider their wisdom or to ignore a procedure, unless the employer's actions have shown that the rule was unimportant. A failure to follow directives or carry out important duties can be just cause even without a warning, where the combination of actions and inactions is inconsistent with proper discharge of the employee's duties. See also Chapter D-11, "Attendance and Substance Abuse", for cases where an employee totally refuses to attend work.

Need for warning — In less severe cases, or where there is some justification for the neglect or refusal, a warning may be required.

Reluctant performance — An employee who develops a pattern of not working effectively or performing reluctantly can give just cause for dismissal if the net result amounts to conduct incompatible with the job and prejudicial to the employer's business.

Examples — just cause — Claims for wrongful dismissal were unsuccessful where:

- A worker, anticipating his dismissal, abandoned his position.
- A worker left his job claiming constructive dismissal without justification.
- A worker walked off the job after an angry dispute. His failure to return to work or inquire about his status was taken as a resignation.
- A worker walked off the job rather than perform an unpleasant duty.
- An employee refused to perform an important duty unless an outstanding expense account was immediately paid.
- An employee left for vacation despite having been refused permission.
- Employees committed themselves to something which made it impossible for them to fulfill their time commitments to the employer.
- An employee failed to perform duties with important health and safety implications.
- An employee unreasonably and persistently refused to perform specific job duties, even after warnings.
- An employee completely refused to co-operate.

Examples — no just cause — Claims for wrongful dismissal succeeded where:

- The employee left work but pursued a reconciliation.
- An employee was unable to return to work for health reasons.

- A neglect of duties, even after warnings, was caused by acute stress-related illness due to the job's pressures.
- An employee refused an assignment due to a physical inability to do the job.
- A long-term employee refused to report to work for one day after a two-day suspension.
- An employee with 13 years of excellent service was dismissed for repeated failures to complete his assignments, but the failures were due to carelessness rather than attitude.
- An employee failed to keep a stamp under lock and key, but the employer had never given a direction to do so.
- An employee delegated an important duty to a subordinate who performed it improperly.
- There was a reasonable business explanation for refusing to perform a certain task.

D-7.3 BREACH OF RULES

General principles — While an employer is entitled to set rules, a breach of a rule or a failure to perform the job exactly as specified is often not serious enough to amount to just cause. A rule infringing the *Canadian Charter of Rights and Freedoms* will not be enforceable.

Contractual force — Some employers attempt to make their rules more enforceable by making them part of a contract or other document with contractual force. This may strengthen the ability to dismiss for breach of a rule. However, any procedure required by the contract for handling breaches must be complied with. For example, a rule requiring a written warning will not permit dismissal unless a warning has been given.

Just cause — A failure to comply with rules may be just cause if:

(1) the employer's business is prejudiced by the refusal;
(2) constant supervision would be required to ensure compliance; or
(3) the refusal is incompatible with the faithful discharge of the employee's duties.

Intention — Intention or wilfulness seems to be required. Dismissal was not justified in one case where a long-term employee had no intention of harming the employer and acted in what he thought was the employer's best interests, without profiting from his actions.

Communication of rule — An employee must be aware of the rule and its application to him. The rule need not have been formalized if failure to comply is inconsistent with faithful discharge of duty, and the rule represents the reasonable standard of conduct expected of someone highly experienced in the field.

Rule must be specific — To warrant dismissal, a rule must be specific and clear. A general policy that allows for individual discretion, or one that provides a guideline but not a firm rule, may not be enforceable. Similarly, a warning that is not consistent with a rule may require an explanation as to how the warning fits with the employer's policy.

Reasonableness — An employer may have to show that a rule is reasonable, and that employees have been warned of its seriousness and the consequences of breach. Where a rule allows for discretion, it must not be exercised capriciously.

Inconsistent application — The breach of a rule that has been inconsistently applied may not justify dismissal without a warning. A dismissal will not be justified where an employee reasonably believed that the employer was aware of his activity and tolerated it. See also Chapter D-3, "Condonation of Misconduct".

Non-enforcement by supervisor — A supervisor, who not only fails to enforce the employer's rules among his subordinates but breaches them himself, may be dismissable for conduct incompatible with his duties. However, in one case, a manager who breached a rule that he strictly enforced among other employees had shown poor judgment, but he could not be dismissed for just cause.

Examples — just cause — A failure to comply with these reasonable company rules has justified dismissal:

- Attendance rules such as medical leave, lateness, and time card procedures (although this was not cause in another case).
- Financial rules, such as loan and credit authorization, cash handling procedures, expense account rules, investments with customers and financial dealings with clients.
- Anti-theft measures such as store security, sale of damaged product, and removal of company property.
- Safety issues, including drinking on the job.
- Order processing, which led to an unauthorized commission.
- Grant application and processing procedures.
- A prohibition against insurance appraiser staff purchasing salvage vehicles.
- Employment of a spouse.
- Failure to disclose a client complaint, contrary to the employer's and professional association's code of conduct.
- Sexual harassment.

D-7.4 INSOLENCE AND INSUBORDINATION

D-7.4.1 General Principles

Insolence vs. insubordination — Insolence (the use of insulting, abusive, threatening or unreasonably violent words) and insubordination (rebellion or refusal to follow a proper direction) are similar in that they both challenge the employer's authority. They can occur separately or together. There can be no insolence or insubordination where the employee is not aware that the person to whom he speaks is a person of authority.

Standard for just cause — Insolence or insubordination will justify dismissal where the remarks made or language used are incompatible with continuing the employment relationship. They may also justify dismissal if the insolence or insubordination amounts to a refusal to submit to authority or to do the job requested. A refusal to acknowledge the inappropriateness of the behaviour or to give an assurance that it will not be repeated may also justify dismissal.

Private disagreements — Disagreements, criticisms and debates carried on in private have not been cause for dismissal where the employee made it clear he would accept whatever decision was made, where the resistance was temporary and was never carried into effect, or where the complaints were valid.

Public complaint — Making a complaint public, refusing a direction or uttering insolent words in front of others, may make the conduct more damaging to a continuing employment relationship. It has been said that an employee is entitled to complain about management to his co-workers, but this can give just cause for dismissal if the complaints are serious or numerous enough to harm the company's well-being or prejudice the employer's interests.

Breaking chain of command — A number of cases have held that an employee is not entitled to go over the heads of his supervisors, or go to the government, public or press, to promote his own views. A reasonable justification may remove the right to dismiss for just cause, for example, where an employee fearing dismissal seeks reassurance as to his job security, or where his boss shows a lack of good faith.

Single incident — Even a single or isolated incident can justify dismissal if the conduct:
(1) is so serious as to destroy harmonious relations between the parties;
(2) is incompatible with the employee's duties and prejudicial to the employer's business; or
(3) seriously undermines management's authority.

Otherwise, one or more warnings will be necessary.

Condonation — Accepting an employee's apology may bar the employer from relying on the event. These types of incidents must be acted upon quickly; otherwise, condonation may be implied. See Chapter D-3, "Condonation of Misconduct".

Character of words — Where there is reasonable justification for the employee's words or actions, they may not amount to just cause for dismissal. Similarly, if they can be characterized in an innocent way, such as poor judgment, insensitivity, resentment or persistence rather than stubbornness and disobedience, just cause may not exist.

Context is important — The context in which the words are uttered is important. Words said in anger or in the course of a momentary flare-up are sometimes excused by judges. Just cause may not arise if the words were spoken at a time when the employer knew the employee was suffering from emotional illness. A court may consider the relationship between the people involved. The manner of refusing a request or responding to a demand can justify dismissal if it would destroy the parties' working relationship.

Profanity or vulgar language — Language that is particularly offensive or damaging to the working relationship may constitute just cause. Use of profanity or foul language in itself will not justify dismissal if it is commonly tolerated in the workplace or where the employee is simply expressing himself in his everyday vocabulary.

Provocation — There will be no just cause where an employee's insolence has been provoked or aggravated by the employer or caused by conduct amounting to constructive dismissal.

Contractual disputes — An employee involved in a contractual dispute is entitled to verbally present his viewpoint or question management about what is happening to his job. An employee may even be entitled to start a lawsuit over a contractual dispute without giving just cause for dismissal, although other cases have disagreed; see Chapter B-5, "Repudiation by Employee". An employee is entitled to enforce his or her statutory rights. In one case, an employee was wrongfully dismissed where he was chosen for layoff because he had threatened to file a legitimate statutory health and safety complaint.

Dispute outside of employment — A dispute on a matter outside the scope of employment will not give just cause for dismissal. Nor will insolence that occurs after the employer's breach of contract.

D-7.4.2 Examples

Insubordination — just cause — Dismissal was justified where:

- Employees perpetuated a dispute about their reporting structure.
- An employee continually argued and criticized his supervisors.
- A manager challenged management plans and took the side of local employees, in front of many lower-ranked employees.
- An employee harangued his manager for half an hour in front of other employees by swearing, insulting him and the company, and using aggressive and abusive language.
- An employee did not speak out as invited to do at the annual sales meeting, but sent an e-mail to all staff across the country containing hyperbole and inaccuracies about what the president had said at the meeting.
- An employee removed a memo from a bulletin board. In one case, this was an insolent act contributing to just cause for dismissal; but in another case, the totality of the conduct was not enough to amount to just cause.
- An employee criticized the employer to customers, although no cause was found in another case.
- An employee made derogatory comments about the employer to the public and his co-workers.

Insubordination after warning — just cause — Dismissal for insubordination after a warning was justified where:

- An employee pursued a complaint to the board of directors for the second time, after being warned not to do so.
- An employee continued to criticize the employer's handling of a matter, both publicly and with other staff members, after being told to drop it.

Insubordination — no just cause — There was no cause where:

- An employee delivered a letter to an employer at home.
- Two employees had an on-going pay dispute and had threatened not to be available for emergency overtime, but had never carried out the threat.
- An employee refused to drop a complaint where the concerns were justified, or where the employee reasonably believed they were justified.
- An employee took the position that the employer's son was not appropriate for a senior role. The employee was acting in the best interests of the employer.
- An employee refused to sign a release.

Public complaint — no just cause — There was no just cause without a warning where:

- Employees refused to speak to a supervisor at a public meeting, or walked out of a meeting in protest, or spoke out about the impossibility of attaining unrealistic goals, or were amused and critical about new policies.
- A manager allowed employees to air their criticisms of the board of directors at a staff meeting.
- An employee discussed concerns and criticisms at a meeting called for that purpose.
- In a conflict situation, an employee appealed his instructions from the executive committee to the full board of directors.
- An employee got into an argument with her supervisor in front of customers.
- An employee encouraged unhappy customers to complain to management.
- A private school teacher sent a letter to all parents complaining of her treatment.
- A public petition was circulated on an employee's behalf, without her participation.
- An editor publicly sought to justify his performance after he was given notice of dismissal.
- An employee criticized the employer by writing letters seeking alternative employment which contained unfavourable comments.

Insolence — just cause — The following examples of insolence have justified dismissal:

- Hanging up the telephone on a supervisor.
- Ignoring a superior and turning one's back to a superior when spoken to.
- Refusing to speak to the general manager.
- Imputing the supervisor is dishonest, incompetent, or mentally ill.
- Telling the employer that he was thinking of telling them to take their job and stuff it. This insolence, along with other disobedience and attitude problems, justified dismissal.

Insolence — no just cause — There was no just cause for dismissal where:

- An employee misspelled the boss's name Ash as "Ass". It was not sufficiently insolent, even if intentional.
- An employee issued a death threat but quickly retracted it, and it was not considered a real threat in any event.
- An employee challenged a supervisor he did not respect. He acted out of genuine concern for his own and the employer's reputation.
- A long-term executive vice-president refused to accept a new president's authority by addressing the previous president as "President".

D-7.5 DISLOYALTY

General principle — Disloyalty (breach of the duty of faith or fidelity) can be cause for dismissal, if it would prevent the employee from fulfilling his obligations. See also Chapter D-6, "Conflicts of Interest and Abuse of Authority".

Competing duties — Testifying against the company in an action by a client was not just cause where the employee's first duty, as an insurance agent, was to the client.

Airing complaints not disloyalty — While disloyalty by an employee or encouraging disloyalty in other employees could be cause for dismissal, the fact that a manager permitted the airing of complaints at a staff meeting did not justify dismissal. See also the discussion of public complaints earlier in this chapter.

Suing employer while employed — The effect of filing a constructive dismissal lawsuit while continuing to work for the company is a matter of dispute; see Chapter B-5, "Repudiation by Employee".

Examples — no just cause — There was no just cause where:

- An employee was a friend of one brother who sold his business to another brother as a result of a dispute. The purchasing brother's concerns about the employee's loyalty were not grounds for dismissal, given that no visible animosity was shown.
- An employee met with a company that was interested in a friendly takeover of the employer.
- An employee promoted one acquisition group over the group that eventually succeeded in taking over the employer.
- An employee provided a supplier with a copy of a report which changed company policy regarding the use of suppliers.
- An employee accepted an appointment to a commission whose principles were opposed by the employer.

Chapter D-8

WORKPLACE CONFLICTS AND HARASSMENT

TABLE OF CONTENTS

D-8.1   Personality and Workplace Conflicts: General Principles
D-8.2   Workplace Conflicts: Managerial Standards
D-8.3   Sexual and Other Harassment
D-8.4   Age and Other Discrimination
D-8.5   Personal Appearance and Habits
D-8.6   Customer Relations

D-8.1 PERSONALITY AND WORKPLACE CONFLICTS: GENERAL PRINCIPLES

Behaviour justifying dismissal — Dismissal is not justified for a minor personality conflict with one's superior or staff, personal incompatibility, disagreement over policies, or a bad attitude. However, dismissal may be justified when a personality conflict or attitudinal problem prejudices the employer's business — that is, it causes harm or a serious risk of harm — or where it is inconsistent with the proper discharge of the employee's duties. This can happen, for example, where the conflict:

(1) escalates to the level of total inability to get along with superiors, co-workers or subordinates;
(2) puts the employee into constant conflict in the workplace;
(3) substantially interferes with production;
(4) causes large staff losses (although not all cases agree on this point); or
(5) makes essential co-operation impossible.

As was stated in one case:

> Clearly, an employer is entitled to dismiss an employee who has been warned from time to time that he has an incompatible personality conflict but refuses or is unable to improve or correct his relationships and similar incidents occur later. (*Fonceca v. McDonnell Douglas Canada Ltd.* (1983), 1 C.C.E.L. 51 at 57 (Ont. H.C.).)

Disagreement — Disagreement with policies, a critical attitude and even half-hearted compliance have not been just cause as long as there was no outright disobedience or opposition in a contentious manner, as discussed in Chapter D-7, "Disobedience and Disloyalty".

Fault — Judges seem inclined to look at the equities of these kinds of situations, including who bears the true responsibility for the conflict. For example, an employee's negative attitude was not cause for dismissal when it was partly justified by the employer's treatment of him, and where it was not incompatible with his duties or prejudicial to the company's business. An inability to get along with co-workers or superiors will not be grounds for dismissal where the fault for poor relationships lies at least partly with the other workers, or with a lack of guidance and support by the employer.

Contract — A contractual clause allowing termination for incompatibility cannot be used capriciously, although a term providing for recall in the event of client dissatisfaction was enforceable when the client cited a personality conflict.

Employer size — In a small business, good employee relations may be so crucial that an inability to get along may justify dismissal. For example:

- A doctor's abrasive personality was just cause where he was working in a small professional office, which required trust, mutual respect and compatibility.
- A manager refused to speak to one of two other employees, had assaulted the other employee in front of a customer, and told the employer "either he goes or I go".
- A plant manager was both argumentative and unco-operative and had complained about the new general manager to other employees at the small workplace. Given his long service, however, a warning was required.

Examples — just cause — Just cause for dismissal was found where:

- An employee, with a record of fighting, instigated a fight with a fellow employee.
- An employee posted an e-mail describing a co-worker in a vulgar and derogatory fashion.
- An employee threatened co-workers who were investigating allegations of misconduct.
- An employee falsely accused his supervisor of theft.
- An employee threatened to ruin a superior's reputation if he did not get promoted.
- A probationary employee was totally unco-operative, even though it was later discovered his behaviour was due to a serious mental illness.
- A probationary employee was unable to get along with her co-workers, and she had been told upon hiring that working as a team was expected.

- An employee displayed a bad attitude toward the public and co-workers, after warnings.
- An employee was rude to management and made derogatory comments about management to his co-workers and the public.
- An employee was warned but did not change his hostile attitude toward his co-workers in general and his supervisor in particular.
- Two employees engaged in constant complaints and arguments.
- An employee was disruptive and domineering at meetings, would not let go of complaints, refused to work with other employees and frequently called her supervisor at home; however, she was said to have been entitled to a clear warning.
- An employee harangued his manager for half an hour in front of other employees by swearing, insulting him and the company and using aggressive and abusive language.

Examples — no just cause — There was no just cause for dismissal where:

- An employee shouted at someone in a noisy work environment where it was no more than the pitch required by the circumstances.
- Employees interfered in internal power struggles or got caught in political disputes and were made scapegoats.
- The employee threatened to file a legitimate health and safety complaint.
- An employee issued a death threat, but it was not considered serious and the employee was under a lot of strain caused in part by the employer's antipathy to him.
- An employee was difficult and disrespectful to his superior, but he was being asked to engage in unethical conduct and his opposition was due to genuine concerns.

D-8.2 WORKPLACE CONFLICTS: MANAGERIAL STANDARDS

General principle — Good employee relations are an implied part of most managerial jobs. Failure to maintain good relationships with and between staff may justify dismissal in some cases. Unfair favouritism is a particular problem that can harm employee relations and entitle the employer to dismiss the manager.

Requirement to warn — Where employee relation problems are not severe, are not wholly a manager's fault, or have been overlooked for some time, a warning will be necessary before the manager can be dismissed for just cause.

Examples — just cause — Dismissal was justified where:

- Problems with staff relations led to three union grievances against a manager, particularly since he had been warned to improve his personnel skills.
- A manager had an affair with a subordinate and showed her favouritism in the office, creating a poor working atmosphere.
- Managers were warned but failed to improve their interaction with staff and/or customers. However, in similar cases where no warnings had been given, there was no cause for dismissal.
- A hostile working environment had been created due to repeated non-sexual harassment, although the effects of favouritism and non-sexual touching did not amount to just cause.

Examples — no just cause — There was no cause for dismissal where:

- A manager showed a preference for lunching with some staff rather than others.
- A manager showed favouritism of one subordinate over others, although it was cause for criticism or a warning.
- A manager created a terrible working atmosphere that led to a successful union organizing drive.
- Poor relations with the union were not the employee's fault or had improved in the period right before termination.
- The manager's attitude toward staff was negative.
- A manager required staff to work before punching in or after punching out, even though this practice was forbidden in the employer's manuals and handbooks.
- A manager hired family members but there was no unfair favouritism, as 95 per cent of the community was related in some way.
- Interpersonal skills were not part of a manager's job description and the problems with staff were only partly her fault.
- A manager was curt with her staff. She was entitled to demand production from them, and there was no evidence of unnecessary staff turnover.
- A manager's abuse of staff was reprimanded in some cases, but he received several promotions and raises. His misconduct had been condoned.
- A manager verbally abused staff and customers but was not wholly unjustified. He could not be dismissed for just cause without prior warning.

D-8.3 SEXUAL AND OTHER HARASSMENT

General principles — The fact that an employee, even a manager, is guilty of harassment has not automatically led to a finding of just cause for dismissal. It has depended on all the circumstances, including the severity and frequency of the harassment.

Time of harassment vs. time of discovery — In one case, summary dismissal for sexual harassment was justified even though the conduct had stopped some time before the employer learned of it.

Harassment policy — The right to dismiss for just cause may be strengthened where a harassment policy is in place. Even if a policy has not been implemented, its existence may help strengthen an employer's claim of just cause, especially against a manager who should have been aware of and enforcing the policy.

Condonation — Condonation seems less likely to excuse this type of misconduct, perhaps due to the perceived future risk to other employees. One judge said that an employee can be properly dismissed for cause even though the employer had done little to change an offensive workplace atmosphere, i.e., even though there had been condonation. Condonation did not deny the employer the right of dismissal where the behaviour justified summary dismissal.

Need for and effect of warning — Although a warning is not always needed, where it is needed, or where a warning has been given and the employee has improved his behaviour, he cannot later be dismissed without fresh misconduct. In one case, this was upheld even though the employer had not known about some of the earlier harassment at the time it gave the warning.

Examples — just cause — There was just cause for dismissal where:

- An employee sexually harassed his secretary, causing her to file a complaint with the Human Rights Commission.
- Managers left the employer open to a human rights complaint or a civil suit by sexually harassing co-workers, even though no such complaint or suit was filed.
- An employee did not admit sexual harassment, but he admitted repeating the behaviour about which he had been warned in the past.
- An employee had touched the breasts of a subordinate, even though he had stopped the misconduct seven months before. His denial of the subordinate's allegations gave the employer no choice but to dismiss him.
- The victim was intimidated and feared losing her job, even though the conduct had stopped some months before the employer learned of it and acted upon it.
- A manager denied the harassment and showed no remorse. Given that it was a second incident, that most of the staff was female and they often worked alone in the evening, the employer was justly worried about further incidents in the future.

Examples — no just cause — Dismissal for sexual harassment was not justified where:

- An employee took a minor part in a tasteless prank carried out by another employee, especially given the lax attitude toward sexual conduct in the workplace, despite a formal policy against sexual harassment.
- A customer service manager made inappropriate sexual remarks to a client.
- A male manager touched female clerks. This was not sexual harassment, as it was minor, non-sexual and he did not persist if they objected.
- A sexual advance was made while two employees were on a business trip. The man did not pressure the woman, demand sexual favours or threaten her job.
- A brief, unwarranted and crude sexual advance was made but was not repeated.
- An employee carried on a consensual affair with a superior. The affair did not significantly disrupt the employer's operations or the morale in the workplace.

Dismissal of victim — Retaliation for ending a consensual affair, in the form of a salary decrease, a negative evaluation and other changes, was sexual harassment, and the victim was not dismissed for just cause for threatening to reveal her claim of harassment.

D-8.4 AGE AND OTHER DISCRIMINATION

General principles — Dismissal due to discrimination based on the employee's age, race, gender or another protected human rights ground, or on refusal of the employer's sexual advances, is not justifiable. This type of dismissal can support a wrongful dismissal action independent of human rights laws.

Age discrimination — Dismissal due to an employee having reached age 65 was not justifiable where this was age discrimination contrary to the provincial human rights law. This was the case even where the parties had had an understanding for many years that the employee would be required to retire at age 65. See also Chapter C-4, "Other Constructive Dismissal Situations".

Pregnancy — Dismissal for illness and absence due to pregnancy was not justified where a statute prohibited dismissal for pregnancy itself.

Failure to pay equally for equal work — Where there is an allegation of failure to pay equally for equal work, the amount the employee should have been receiving prior to dismissal would be relevant in assessing the employee's damages.

D-8.5 PERSONAL APPEARANCE AND HABITS

General principles — Dismissal can be justified if the problem is serious and causes harm or the risk of harm to the employer. In most cases, however, a failure to improve after one or more warnings will be needed to justify dismissal.

Examples — no just cause — Just cause did not exist without warnings based on:

- Sloppy appearance.
- Untidy offices or workspaces.
- A flashy and aggressive image that was not right for the employer's market.
- Obesity which interfered with job performance. The employee had lost some weight after being warned, and he had also received the required annual medical certificate of fitness.

Examples — just cause — Just cause was found, however, where:

- A hairdresser's appearance and demeanour offended clients.
- A perfume demonstrator occasionally had a body odour problem, plus other problems with her behaviour. However, she was entitled to clear warnings before she could be dismissed without notice.

D-8.6 CUSTOMER RELATIONS

General principle — Customer relations is an area of frequent concern to employers. A single customer complaint or minor complaints usually would not be sufficient to justify dismissal, nor would there be cause where:

(1) the employer's business had not suffered;
(2) the employee had a large number of customer contacts so some complaints would be expected;
(3) the problems were not the employee's fault;
(4) the problems were the result of normal human error; or
(5) there was a chance the situation could have been resolved if the employee had been warned.

Must be prejudice to employer — As with other just cause situations, for dismissal to be justified it may be necessary for the employer's business to be seriously prejudiced. There will be no right to dismiss for cause where there is any justification or indication that the employer has not been injured by the behaviour.

Need for warning — Cases vary as to whether a warning is required. It has been said that arguments with customers and verbal abuse of staff are not cause for dismissal without a warning, at least where they are not wholly unjustified, or performance was not affected. However, a warning was not required where the conduct showed a lack of basic skills to be expected of any manager dealing with the public.

Failure to improve after warning — Failure to improve after a warning may justify dismissal. For instance, an employee whose continued pattern of customer complaints was incompatible with the employer's need for good customer relations was justly dismissed.

Complaints to customers — An employee who criticizes the employer to its customers may or may not be dismissable for just cause. See Chapter D-7, "Disobedience and Disloyalty".

Examples — just cause — Dismissal was justified where:

- A baker allowed the bakery to become so filthy that it represented a menace to public health.
- An insurance adjuster engendered many customer complaints and some loss of business.
- An untidy hairdresser smoked and drank coffee on the job.
- A town manager was insolent, intemperate and incompetent in dealing with town merchants.
- A personnel agency manager lied to a client about the reason for not fulfilling the client's request.
- A marketing director was rude and abusive on business trips, and assaulted staff and damaged property at a company dinner.
- An employee misrepresented a product to clients and misrepresented the clients to the employer for insurance purposes, even though the misconduct occurred at a time of personal difficulty.
- An employee forged customers' signatures to service contracts. Even though there would be no charge to the customers, the conduct would put the employer's integrity into question.
- A manager placed misleading advertisements.

Examples — no just cause — Just cause was not found where:

- An employee engaged in a display of temper in front of customers, including swearing and breaking a display rack. It was a momentary flare-up and was partly provoked by his supervisor.
- An employee made off colour remarks to female customers.
- Customer complaints were caused by a long-term employee's mental illness.

- Customer complaints were made against a warranty clerk, since some complaints were to be expected given the nature of the job.
- Complaints were made against a sales manager who had made thousands of sales calls. A few complaints were to be expected, given the volume of calls.
- An employee told a customer to "shove it". It was a single incident by a long-term employee in a senior position.
- A customer asked for a new exclusive representative. Something more than the customer's desire was required for there to be just cause for dismissal.
- A manager's actions upset the company's bank. His actions were authorized by his superiors, and there was no evidence that they had jeopardized the company's relationship with the bank.

Chapter D-9

ATTENDANCE AND SUBSTANCE ABUSE

TABLE OF CONTENTS

D-9.1　Absence from Work Generally
D-9.2　Absence Due to Illness
　　　　D-9.2.1　General Principles
　　　　D-9.2.2　Mental Illness
　　　　D-9.2.3　Failure to Return to Work; Malingering
D-9.3　Vacations
D-9.4　Lateness
D-9.5　Substance Abuse

D-9.1　ABSENCE FROM WORK GENERALLY

General principles — Attendance at work is an implied requirement of all employees. Absence from work without the employer's permission may amount to just cause, depending on the circumstances. The cases seem to focus on:

(1) the reasonableness of the employee's decision to take time off;
(2) the harm done to the employer;
(3) the amount of time taken; a smaller amount of time away is less likely to amount to just cause;
(4) whether absences are occasional or frequent. Occasional absences might not justify dismissal, but frequent unauthorized absences may;
(5) whether the absence remains unexplained;
(6) the timing of the absence, such as a brief, unjustified absence at a critical time; and
(7) whether a warning had been given.

Condonation — Absences taken with the employer's knowledge and tacit consent generally are not cause for dismissal, even if the employee has failed to follow formal procedures.

Onus — The onus of proving authorization for an absence would appear to fall on the employee.

Examples — no just cause — There was no just cause for dismissal where:

- A manager had apparent authority to assign hours and assigned his own hours in a manner that was never forbidden by senior management.
- An employee returned early from business travel and did not contact the employer for several days, but did try to contact the employer before he was scheduled to work again.

Examples — just cause — There was just cause for dismissal where:

- An employee took time off while the request for approval was still pending or where authorization had been refused.
- An employee refused to give up a commitment which would overlap with his regular work hours.
- An employee walked off the job without telling anyone and left a potentially dangerous machine unattended.

Lying — Providing false reasons for an unauthorized absence, or obtaining authorization through false reasons, has also been held to constitute just cause. See also Chapter D-5, "Dishonesty". For example, there was cause where:

- An employee claimed to be totally disabled when actually capable of returning to work.
- An employee left early for a business trip, took unauthorized time off work and lied about his whereabouts.

Excusable absences — Taking unauthorized time off may be excused if it was reasonable in the circumstances. Examples include:

- An employee who took a leave of absence upon short notice due to his daughter's serious illness.
- An employee who was absent while serving an unrelated jail sentence. See also Chapter D-10, "Off-the-Job Conduct and Other Just Cause Situations".
- An employee who played golf rather than attending to his duties over several weeks, but he had personal problems at the time and no warning had been given.
- An employee who failed to attend a product meeting one weekend.
- An employee who failed to seek authorization before taking a vacation to which he was entitled.
- An employee who refused to give up a break to which he was entitled, or who took time off in lieu of missed breaks.
- Employees who left work in response to a dispute or a claimed constructive dismissal, although this may not always be the case.
- An employee who provided false reasons for an absence while suffering from emotional strain.

D-9.2 ABSENCE DUE TO ILLNESS

D-9.2.1 General Principles

Permanently incapable — An employee who has become permanently incapable of fulfilling his duties may properly be dismissed, as may one who has become permanently incapable of performing one essential job duty. Whether illness entitles an employer to terminate a contract depends on a number of factors, including:

(1) the terms of the contract;
(2) availability of sick leave and pay;
(3) how long the employee is likely to remain sick;
(4) the nature of the job;
(5) the nature of the illness;
(6) the length of service; and
(7) how long the employer should reasonably be expected to await the employee's return.

Issue — The question is whether the employee has been incapacitated to such a degree that further performance of his obligations would be impossible or would be substantially different than was originally intended.

Temporary illness — Temporary illness generally is not just cause for dismissal, particularly if the injury or illness is job-related. For example:

- An employee was found to have been wrongfully dismissed due to her illness where she was entitled to sick leave which had not yet expired.
- An employee who refused a job assignment because she was unable to do the work due to injury was wrongfully dismissed.
- A short-term illness was not just cause, even where it was known that the employee had a chronic and progressive disease.
- An employee who left immediately when advised by his doctor to take time off had not abandoned his job, as he was entitled to sick leave and had made it clear that his absence would be temporary.

Long-term illness — Even illnesses which last a substantial amount of time may not be cause for dismissal if they are not permanent. Long-service employees may be entitled to a longer period of illness before dismissal than short-service employees.

Time for assessing permanence — Most judges assess the permanence of an illness as of the date of dismissal, not the date of trial. In other words, the test is objective, based on the circumstances at the time of dismissal and not on the subsequent length of the illness. For example, an employee could not be dismissed after only a few days' illness where it was not yet known whether the illness would leave him unable to do his job on a permanent basis.

Duty to communicate — An employee, claiming absence due to illness rather than an unauthorized absence, must communicate with the employer about the reason for absence. Dismissal was justified where:

- An employee claimed he left work due to job-related stress, but he had never discussed the problem with the employer and the employer had accommodated that type of problem in the past.
- An employee failed to report for work, seek a leave of absence or communicate her intentions after expiry of a sick leave.
- An employee failed to respond to requests for information and failed to return to work as soon as he had recovered.
- An employee's lawyer wrote that she was on sick leave, with no indication of a date of return.
- An employee on workers' compensation failed to report regularly on his condition, as required, where other misconduct was also involved.

Failure to communicate — no just cause — Just cause was not found where:

- An employer knew the employee was still receiving disability benefits, despite her failure to communicate.
- A senior employee was stressed from long hours, the death of her mother and her own illness, and communicated her intentions to a colleague rather than a superior.
- An employee returned from a sick leave to find his job had been filled. He had communicated with the employer during the sick leave.
- An employee complied with her employer's request for a medical certificate. The employer's order that the employee return to work was not lawful or reasonable.

Statutory duties — Human rights, health and safety and workers' compensation laws require accommodation of illness or injury in certain situations. These requirements may affect judges' views under the common law.

Frustration — The right to dismiss may be based on the principle of frustration rather than just cause, as discussed in Chapter B-3, "Frustration of the Employment Contract".

Written agreement — In one case, an employee signed a contract that provided for dismissal if he became incapable of performing the job. A judge ruled that the contract did not apply to a pre-existing medical condition, since it could not be said that the condition interfered with the proper discharge of his duties.

Disability during notice period — Judges have differed on whether an employee who becomes disabled during the notice period should receive reasonable notice in addition to disability pay or sick leave benefits. See Chapter G-11, "Deductions from the Damage Award".

D-9.2.2 Mental Illness

Behaviour caused by mental illness — Whether just cause can exist due to behaviour caused by mental illness is in dispute. The result seems to depend on the degree of misbehaviour, and the severity and permanence of the illness. For example, there was just cause for dismissal where:

- An employee's attitude, attendance and insubordination were unacceptable, even though it was later learned that his behaviour was caused by a serious mental illness.
- A fire chief committed arson under the influence of early Alzheimer's disease. However, he should not have been denied his pension.
- An employee's alcoholism caused unacceptable performance. He had been given second chances but was unable or unwilling to control his addiction.
- An employee claimed job-related stress, given that he had never discussed the problem with the employer and the employer had accommodated that type of problem in the past.

Examples — no just cause — Just cause was not found where:

- An employee had personal and emotional problems but her performance was good.
- An employee's poor performance was due to an acute stress-related illness caused by the pressures of the job.
- An employee's poor performance was a result of depression.
- An employee took unauthorized time off due to mental strain caused by the employee's heavy work schedule, since the employee was suffering from a real illness.
- The parties agreed that an employee's performance due to the early stages of AIDS-related dementia was not so poor as to give rise to just cause for dismissal.

D-9.2.3 Failure to Return to Work; Malingering

Malingering — An employer must be cautious when dismissing for malingering. Mere suspicions are not enough; the employer must ensure that it acts on accurate medical information. An employee may be capable of some activities without being capable of returning to work; and being seen out and about does not equate to malingering. However, where an employee claimed to be totally disabled when he was actually fit to return to light duty, he was properly dismissed.

Ultimatum in absence of information — An employer wrongfully dismissed an employee when it sent him a letter stating that he would be terminated if he did not return by a certain date. Although the employer asked for medical information, the letter did not say that he would not be dismissed if his absence was medically justified.

Absenteeism control — An employee was wrongfully dismissed for absenteeism even though she had been warned that no further absences would be allowed. It was not clear how a ban on all absences, even medically required ones, could be reconciled with company policy allowing medically justified absences.

Inappropriate accommodation — Where an employee was fit to return to work, but the employer believed she was not well enough to perform her old job and therefore offered her a lesser job, she had been constructively dismissed.

Workplace safety, accommodation issues — Where the employee's refusal to work was protected by the *Occupational Health and Safety Act* and the employer had not followed the Act's provisions for challenging the refusal, dismissal was unjust. Similarly, dismissal was wrongful where:

- An employee refused a work assignment because she was physically unable to do the job due to injury.
- An employee was unreasonably refused accommodation for her disability as required by statute.
- An employee had been ruled fit to work by the Workers' Compensation Board but had refused to return to work, to take an unpaid leave of absence or to provide medical proof of his inability to work.

Examples — no just cause — Dismissal was wrongful where:

- It was shown that an employee was still injured, and his request to return to a lighter-duty job had been refused.
- An injured employee played in a softball tournament with his doctor's permission, even though playing had delayed his return to work.
- An employee was suffering from mental illness, and there was no evidence that he was working elsewhere, but rather that he was following his doctor's advice to get out as much as possible.

D-9.3 VACATIONS

General principle — Although employees are entitled to vacations by statute and by contract, they must be taken within the employer's rules, which generally involve permission as to the timing and the amount of vacation taken. Taking vacation outside the rules will generally only give just cause for dismissal if the circumstances were egregious and the employee's actions had serious business consequences for the employer. For example, just cause was found where:

- A baker took a vacation despite permission having been refused, and left his employer short-staffed at a critical time.
- A property manager left on short notice for his vacation, without ensuring that buildings were looked after or staff were instructed in his absence.

Examples — no just cause — Dismissal was not justified where:

- An employee who worked independently took his accrued vacation without seeking permission or informing his employer of the details.
- An executive took an extended vacation without having obtained authorization, given the combative atmosphere between the parties at the time.
- A manager took an unauthorized weekend off after working many weekends in a row.
- An employee refused to change his long-standing, pre-authorized vacation plans on short notice, even though his absence would affect production at a critical time. The employer's demand that the employee change his plans was unreasonable.
- A managerial employee left early on vacation, where he had arranged for a substitute.
- An employee failed to leave a telephone number where he could be reached during his vacation.

D-9.4 LATENESS

General principles — A single incident of lateness is seldom serious enough to warrant dismissal. More often, lateness will require one or more warnings and a chance to improve, before dismissal will be justified. It may be necessary to show harm, or risk of harm, to the employer's business, especially in the case of long-term employees.

Condonation — Condonation may exist where there was a leisurely workplace atmosphere; an employee was given a promotion, raise or positive performance review without mention of previous lateness; or the employer allowed the employee to make up missed time.

Examples — just cause — Dismissal was justified where:

- A short-term employee was chronically late, missed important meetings and took a great deal of unauthorized personal time.

- An employee was given several warnings to cease his chronic lateness, which was prejudicial to the employer since it was visible to 40 other employees.
- A production worker's chronic lateness delayed work on the entire production line.
- A long-term employee was frequently tardy and overstayed her breaks, in combination with other misconduct and poor performance.
- An employee often arrived late, left early, and engaged in other misconduct. He was guilty of habitual neglect of duty and other conduct incompatible with his duties.
- An employee repeatedly overstayed his breaks in breach of company rules, despite warnings. He was not entitled to decide that he could start earlier in the morning and take extra breaks due to above-average productivity. Given that he often incurred overtime, for which he was paid, his extended breaks were akin to theft from the employer.

Examples — no just cause — Dismissal was not justified where:

- A worker was chronically late by a few minutes. He could not be dismissed for cause without written warnings, given the leisurely atmosphere in his workplace.
- An employee was repeatedly late by a few minutes, the lateness was not her fault and she made up the time at the end of the day.
- An employee usually made up the lost time, and she received good performance reviews without mention of her lateness.
- A long-term employee with some managerial responsibilities was late. He had worked a considerable amount of unpaid overtime. A written warning without a warning that the job was in jeopardy was not sufficient.
- A controller was often late by less than five minutes, and was five to nine minutes late on five occasions in the three weeks before dismissal, but he had made a sincere effort to comply with the employer's directive to be on time.
- An employee was chronically late and failed to ever put in a full day's work over a one and a half year period, given the lengthy condonation and the employee's seven years of satisfactory service.
- A short-term employee was habitually late, had excessive personal phone calls and time off, and showed slow and sloppy work habits. These shortcomings were not enough to amount to just cause, although only minimal notice was required.
- An employee was chronically tardy but the president had told the employee to ignore the warnings she was given.

Late work — Lateness in completing work may also be cause for dismissal in some instances, although not all cases agree. In one case, an employee who was habitually late in handing in work was wrongfully dismissed where his previous performance evaluations were good.

D-9.5 SUBSTANCE ABUSE

Substance use on job — The effect of substance use on the job depends on the degree of intoxication, and the prejudice caused to the employer's business.

Contract — A truck driver who drank while listed on the schedule as "ready for work" was properly dismissed, since the employer had a contractual term with its drivers that they could be dismissed without notice if they consumed alcohol while on duty.

Performance must be negatively affected — Merely having alcohol on one's breath is not cause for dismissal unless performance is negatively affected. Similarly, an employee with a drinking problem whose performance was not affected and who was never under the influence while working could not be dismissed for cause. Excessive drinking in the past, which occurred away from work and was never the subject of complaint or warning, could not be brought up later as cause for dismissal.

Duty to warn — There may be a duty to warn employees that drinking on duty will result in dismissal. For example:

- A hotel manager who did not become intoxicated, but who nevertheless knew he should not drink while on duty, was entitled to a warning.
- An employee who became drunk and abusive at a company dinner was properly dismissed, since he had been warned in the past about similar behaviour.

Proof — An employee accused of smoking hashish at work was not dismissed for cause, as the evidence of drug use was conflicting. However, use of illegal drugs during working hours might have been just cause if the allegation had been proven.

Off-the-job intoxication — Intoxication outside of working hours and away from the employer's premises did not give cause for dismissal in one case, even where the drunk employee got into an altercation with another employee. Similarly, an impaired driving charge which had no bearing on the employee's job was not just cause for dismissal.

Addiction — Modern cases take a sympathetic view of an employee with a drinking problem or an emotional problem causing temporary, excessive drinking, especially for long-term employees. Note also that many human rights statutes would apply to dismissal for the physical disability of addiction. Nevertheless, dismissal may be justified where addiction causes serious performance problems or otherwise prejudices the employer's business, or where the employee has been warned but is unwilling or unable to help himself.

Examples — just cause — Just cause was found where:

- A manager was away from work for a week and a half on a drunken binge.
- A ship's captain became grossly intoxicated while in command of a ship.
- An employee drove a company vehicle while intoxicated.
- There was a strict policy against the use of drugs and alcohol while at work, which was necessary to meet safety concerns, and an employee was found in violation during a routine medical exam.

Examples — no just cause — Just cause was not found where:

- A company encouraged its salespeople to socialize with clients. It could not complain if a salesman occasionally returned from a business lunch somewhat intoxicated.
- An apartment superintendent was on call 24 hours a day. He could not be expected never to have a drink, although the employer could require that he not drink when meeting with tenants and the public.
- There was an isolated instance of drunkenness and misconduct at the company Christmas party, even where the employee assaulted his wife in an attempt to make her leave.
- There was an isolated incident of drinking during working hours, despite a company policy forbidding employees from drinking during the work day.
- There was an isolated act of driving a company car while impaired, during work hours and while engaged in a company activity, by a long-term employee.
- An employee operating heavy construction equipment was accused of smoking marijuana on the job; even if it had been proven, he was entitled to a warning.
- There was drinking on the employer's premises but outside of working hours.
- A manager permitted alcohol to be served at Christmas parties in breach of the employer's policy, but this was known to more senior management.

Chapter D-10

OFF-THE-JOB CONDUCT AND OTHER JUST CAUSE SITUATIONS

TABLE OF CONTENTS

D-10.1 General Principles
D-10.2 Sexual Conduct
D-10.3 Criminal Conduct
D-10.4 Redundancy, Economic Problems, Company Reorganization, Strikes
D-10.5 Driving of Company Vehicle; Loss of Driver's Licence

D-10.1 GENERAL PRINCIPLES

General principles — Judges are reluctant to allow employers to control their employees' private lives, and dismissals based on employees' private conduct seldom succeed. Nevertheless, an employee can be justly dismissed for his private conduct, if the conduct is wholly incompatible with the proper discharge of the employee's duties, or if it would tend to harm the employer's business.

Objective view — The existence of just cause depends on the seriousness of the conduct and the nature of the job. The conduct's seriousness must be judged objectively, in relation to the community's moral standards.

Relationship to job — The fact that an employee's conduct was related to the job, although occurring away from work or outside of the job's duties, may or may not strengthen a claim of just cause. Just cause was found where a demoted employee threatened a subordinate by calling him over the weekend and telling him he had been reinstated and that he intended to fire the subordinate on Monday morning. The personal bankruptcy of a vice-president of finance was said to possibly justify dismissal. In other cases, however, relationship to the job has not been enough to justify dismissal; for example, there was no cause where:

- An employee misbehaved during a company hockey tournament.
- An employee frequently called her co-workers at home while she was off sick; the conduct occurred outside the workplace and sentiments against her had been unfairly inflamed by a co-worker with a grudge.

- An employee parked the company van in front of a bar. He was warned not to do it again, and he did not.
- An employee dragged his intoxicated, brawling wife away from a Christmas party held by the employer.
- An employee hid important computer software and refused to reveal its location unless his severance pay demands were met. His uncharacteristic behaviour was triggered by the employer's unfair dismissal.

Human rights — Where an employee's personal conduct would be protected under human rights laws, it is unlikely to amount to just cause for dismissal. For example, an employee of a public utilities commission who was active in the campaign for election of the commission's officers would likely be protected by human rights law from dismissal due to political activity. Similarly, a doctor working for a Catholic hospital was entitled to publicly state his personal views in favour of euthanasia.

D-10.2 SEXUAL CONDUCT

General principle — In modern times, sexual conduct has been treated with tolerance where there are no work-related repercussions. For example, there was no cause where:

- A salesman had an affair with a woman who was separated from a co-worker of the salesman.
- An employee made a sexual advance to a co-worker while they were on a business trip.
- Employees were involved in a consensual affair, without negative effects at work.
- A woman was romantically involved with an employee who had been dismissed.
- An employee had an abusive partner who was accused but acquitted of sexually assaulting a client of the employer.

Examples — just cause — Just cause was found where:

- An employee had an affair with the wife of one of the business' owners, and the employee and the wife were often alone together in the office, which could affect the employer's reputation in a small rural setting. However, it was said that this same conduct would not be just cause in an anonymous urban setting.
- A manager had an affair with a subordinate and allowed their personal relationship to affect the working atmosphere.
- A social worker had a relationship with a client who was being counselled about sexual abuse.

- An employee had engaged in a sexual relationship with a ward of the child welfare department 13 years earlier, when he had been a youth care supervisor.
- A high-profile employee used the employer's premises for assignations.

Sexual harassment — Note that sexual harassment may amount to just cause, where the advances are persistent and unwelcome. See Chapter D-8, "Workplace Conflicts and Harassment".

D-10.3 CRIMINAL CONDUCT

General principles — Again, the issue is whether the criminal conduct might significantly harm the employer's business or reputation. Just cause was found where:

- A supervisor was convicted of the sexual assault of a minor. The confidence and respect of his subordinates had been destroyed, and this would have serious production and safety considerations in a dangerous workplace.
- A supervisor had a personal relationship with his secretary, and he assaulted her. His behaviour and the character it revealed were unacceptable from a member of management.
- A restaurant manager drank too much and got into fights at other bars. His conduct threatened the employer's reputation and raised concerns about licensing problems.
- A probationary constable committed perjury.
- A university business school lecturer committed criminal insurance fraud. Teaching ethics was an important part of the school's curriculum.
- A superintendent of schools defrauded the province. This was just cause given his position of trust within the community.
- A securities fraud investigator cheated on a qualifying exam. The job required a person of the highest moral character.
- A corporate lawyer failed to disclose a pending investigation of himself for influence peddling. The charges could have affected his ability to perform the job's duties.
- An employee was convicted of fraud, even though the fraud was committed at the behest of her supervisor.
- A controller advised another employee to pay illegal bribes.
- A seasonal employee was serving a criminal sentence when he was recalled for work, and therefore was unavailable to work.

Examples — no just cause — Just cause was not found where:

- An employee beat up his common-law wife, even though she was a co-worker of his, because the incident happened at home and involved a purely domestic dispute.

- An employee was convicted of gross indecency for conduct occurring away from work.
- An employee was charged and later convicted of assault causing bodily harm involving a transvestite prostitute.
- An employee vandalized a taxi after getting drunk at an office Christmas party.
- An employee failed to inform his employer of the loss of his driver's licence due to drunk driving, as driving was not part of his job and his right to receive a car allowance had not been affected.
- A criminal charge for drug trafficking was laid against an employee relating to activities away from work.
- An employee purchased marijuana from a co-worker, but he never used or possessed the drug at work.
- An employee was arrested for trafficking in narcotics, but the charges were later stayed. The employer was found to have dealt unfairly with the employee by dismissing him without proof of criminal activity and despite his previous good record.
- An employee had failed to disclose a pending fraud charge. He was not in a special position of trust, and the employer had done nothing when it learned of the charge and eventual conviction.
- A police constable was charged but acquitted of fraud. The employer should have awaited the outcome of the criminal charges before dismissing him.

D-10.4 REDUNDANCY, ECONOMIC PROBLEMS, COMPANY REORGANIZATION, STRIKES

General principle — Redundancy or loss of a job due to the employer's economic difficulties does not amount to just cause for dismissal. Harsh as it may seem to an employer, an employee being dismissed under these circumstances still must be given reasonable notice. In most cases, a company's reorganization will not justify dismissal without reasonable notice or pay in lieu, although sometimes there may be a contractual term that an employee will accept reasonable reassignments, as discussed in Part C, "Constructive Dismissal".

Examples — no just cause — There was no just cause for dismissal where:

- An employer ceased his business due to health problems. The cessation of business did not eliminate his employee's right to reasonable notice of dismissal, as the employer's eventual retirement was foreseeable.
- The employer lost funding for two employees' jobs, as the employer could have made their employment conditional on receiving continued funding, but it had not done so.

Effect of statute — In some cases, statutes may reduce or eliminate the right to reasonable notice, or at least to statutory notice, where termination is due to reorganization or economic circumstances. For example, Newfoundland's *Labour Standards Act* exempts employees terminated due to economic conditions beyond the employer's foreseeable control from the right to statutory termination notice. Some statutes, particularly those governing public employees, may affect just cause and the right to notice in reorganizations. In these cases, the court may still be asked to decide whether reorganization was the true motive for the termination.

Strike — In one case, a strike by other employees was not just cause for dismissing employees who were not on strike, where the employer could still have provided the proper facilities for the non-striking employees to perform their jobs. See also Chapter B-3, "Frustration of the Employment Contract".

D-10.5 DRIVING OF COMPANY VEHICLE; LOSS OF DRIVER'S LICENCE

Required part of job — Improper driving of the employer's vehicle may be just cause if driving is a required part of the job and if the driving behaviour was clearly unacceptable. However, where the behaviour is less serious or driving is not an integral part of the job, dismissal may not be justified.

Examples — just cause — Just cause for dismissal was found where:

- Along with other misconduct, an employee prejudiced the employer's insurance by driving a company vehicle while intoxicated.
- An employee negligently drove the employer's fire truck.

Examples — no just cause — Just cause was not found where:

- The misconduct was an isolated act after almost 30 years' employment.
- An employee took the company van from work to home, despite it being against company policy. The employee thought his behaviour was authorized and he was too unsophisticated to think about insurance factors or legal liability.
- An employee who was warned not to park the company van in front of a bar did not do so again.

Loss of driver's licence — A truck driver was wrongfully dismissed for temporary loss of his driver's licence where he had been kept on performing other duties for two months, and he could have been kept on alternate work for the remainder of the suspension.

Chapter E-1

COLLECTIVE AGREEMENT, ARBITRATION OR APPEAL PROCEDURES

TABLE OF CONTENTS

E-1.1 Existence of Collective Agreement
E-1.2 Existence of Arbitration or Appeal Procedure
    E-1.2.1 General Principles
    E-1.2.2 Statutory Procedure
    E-1.2.3 Contractual Procedure

E-1.1 EXISTENCE OF COLLECTIVE AGREEMENT

General principle — Employees who are covered by collective agreements generally will not be permitted to bring wrongful dismissal actions at common law. They are limited to the remedies set out in their collective agreement. As stated by the Supreme Court of Canada:

> The courts have no jurisdiction to consider claims arising out of rights created by a collective agreement. Nor can the courts properly decide questions which might have arisen under the common law of master and servant in the absence of a collective bargaining regime if the collective agreement by which the parties to the action are bound makes provision for the matters in issue, whether or not it explicitly provides a procedure and forum for enforcement. (*St. Anne Nackawic Pulp & Paper Co. v. Canadian Paper Workers Union, Local 219*, [1986] 1 S.C.R. 704 at 720.)

No peripheral actions — A collective agreement will also bar a common-law action in matters peripheral to the employment; for example:

- Actions against a fellow employee.
- Actions dealing with a matter not covered by the agreement, if it is part of the terms and conditions of employment, such as a relocation directive.
- Actions following decertification of the union where the employer has agreed to continue to abide by the terms of the collective agreement.

Parties' agreement — Where the parties specifically state that a matter is outside of the collective agreement, the existence of the collective agreement does not bar a common-law action. However, this is unlikely to be the case with dismissal.

Examples — common-law action permitted — Common-law claims were permitted where:

- An employee had not been told when hired that he would be covered by a collective agreement, and had not consented to it.
- An employee was dismissed before starting his employment, and therefore was not yet covered by the collective agreement.
- An employee's coverage by the collective agreement was in dispute.

Probationary employees — In some cases, probationary employees who were not yet entitled to grieve under the collective agreement have been held to be entitled to sue, while in other cases their claims have been barred.

Tort or statute claim — Where an employee's claim is based purely in tort or under a statute, not contract, some cases have allowed claims to proceed, although others have ruled the collective agreement still bars the claim.

Misrepresentations during hiring — A collective agreement may not bar an employee's claim based on a pre-employment contract or misrepresentations made during hiring.

Breach of settlement — A claim that the settlement of a grievance was breached did not revive the employee's original wrongful dismissal claim; the employee's remedy was still through the arbitration procedure.

Charter of Rights and Freedoms — Neither a collective agreement, which bars a wrongful dismissal action, nor the *Canada Labour Code*, which requires all collective agreements to provide for final settlement of all disputes, breaches an employee's equality rights under s. 15 of the *Canadian Charter of Rights and Freedoms* by depriving him of his common-law rights. Claims to enforce alleged rights under the *Charter* must still be pursued under the collective agreement, according to the Supreme Court of Canada.

Non-unionized employees — A common-law action may be brought by a non-union employee whose contract includes an implied term based on a term of the collective agreement. For example, a common-law action was permitted where:

- Some management employees who had been promoted out of the bargaining unit claimed to have a right, based on the collective

agreement or on a specific promise made to them, to be returned to the bargaining unit rather than be dismissed.
- An employee who had a right to return to the bargaining unit, but who was not required to do so, chose not to return and instead brought a wrongful dismissal action.
- An employee brought a defamation action in a dispute involving another employee who belonged to a separate union with a separate collective agreement. It was found that the "essential character" of the dispute did not involve the interpretation, application, operation or violation of the collective agreement.

Union employees without collective agreement — Employees of unions who are not themselves covered by collective agreements generally are entitled to sue for wrongful dismissal. However, a union may be impossible to sue if it is an unincorporated entity.

Claim against bankrupt employer — Employees covered by collective agreements are entitled to claim as unsecured creditors for severance and termination pay upon a bankruptcy, and are not barred from bringing a claim because they are covered by a collective agreement.

E-1.2 EXISTENCE OF ARBITRATION OR APPEAL PROCEDURE

E-1.2.1 General Principles

Alternative dispute mechanisms — Some contracts and some statutes provide other ways of settling disputes; for example, an internal appeal or grievance procedure, or the right to submit disputes to arbitration. Whether or not these alternatives are mandatory (therefore ousting the courts' jurisdiction) or optional depends on a number of circumstances, including the nature of the dispute; the nature of the scheme providing for adjudication; and whether giving jurisdiction to the courts would do violence to a comprehensive scheme designed to govern all aspects of the relationship between the parties.

Choice of forum — Where an employee has a choice of where to proceed, choice of one forum may exclude the option of a later proceeding in the other forum. See Chapter E-2, "Issue Estoppel: Previous or Concurrent Actions".

E-1.2.2 Statutory Procedure

Statutory procedure — The effect of a statutory grievance or appeal procedure is not as clear as the effect of a collective agreement. Generally, courts will not defer to an alternative procedure unless the grievance panel is better equipped to deal with the particular issue. In most cases involving dismissal, the courts have not considered a grievance panel to be better equipped to deal with the issue.

Wording of legislation — Many statutes which provide alternative remedies expressly state that employees' common-law rights are not affected. In other cases, it has been said that a statute need not specifically preserve common-law rights in order to maintain the right to sue for wrongful dismissal, given the courts' inherent jurisdiction to hear wrongful dismissal claims. As long as there is no privative clause or requirement for mandatory dispute resolution, the panel will not have exclusive jurisdiction. In those cases, an employee would have an option as to which procedure to follow. However, in other cases where the statute is silent, it has been said that unless a statute explicitly preserves common-law rights, the courts' jurisdiction is excluded by necessary implication, especially where the statutory remedy is adequate on its own.

Where courts have jurisdiction — Generally, a wrongful dismissal action will not be barred where:

(1) the statutory scheme is not explicitly mandatory;
(2) the statutory procedure provides no real powers or remedies and does not specify that it is mandatory;
(3) the statutory procedure does not give the other forum exclusive jurisdiction; or
(4) the statutory procedure does not permit the employee to take the matter to binding adjudication by a third party.

Public servants — In some cases involving public servants, a grievance procedure under a regulatory process was held to bar a wrongful dismissal action or to limit the court's powers. However, other cases have said that the existence of a grievance procedure does not necessarily oust the courts; it depends on the subject-matter of the dispute.

Examples — Deference was given to a tribunal where the members of the appeal tribunal were members of a hospital board and would have knowledge of how hospitals functioned, and would also have a better appreciation of hospital congeniality than would a judge. However, common law actions were permitted even though an alternative remedy was available where:

- The grievance procedure would have been useless due to bias against the employee.
- Regulations authorized the employee to choose between the grievance procedure or an independent action.
- The legislation did not permit a grievance over the particular issue, for example, constructive dismissal.

E-1.2.3 Contractual Procedure

Contract or policy — Where an employee's individual contract, or the employer's general policy, provides for a grievance or arbitration procedure, the case law has varied on whether the court's jurisdiction is ousted. A lot depends on the clause's wording. Where a contract was ambiguous as to whether termination was to be dealt with under an arbitration clause or in the courts, a court held that it was appropriate that the matter proceed in the courts.

Examples — In one case, a court action was not allowed because it was said that differences relating to termination of employment were within the range of matters to be settled by arbitration. The court refused to stay the arbitration proceedings to allow a court action. However, in other cases, court actions have been permitted where:

- A clause provided for the employee to continue working during the grievance process. This could not be said to apply to a dispute over termination, so it must have been intended that termination issues would be dealt with in court.
- A union employee was entitled to pursue the union's internal appeal procedure, since it was said the internal procedure did not oust the court's jurisdiction.

Chapter E-2

ISSUE ESTOPPEL: PREVIOUS OR CONCURRENT ACTIONS

TABLE OF CONTENTS

E-2.1 Issue Estoppel Generally
E-2.2 Employment Standards Rulings
E-2.3 Employment Insurance (EI) Rulings
E-2.4 Human Rights Complaints
E-2.5 Other Adjudications
E-2.6 Previous Civil Action

E-2.1 ISSUE ESTOPPEL GENERALLY

General principles — Issue estoppel can arise any time there are multiple formal decisions, whether by adjudication, statutory decision, common-law action or otherwise, and the same issue arises in both actions. For example, the wrongfulness of a dismissal may be considered under the *Employment Insurance Act*, employment standards legislation, and under the common law in a wrongful dismissal action. Where an issue has already been decided in a previous forum, the person is said to be "estopped" or forbidden from relitigating the issue. Issue estoppel may bar an action altogether or may simply bar a new decision on the particular issue.

Requirements — For issue estoppel to apply in a later proceeding, the earlier proceeding must involve:

(1) the same issue, whether of fact or law or a mixed question of fact and law;
(2) the same parties;
(3) a judicial decision; and
(4) a final decision.

Test of judicial decision — To be "judicial" the decision must be:

(1) made by an institution capable of receiving and exercising judicial authority;
(2) required to be made in a judicial manner; and
(3) made in a judicial manner.

For example, the employee must know the case he or she has to meet, and must be given a reasonable opportunity to meet it and to state his or her own case.

Judicial discretion — Even if the tests have been met, the courts have the discretion to refuse to apply issue estoppel to avoid unfairness or commit an injustice. The courts will seek to balance the public interest in the finality of litigation with the private interest of achieving justice between the litigants. Procedural differences and the financial stakes are considerations which may result in a refusal to order issue estoppel.

Onus — The party seeking to invoke estoppel has the onus of showing injustice if it is not applied.

Rule against double compensation — Where two or more actions do proceed, there is a rule against double compensation for the same "wrong". This is possible, for example, where termination pay is awarded under an employment standards statute, and damages are awarded for wrongful dismissal in a civil action. Where there is a possibility of double compensation, one action may be stayed. If both are allowed to proceed, the damages awarded in the first action should be deducted from the damages in the second action that arise from the same issue.

E-2.2 EMPLOYMENT STANDARDS RULINGS

Wording of statute important — Most Canadian employment standards laws preserve the right of civil action, or preserve more favourable common-law remedies. Wrongful dismissal damages, being broader than most statutory terms, are regarded as more favourable. Thus, civil actions may be allowed to proceed in these cases, even though there was a previous employment standards ruling, as long as something potentially "more favourable" can be found in the court action. Some statutes, like Ontario's *Employment Standards Act*, force employees to make a choice between statutory proceedings or civil actions in the courts. In Ontario, an employment standards decision generally bars a later civil action for wrongful dismissal, although a ruling by the Supreme Court of Canada has left the door open for more challenges of this rule (*Danyluk v. Ainsworth Technologies Inc.*, [2001] 2 S.C.R. 460).

Issue estopped but action not estopped — Where one part or issue in a claim is the same as in the previous proceeding, a new decision may be barred on that one issue, but not on others. In one case, it was found that the employment standards ruling had determined the issue of wrongful dismissal, which could not be challenged anew in court; but the measure of damages was not decided by the earlier ruling, so the court action could proceed on that basis.

Applies to both parties — Issue estoppel has been applied to claims by employers as well as employees. For example, an employer was barred from arguing that there had been no constructive dismissal where an employment standards officer had already made a finding on the same issue.

Examples — civil actions allowed to proceed — Actions were permitted where:

- The later civil suit included a claim for punitive and aggravated damages.
- An employee was claiming back commissions that had not been paid for a number of years, and the amount at issue was significantly larger than the amount the employee had been permitted to claim under the legislation.
- The employee had not been given a proper opportunity to respond in the statutory decision, or there was other procedural unfairness involved in the earlier decision.
- A statutory severance pay claim within a court action had been dismissed without dealing with the merits; the employee could proceed with a statutory application.
- An employment standards finding had awarded nothing for termination pay because the employee had been primarily seeking overtime pay.
- An employment standards officer had not reached a decision, but had merely passed along an offer from the employer to the employee. Even though the employee had accepted the offer, he was not barred from bringing a civil action.
- An employment standards officer found that the employment contract had been frustrated, so made no ruling on the question of just cause for dismissal.
- An employee failed to seek an administrative appeal (which, in any event, was discretionary). The failure did not preclude the employee's civil action where the issues were too complex to be dealt with by the administrative tribunal.
- An employee's statutory entitlement was still under appeal. It was held that the employment standards matter was not yet final.
- The employee sued for wages under a verbal contract. While issue estoppel applied to the employment standards order for overtime and vacation pay, it did not apply to the claim for wages.

Consent required — A lawsuit was barred in British Columbia where its *Employment Standards Act* required the written consent of the director before a claimant under the Act could pursue a civil remedy, and the employee had not obtained the required consent.

Multiple employment standards actions — In Quebec, a complaint of dismissal without cause under s. 124 of the *Labour Standards Act* was not barred even though the employee had already brought a complaint for illegal dismissal under s. 122, as the two sections create separate rights and remedies.

E-2.3 EMPLOYMENT INSURANCE (EI) RULINGS

Employment insurance ruling — Most judges have resisted treating Employment Insurance (EI) rulings as decisions that create an issue estoppel in a later civil action, whether they involve findings of just cause or of constructive dismissal. The main reasons for this are three-fold. First, many judges do not regard the EI process as "judicial", either because it is administrative or investigative, or because parties are not necessarily given an opportunity to be heard. Second, the legal issues are not necessarily the same, even though they may go by the same name, such as "just cause". Usually, it is thought that the common law involves broader tests than are required under the *Employment Insurance Act*. Third, the employer is often not treated as a full party in an EI determination, and may not be involved at all. For these reasons, the tests for issue estoppel are not usually met.

Issue estoppel applied — The occasional case has applied issue estoppel in civil cases based on EI findings. Each case has to be determined on its facts. Where the parties have participated fully and the process was sufficiently judicial, with each side having a full opportunity to present its case, and where no special expertise was needed for deciding the claims, it may be fair and reasonable to apply issue estoppel so as to prevent the same issues from being relitigated.

E-2.4 HUMAN RIGHTS COMPLAINTS

General principle — Employees who claim their dismissals were discriminatory on human rights grounds, and who file both a human rights complaint and a lawsuit for wrongful dismissal, have generally had one claim stayed until the first one is resolved. Sometimes, the employee has been given the choice of which claim to pursue first; in other cases, the court has decided. For instance, a wrongful dismissal action was stayed in light of a pending human rights complaint where it was held that there was an element of possible double compensation. The judge said that the Human Rights Commission had broader powers than the court, so the human rights complaint should be dealt with first.

Stay not granted — Some judges have disagreed, however, holding that human rights and contractual rights are separate, and can be pursued simultaneously. In other cases, stays have been refused due to the particular facts of the situation, especially given the lengthy delays that often face human rights complainants. For example, a stay was refused where the potential harm to the employee outweighed the prejudice to the defendant. The Human Rights Commission had not yet started to investigate the complaint and the employee, who was HIV positive with a short life expectancy, was aggressively pursuing his civil case and wanted control of the proceedings.

Where previous human rights complaint — In one civil action in British Columbia, it was held that there was no issue estoppel. The fact that the *Human Rights Act* was satisfied did not preclude the employee from pursuing a common-law remedy.

Double compensation may arise — Recovery under human rights statutes is not limited to the damages available in a wrongful dismissal action, because the issue of intention is relevant and can lead to different claims. In one case, it was held that damages in a human rights matter are not limited to the period of reasonable notice, and can be awarded for the entire period of unemployment. Another case has held, however, that there must be "some congruence" between the loss of wages and the duration and quality of the complainant's employment.

E-2.5 OTHER ADJUDICATIONS

Unjust dismissal adjudication — Adjudication of an unjust dismissal complaint under the *Canada Labour Code* may give rise to an issue estoppel where damages in lieu of reasonable notice were awarded, or may bar a subsequent wrongful dismissal action altogether where the question posed is the same as in the adjudication. The adjudication is a judicial decision and, subject to the right of review, is final. This was the case where:

- The claim was dismissed.
- Reinstatement was ordered.
- Damages in lieu of notice were awarded.

Pay equity complaint — In a conflict between a civil action and a pay equity complaint, Ontario's Pay Equity Hearings Tribunal allowed the pay equity complaint to proceed, as it was said that the two actions were different and double recovery could easily be avoided.

Contractual restrictions — Note that civil actions may be restricted by contract. Many contracts provide for another means of dispute resolution, as discussed in Chapter E-1, "Collective Agreement, Arbitration or Appeal Procedures". The fact that the contract provides an alternative may or may not foreclose a civil action in the courts. For example, resort to the courts was restricted where:

- A contract contained an agreement that disputes would be settled by arbitration and it also contained a privative clause. The employer could only turn to the courts for judicial review if the arbitrator's award was patently unreasonable.
- A grievance was settled. The grievor was not entitled to revive her common-law claim when the settlement was breached. Rather, her remedy was enforcement of the settlement through the arbitration procedure.
- An employee had already had his discipline grievance arbitrated. He could not pursue a civil action based on the same facts, even by claiming the new ground of defamation.

E-2.6 PREVIOUS CIVIL ACTION

General principle — Generally, an employee cannot bring two court actions based on a breach of the employment contract, unless the two actions arise out of different facts at different times, or clearly involve totally separate rights. For example, an employee, who had already sued and lost a claim for breach of an implied covenant of good faith not to terminate his employment, could not then bring a wrongful dismissal action.

Second action permitted — A second action was permitted where an employee had started a constructive dismissal action while continuing in his job, but he was then dismissed outright and started a second action for wrongful dismissal. The two actions arose from different conduct and were separate in time, so the employee could pursue both actions.

Chapter E-3

SETTLEMENTS AND DELAYS

TABLE OF CONTENTS

E-3.1   Settlements
E-3.2   Accord and Satisfaction
E-3.3   Releases
E-3.4   Delay and Limitation Periods

E-3.1 SETTLEMENTS

General principle — A settlement accepted voluntarily, with full knowledge of its effect, amounts to accord and satisfaction and bars a subsequent court action. However, there must be a true meeting of the minds to create a binding agreement. There was no binding settlement, for instance, when an employee was merely told what he was getting. There was no opportunity for negotiation and no attempt was made to reach an agreement.

Release — A formal settlement usually includes a release, which the employee signs to release all claims in exchange for the settlement. Releases are discussed later in this chapter.

Undue pressure — Severance pay that was accepted due to undue financial or other pressures may not create a binding settlement, especially if the amount is grossly unfair and is accepted without legal advice. Money, however, that is received will be credited to the employer in assessing reasonable notice.

Inequality of bargaining power — A settlement or release will be unconscionable where there is inequality in bargaining power. Where the stronger party uses its position of power to gain an advantage, there is substantial unfairness to the weaker party. Malice is not required. For example, settlements were not binding where:

- An employee was unsophisticated in business matters and was not thinking clearly due to his panic about being without an income, the employer had given little thought to his circumstances or the proper amount of reasonable notice, and the settlement amount was substantially unfair.

- An employer did not make it clear at the time of negotiation or payment that a settlement would be final, the employee had not obtained legal advice, and no release was signed.
- An employee was told to sign a letter of resignation and receive one year's pay or be fired with no pay.

Independent legal advice — Where an employee has received independent legal advice on a settlement, it may be difficult to argue that he or she has been unduly pressured into signing. However, legal advice is not always required to make a settlement valid, especially where the employee is experienced in business and negotiates his or her own terms, and where those terms are met by the employer.

Duty of disclosure — An employer owes a duty of care to its employees not to withhold vital information when discussing settlement, particularly with regard to pensions and benefits. Where an employer failed to convey highly relevant information that led an employee to choose an option which seriously decreased his pension, the employer's non-disclosure made the settlement non-binding, despite the employee having signed a release.

Unaccepted offers — Settlement offers that are not accepted can be withdrawn, and the offering party will not be bound by the offer, particularly if it is marked "without prejudice" or "draft for discussion", or other such language.

Agreements in principle — An agreement in principle may include an implied agreement to provide a simple release.

Oral acceptance — Oral acceptance of an offer may create a valid settlement, even without acceptance in writing. Even if no formal settlement has been agreed to, the existence of accord and satisfaction can bar a claim.

Breach of settlement — An employer's failure to abide by the terms of the settlement may make the settlement invalid, and may entitle the employee to sue for wrongful dismissal as well as for enforcement of the settlement. An employer's unilateral deduction of income tax from a settlement did not vary the terms of the settlement so as to make it unenforceable.

E-3.2 ACCORD AND SATISFACTION

General principle — Even if no formal settlement has been agreed to, the existence of accord and satisfaction can bar a claim. The accord is the agreement by which the obligation is discharged. The satisfaction is the consideration which makes the agreement operative. Whether or not there has been accord and satisfaction, or an implied settlement, depends on an assessment of the employee's actions.

Cheque cashing — There was no accord and satisfaction (and wrongful dismissal actions were therefore permitted) where:

- An employee merely cashed a "severance pay" cheque, there was no agreement between the parties that it would act as a release of the employee's claims, and the employee did not comment for five months.
- A cashed cheque stated "this cheque accepted in settlement of all claims" where the employee had already disputed the amount and where no letter accompanied the cheque to set out the employer's views.
- An employee resigned and cashed a severance paycheque, after being told to resign and take the money or be fired.
- "Everyone knew" that the employee was disputing the amount of her severance pay, even though she cashed the cheque.

Effect of negotiations — In one case, an employer unilaterally increased the amount of pay in lieu of notice in response to the employee's claim, but the employee never expressly or impliedly agreed to accept it in satisfaction. His claim over five years later was not barred. In another case, however, an employee tried to negotiate for more notice, but then gave up and took no action for more than three years. His conduct implied accord and satisfaction.

Pension payments — An employee, who applied for and received pension payments during the notice period, had not indicated accord and satisfaction on his wrongful dismissal claim. He was legally entitled to the pension payments, and they were separate and apart from his right to reasonable notice upon dismissal.

Examples — accord and satisfaction — There was accord and satisfaction (and the employees' actions were therefore barred) where:

- An employee was given six months' working notice with an offer of 50 per cent of the balance if she left earlier, and she left after two months and requested and cashed a cheque for two months' pay. Her request for 50 per cent indicated "unhurried and considered acceptance" of the employer's offer.
- An employee went to her employer for the purpose of negotiating an agreement. The agreement was negotiated and agreed to. It did not matter that she had not sought legal advice.
- An employee complained that he had lost out on the increased value of shares because he had sold his shares in order to accept a transfer desired by the employer. The employer then sent him a cheque for $50,000 in U.S. funds. It was held that, by cashing the cheque, he had settled any claim he might have had about the shares.

- An employee was given an extra-large salary increase in compensation for unpaid overtime. She was barred from suing for compensation for the overtime after her dismissal, because the raise was accord and satisfaction.

Salary continuation — Where an employer unilaterally continued an employee's salary after termination, there was no accord and satisfaction and the employee was not barred from suing, although the amount paid was deducted from any damages found owing.

E-3.3 RELEASES

General principle — The existence of an effective release will bar a subsequent wrongful dismissal action. A release may be invalid, however, if obtained through duress, inequality of bargaining power or other unconscionable circumstances. See the discussion under Section E-3.1, "Settlements", earlier in this chapter.

Examples — release binding — The following releases were valid:

- A release that was stated to be "in full satisfaction of all claims arising out of the termination of your employment". It was not ambiguous and included a claim for failure to give notice.
- A release that included words contemplating any "agreement or arrangement" with the employer barred further claims as to pension rights. The words were clear on their face, and evidence of the parties' discussions confirmed that the pension was covered by the release.
- A release found to have been based on fair and just treatment of the employee, where notice was reasonable and sufficient.
- A release that was signed upon the sale of a company; it released the new employer from liability under an existing written employment contract.

Examples — release not binding — Releases did not bar a subsequent action where:

- The release was signed merely to acknowledge a transfer and facilitate the employer's reorganization.
- An employee made a claim for a bonus, where the release included "all claims". It was held that the general words were limited to those things specifically in the minds of the parties when the release was signed. The release was signed before the amount of the bonus could be calculated, and therefore before it was in dispute. The surrounding circumstances made it clear that it had not been the parties' intention to deal with the bonus in the release.

- An employee was pressured to sign overnight or risk a worse deal, and was misled into thinking his termination was due to downsizing. The amount offered was "substantially unfair", and the employee's bargaining power was impaired by ignorance of his rights, his family needs and an employer whom he trusted to be fair and who was a friend upon whom he relied to get him the best deal.
- An employer substantially breached a settlement agreement. The employee's wrongful dismissal action was allowed for a higher amount, as the breached settlement no longer barred an action.
- A settlement released "all causes of action arising ... by reason of dismissal". This did not include an action against individuals for conspiracy and inducing breach of contract.

Demanding release before payment — Employers, who have refused payment of monies owing until a release has been signed, risk having the release ruled invalid due to duress or undue pressure, or risk other signs of the courts' displeasure. However, employees who obtain legal advice before signing the release are less likely to have the release overturned, or to be compensated in other ways. For example:

- An employer, who would not advance the sum offered in lieu of notice unless the employee signed a release, was penalized in costs and an order to pay prejudgment interest.
- An employer who withheld a severance payment until the delivery of a release was considered high-handed and ordered to pay an additional amount in damages.
- An employee was held to have been wrongfully dismissed for refusing to sign a release accepting a proposed settlement.
- An employer could not insist that an employee release all claims with respect to his position as an employee before the employer would honour its obligations to purchase the employee's shares.
- An employee, who had been given and had taken the opportunity to obtain legal advice before signing the release, was not under duress due to the withholding of severance pay. The release was valid.

Need for consideration — An employer must give something of value in return for a release. Where an employer did not make a release a precondition for payment but merely paid an employee in accordance with a standard company policy, and there were no negotiations as to the final amount, it was held that the release was not binding.

Effect of release on human rights claim — A release may not bar a human rights claim, depending on the circumstances. Where a release was general, it was held that the human rights legislation took precedence over the parties' contractual arrangements.

E-3.4 DELAY AND LIMITATION PERIODS

General principle — Delay within the limitation period generally will not bar a claim. This was the case where an employee's delay in bringing his action was caused by the employer implying that failure to settle his claim might harm his reputation with his new employer.

Implied abandonment of claim — The question is whether the employee's delay and other actions have led the employer to believe that the employee has abandoned his claim. A settlement was valid where the employee had obtained a new job after two months, which removed any fear of not getting a reference or being without income, yet he continued receiving payments under the settlement for eight more months before challenging the agreement.

Limitation period — It is important to make sure that an action is filed before the limitation period expires, or the action will be barred. The limitation period applying to breach of contract actions usually applies to wrongful dismissal actions. This period varies by province, and may be as short as six months or as long as six years. Some employees, such as public employees, may have special limitation periods in some jurisdictions. These periods are set by statute, and the applicable statute for the jurisdiction should be checked as soon as possible after dismissal.

Chapter E-4

WRITTEN EMPLOYMENT CONTRACTS

TABLE OF CONTENTS

E-4.1   Written Contracts: General Principles
E-4.2   Parol Evidence Rule
E-4.3   Matters of Form
E-4.4   Failure to Enter into Written Contract

E-4.1 WRITTEN CONTRACTS: GENERAL PRINCIPLES

Express agreements — The right to reasonable notice of dismissal is an implied term of employment contracts. As with any implied contractual term, however, it can be negated by an express contractual term, whether oral or written. The matters affecting wrongful dismissal that are commonly dealt with in express agreements include: the right to dismiss, with or without cause; the manner of termination; and limits on the amount of dismissal notice to be given.

Written vs. oral agreement — Written agreements are the most common express agreements affecting terms of employment. This is simply because written agreements are easier to prove. Consequently, this chapter refers mainly to written agreements. However, it should be noted that the same considerations may also apply to express oral agreements. It also should be noted that documents other than formal written contracts can also be contracts, as discussed in Chapter E-5, "Standard Form Contracts, Employers' Policies and Other Documents".

Definite-term contracts — Definite-term contracts are often reduced to writing. For issues affecting these contracts and other issues affecting indefinite and definite terms of hire, see also Chapter A-2, "Employment Status and Types of Employment Contract".

Express agreements strictly interpreted — Since express agreements usually limit the employee's common-law rights, courts tend to interpret them very strictly and will not imply a term if an express term exists. For example, in one case a strict interpretation led to the finding that while an employee was obligated under his contract to give 12 months' notice, he was not obligated to work during that period. Yet, in another case, a clause stating that the employee could be let go if he proved unsatisfactory "in the opinion" of the employer was held to mean that no warning was required, and dismissal could be purely subjective.

Ambiguous terms interpreted against drafter — Where there is more than one reasonable meaning of a contractual term, it will usually be interpreted against the party who drafted the contract; in other words, the interpretation of the person who did not write the contract will be favoured. This is also known as the principle of *contra proferentum*.

Normal contract rules apply — The normal rules of interpretation of contracts apply to express employment agreements. These include:

Offer and acceptance. There must be an offer and an acceptance before a contract will be binding. In some cases, acceptance may be implied based on a party's conduct.

Consideration. Each party must give and get something from the agreement. A wholly voluntary promise that is one-sided will not be enforceable.

Inequality of bargaining power and unconscionability. The parties should both have real input into the terms of the contract, rather than everything being dictated by one party. An unconscionable term — one that is unduly harsh or one-sided — may not be enforceable, especially if there was an inequality of bargaining power.

Duress. An agreement or a term of an agreement must not have been forced upon anyone by threats or undue pressure. Contracts must be voluntary to be valid.

Non est factum. Each party must know and understand what they are agreeing to do. Terms cannot be hidden in a contract or inserted without a party's knowledge. However, wilful ignorance may not be excusable.

Illegality. Contracts that are illegal — for example, in breach of statute or made without authority — generally will not be enforceable. In Saskatchewan, for example, *The Crown Employment Contracts Act* rescinds the terms of all written contracts relating to termination payments and leaves the employees' claims to be determined on the basis of the common law.

E-4.2 PAROL EVIDENCE RULE

Parol evidence rule defined — The parol evidence rule states that a written agreement is the final expression of the parties' agreement, and that document is not to be varied or contradicted by oral or written statements. As a result, evidence of conversations or oral reassurances cannot be used to contradict the terms of a written contract.

Exceptions — There are a number of exceptions to the rule that permit the introduction of oral evidence: whether there has been an offer and acceptance; preparation of the agreement; its execution; and the parties' intentions. Parol evidence may also be allowed if the contract's terms are ambiguous. Where there is ambiguity, it has been held appropriate to consider evidence as to the parties' intentions and reasonable expectations. Parol evidence will also be allowed where there is a claim of fraud or misrepresentation. As a result, sometimes courts will look beyond the four corners of the agreement and will not enforce its strict provisions.

Examples — parol evidence rule not invoked — Evidence of a collateral verbal agreement has been admitted where:

- Employees were assured, at the time they signed standard form contracts, that the termination clause would not apply to them.
- The employee was promised job security. An employment contract providing for dismissal on 30 days' notice was not upheld.
- A written contract was silent on the issue of termination notice. It was found on the basis of the parties' intentions that there was an implied right to reasonable notice.
- A contract resulted from misrepresentations made by the employee upon which the employer clearly relied. Evidence of the misrepresentations was permitted and the employee was not entitled to rely on the wording of the contract.
- A fixed-term contract was a "charade" for the benefit of third parties, and both parties knew the employee had been hired indefinitely. The contract was ignored.

Example — evidence of intentions not permitted — Extrinsic evidence was not permitted where an employer claimed a contract was based on certain misrepresentations made by the employee, but these representtations were not mentioned in the contract, and it had been negotiated by skilled businessmen and prepared by a lawyer. The judge did not accept that there had been any misrepresentation that made the contract invalid.

E-4.3 MATTERS OF FORM

General principles — Generally, an employment contract need not take a specific form to be enforceable. Usually, it must be signed by both parties. The person acting on behalf of the employer must be acting with proper authority, but this need not always require affixing a corporate seal or approval by the corporate board of directors, depending on the circumstances. Challenges to employment contracts on the basis of form are rare.

Onus — The onus may be on a party relying on a written contract to prove the authenticity of the contract by leading evidence about the circumstances of its signing.

Examples — contract not enforced — The following contracts were found not enforceable:

- An agreement between a group of employees with their employer about termination pay, which was only signed by the company, and not by the employees, was held to be more a series of gratuitous proposals and was not a binding contract.
- A provision in the corporate articles providing for immediate removal without cause of any officer did not take away an employee's right to reasonable notice, as he had never been appointed by directors' resolution.
- A CEO's contract that was not considered and approved by the board of directors, especially since there was no evidence that the proposed terms had ever actually been accepted by the company.
- A contract in which the president and the second director consulted no one when the president's employment contract was drawn up. The contract had no earmarks of an arm's length transaction and was not one that an independent board, acting in the best interests of the corporation, could have approved.
- A contract prepared and executed by the employer's local manager without its authority or knowledge, in a conflict of interest and clearly against company policy.

E-4.4 FAILURE TO ENTER INTO WRITTEN CONTRACT

General principle — Where parties intended to enter into a written employment contract but never did so, the terms of the agreement may still be enforceable. If there has been any detrimental reliance by the employee upon the existence of an employment contract, a defence based on failure to enter into a contemplated written contract will likely fail. The exception is where execution of a formal document has been made an essential term of the parties' agreement.

Remedy — Where the parties have agreed to enter into an agreement on a specific provision, but have not done so, a court may award damages based on a fair provision in all the circumstances, or on the basis of *quantum meruit* (i.e., on what the work deserved). For example, where:

- The parties had never agreed on a formula to be used for calculating a bonus, the court awarded a fair payment.
- The parties had agreed to negotiate severance pay, this meant they had agreed to negotiate reasonable notice. Where they had not done so, reasonable notice was to be decided by the court. (Note that, in a

similar case, the judge said his job was to decide what the parties likely would have negotiated.)
- The parties had entered into a personal services contract as a "charade" and had really agreed to indefinite employment. The employee was awarded damages on that basis.

Chapter E-5

STANDARD FORM CONTRACTS, EMPLOYERS' POLICIES AND OTHER DOCUMENTS

TABLE OF CONTENTS

E-5.1 Standard Form Contracts
E-5.2 Employers' Policies
E-5.3 Application Forms
E-5.4 Offers of Employment
E-5.5 Other Documents

E-5.1 STANDARD FORM CONTRACTS

General principles — Courts have shown reluctance to enforce standard form contracts in some cases, perhaps because of fears that they reflect an inequality of bargaining power. However, a standard form contract can be enforceable, as long as the important terms are clearly set forth and there is no undue influence, coercion or other improper behaviour. See Chapter E-4, "Written Employment Contracts".

Examples — standard form contracts not enforced — The following standard form contracts were not enforced:

- A contract that clearly did not cover the whole agreement between the parties, and that included terms contradicted by other evidence.
- A contract that was purely administrative or procedural with no real intention that it be binding.

Parts unenforceable — Clauses that were never actually agreed to by the parties, and ones that are inappropriate in the job's context, may not be enforced by the courts.

E-5.2 EMPLOYERS' POLICIES

General principles — Employers' policies can take many forms, from personnel manuals to benefit policies, from employee handbooks to more general corporate documents. They may also include a code of ethics from the employer or the relevant industry association. As with standard form contracts, courts seem to be concerned that the lack of negotiation of these "contracts" reflects an inequality of bargaining power or other unfairness to the employee. Several judges have said that a policy does not automatically form part of any contract.

Knowledge and agreement — Generally, a provision contained in a personnel manual or a company rule or by-law will not be enforceable unless the employee knew about it. Usually, the policy must be drawn to the employee's attention before he begins his employment. Courts are often reluctant to enforce policies that were unilaterally imposed on an existing employment relationship, although some cases have ruled otherwise. In that situation, evidence of agreement to be bound by the policy may be needed.

Proof of acceptance — There must be evidence that the policy was accepted by both parties as a term of the contract, and the onus of proving that is on the person seeking to rely on it. A court must examine all the surrounding circumstances, including the policy's nature, how it came into effect, how long it has existed, context, what a reasonable person would conclude and what it was reasonable to expect of the party. If a policy was not always followed, that may be evidence against its having contractual force. In some cases, however, policies have been applied without discussion of whether they were accepted by the parties as a part of their contract.

Examples — no knowledge or agreement — Policies did not become part of an employee's contract where:

- The employee never knew of them, had never received a copy of the policy manual or read it, and had signed a contract with very different terms in which the policy manual was not mentioned.
- A new policy was presented without any request that the employee read it, and the employer never indicated that it relied on the policy as part of the employee's contract.
- A copy of the policy was not provided to the employee. There was no evidence that the parties had adopted the policy to govern their relationship. There was no signed acknowledgment that the employee would be bound by the policy and there was no evidence that the documents were ever discussed with the employee.
- A policy handbook stated clearly on its face that it applied to staff but not management. It did not apply where the employee was clearly a member of management.

Examples — policies upheld — Some policies have been given contractual force by the courts. For example:

- A policy incorporated by reference into a job offer letter.
- A policy manual had contractual force even though the employee never received a copy of it but, rather, only received amendments to it from time to time.

Employee conduct — The employee is not taken to have agreed to a term just because he or she continues in the job after becoming aware of it. However, where it is clear that the parties did agree or conducted themselves so as to show they regarded a policy statement as part of their contract, or where the employee clearly knew of the provision throughout his employment, it may be binding. This will be the case as long as it is not ambiguous or inconsistently enforced. The fact that an employee himself applies the policy as part of his job may strengthen the claim that it is part of his contract.

Examples — policies binding due to employee conduct — Policies were enforced where:

- A policy set out an employee's benefits entitlement. It was clearly intended to form part of the employment contract.
- A policy was designed to protect a commissioned employee's accounts, even though its strict application seemed capricious and unfair in the circumstances.
- The employee had a copy of the company's policy and he agreed, in a disciplinary discussion, that he would be more careful in the future.
- An employer acted at all times in accordance with a policy and all representations made to the employee reinforced that policy.

Interpretation — Policies may be strictly interpreted and may not be enforced where the language did not clearly indicate that the employer intended it to have contractual effect, even where the employee knew about and agreed to the policy. If a policy is not enforceable, a court may use it as an indication of what the parties considered reasonable. Courts are reluctant to enforce unreasonable policies, holding that breach of all policies should not necessarily result in termination.

Interplay between policy and contract — Where the terms of an individual employment contract and an employer's policy conflict, cases have gone both ways as to whether the policy takes precedence over the contract, or the contract takes precedence over the policy. For example:

- Where a contract was so stringent on its face that it was clearly unreasonable, it was interpreted in accordance with the employer's much more reasonable policy, thereby excusing the employee from not complying with the strict words of the contract.
- Where a policy conflicted with the terms negotiated with the employee, the terms in the employee's own agreement overrode the policy.

- Where one employee's contract entitled her to a specific benefit, the fact that the employer changed its policy to eliminate that benefit did not affect her entitlement, as her contract did not tie her rights to the employer's policy.

Unilateral change — Courts are especially reluctant to enforce policies that can be unilaterally changed by the employer. Also, policies imposed after the start of employment may not have contractual force or may constitute a constructive dismissal.

Policy changes after hiring — In some cases policy changes have been upheld, particularly where the employees are made aware of the change and their employment continues for long enough that it can be inferred that they accepted the change. For example, a policy manual became part of an employee's contract where she received it during her first week of work. One case held that a policy permitting future changes will only be enforceable if it clarifies how future changes will come about, or if it expressly states that the employer may change the policy for the worse. A letter confirming a promotion which stated that all policies in effect would apply to the employee did not bind him to future changes.

Standard of conduct policies — Courts may be somewhat more willing to enforce policies that detail the standard of conduct expected of an employee, even if they are imposed unilaterally on existing employment relationships, because they are more like the employer giving guidelines on job performance.

Absence of policies — The absence of policies may be significant, particularly where they affect the courts' perception of employee fairness or due process for employees. In one case, the lack of a policy against a certain practice contributed to a finding that there had been no just cause for dismissal.

Union policies — Decisions vary on whether an employee of a union is bound in his employment by the terms of the union's constitution and by-laws. One case enforced a severance pay policy adopted by membership vote. Other cases have refused to enforce claims of employment at will or complete subordination to the union executive's decisions that have been based on the constitution or by-laws. A lot seems to depend on the provision relied upon and the circumstances of its application to the employee.

Termination policies — Some cases have ruled that a termination pay policy is a contractual right enforceable by an employee or by an employer. Other cases have regarded termination policies merely as discretionary guidelines that may not be enforceable at all. As with employment contracts generally, a termination policy must be clearly worded to rebut the common-law presumption of reasonable notice.

Policy binding upon employer — Sometimes employees wish to enforce policies against employers. Since the employers generate the policies, courts usually seem more willing to enforce policies (or to interpret them broadly) where the clause is to the employee's advantage under the circumstances. This will be the case unless the policy statement or personnel manual was clearly not intended to have contractual force. However, the employee may still have to prove that he or she falls within the strict words of the policy.

Examples — policy enforced against employer — The following policies have been upheld in favour of employees:

- In one case, an employer had made a payment under its policy but had not included certain benefits that a court found should have been included. The court refused to allow the employer to argue that the notice period should have been shorter than provided by its policy, and awarded the employee damages for the benefits that should have been provided.
- Where an employer failed to follow its own rules for dismissal, as set out in its policy manual, the dismissal was held to be in breach of the employee's implied contractual terms.

Examples — policies not binding on employer — Policy-type documents that have not been upheld against employers include:

- A written document outlining early retirement options. It was held to be an information package rather than an offer that the employee could accept and enforce against the employer.
- A broad statement of company policy to avoid capricious firings, and memos saying the president was committed to job security by way of a "core staffing strategy". They were not enforceable by employees as they were not made with contractual intent, despite the use of certain words with a contractual flavour.
- An employment equity policy did not bind the employer to make job sharing available, or to find another job sharer when one quit.
- A termination policy negotiated with the employer by a group of non-unionized employees. The employer signed a document acknowledging the policy but the employees did not sign it. It was held that there was no enforceable contract against the employer's receiver or trustee in bankruptcy.

E-5.3 APPLICATION FORMS

General principle — A limit on an employee's common-law rights which appears in an application form may not be enforceable. It may be unconscionable in that the employee's attention was never drawn to it and he never truly consented to it, or it may simply lack contractual force, since no contract is in existence at the application stage.

Examples — A limit on the right to reasonable notice or amount of reasonable notice was not enforceable where:

- An application form was signed after the employee had already started work, and the limitation was never read by the employee or drawn to his attention.
- A term in an application form conflicted with the terms of an individual letter offering employment, particularly where the application was signed after the employee had received the job offer.

E-5.4 OFFERS OF EMPLOYMENT

General principle — A letter offering employment or setting out terms and conditions of employment may in some cases amount to an enforceable agreement, even if it does not describe itself as a contract or require the employee's signature in acceptance. See also Chapter E-4, "Written Employment Contracts".

Examples — contract upheld — For example, it has been held that:

- Where an employer's separation policy was incorporated by reference into an employment offer, it became a contractual term.
- A letter sent upon hiring which stated an employee's hours of work created an enforceable contract. The employer could only change the hours of work upon agreement or with reasonable notice.
- Where the parties had exchanged letters offering and accepting the job, these letters formed a contract. A different written contract signed by the employee on his first day of work was not effective because the essential terms of his contract had already been set and there had been no new consideration.

Parties' intentions — The intentions of the parties may govern. A written document will not necessarily preclude a court from considering parol evidence of the parties' discussions. See also Chapter E-4, "Written Employment Contracts".

Parties' conduct — The parties' conduct can affect the court's finding on whether the parties had an enforceable agreement. For example:

- Where an employee did not agree with the terms of employment set out in a letter written by the employer, it was incumbent on him to say so. Where he remained silent, he was held to have agreed to the terms. An employer has also been held to have agreed to terms where it did not communicate its intention to the contrary. However, a letter signed by an employee confirming a specific agreement was not enforced, even

though the employee had not voiced his disagreement with it. The letter had not been intended to be an employment contract and was overruled by the parties' oral agreement.
- Where an employee asked for certain terms but the employer then sent a letter of offer setting out different terms and made it clear it would not agree to the employee's terms, the employee accepted the employer's terms by accepting the job.
- Where an employee himself wrote a letter confirming the parties' agreement, he was bound by the letter and was not allowed to allege the existence of additional agreed terms.
- Where the parties discussed a new term and the employer then sent a letter confirming the change and including another change that had not been discussed, the change that had not been agreed to was not binding on the employee.

E-5.5 OTHER DOCUMENTS

Memoranda or letters to employees — Despite the use of certain words with a contractual flavour, neither a letter sent to all employees expressing a general corporate policy to avoid capricious firings, nor memos saying the president was committed to job security by way of a "core staffing strategy", had contractual force.

Draft contract — A draft contract prepared but never signed likely will not be enforceable in the absence of other evidence that one party accepted the other's terms. See also Chapter E-4, "Written Employment Contracts".

Exchange of legal correspondence — When an employee's solicitor protested a proposed change in the terms of employment, the employer agreed not to change the terms and confirmed this by letter. The letter amounted to an enforceable contract that the terms would not be changed in the future without agreement or reasonable notice.

Employer brochure — A provision in a brochure about an employer could not be used to impose an obligation on the employer by an employee who was hired without reliance on the brochure. On the other hand, limits may be enforceable where the employee clearly knew of the term or had ample opportunity to read it. The fact that employment is only available on those terms does not constitute undue pressure.

Corporate or organizational documents — Courts may be reluctant to enforce other corporate or organizational documents against employees. For example:

- An employee and officer was not bound by a provision in the corporate articles providing for immediate removal without cause of any officer, since he had never been appointed by directors' resolution.
- A unilaterally adopted by-law did not apply to an employee where there was no evidence that it ever became part of his contract.

Shareholder agreements — Where an employee is also a shareholder and has signed a shareholder's agreement, its terms as they relate to employment may create an enforceable employment contract, unless it is clear that the agreement is not intended to affect the employment relationship. See also Chapter A-4, "Dismissal Rights of Specific Types of Workers".

Sales documents — Where a commissioned sales agent did not have an employment contract but had been told that trade record sheets filed on each sale would form her contract, a unilateral change to the form of trade record sheet was not binding on her. Another commissioned salesman was entitled to a standard commission of 10 per cent when the employer sent a letter agreeing to pay a commission "not to exceed 10%" and did not communicate its intention to pay any less.

Transfer agreement — Where an employee accepted an overseas transfer for a specific project and signed an agreement in connection with the transfer, the cancellation of his appointment did not amount to termination of his employment. The underlying employment contract remained in force.

Training agreement — A training program agreement did not terminate the employment upon its conclusion where it did not specifically address the subject of termination.

Indemnity agreement — An indemnity agreement failed to protect an employee who engaged in a fraudulent scheme at the request of her supervisor, as there had been no consideration for the indemnity and as there would be no need to invoke it but for the fraud. The employer was not responsible for the supervisor's fraud. Conversely, a letter agreement promising to make an employee whole, containing the president's personal guarantee, for an employee who gave up share options to save the employer from embarrassment, was enforceable. It was not void for lack of consideration, as the employee gave consideration by forbearing to sue to enforce the employment contract, and the agreement was not a financial assistance provision forbidden by the *British Columbia Company Act*, and so was not illegal.

Retirement documents — Where an agreement providing for a retirement allowance was said to supersede all other clauses, the clause providing for a limit to the employer's cost, which would have applied had the employee retired before he was 65, did not apply when the employer asked him to stay beyond the age of 65. It was held that the employee's retirement was within the employer's control. In another case, a "bridging agreement" designed to cover the four-year period between an employee's early retirement and the retirement age of 55 limited the employee's long-term benefits claim to the amount payable under the bridging or severance agreement. He was not entitled to a calculation based on the salary he was earning before entering into the agreement. Where a pension bridging offer was based on a mutual misunderstanding as to the amount of money involved, the employer was entitled to pay the correct, lower amount. Where an agreement merely provided for the terms of a pension to be agreed upon, and this was not done, it was unenforceable because it was too vague.

Voluntary retirement agreement — An agreement to voluntary retirement forms part of the employment relationship and has to be considered in light of that relationship. For example, an agreement providing for an extra payment upon retirement in exchange for an agreement not to compete was evaluated as if it were a restrictive covenant in an employment contract, even though it was tied to a retirement benefit.

Chapter E-6

EXPRESS TERMINATION PROVISIONS

TABLE OF CONTENTS

E-6.1   Expiry and Extension of Fixed-Term Contracts
E-6.2   Effect of Promotions or Lapse of Time
E-6.3   Severance Clauses vs. Termination Clauses
E-6.4   Termination Agreements

E-6.1 EXPIRY AND EXTENSION OF FIXED-TERM CONTRACTS

Extension of contract — A fixed-term contract can:
(1) cease at the end of the fixed term, along with employment ceasing;
(2) be orally extended on the same or amended terms, and the extension will be effective even where the parties did not confirm it in writing before the employee was terminated; or
(3) be renewed impliedly.

A contract was found to be renewed impliedly in the case of a teacher who ordered supplies for the following year, was paid after his first contract had expired and whose employer knew he was in the classroom continuing to prepare for the coming year. The employer was held to have acquiesced in the renewal.

Expiration with continued employment — Case law differs as to the effect of employment continuing after a fixed term ends. In most cases, the contract will no longer be in force and none of its terms will continue except those confirmed by the parties' conduct. However, in other cases, it has been held that in the absence of a specific or clearly implied provision in the contract, all provisions of the written contract, save the provision as to the term, continue to govern the employment relationship. Once the fixed term expires, the employment becomes indefinite, and the employee becomes entitled to reasonable notice of dismissal.

Notice where employment continues — The effect of continued employment after expiry of a fixed term varies:

- In some cases, an intended renewal term of a contract that was never signed may be considered as a factor affecting reasonable notice.

- An employee who was paid for the termination of a written commission agency agreement but then worked several more years without a written agreement was entitled to reasonable notice based on his entire service with the employer. The earlier payment had related only to the terms of the agreement and had not been related to the employee's years of service or to pay in lieu of notice.

Series of contracts — Where the last in a series of similar written contracts was never signed by the employee, its terms were not enforceable against him. In another case, however, the existence of offer and acceptance was enough to create an enforceable contract, even without execution of the document.

Contractual changes during renewal — Contractual changes during contract renewals may be subject to suspicion, especially where they are imposed on long-term relationships and are concluded shortly before termination. For instance:

- Where a term in the original contract appeared only in a more limited way in a later contract, the employer could not rely on the original term, as it no longer applied.
- A written contract was not enforceable to limit the term of the employment to one year where it was one of a series of annual contracts, some of which were never executed and some of which were presented and signed while the employee was in the midst of teaching a class, and where the employee was led to believe the relationship was one with an indefinite term.

Automatic renewal clause — Where a contract stated that it automatically renewed for a second five-year term unless at least six months' notice was given, notice to terminate the contract was given by the employee's wrongful dismissal within the first five-year term. The employer was liable for damages only for the balance of the first five-year term.

E-6.2 EFFECT OF PROMOTIONS OR LAPSE OF TIME

Time — The mere passage of time may not be enough to make a contractual limit on notice unenforceable. However, if the nature of the employment or the position has changed drastically since the contract was signed, such that the substratum of the contract has disappeared, the contractual limit may no longer apply.

Promotions — Similar results are found where there have been one or more promotions after the contract was signed. In some cases the contract has been upheld notwithstanding the promotion and in some cases it has not.

Examples — contract overturned — Contracts were not enforceable where:

- An employee signed an agreement, which, after six years, while primarily concerned with maintaining confidentiality, also provided for dismissal upon three days' notice. Eighteen years later he was dismissed without any notice. The trial judge felt that the notice part of the contract was not really agreed to by the employee, and overturned it, awarding the employee reasonable notice of dismissal.
- An employee's contract had become out of date due to the passage of time and successive promotions. However, the employer told him there was no need to prepare a new contract, the contract was not part of his personnel file, and it was never mentioned when the employee was dismissed. In these circumstances, it was held that the parties had treated the contract as being at an end; it was no longer binding

Examples — contract upheld — Contracts were upheld where:

- An employee was fired after seven years and several promotions. The contract he had signed when he first began his employment, which limited his notice to four weeks, was enforced, because the term was standard to all the employer's contracts. The employer was a manager who was required to be familiar with the employment manual and therefore he could not claim that the clause had escaped his attention.
- The employee had signed a contract which contemplated promotion, so that it could not be said there had been such fundamental changes as to remove the entire substratum of the contract. Furthermore, the termination clause was not objectively unconscionable at the time of signing or at termination.
- The employee had signed a new contract every year and with every promotion.
- The employee held the same position throughout his employment and the mere passage of time did not remove the entire substratum of the contract.
- The employee had been transferred from Ontario to Vancouver. The basis of the contract had not been lost in the transfer.

E-6.3 SEVERANCE CLAUSES VS. TERMINATION CLAUSES

Definition — While a termination clause provides for notice to the employee or payment in lieu of notice, severance clauses are designed to provide an employee with a fixed payment upon termination. As a result, there is no express or implied duty on the employee to mitigate his damages. See Chapter H-1, "Mitigation of Damages". It should be noted that the terms "termination clause" and "severance clause" are often used interchangeably.

Differences — Where a clause was specifically negotiated as a genuine pre-estimation of damages, or where it was part of a severance policy applying to all employees, the courts may not imply limits on the employee's right to the specified notice. The question is whether the agreement was for a set amount of notice, or for a set amount of pay. Earnings in mitigation may be deducted where termination clauses, but not where the clause is deemed a severance clause, unless the agreement specifically states a duty to mitigate.

Examples — severance pay granted — An employee was entitled to severance pay where:

- The employer had offered and the employee had accepted six months' working notice plus one month's pay. When the employee resigned four months into the working notice, he had forfeited the right to compensation for the rest of the working notice period but was still entitled to the one month's pay which was not tied to working.
- A clause provided for a set severance payment upon termination "for any reason". It was held to apply to a wrongful dismissal. The employer was not entitled to restrict the employee to his common-law rights.

E-6.4 TERMINATION AGREEMENTS

Definition — A termination agreement or severance agreement is entered into upon termination, and often settles a potential claim at the time of dismissal or another time prior to legal proceedings being started. These agreements are interpreted much like any other contract or settlement.

Separate contract — A severance or termination agreement is a separate contract, not merely an extension of an existing employment contract. For example:

- Where a severance agreement did not provide for termination for just cause, the employer could not terminate it for cause based on a just cause provision in the employment contract.
- An employer who entered into an agreement that differed from the terms of a collective agreement could be sued on the agreement, as it was arguable that it was separate and independent from the collective agreement.
- A party to a termination agreement did not remain an employee so as to be entitled to statutory termination pay or long-term disability payments.

Examples — termination agreements upheld — Termination agreements have bound the parties where:

- The agreement was negotiated with the employer's president, as the president had ostensible authority despite the fact the employer was a subsidiary of another company.
- The owner was acting within the scope of his authority on behalf of the corporation.
- There was no mistake, but rather a deliberate offer based on incorrect information. The employer was held to the higher amount it had offered and the employees had accepted.
- An employee entered into a severance agreement and became disabled. He was only entitled to long-term disability payments based on the amounts due to him under the agreement, not his salary at the time the agreement was entered into. He was more sophisticated than management in these matters and should have drafted his severance agreement differently if he wanted the calculation to be based on the higher amount.
- An unusual shareholder agreement provided for salary continuation payments pending a wrongful dismissal determination, with the amount to be deducted from the repurchase price of the shares. It was enforced, as it was sufficiently clear, despite the employer's argument that it was only intended to apply if the shares' value was greater than the amount of salary continuation.

Examples — termination agreements overturned — Agreements were not upheld where:

- The agreement was the product of a casual discussion with the president, and the employee knew an agreement would have to be authorized by the board of directors, which was never done.
- A contractual term was obtained by virtue of the employee's fraudulent misrepresentation or the employer's unilateral mistake; it was also said that an employee has a duty to disclose material information, even when it relates to his termination.
- An employer offered two severance packages in a mass termination situation, one for non-union and one for union employees. An employee who was wrongly treated as a union employee was entitled to the more generous non-union package.

Duty to disclose job prospects — Failing a specific term, a termination agreement does not include a general duty to disclose developments in an employee's job search. There was no duty to disclose where:

- A termination agreement was being negotiated, even where the employee had already been offered and accepted a new job.
- A former employee began a competing business within the term of the termination agreement.

Examples — duty to disclose — A duty to disclose was found where:

- An agreement provided for payments to continue only until the employee became re-employed or relocated into a new position. He was obligated to disclose his work as a consultant and was ordered to repay the former employer for amounts paid after he began working as a consultant.
- An employee breached his contractual duty to advise the employer of his new employment. He was held liable to repay the employer.

Payment issues — Where a settlement provided for reimbursement of out-of-pocket expenses, with no mention of a deduction for income tax, the entire amount was to be paid to the employee and the income tax liability was to be borne by the employer. Payment of a lump sum instead of periodic payments was a breach of contract; furthermore, where the agreement required payment of a certain amount into an RRSP, the employer could not decrease the amount because the terms of its RRSP plan did not allow such a high contribution.

Employment standards — A severance agreement that does not provide for payment of the employment standards minimum will generally be void for non-compliance with the statute. In one case, an employee signed a termination agreement providing for 15 months' pay, including *Employment Standards Act* requirements, but later claimed that he was entitled to the statutory amounts in addition to the 15 months. His action for the greater payment was dismissed. He knew the employer regarded the settlement amount as including the statutory amount when he signed the agreement. If he was in doubt about the agreement's meaning, it was up to him to check with the employer before signing it.

Chapter F-1

REASONABLE NOTICE: GENERAL PRINCIPLES

TABLE OF CONTENTS

F-1.1   The Parties' Obligations
F-1.2   Purpose of Notice Period
F-1.3   Time for Assessing Reasonable Notice
F-1.4   Factors Affecting Reasonable Notice
F-1.5   Effect of Parties' Expectations
F-1.6   Minimums, Maximums and Formulas
F-1.7   Who Decides the Notice Period: Employer, Judge or Appeal Court?

F-1.1 THE PARTIES' OBLIGATIONS

Reasonable notice required — In a case of indefinite hiring, where there is no express limit on the notice to be provided, there is an implied term that the employee is entitled to reasonable notice of dismissal. The only exception is when the employee's behaviour has given the employer just cause for terminating the contract, in which case the employee may be dismissed without any notice. Even where termination is necessary from a business point of view, there is no right to dismiss without notice. All employers are subject to this rule, including non-profit organizations.

Pay in lieu of notice — The employer's actual obligation is to give reasonable notice and continue to employ the worker until the end of that period. However, few employers want to continue to employ a worker during a lengthy notice period, so most dismiss without notice but pay damages equal to having kept the employee on during the notice period. An employer can also meet its obligations with a combination of working notice and pay in lieu.

Choice of working notice or pay in lieu — It is up to the employer, not the employee, to decide whether an employee works through the notice period or is paid in lieu. An employee does not have the right to withdraw his services and demand pay in lieu instead of working notice. The only exception may be where it is unreasonable to expect an employee to work through the notice period for a particular reason.

Employee's notice — An employee is also obligated to give the employer reasonable notice of resignation, to allow the employer to find a replacement. An employee who terminates the employment without reasonable notice can be held liable for damages, if the employer can show it suffered damages.

F-1.2 PURPOSE OF NOTICE PERIOD

Purpose of notice — The purpose of the notice period is to give the employee time to look for a comparable job. One judge has described the notice period as "... 'the length of time reasonably required to disengage oneself from the employment' and set up again elsewhere" (*Tannahill v. North Battleford (City)* (1989), 72 Sask. R. 302 at 306 (Q.B.)).

Purpose of court award — The goal of a court award for reasonable notice is to put the employee in the same position he or she would have been in if the employer had honoured the contract by giving working notice. Liability is limited to the damages which would be incurred within the period of reasonable notice. An employer has a right to terminate employment and is not required to subsidize the full period of unemployment.

Notice based on estimate — To properly compensate the employee, the notice period must be an estimate of the time it will take the employee to obtain a similar job with similar pay in the same geographical area. The fact that the employee could more quickly find a different type of job, or a job with lower pay, or even the same type of job in a different location, will usually be irrelevant. The purpose of the notice period is not to guarantee the finding of new employment, however, so the actual time necessary to find a new job is not always the same as the length of reasonable notice.

F-1.3 TIME FOR ASSESSING REASONABLE NOTICE

Views upon hiring irrelevant — The amount of notice that is "reasonable" normally depends on the circumstances at the time of dismissal, not on what the parties would have agreed to at the time of hiring. The exception is where the parties have expressly agreed to a length of notice, or there are other clearly-understood factors in operation, as discussed later under Section F-1.5, "Effect of Parties' Expectations".

Notice fixed upon termination — The period of reasonable notice is a question of law, not fact, and is fixed at the time of contract breach. Thus, the notice period should be based on the employee's re-employment prospects as of the time of termination. Where it is known that there is a strong prospect of a new job, judges have disagreed on whether this should be considered in assessing notice. A planned end to the employment, such as a planned resignation or retirement, has been said to be a proper consideration in setting the notice period. Similarly, an anticipated absence without pay during the notice period was subtracted from a notice period award.

Post-termination events — Events occurring after termination may affect the assessment of damages, but should not affect the notice period itself. For instance, a progressive illness that was not diagnosed until after dismissal was not a proper factor to consider in setting the employee's notice period.

Where re-employed before trial — In many cases, the actual time needed to find other work is known by the time the case is tried; but it should not affect the judge's decision, since the judge should make a decision as of the termination date, without the benefit of hindsight. The time taken to find a new job may be used as evidence of the re-employment market for a person with those qualifications, but the notice period will not necessarily be as long as the full period of unemployment. The notice period may actually be longer than the time taken to find a new job, particularly where the new job is lower paying, less desirable or farther away. In reality, the actual time needed to find a new job does seem to influence many judges, given the number of cases where the two periods of time are remarkably similar.

Cutting off notice period — Some judges purposely cut off the notice period when an employee becomes re-employed. However, this would seem to be improper in law, since the new employment should be regarded as a matter of mitigation, not notice.

F-1.4 FACTORS AFFECTING REASONABLE NOTICE

Individual decision — The amount of notice which is reasonable will vary from case to case, and the decision must be made individually, based on all the circumstances of the employment and the employee. The classic statement appears in *Bardal v. Globe & Mail Ltd.*, [1960] O.W.N. 253 (H.C.):

> There [can] be no catalogue laid down as to what [is] reasonable notice in particular classes of cases. The reasonableness of the notice must be decided with reference to each particular case, having regard to the character of the employment, the length of service of the servant, the age of the servant and the availability of similar employment, having regard to the experience, training and qualifications of the servant.

These factors remain the most important in setting the notice period, likely because they all relate directly or indirectly to the chances of re-employment. Many judges now accept that there may be a "range of reasonableness" rather than one right answer. This issue is one of the most difficult and most frequently litigated of all wrongful dismissal issues because the assessment of reasonable notice is so individualized.

Other factors — The *Bardal* factors are not exhaustive and a number of other factors have been identified. Most relate to the expected ease or lack of ease with which the employee will be able to find equivalent work. An employer's bad faith has also been identified as an important factor, even if it does not directly affect the employee's future employment prospects, as discussed in Chapter F-5, "Effect of Parties' Conduct on Reasonable Notice".

Quebec approach — In Quebec, at least one case has said there is no "wrongful" element involved in an action for dismissal without cause, so notice periods tend to be shorter. However, the purpose of notice is the same — to allow the employee time to find a new job without suffering financial loss. Quebec courts consider factors similar to those considered in the rest of Canada, including age, status of position, length of service, salary, and the time required to find new work. Recent court awards also seem to be similar to the rest of Canada in the length of notice required.

F-1.5 EFFECT OF PARTIES' EXPECTATIONS

Influential factor — The parties' expectations about the length of notice have often been given weight in setting the notice period. Sometimes the parties, especially the employee, have expectations about the job itself — for example, expectations of job security or the length of employment. These are discussed in Chapter F-3, "Reasonable Notice Factors: Age and Service Length".

Amount claimed by employee — In one case, the amount claimed by an employee was regarded as evidence of what he regarded as reasonable, although it was not binding. However, where an employee stated his claim without having received legal advice, it was given little weight.

Notice upon resignation — The amount of resignation notice to be given by the employee to the employer may be considered, although resignation notice is usually shorter than dismissal notice, so it may not be binding. Where an employee gave notice of resignation in response to a constructive dismissal, it did not limit the amount of notice to which he was entitled for that constructive dismissal.

Planned departure — The fact that an employee had planned to resign or retire in several months' time may limit his notice to that amount of time, although not all cases have limited notice. Where there was no policy of retirement at age 65 and there had been no indication by the employee that he intended to retire, a cap on damages was refused. The fact that an employee has given notice of resignation does not entitle the employer to terminate earlier with only the minimum notice required by employment standards law.

Previous notice period — An employee who had been given a one-year period of working notice, and then was constructively dismissed one month into the year, was awarded the balance of the one-year notice period, presumably on the basis that the parties had treated this notice period as reasonable. The fact that an employee had been entitled to a certain amount of notice at his previous job, which was known to the employer, was considered in one case.

Third-party notice — The fact that the employer, a management company, was itself entitled to three months' notice of termination of its contract was considered in setting the employee's notice period.

Length of probation — In one case, the length of an initial probationary period was used as an indicator of a reasonable notice period, even more than seven years later. When an employee is dismissed during an initial probationary period, the length of the probationary period may or may not affect the employee's notice period, as discussed in Chapter A-3, "Probationary Employment".

Contracts — Normally, a valid contractual limit on notice will be upheld. Where the contract has expired or is otherwise invalid, its terms may still be considered as indicating an intention about the range of notice that the employee should receive. Where a contractual limit on notice had expired, the judge said that it was up to the employer to bargain for a limit on notice if it wanted one; since it had not done so, full reasonable notice was awarded.

Collective agreement — The notice period in a collective agreement, which would have applied to the employee if his employment had continued, was a factor in limiting his notice. The notice period in a collective agreement that did not apply to the employee in question was disregarded in one case; in another case, the judge said that the non-bargaining unit employee should receive at least as much notice as the bargaining unit employees.

Non-competition agreement — Some judges have treated the length of a restrictive covenant or non-competition agreement as a relevant factor in setting notice.

Employer's policy — The notice period in an employee handbook, of which the employee was clearly aware, can influence or even limit the notice awarded by a court. Whether an employer's policy is enforceable against the employer or the employee is discussed in detail in Chapter E-5, "Standard Form Contracts, Employers' Policies and Other Documents".

Employer's other judgments — The British Columbia Court of Appeal has said that where several judgments are pronounced against the same employer around the same time, the reasonable notice period for each employee should reflect a fair comparison between them. An award in another case involving the same employer, however, was not a proper consideration where it arose in another province because the conditions in that province might be quite different, and there might also be variations among some courts as to the proper factors to consider.

Employer's other settlements — Some judges have said that the settlements reached by the employer with other employees are irrelevant, however, other judges have said that the notice provided to other employees may be a factor to consider. The amount of notice offered to an employee in a previous buyout offer to all employees was used as the basis of an award in one case, with an additional amount of notice added to reflect his additional three years' service since the offer. The amount of pay under a voluntary separation plan that became available four months after an employee's dismissal was not considered, as it was not available at the time of his termination.

Industry custom — Since reasonable notice is based on the implied understanding between the parties, it is reasonable that industry custom should be taken into account, as long as no express agreement exists. "Custom" implies a usage so general and well-understood that the parties are presumed to have intended it. The custom must also be reasonable. The onus is on the employer to prove that the custom is so certain, notorious and reasonable within the industry that the employee is deemed to know about it.

Illegality of custom — It has been said that custom cannot be established by a past improper practice. The fact that an industry was exempt from statutory notice requirements was evidence of legislative support for the industry's custom of dismissing without notice.

Financial circumstances important — A custom which may be reasonable in normal economic circumstances may be unreasonable where other employment is scarce due to the state of the economy, and a longer notice period may then be justified.

Custom applied — Custom has been used successfully to decrease the notice period in several older cases, and in a few more recent cases involving: the construction industry, a project-based consulting engineering company, a professional sports team, and a commissioned salesman for a new home builder.

Custom not applied — An argument of industry custom has been unsuccessful in many other cases, and one decision has declared that custom is not binding on the courts in setting reasonable notice. The difference between these cases seems to turn on the employee's knowledge of the industry custom, and hence on the implied understanding between the parties. One recent case stated that it considered it an industry standard to dismiss with the statutory minimum of severance pay; however, the judge still awarded 12 months' notice to the long-service employee.

Other industry awards in area — The notice awarded to similar employees in the geographic area may be an important consideration, presumably because it would affect the parties' expectations. Even where the awards do not involve the same employer, a similar employer and employee in the same geographic area may be used as a comparator.

F-1.6 MINIMUMS, MAXIMUMS AND FORMULAS

Minimum notice — The idea of a minimum amount of notice has been suggested a number of times, but has not received general favour among judges. The statutory minimum in each province thus remains the only recognized minimum amount of notice.

Effect of statutory period — There is disagreement about the effect, if any, of the notice periods required by employment standards laws. Most statutes state that their standards are a minimum only, and that employees' civil rights are preserved. Thus, a number of cases have rejected the idea that the amount of notice required by statute is reasonable under the common law, even in the case of low-level employees. However, a few cases have considered the amount of statutory notice to be one factor influencing the common-law notice period. A few others have ruled that in some cases of short-term or low-level employees, the amount of notice required by statute may also be reasonable under the common law. Still others appear to accept that low-level employees may only be entitled to the statutory amount of notice, but distinguish their cases on the basis of facts such as higher responsibility levels or salaries, long service or the employee's age.

Maximum notice — Most judges agree that there is no absolute maximum period of reasonable notice. However, many have cited a rough upper limit of 18 to 24 months unless there are exceptional circumstances, since there is a cap of reasonableness even if there is no chance of re-employment. Others have expressed discomfort with a limit that high, calling such lengthy notice periods "inflated" and "excessive". At least one case has stated that the trend is toward "moderate" awards.

Notice formulas — Judges have long searched for an easy, mathematical formula based on service length or a combination of service length and the job's character. Many judges have mentioned a rough guideline of one month per year of service, at least for middle managers, or at least for middle managers with years of service in or near the double digits. Some judges have suggested a formula of two to three weeks per year of service for non-managerial or lower-managerial employees. However, other judges have rejected the idea of a simplistic formula, since much depends on service length, age, status of the employment, and many other factors. Some judges use a formula, such as one month per year of service, as a preliminary estimate of the notice period, and then adjust based on additional factors.

F-1.7 WHO DECIDES THE NOTICE PERIOD: EMPLOYER, JUDGE OR APPEAL COURT?

Employer in the ballpark? — Many judges have said that courts should first consider whether the employer's severance arrangements were fair. If the notice or pay in lieu was within a reasonable range, the court should not second-guess the employer's assessment. Similarly, where an employer has made an offer at the high end of the range, the court may award the amount of the employer's offer. This approach would encourage employers to make reasonable offers and encourage employees to accept them, and add some needed certainty to the end of employment. However, one judge has cautioned that this "ballpark" doctrine should not be used to justify deliberately bottom-edge offers. Of course, if an offer is outside the range, a judge will ignore it and set the notice period in court.

No deference to employer — Some judges are uneasy with this approach, or with the idea of putting the onus on the employee to prove that the employer's offer was unreasonable. Others deny it altogether, stating that there is no rule of deference to the employer's decision on notice. The judge is in as good a position as the employer to assess the factors affecting notice. Therefore, nothing prevents the court from overturning the employer's decision on the notice period. Other judges have said that, even if there is a range of reasonableness, there is no justification for permitting the employer to choose the point within that range which is appropriate.

No deference in circumstances — One judge refused to apply the "ballpark" approach where the employer offered a reasonable severance package but paid only a smaller, clearly unreasonable amount when the employee refused to accept the package.

Deference on appeal — Many appeal judges have declined to "tinker" with trial judges' awards where they are at one end or even slightly outside the range of reasonableness. Others have said a trial award should stand unless there was an error in principle, a wrong test was used or the award is outside the range of reasonableness. An appeal judge will often refuse to interfere with a trial judge's assessment of proper notice because it is said that the trial judge is in the best position to evaluate the human aspects of the case. Similarly, it has been said that as long as a jury was given proper instructions, its award should not be varied on appeal unless it is inordinately high.

No deference on appeal — Other appeal judges, however, have insisted that the trial award must be right or it will be varied on appeal.

Chapter F-2

REASONABLE NOTICE FACTORS: CHARACTER OF THE EMPLOYMENT

TABLE OF CONTENTS

F-2.1   Significance of Job Character
F-2.2   Job Status
F-2.3   Degree of Specialization
F-2.4   Nature of Job
F-2.5   Nature of Industry and Employer
F-2.6   Where Job Precarious
F-2.7   Time of Assessing Job Status

F-2.1 SIGNIFICANCE OF JOB CHARACTER

Traditionally important — Job character has traditionally been a major consideration in setting a dismissed employee's reasonable notice period. Judges have typically considered a job's level, and degree of specialization, and the industry's nature and size, and have tried to award notice periods that accord with the employee's place in the employer's hierarchy.

Weight given to job status — Recently, some judges have stressed that courts should not make minute distinctions between the importance of various employment functions. Even a distinction based on the supervisory duties of some professionals as opposed to others may be too fine a difference. Although some have rejected the emphasis on a job status "caste system" that reserves the highest amount for the most important employee, other judges have affirmed the traditional approach. Still others have said that while there is a hierarchy based on job status, it can be outweighed by other factors in an individual case, such as service length, age or the availability of similar employment.

Actual duties vs. job title — A court will look at the employee's actual duties to determine the character of the employment. Most judges have said that the court need not be bound by the job title given by the parties, although a few have said the parties should be held to their characterization of the job.

Employment status — Considerations of job status can also include a worker's employment status. Independent contractors, assignment employees and workers of an "intermediate status" may be entitled to somewhat less notice than regular, full-time employees. See the discussion in Chapter A-4, "Dismissal Rights of Specific Types of Workers".

Part-time employees — Some cases have ruled that a part-time employee may be entitled to less notice than a full-time employee. Others treat part-time employees the same as full-time employees but simply base damages on their shorter hours. One employee, who was part-time for part of his employment, was awarded less than he would have received if all his service had been full-time, although this approach is not common.

Change in employment status — Part-time or temporary employees, who had previously been permanent and whose status had been changed by the employer shortly before termination, have not been treated like employees who were always part-time or temporary. Similarly, the fact that an employee had previously been an independent contractor did not affect her notice when she was a permanent employee at the time of termination. Where an employer creates expectations of long employment or changes an employee's status without clearly advising that reasonable notice rights will be affected, judges may refuse to shorten the notice period. One employee whose status had changed back and forth from permanent to contract employee, depending on the employer's tax purposes, was treated the same as a permanent employee, since he was doing essential work in a senior position.

F-2.2 JOB STATUS

Higher level gets more notice — Generally, a senior, high-level or management employee will be entitled to a longer notice period than a junior, non-managerial employee. Similarly, an employee in a highly skilled, technically demanding position will usually be entitled to more notice than one in a semi-skilled job. This is sometimes expressed by asking whether or not the employee held a key position with the employer. Any position in management may make re-employment more difficult, as it may lead future employers to consider the employee unsuitable for non-management positions. This factor can, however, be offset by length of service and age in some cases.

Hierarchy questioned — Some judges have argued that fine distinctions between senior executives and middle managers, or even between managers and non-managers, are not that important. It is not always more difficult for a senior-level employee to find new work, so the facts of each case should govern the length of notice. For example, one judge has said that re-employment may actually be more difficult for a foreman than for a senior executive, because the foreman may lack the mobility and contacts that the executive has. There is not necessarily more stigma for a senior manager who is dismissed than for anyone else; nor is it necessarily easier to find a job at a lower level, especially in modern job markets. Other judges disagree, however, and even those who say fine distinctions are not called for often use them to award notice periods in keeping with the employer's hierarchy.

Supervisory duties, management functions — While some judges treat supervisory duties as being significant, others have stated that supervisory duties alone do not make people part of the management team or entitle them to special consideration. Participation in management groups and decisions, and the perceptions of others, are other factors leading to a finding that an employee was a manager. Even where an employee was part of management, the fact that he had no supervisory duties, no input into policy decisions, or only limited managerial responsibilities tends to decrease notice. The fact that a manager worked in a very small office with few employees to supervise offset the fact of management status in one case. In other cases, however, managers have been given increased notice even where supervisory duties or other typical management functions were not part of their jobs.

Non-management employees — Some judges treat non-management status as a factor restricting notice, but others stress the responsible nature of a position in setting the notice period. The fact that a position is not managerial or supervisory can still be offset by the job's specialization or other factors making re-employment difficult. A few judges have said that a minimally-skilled position calls for no more than the minimum notice required by statute, but others have said that notice should be assessed on the usual factors. Where an employee has more than minimal skills, service or pay, chances are that he or she will be entitled to more than minimal notice, since employment standards laws set minimums only.

Probationary employees — Probationary employees may be entitled to less notice than short-term permanent employees. But a new employee who was not hired on a probationary basis was entitled to full reasonable notice, even where the contract was breached before employment started. An employee hired on a probationary basis, and who was terminated before starting work, was entitled to damages for the full probationary period. An employee dismissed during a probationary period for reasons unrelated to her performance was awarded full reasonable notice. While damages for probationary employees may be smaller because of the short term of employment, the fact that the employee has given up other job-finding opportunities must be weighed against that fact.

Seasonal employees — Some judges have said that the fact of seasonal employment shortens notice; others have said that the time remaining until the start of the next season is an important factor, which may actually lengthen notice, depending on the circumstances. One season seems to be a fairly common measure of the notice period for a seasonal employee.

F-2.3 DEGREE OF SPECIALIZATION

Specialization — Usually, the fact that an employee is in a highly-specialized or unique position is thought to increase the length of notice — especially where there are no other comparable jobs in Canada, or there is a shrinking demand for the specialty. Where an employee has been able to translate specialized experience into success in a new area, however, the lack of similar work will be less significant.

Lack of specialization — A lack of specialization may decrease notice, since there may be a broader job market open to the employee, although in one case a judge seemed to increase the notice period due to the employee's experience as an all-around employee performing whatever task was needed. In several cases, the fact that the employee had become a generalist and would no longer possess the specialized skills he had been trained in justified a lengthy notice period. The fact that an employee had not been a manager for long and still had invaluable, specialized, practical skills decreased the notice period.

Long-term sales — Where a job involved complex, specialized, long-term sales projects, the notice period reflected the time which would have enabled the employees to complete the sales they had started. However, regular salespeople not required to concentrate on long-term sales have not received extra notice. The special circumstances of a commission salesman, including the time needed to build up new clientele, may also lengthen notice, as may dealing with highly specialized products with a limited market.

F-2.4 NATURE OF JOB

Income level — Judges may look at an employee's income level as an indicator of job responsibility as well as a factor affecting re-employability. In many cases, although not all, the fact that an employee was earning a "relatively high salary" has been a factor that increased notice. In one case, however, an employee's sole concern with salary seemed to decrease his notice, presumably because he had no emotional investment in the job.

Commission — The fact that an employee earned a large part of her income through commissions, which she could not duplicate in a new job, was a factor in one case. The time required to re-establish himself in a competitive, commission-only sales job was a factor in another case.

Individual characteristics — Some judges stress individual characteristics in increasing notice, such as the fact that:

- A job required experience and special personal traits even though it did not require special education or training.
- An employee had reached a particularly high position for his age.
- The employee was the only full-time staff member and had more training and experience than any other employee.
- A worker particularly enjoyed his job, but other enjoyable positions would be rare.
- A position was demanding and involved long hours.
- A job required extensive travelling.

Public visibility — A job which by its nature is publicly visible may require a longer notice period, due to the effect of visibility on the chances of re-employment.

Unstable job — The fact that the job itself is cyclical, as in seasonal employment, may be a proper consideration in setting the notice period. An argument that a particular type of position was known to be more unstable than others was said to be without merit. The fact that an employee was subject to layoffs was said to affect notice in one case.

F-2.5 NATURE OF INDUSTRY AND EMPLOYER

Small industry — The fact that a worker is employed in a small or limited industry will tend to increase the notice period, especially where the worker:

- Has been employed in that industry for a substantial length of time.
- Has worked for other industry employers in the past.
- Has no training for any other type of work.
- Is unemployable in the industry due to the manner of termination.
- Will need to start his own competing business or adjust to a different type of employment.

The fact that an employee was employed in a particularly competitive industry, or an industry that was depressed or shrinking, or one with a local or provincial monopoly, has also been mentioned.

Skills transferable — Increased notice may not be needed if the employee's skills are easily transferable to other industries or the employee is otherwise able to readily get a new job.

Unstable or cyclical industry — Some judges have said that an employee should get less notice if he was employed in an industry which was known to be unstable, but other judges have said that the employee should get more notice. One employee who was never laid off in 15 years had no reason to believe his industry was volatile or that he was subject to the risk of layoff. In another case, it was said that the construction industry's volatility cut both ways, hurting both employer and employee; notice was increased slightly due to the unavailability of similar work. Where an employer showed that the employee would only have worked 10 weeks in the year following termination, because of the decline in the employer's business, this was a factor that reduced his damages.

Employer size and sector — Some judges have said that an employer's small size should increase notice, while others have said it should decrease notice. A few judges have said that an employer's large size should increase notice, since there would be more expectation of job security. Still other judges say size is not a proper consideration at all. It has been said that a non-profit organization is not entitled to be treated any differently than any other employer.

F-2.6 WHERE JOB PRECARIOUS

Precariousness as notice factor — The rationale for requiring reasonable notice is to allow the employee time to find a new job. Several courts have mentioned this as a factor against long notice where the employee should have known the job was precarious, such as where:

- An employer was in receivership or other financial trouble.
- The venture was speculative.
- The employer had lost its major contract.
- The position was experimental.
- The employee knew that the employment relationship was deteriorating.
- The employee was the last one to be kept on pending sale of the business.
- The employee knew that the business was being sold and his job would disappear.
- An employee was told far ahead of time that his job, or a significant aspect of his job, would be phased out.
- The employee had accepted probationary employment, as discussed earlier in this chapter.

- The industry was known to be volatile, as discussed earlier in this chapter.

Precariousness not factor — However, several judges have held that knowledge of the employer's financial instability should not shorten the notice period. The fact that an employee knew her job was being eliminated did not affect her notice period where, due to delays and lack of communication, she was left unsure of her status for a year. An employer's bankruptcy several months after an employee's dismissal did not decrease the employee's notice.

Known insecure position — An assignment or temporary employee who knows his job will end may be entitled to less notice than if the job was permanent, as may probationary employees and part-time employees; see the discussion earlier in this chapter. To affect notice, however, the insecurity must be obvious to the employee.

F-2.7 TIME OF ASSESSING JOB STATUS

Time of termination — Normally, notice is based on the job at the time of termination. For example, a former senior manager who had requested a transfer to a non-management position had his notice based on his non-management job, not his previous higher-level job. Where an employee was hired as a salesman with the expectation that he would become the sales manager, his future expectations were taken into account in setting his notice period.

Change in job — Where an employee's change of job was requested by the employer, the former position has been taken into account in setting notice. Where an employee had progressed through the ranks from "humble beginnings", this contributed to increased notice. However, where a manager had only recently been promoted to management, his role throughout his entire employment was considered in setting his notice. In one case, an employee who voluntarily accepted a promotion shortly before dismissal was entitled to less notice, even though there was no formal probationary period, because he should have known that there was a chance that it would not have worked out.

Switch from union — The fact that an employee gave up a unionized position with greater job security, has been mentioned, but its influence on notice seems minor. In one case, the employee had spent most of her service in a unionized position, before becoming a manager, but this was said not to be relevant; all of her service was treated equally for notice purposes, rather than just looking at the time spent in management. In another case, however, an employee who gave up substantial rights to take a management job at the employer's behest was awarded increased notice beyond the normal upper limit for professional or managerial employees. Note, however, that the appeal court disagreed, as the employee was not induced to take the supervisory position.

Last employee — Where the last employee of a company worked in many positions over the years, and lastly worked as a security guard to protect the employer's property until it could be sold, there was an implication that the position would be short-term. Thus, he was entitled to only a brief period of reasonable notice.

Chapter F-3

REASONABLE NOTICE FACTORS: AGE AND SERVICE LENGTH

TABLE OF CONTENTS

F-3.1   Age
F-3.2   Service Length
F-3.3   Calculating Service Length
    F-3.3.1 Interruption in Service
    F-3.3.2 Change of Employment Status
    F-3.3.3 Change in Employer
F-3.4   Enticement by Employer

F-3.1 AGE

General rule — Usually, the older the employee, the more age tends to lengthen notice. Note, however, that judges are not always consistent in their treatment of age. One judge described a 45-year-old employee as being at his prime in terms of job capacity and experience, while another described a 40-year-old as "young". In another case, a 52-year-old employee was said not to be at a disadvantage in a profession (human resources) that depended more on maturity and experience than technical skills, while other 50-year-olds have been treated as virtually unemployable.

50s and up — For most employees in their 50s or above, age tends to increase the length of the notice period, presumably due to the well-known problems for older people to find new work. Employees dismissed in their mid-50s may be particularly vulnerable, as they may be too young to retire but too old to easily retrain. Employees dismissed in their 60s may in effect be forced into early retirement.

Employees in their 40s — Age probably will not affect the re-employment chances of employees below age 50. Several judges, however, have extended extra notice to employees over age 40, on the basis that they have a more difficult time changing jobs than younger people. This seems more likely to happen where the employee has long service with the employer, or where age is a particular concern for the type of job, as with firefighters, for example.

Employees under 40 — Most courts award relatively short notice periods to employees in their 20s and 30s, unless it is shown that jobs are not available despite their young age. Treatment of employees in their 30s tends to be inconsistent. One 38-year-old was described as being at the young end of the "difficult to get re-established" age bracket, while a 37-year-old was called "relatively young". Again, service length can influence how a judge reacts to age. One judge referred to a 35-year-old employee's age as being a neutral factor in assessing notice, while another considered the 30-year-old employee's youth to be partly offset by the fact that he had worked for the employer almost his entire adult life.

Service length and age — Judges have distinguished between older employees with short service and those who spent a large part of their careers with one employer. Judges seem increasingly willing to discount age for older employees with very short service, perhaps with the view that employers who are willing to hire older workers should not be penalized for it, or that the employee's marketability would not have changed during the employment. Short service, however, can be offset by an employee who was enticed away from a secure job.

Age no hindrance — When it is clear that age is not a hindrance to the employee's job search, it should not affect the court's award. For example, a 70-year-old pharmacist who found other work right away was entitled to only three months' notice, which was rather short for an employee of 18 years. Where an employee conducted most of his business by phone and fax and there was no evidence that age was a disadvantage, it was said to be unimportant in setting notice. Similarly, where it is clear that young age is not a help to the employee's job search, notice will not be decreased.

Over age 65 — Where there has been no agreement that an employee will retire at age 65, and there is no retirement policy, an employee dismissed shortly before reaching 65 is entitled to full reasonable notice; damages will not be capped on the employee's 65th birthday. The fact that an employee is past age 65 when dismissed does not mean he is automatically unemployable. As long as he is in good health and capable of working, the employer must still give him sufficient notice to enable him to find a new job. The fact that an employee is already receiving a pension from a previous job does not reduce his notice entitlement.

Planned retirement — Where the parties had agreed that the employee would retire at a certain age, this may limit the notice period, if the employee is dismissed shortly before reaching that age. An employee, who knew he required yearly permission from the chief executive officer to continue working past age 65, was entitled to shorter notice than would otherwise be the case.

Pension and benefits vesting — The time remaining until an employee's pension would vest was held to be a proper consideration in the case of a 62-year-old employee who reasonably expected that he would not be let go on the eve of vesting. His notice period was increased one month, to allow pension vesting. However, extending a notice period eight months to include a planned retirement date was said to be too much in another case. The fact that a short-term employee's pension would have vested nine months after termination did not call for increasing the notice period; it was said that this would be a consideration only in the case of a long-term employee who was fired on the eve of vesting.

F-3.2 SERVICE LENGTH

Importance of service length — Length of service seems most influential when it is either very long or very short. Some judges have cautioned that it is still only one factor to consider, and that it should not be given undue weight. Although it is common for employers to base severance packages solely on service length, this is not always sufficient where other factors would require a longer or shorter notice period.

Long service — Long service is generally related to breadth of experience. Judges tend to believe that an employee who has been in one job or with one employer for many years will have narrower experience and hence will be less employable and will require more notice. Long notice often seems to be given as a reward for long service, too, and a few judges have explicitly recognized a moral claim. Many others seem to implicitly consider moral claims based on long service, as indicated by remarks such as "the plaintiff devoted his entire working life to the defendant". Where it is clear that long service has not damaged re-employment prospects, however, notice may not be lengthened.

Short service — Judges tend to believe that short service will not harm a worker's ability to find a new job, so less notice will be required. However, one judge has pointed out that short service must be weighed against the fact that the employee has given up other job finding opportunities during the employment.

No service — In anticipatory breach situations, where the employee is dismissed before starting work, full reasonable notice or notice for the entire probationary period may be called for, despite the total lack of service.

How long is long? — In general, it seems that service lengths of 20 years or more tend to result in extra notice. Some judges may award extra notice for service in the double digits. For example, one judge stated that it did not matter whether an employee's service length was 13 years or 20 years, since both were long and would lead to the same notice period.

How short is short? — Service of seven-and-a-half years was said in one case not to be long enough to raise a moral claim or entitle the employee to special treatment. However, in another case, a five-year length of service was described as "moderate" rather than "short".

Middle ranges — The effect of service length seems to be unpredictable in the middle ranges, and is greatly affected by age and circumstances. For example:

- A 56-year-old nurse employed for 13 years was awarded a relatively short notice period of nine months, since her service to the employer, while fairly long, represented less than half her working life.
- By this same reasoning, the 28-year-old salesman who had worked eight years for the same employer, nearly his entire working life, should have been given fairly substantial notice, but he was awarded only four months.
- One case involved a 52-year-old with six years' service, who had just obtained his Ph.D. before starting the job. It was said that while six years was not that long, it was a significant period of time for the plaintiff, because it was his first job after obtaining his Ph.D., and because his career as a professional engineer would be shorter than most due to starting later in life.

Interaction with character of job — The effect of service length is also affected by the character of employment. A short-term, high-level employee may be entitled to more notice than a long-term, low-level employee. Where an employee accepted an assignment with the implication that his employment would soon end, he was entitled to less notice than otherwise would have been reasonable for a long-term employee.

Total service counts — The fact that an employee was only a manager for the last part of her employment was not relevant; her full service was counted for purposes of assessing reasonable notice. An employee who had worked for the civil service for 10 years was treated as a 10-year employee even though he had only been in his present position for one year. An employee's service in both unionized and management positions was included in calculating her service for notice purposes. An employee who spent her first few years in training still had those years counted in her service, as the employer had obtained full value in the form of service after the training.

F-3.3 CALCULATING SERVICE LENGTH

F-3.3.1 Interruption in Service

Parties' treatment important — Calculating length of service for the purpose of reasonable notice can be difficult where there has been a hiatus in the middle of the employment. The effect of an interruption depends on the parties' treatment of it when employment resumed.

No recognition of past service — Where there has been a resignation or termination and a later rehiring with no special treatment due to the previous employment, length of service will generally run from the rehiring, not from the original hiring. Some judges refuse to ignore earlier service, even if the employee was rehired in a totally different position with different pay and benefits and was given no credit for his previous service. However, in those cases, judges may give the earlier service less weight than would otherwise be the case.

Rehiring with recognition — Where the employee is rehired with an understanding to recognize past service in some way, such as an increase in salary or the same vacation entitlement based on length of service, the earlier service will be included for notice purposes. Employees rehired at the employer's direct invitation were treated as long-term employees even though there was a three-year hiatus in employment, and a wrongful dismissal settlement from the previous termination. Occasionally, a judge will recognize the earlier service, but will give it less weight than if the service had been continuous. Employees who are rehired and given recognition of previous service for pension purposes will not necessarily be entitled to recognition for notice purposes, if there has been no other recognition of the past service for salary or benefits purposes.

Frequent layoffs — Employees who are frequently laid off and rehired may have their service treated cumulatively, as may seasonal employees. However, an employee who had worked for another employer for months after layoff, before returning to the first employer, and who was then laid off again after only nine months, was treated as a short-term employee only.

Length of gap — Sometimes judges seem more influenced by the length of the hiatus than by the parties' actions, especially when the gap is short in relation to the total length of employment. Where only a few days elapsed between an employee's resignation and her starting a new job with the employer, her service was treated as continuous even though the parties had not dealt with the issue. Two brief absences of less than two months each in 20 years, each of which was "no longer than a long vacation", did not affect an employee's service length. A 16-month hiatus due to sickness in the middle of 20 years' total service was said to be meaningless. Where a woman resigned to have a child and then worked for the employer as a casual employee through an agency before returning to work full-time, her two periods of full-time employment were treated as cumulative. (Although a similar case did not treat service as cumulative, because the employer did not seek the woman's return.) Where a gap is lengthy, recognition is less likely. Where the parties were silent about the effect of the employee's service "some years earlier", he was not given credit for the earlier service.

F-3.3.2 Change of Employment Status

Parties' intentions important — The calculation of service length can also be difficult where there has been a change in employment status. Again, the effect seems to depend on whether the change was mutually agreed to, and on how the parties treated the change.

Change to employee — In most cases, when a non-employee becomes an employee, he or she has been given credit for the past service, including:

- An independent contractor who had his status changed to employee four months before dismissal.
- An employee who spent his first few years on short-term contracts before obtaining a permanent position.
- A lessee/commission agent who became an employee and was given vacation entitlement based on his long service.

Exception — An employee who first worked as a volunteer before starting paid employment did not have her volunteer service taken into account in calculating her notice, because her volunteer duties had been somewhat different and she was still in the probationary period of her paid employment.

Change to full-time — Part-time and seasonal employees may be entitled to less notice than full-time employees, as discussed in Chapter F-2, "Reasonable Notice Factors: Character of the Employment". A part-time employee who became a full-time employee was given partial credit for his part-time years of service for notice purposes; the judge said that the weight to be given would depend on the extent and duration of the part-time work. However, one seasonal employee, who eventually became permanent, did not have her earlier service considered at all.

Change to part-time — Where a full-time employee had her hours reduced to part-time for several years before dismissal, her 10 years of service were found to be equivalent to nine years of full-time service. A previous full-time employee who was rehired part-time on-call had her earlier service ignored in assessing her notice. In another case, however, a full-time employee who retired and then returned as a seasonal employee had her earlier service considered in assessing her notice.

Change to non-union — Although persons covered by collective agreements may be excluded from some employment standards provisions, time spent in a bargaining unit still counts in a person's calculation of service length for statutory and common-law purposes.

Change from employee to business owner — Where parties mutually agreed to end the employee's employment so that he could become manager and part owner of a new company, his 30 years with the original employer were not taken into account, as he had voluntarily ended his employment.

Change from business owner to employee — Where an employer sells his own business and becomes an employee of the purchaser, some judges have ruled that there should be no credit for past service, since the change was within the employee's control. Other judges have given credit for past service, since the service was continuous.

F-3.3.3 Change in Employer

Depends on arrangements — Where the employing entity has changed, the effect on service length depends on the arrangements between the parties and the surrounding circumstances.

Credit denied — Credit for past service is sometimes denied regardless of the circumstances. It has also been denied where:

- An employee previously worked for his father.
- The business was sold after a bankruptcy or receivership.
- The previous employer gave termination notice and refunded pension contributions.
- An apartment building manager worked in the same building under three unrelated management companies, and transfer of his employment was not automatic.
- A written contract overcame any implication that credit for past service would be given.
- An employee left his old company and his new company later bought the old company.
- An employee accepted a lower position with a new owner in a new venture, with substantially different terms of employment.
- A senior manager signed a release of all claims against the original employer upon accepting a job with the new corporate entity.

Credit given — Employment was regarded as continuous where:

- The employee's status, including responsibilities and remuneration, did not change.
- The employee was to be kept on with terms and conditions "at least as favourable" as with the old employer.
- The employer treated the employment as continuous for pay or benefits purposes.
- An employee was transferred to a new corporate employer with an agreement that his past service would be recognized.

Transfer between related entities — Where there is a transfer or sale of a business, or an employee is transferred between related entities, service is usually treated as continuous. An employee who spent 10 years in several civil service jobs had all his service counted, even though he had only been with the last government agency for one year.

Sale as going concern — There is a presumption of credit for past service whenever a business is purchased as a going concern, unless the purchaser gives express notice otherwise. Note, too, that many employment standards statutes treat service as continuous where a business is sold and the employee continues on with the purchaser. However, full credit for all past service may not be given.

F-3.4 ENTICEMENT BY EMPLOYER

Offsets short service length — The circumstances of hiring are generally not relevant in setting the notice period. However, enticement or luring away by the employer at the time of hiring may offset the effect of a short period of employment. An employee's expectations based on the employer's representations at the time of hiring may also offset the effect of a short period of employment (see also Chapter F-5, "Effect of Parties' Conduct on Reasonable Notice"). The fact that an employee was hired away from another job did not entitle her to add her service with the previous employer to her service with the dismissing employer. However, it would merely slightly lengthen the notice period.

What enticement is — In some cases, an enticement claim is similar to a claim of misrepresentation. Enticement has been found where:

- The employer recruited or solicited the employee specifically, particularly if these efforts were aggressive.
- The employer gave assurances of long, secure employment, higher income or improved opportunities, especially if these promises were not kept.
- Shares in the employer were offered to the employee at the time of hiring, indicating an intention for a long relationship.
- The employer gave assurances of fair treatment.

- The employee gave up a secure job or the right to a lengthy notice period, to the employer's knowledge.
- The employee gave up his own company, or other better-paying or more secure offers, to join the defendant employer.
- The employee relocated for the employer, as discussed below.

What enticement is not — For enticement or inducement to be a factor in the length of notice, something beyond the ordinary degree of persuasion must be shown. The mere fact of recruitment is not enough, and not all inducements will carry equal weight. An employee who willingly leaves a secure job (or an insecure job), or who gives up his own business, for a new opportunity has not necessarily been enticed. Where the employee did not relocate, left an insecure position, remained with the employer for several years or there was otherwise only a slight element of enticement, it may receive little weight in setting notice. The enticement of an employee was said not to be significant where the employee was paid by commission and therefore enjoyed mobility of employment.

How long is enticement a factor? — Previously, enticement was regarded as something that lost its importance after a few years of employment. However, the Supreme Court of Canada has confirmed that inducement and promises of job security can influence notice even after 14 years of employment, although the court also said that not all inducements carry equal weight.

Relocation — Relocation often indicates enticement or an employee's special reliance on the continuation of the job. This is particularly so where the employment was brief, or the job involved an overseas or out-of-province move. The fact that an employee's spouse gave up a secure job to move with the employee has been mentioned. The existence of a mortgage assistance plan, which the employee relied on in relocating at the employer's request, was said to be a factor to consider in setting notice, since the plan would cease upon termination.

When relocation less important — Relocation seems to be less influential where:
- The employee had a history of job-related moves.
- The relocation was temporary and was readily agreed to by the employee.
- The relocation was agreed to at the time of hiring and the employee was retained for several years afterwards.
- The employee intended to relocate anyway.
- The move was otherwise wholly voluntary.

The fact that an employee had relocated four times during his 33 years of employment did not entitle him to any extra notice in one case.

Chapter F-4

REASONABLE NOTICE FACTORS: AVAILABILITY OF A NEW JOB

TABLE OF CONTENTS

F-4.1   Training, Qualifications and Experience
F-4.2   Job Characteristics
F-4.3   Personal Characteristics
F-4.4   Geographic Location
F-4.5   Economic Climate
F-4.6   Employer's Financial Problems
F-4.7   Proving Job Availability

F-4.1   TRAINING, QUALIFICATIONS AND EXPERIENCE

Related to job availability — Experience, training and qualifications are identified as important factors in *Bardal* and in many other cases. Obviously, they are closely tied to an employee's chances of finding a new, similar job.

Lack of formal education — Most judges view a low level of education, or a low level of education relative to the job status achieved, as a factor that will increase notice because new work will be less available. For example, a woman who had no formal training for her long-term job as a dental assistant could be expected to have a hard time finding a similar job, so she would need more notice. However, this is not always the case. A woman with limited skills who could earn a particularly good living at one job, which would not be readily available to her elsewhere, was said not to require extra notice.

Technological, teamwork skills — A lack of computer skills may be a hindrance to some employees' job searches. So was the fact that an employee's skills were in obsolete technology. The fact that an employee was not used to working as part of a team was mentioned as a factor lengthening notice.

Generalists — A man trained as an engineer whose skills had grown rusty in his position as a generalist was said to need extra notice.

However, an employee who has broad experience in many kinds of work may need less notice, as may an employee whose job is not particularly unique, whose experience is not particularly specialized, or whose skills are portable. A woman who had training and experience as a nurse, and whose profession was in demand, was given a fairly short notice period despite her age and length of service.

Salespersons — A salesman was said to have general skills and experience that were transferable to other industries, although some salespeople have been treated as having skills that are not easily transferable.

Progressed through ranks — An employee's beginning in a lower position, with movement upward through the ranks, has been mentioned as a factor, although it is not clear whether that should increase or decrease an employee's notice entitlement.

Experience limited — Experience can be an important factor where the employee's experience is limited to a particular field or industry, especially if the employee has already worked for other employers in that industry. Similarly, an employee with long service with one employer will generally have limited experience and require more notice. The fact that a long-service employee had no other job experience in Canada was mentioned as a factor increasing her notice requirements. See also Chapter F-2, "Reasonable Notice Factors: Character of the Employment" and Chapter F-3, "Reasonable Notice Factors: Age and Service Length".

First job in industry — The fact that a short-service employee had no previous experience in an industry seemed to decrease his notice entitlement, although it would seem that that might make re-employment in the same industry all the more difficult.

F-4.2 JOB CHARACTERISTICS

Specialized, high-level or visible job — An employee in a unique or very specialized position may need more notice to compensate for the small number of such positions in existence. A high-level employee in a limited industry, or an employee in a high-profile, publicly visible position may also need more notice. See also Chapter F-2, "Reasonable Notice Factors: Characters of the Employment".

Union job — Where an employee's important position with a union had damaged his chances of re-employment in the industry, this was a factor tending to lengthen the notice period.

Commission salesman — Where alternative employment as a commission salesman was available, but it would take two years to establish comparable customers due to the limited market in the area, this was reflected in the notice period.

Non-competition clause — The length of a restrictive covenant or non-competition clause that restricts an employee's ability to look for new work may be a factor in setting notice.

Industry hiring practices — The custom in an industry to promote from within rather than to hire from outside was a factor increasing a dismissed employee's notice period.

Timing of dismissal — A college that dismissed its principal should have realized that he probably would not find new employment until the next academic year, and this was a factor in setting reasonable notice. The fact that a university student was dismissed in mid-summer, when there would be few other summer jobs available, was also considered. A radio announcer who was terminated at the start of a ratings period, when other stations would not be hiring, had this fact considered. An employee dismissed during the Christmas season was entitled to extra notice, since this made his job search harder.

Seasonal employment — A seasonal employee is often entitled to one season's notice of dismissal. If off-season unemployment is usual in an industry, however, the fact that an employee was let go at the end of the season need not lengthen the notice period.

Salary, benefits level — An employee's very high salary was mentioned as a factor in setting notice, presumably because it would be difficult for him to find another job that paid as well. Similar consideration was given to the fact that an employee had been overpaid by her employer. In another case, the fact that an employee made a relatively good living compared to her skill level was said not to be a proper consideration in setting notice. An inability to find a new job that would provide the same benefits was said to be a factor in setting notice in one case.

F-4.3 PERSONAL CHARACTERISTICS

Marital status — An employee's married status or the fact that the employee has dependent children is often mentioned, apparently to increase notice. Presumably this is because it may affect the employee's ability to relocate. Yet, one employee's inability to relocate due to her family obligations was mentioned as a factor decreasing notice. The fact that an employee is single or has no dependents, and so can easily relocate, has also been mentioned as a factor to shorten notice. See the discussion under Section F-4.4, "Geographic Location" later in this chapter. The fact that an employee was terminated just after separating from his wife and injuring his back was mentioned, presumably to increase notice.

Pregnancy — The fact that an employee was pregnant when dismissed may increase notice, although at least one case seems to have ignored pregnancy as a factor. In other cases, it was said that a dismissed employee's pregnancy did not entitle her to any extra notice. The fact that an employee was dismissed during her maternity leave was mentioned in one case, but the employer was still given credit for the notice that coincided with the maternity leave. The fact that an employee's wife was expecting a child and she had already given up a well-paid job in order to relocate with him was mentioned in one case.

Poor health or disability — The employee's poor health or disability may need to be taken into account in setting reasonable notice, as this may affect the employee's ability to find a new job. However, some judges have said that this may not be a proper consideration if the employee is still fit to work. Other judges have said that it is not to be given undue emphasis, but simply treated as part of the greater question of availability of new work. The fact that an employee is totally disabled and may never return to work does not eliminate the entitlement to reasonable notice. The fact that an employee's poor health was caused by the job itself does not increase notice, although it was mentioned in one case where the employee would require retraining in order to become re-employed. An employee's good health has also been mentioned as a factor shortening notice.

Disability arising after dismissal — Where an employee's health problem had not been identified at the time of firing, it was not considered in setting notice. The fact that an employee was undergoing tests for permanent disability at the time of firing did not obligate the employer to confirm his health status before dismissing him.

Accumulated sick leave — The fact that an employee had a large amount of accumulated sick leave which was not compensable, even though he had been ill during the notice period, justified increasing his notice period by two months.

Personality — Where an employee's personality would likely hinder his chances of re-employment, it was taken into account. On the other hand, an employee's physical and temperamental attractiveness was mentioned as a factor shortening notice, since it would reduce the time he would need to find new work.

Race — Racial origin was mentioned in one case as a possible factor, but it was rejected in another case. One judge refused to increase notice based on systemic racism against black women, as no evidence was provided for the claim and the plaintiff's own job history showed that no increase in notice was needed.

Criminal charges — Pending criminal charges arising from the employee's job, which prevented the employee from getting a similar job, were mentioned in one case. In another case, charges that were laid while the employee was employed, and which prompted his dismissal, were a factor in setting notice, since the employer should have known that they would hamper his job search. However, the notice period was not extended to cover the full time needed to resolve the charges.

Transience — An employee's tendency to change jobs frequently, and the transience of an industry's workforce, have also been mentioned as affecting notice. The fact, however, that an employee had applied for other jobs during his employment merely showed ambition and was not a sign that he did not consider his employment permanent. The mere fact that an employee had held several jobs during his career did not indicate that he was "on the move", when he had stayed in each job for an average of over five years. An employee's "strong tendency to cling to the familiar", which would make her less likely to change jobs on her own, was mentioned as a factor increasing her notice. The number of times a person has been terminated from previous jobs was rejected as a proper factor in one case.

Late career change — The fact that an employee had received his Ph.D. relatively late in life, which therefore would make his professional career shorter and his six years with the employer more significant, was stressed in one case.

Finances — Employees' finances have been considered in a few cases, although the rationale for doing so is unclear. Where an employee had a large capital sum available due to his investment in company shares, this was taken to reduce his notice, since his financial ability should make it easier for him to find a new job. An employee's own business, which enabled him to generate extra income right from the time of dismissal, has also shortened notice. The fact that an employee had a pension from an earlier job and was financially self-reliant was considered in one case; but another case said this was not a proper consideration, since an employee's ability to retire, even on full pension, did not take away his right to notice.

Self-imposed limits — An employee's desire to be semi-retired and avoid business travel was mentioned in one case, but these self-imposed limits on employment seemed to shorten the notice period rather than lengthen it.

F-4.4 GEOGRAPHIC LOCATION

One-industry town — Geographic location is a factor in setting notice, as it can affect the availability of other work. A worker in a one-industry town, or one with special training who is dismissed by the only employer of that type in the area, may need extra notice. Where the employee will have to relocate, this may be considered because it involves extra time and disruption to the employee's life.

Depressed area — An employee dismissed in an area of high unemployment, either generally or in his industry, usually will also receive extra notice. An employee who had recently moved at the employer's request, to an area of high unemployment, was entitled to notice based on the job market in that locale.

Earlier move — The fact that an employee was dismissed soon after being enticed by the employer to move from Edmonton to Toronto lengthened notice, as did the fact that an employee was dismissed after selling his house in anticipation of a promised transfer.

Need to relocate — In one case, the need to relocate did not affect notice, since the employee had been planning to move anyway. An employee's willingness to search for jobs in other locations was mentioned as a factor in setting her notice, but it was not clear whether it should increase or decrease her notice. An employee employed outside Canada at the time of dismissal was entitled to extra notice.

Refusal to relocate — Some judges are not sympathetic to employees who insist on staying where there are no jobs. In some cases, the fact that similar jobs were available, although the employee would have to relocate, has shortened the notice required. Where an employee is unable or unwilling to relocate due to family concerns, some judges have increased notice, while others have decreased it. In one case, where an employee would have had trouble relocating due to his business investments, his notice was increased. See also the discussion in Chapter H-3, "Career Changes and Relocating".

F-4.5 ECONOMIC CLIMATE

Bad economy increasing notice — Many cases have mentioned poor general economic climate as a factor that increases notice, especially where the entire industry is economically depressed or there is a particularly poor market for that type of position. Notice also may be lengthened where the employer has flooded the market by terminating a large number of employees with similar qualifications.

Bad economy not increasing notice — However, other cases have denied that the economic climate is a proper factor, or have downplayed its importance, because the poor economy will have hurt both parties equally. At least one judge has said that evidence is required of the poor economy's particular impact on the parties before this factor should be given weight. Where an employee was hired during a downturn and then dismissed a short time later, the judge said the industry's problems had not really gotten worse between hiring and firing, so they should have little impact on notice.

Bad economy decreasing notice — In one case, the fact that an employer's entire industry was struggling was applied as a factor limiting notice, rather than increasing it.

Proving bad economy — An employee who alleges that an entire industry is depressed, thereby affecting his job prospects, may have the onus of proving it. Evidence of an employee's job search efforts may be sufficient evidence in some cases.

F-4.6 EMPLOYER'S FINANCIAL PROBLEMS

More, less or the same? — The effect of an employer's own economic problems remains controversial. The idea that an employer should have to give less notice due to its own financial woes conflicts with the principle behind wrongful dismissal cases, which is to compensate the blameless employee. Yet, it is widely accepted that the notice period must be reasonable to both the employer and the employee. Some judges deny that notice should be reduced because of the employer's financial troubles, while other judges allow it. An employer's financial problems may reduce notice, but they do not remove the employee's right to reasonable notice altogether.

Limits on reduced notice — Some discomfort with reducing notice remains, and this has caused attempts to limit the situations in which notice will be reduced. The fact that an employer was in receivership was not a sufficient reason to reduce notice where the employer was still operating. Where an employer went bankrupt, but not until several months after dismissing an employee, notice was not reduced. One case said that reducing notice may be appropriate in cases of cyclical or seasonal employment.

Employer and industry suffering — Where an employer was suffering depressed economic conditions but the entire industry was affected, which would hamper the employee's job search, one case said that these factors could increase the notice period but could not decrease it, and they were not to be given undue influence — in other words, they cancelled each other out.

Proving economic problems — The employer must prove that the dismissal was required by economic circumstances, and that it was not the employer's own fault. Direct evidence and financial statements may be needed to do this, not just a statement in the termination letter that the dismissal was for financial reasons. The fact that many other employees were terminated at the same time has been accepted as sufficient evidence in some cases.

Seriousness of problems — While some courts have been willing to defer to management prerogative or take judicial notice of an industry's problems, others have refused to reduce notice where a basically sound company has suffered a short-term loss. For example:

- The company is still paying high share dividends.
- The employer is an unprofitable subsidiary of a profitable parent company.
- The financial situation is not sufficiently serious.
- The financial downturn was not unexpected.
- The employer's business tends to be cyclical.
- The employer is simply trying to obtain labour at a cheaper rate.

Reduced earnings during notice period — Where an employer showed that an employee's earnings would have been severely cut during the notice period due to the employer's lack of business, his damages were reduced. However, where an employer's financial situation had already been considered in setting the notice period, an employee was awarded damages at his regular rate, before a pay cut that was prompted by the same economic problems.

F-4.7 PROVING JOB AVAILABILITY

Evidence of availability — Where a party needs to prove that new employment was or was not available, the case law has suggested the following methods:

- Testimony of a local Canada Manpower director.
- The opinion of an employment and relocation counsellor.
- Statistics on job availability.

Copies of newspaper ads are generally not given much weight by judges because there are too many unknowns involved. Some industries' problems have been sufficiently well-known to be considered by judges without requiring proof.

Employer's duty to check availability — One case has implied that it is the employer's duty to check on an employee's re-employment prospects when providing notice or pay in lieu. While this may not be a legal duty, it is a practical duty if the employer is to assess the notice period accurately. Often, the lack of evidence about available jobs seems to be taken as proof that there were none available to an employee.

Chapter F-5

EFFECT OF PARTIES' CONDUCT ON REASONABLE NOTICE

TABLE OF CONTENTS

F-5.1   Assurances of Job Security
F-5.2   Manner of Dismissal
F-5.3   Employer's Bad Faith
F-5.4   Employee's Near Cause
F-5.5   Employee's Merits

F-5.1 ASSURANCE OF JOB SECURITY

Representations upon hiring — Statements during the hiring process may affect notice where the employer made representations about job security or the intended length of employment. The employer's unkept promises have been considered as a factor increasing notice in many cases, even where these promises did not amount to enticement, although a minority of judges deny that they should affect notice.

Implied assurances of security — Asking an employee to make a commitment to long-term employment may justify an employee's expectation of long-term employment. An automatic renewal clause in a fixed-term contract also created a reasonable expectation of secure employment. An employer who granted an employee credit for past service for purposes of his seniority and pension was said to have created an "atmosphere of expected longevity". Similarly, where parties had started up a business together in part so that they would have control of their own lives, a lengthy notice period must have been intended. Where the parties had intended a long-term contract that had not in fact taken effect, the intended job security was considered in awarding a very long notice period, although the notice period was lowered on appeal.

Detrimental reliance — Where a plaintiff sold his business to the defendant upon a guarantee of a five-year contract, and the purchaser dismissed him after one year, the plaintiff's detrimental reliance was a factor in increasing notice. Similarly, an employee who brought with him many clients and the goodwill from a previous employer was given extra notice when he was dismissed after a short time. The fact that an employee's contract stated that she could only be dismissed for just cause, which was intended to give her extraordinary job security, was a factor in setting her notice period upon her dismissal without just cause.

Recent assurances — Recent assurances of job security have also been mentioned as a factor increasing notice. So was the fact that the employer had recently urged the employee to stay with the company rather than accepting another job offer. Where an employee had recently been transferred out of province, this gave rise to an expectation of security, at least in the short term. An employee, who was told he would be retrained but was terminated instead, was awarded increased notice.

Expectations based on conduct — Notice was increased where a "paternalistic employer" led an employee to believe there was almost no chance of dismissal, and where a receiver undertook major restructuring and renovations, leading employees to believe the business had a future. An employee's reasonable expectations of long tenure, based on a predecessor's experience, may also justify a longer notice period.

Duty to warn of insecurity — In one case, where the employer knew an employee's job could be insecure, and it knew that security was particularly important to her, the court held that the employer should have warned her of the chance that she could lose her job.

Other expectations — While judges sometimes mention employees' expectations of "lifelong employment" or similar expectations, other judges have said that these are not a proper consideration where the employer did not contribute to them. The fact that an employee regarded her employer as "family" did not obligate the employer to treat her in other than a fair, businesslike way.

Known insecurity — Where an employee knew his job was contingent on satisfactory performance, this was a factor shortening notice. See also the discussion in Chapter A-3, "Probationary Employment", and the discussion of precariousness in Chapter F-2, "Reasonable Notice Factors: Character of the Employment".

F-5.2 MANNER OF DISMISSAL

Harms job search — Where the manner of dismissal harms an employee's chance of finding similar work — for example because of suddenness or harsh and unfair conduct, or untrue claims of poor performance or misconduct — some judges have lengthened notice. The Supreme Court of Canada sanctioned that view in *Wallace v. United Grain Growers Ltd. (c.o.b. Public Press)*, [1994] 4 W.W.R. 86 (S.C.C.), reversing (1995), 14 C.C.E.L. (2d) 41 (Man. C.A.), reversing (1993), 49

C.C.E.L. 71 (Man. Q.B.). Previously, the manner of dismissal often led to an award of aggravated or punitive damages, instead of increased notice, as discussed in Chapter G-9 "Aggravated and Punitive Damages".

Negative publicity — An employee with a high public profile who received negative publicity due to her wrongful dismissal had had her future job prospects interfered with, so her notice period was increased. Where the employer made false public statements or allowed word to get around within the industry, so that the employee's re-employment chances were affected, this also increased notice. The fact that an employee was embarrassed or suffered negative publicity in his small community has also been mentioned. However, an employee was not entitled to extra damages where there was no proof that adverse publicity had actually harmed his job search.

Harm or bad faith — In *Wallace*, the Supreme Court of Canada stated that the notice period can be increased if the employer's actions have affected the employee's ability to find a new job, but it can also be increased to reflect bad faith conduct by the employer. A negative effect on the employee's job prospects is not required if there has been bad faith. A recent case said that an increase under *Wallace* is meant to compensate the employee, not to punish the employer, and should not be awarded unless there was significant mental distress or other harm. However, many other judges seem to view a *Wallace* increase as punitive.

Overlap — Many of the actions that can damage an employee's re-employment prospects have also been treated as bad faith conduct. The two situations therefore are dealt with together in the following Section F-5.3, "Bad Faith".

Good treatment — Where an employee has been treated with consideration and equity throughout, this can minimize the notice period. Comments on the employer's lack of fault include the fact that:

- The dismissal was not unfair.
- The employee was let go due to redundancy or the employer's poor economic position, not through the employer's "fault".
- The employer had honest or good faith motives.
- The employer had previously paid considerable sick pay.
- The employer had been kind and patient during the employment.
- The employer offered to pay for relocation counselling.
- The employer allowed an employee some paid time off to consider a proposed job change.
- An employer had paid for a lengthy retraining program for the employee.

F-5.3 EMPLOYER'S BAD FAITH

One factor — Bad faith is only one factor to be considered, and it will not entitle an employee to greater notice if the amount of notice has already been fixed by contract. Canadian courts have not to this point recognized a separate cause of action for bad faith dismissal.

Bad faith during employment — Unfair conduct prior to dismissal may amount to bad faith that increases notice; for example:

- Failure to provide proper training and a tolerable working environment.
- Inappropriate treatment during employment.
- Underpayment an employee.

No bad faith during employment — The following did not amount to bad faith during employment:

- Reducing a part-time employee's hours and trying to change her status to independent contractor.
- Refusing to meet with a long-term employee to discuss a decrease in his salary and bonus.

Unfair evaluation — Probationary employees who were not fairly evaluated or warned about performance concerns had been treated with bad faith and were entitled to extra notice.

Breach of expectations — Where an employer created expectations and then dismissed instead, bad faith has been found. For instance, bad faith has been found where:

- The employee was replaced without notice, after having been told to expect a short layoff.
- A long-term employee's contract was not renewed, without explanation, when he had been told it was a mere formality.
- An employer lied to an employee about his job security.
- An employer promised an employee a new job and then dismissed him instead.

Delay — An employer's failure to give dismissal notice as soon as possible may affect the notice period. For example, where an employer decided before a temporary layoff to fire an employee, but did not actually fire him until the end of the layoff, the notice period was increased, as the employer's delay meant the employee had lost those months to look for a new job. However, in another case, the fact that an employee was told he was "laid off" instead of "dismissed" was not cause for complaint where the employer had no improper motive.

Failure to explain — Failing to give any explanation for the dismissal of long-term employees, or to express appreciation for their long years of service, was regarded as bad faith in one case.

Untrue allegations — Bad faith has been found in many (but not all) cases where there are untrue allegations of misconduct or poor job performance; where allegations are made public or allowed to persist for a long time; or where the allegations are not raised until much later or until the employee starts a lawsuit. However, allegations of just cause without unreasonable or unfair treatment usually do not, by themselves, increase the notice period, especially if there was some cause for making them, they were not made public, and no "hardball tactics" were used.

Procedural failures — A failure to allow the employee to respond to charges of wrongdoing or poor performance may also show bad faith, although not all cases have agreed. Bad faith has been found for failure to investigate in a timely manner, and for a failure to warn an employee about his performance. The fact that an employer bypassed its own progressive discipline policy and went straight to termination was not in itself bad faith. An employee dismissed merely because he was charged with a serious criminal offence had been treated in bad faith, as he was given no chance to prove his innocence.

Timing — The timing of a dismissal can amount to bad faith. For example, dismissal:

- Shortly after being enticed to relocate out of the province.
- During the Christmas season, which made the new job search more difficult.
- After previous inducement to give up secure employment.

Harsh, callous, high-handed treatment — Although some judges deny it, most agree that harsh, callous, cold, impersonal or high-handed treatment can amount to bad faith that increases the notice period. Termination that is unduly insensitive or abrupt, or which causes the employee serious mental distress due to its manner, may also increase the notice awarded.

Insensitivity — "Insensitivity" to a vulnerable employee — particularly one who is ill — has been found to amount to bad faith under *Wallace*. Dismissing an employee soon after he went off work on sick leave was bad faith in several cases, as was terminating an employee just after a return from a sick leave. Where an employer had changed its sick leave and workers' compensation top-up policies just after an employee was injured, the employee's notice was increased by two months. Insensitivity in announcing a change that amounted to constructive dismissal also increased notice. In other cases, however, insensitive or blunt treatment without malice has not been found to be bad faith, or to increase notice.

Malice — Malicious conduct includes conduct that is intended to harm or upset the employee rather than merely achieve the employer's own aims, such as:

- Threatening to blacklist an employee in a local industry.
- Digging up dirt on an employee after dismissal.
- Interfering with an employee's business relations with others.
- Dishonesty or lack of candour from a manager about his support for an employee.
- Dismissal due to age discrimination.

Constructive dismissal situations are ripe for *Wallace*-type claims, especially where an employer has been indifferent as to whether the employee would be driven out or not. However, behaviour which was due to the "fog of battle" rather than any intention to harm was not malicious.

Severance arrangements — A number of aspects of severance arrangements can lead to bad faith claims: the content of an offer, the timing and circumstances of negotiation, dealing with government agencies and paperwork, and the issuance of payments.

Content of severance offer — An attempt to get a long-service employee to accept the statutory minimum amount of notice was not commendable, but it was said not to amount to bad faith. On the other hand, a clearly unfair offer which the employer could not possibly have believed to be justified was bad faith. Repeated, wrong claims that no severance pay was owed to an employee, which caused her considerable anguish, were found to be bad faith. Offering different severance arrangements to other employees was not considered bad faith in one case.

Timing and negotiations — Requiring quick acceptance of a severance offer, or refusing to allow an employee time to obtain legal advice, may lead to a finding of bad faith. Making one severance offer at the time of termination, and later increasing the offer, was not bad faith where the first offer was not unfair; however, decreasing an offer during negotiations was regarded as bad faith.

Government forms and agencies — Carelessly issuing an incorrect income tax form and failing to advise the employee of later corrections, along with threats made by the employer's lawyer during mediation, was considered minor bad faith in one case. Failing to issue separation papers promptly has also been treated as bad faith, although one employer's five-month delay in issuing a Record of Employment did not warrant increased notice. An employer's appeal of an Employment Insurance claim was found to entitle the employee to extra notice in another case.

Payment — The failure to promptly pay statutory severance pay did not call for an increase in notice, particularly since the jurisdiction did not require severance pay at the time of termination. A delay in paying a severance payment, which was due to a misunderstanding rather than any intent to harm the employee, was not bad faith. In another case, where failure to pay severance pay promptly increased an employee's income tax liability, his notice period was not increased, but his damages were grossed up to offset the tax increase.

References — Some judges have denied that the giving or withholding of references should affect notice, but many others have treated it as bad faith leading to increased notice where the employer has refused a justified good reference, or has given an unjustified bad reference. Even the giving of a "perfunctory" or luke-warm reference has been mentioned as a factor affecting notice. Misrepresenting an employee's position in reference letters, to the employee's detriment, also was bad faith. Failure to give a reference may not count against an employer if the employee never requested a reference.

Job search help — Other instances of bad faith include situations where the employer gave the employee no help in the new job search and it failed to provide relocation counselling.

F-5.4 EMPLOYEE'S NEAR CAUSE

Principle rejected — The principle of "near cause" is that the notice period should be reduced where there has been substantial misconduct that falls short of the degree required for dismissal without notice. Near cause represents a compromise of the traditional black-and-white just cause rules, and thus "moderated damages", as the principle is sometimes called, can be useful to both employers and employees. However, the Supreme Court of Canada has stated that the courts "do not accept any argument relating to near cause" (*Dowling v. Halifax (City)*, [1998] 1 S.C.R. 22), and thus it can no longer be regarded as a proper consideration in setting notice.

F-5.5 EMPLOYEE'S MERITS

Merits relevant? — Some factors relating to the employee's merits have been mentioned in the case law, although as with near cause, the theoretical justification for weighing blame in a breach of contract action is questionable. As several courts have pointed out, the notice period should not be a disguised way to award a performance bonus.

Job performance — In addition to the length of service, which is a proper factor in setting notice, judges often mention the quality of an employee's service. However, at least one case has cautioned against giving too much weight to an employee's performance, and another actually said that an employee's excellent performance would tend to decrease his notice, because it would increase his marketability.

Relocating — The fact that an employee had relocated at the employer's request has not influenced notice in some cases, but in many others it has increased notice. See the discussion of "Enticement by Employer" under Section F-3.4 in Chapter F-3, "Reasonable Notice Factors, Age and Service Length".

Chapter G-1

DAMAGES: GENERAL PRINCIPLES

TABLE OF CONTENTS

G-1.1   General Principles
G-1.2   Damages for Benefits
G-1.3   Time From Which Damages Run
G-1.4   Time at Which Damages End
G.1-5   Early Termination of Fixed-Term Contracts
G.1-6   Contractual Notice Provisions

G-1.1 GENERAL PRINCIPLES

Goal of damages — An employee who does not receive reasonable notice will be awarded damages to put him in the same position as if he had received working reasonable notice. Salary plus all other benefits and special allowances that are considered terms of the employment contract must be taken into account. As stated in the leading case of *Bardal v. Globe & Mail Ltd.*:

> The contractual obligation was to give reasonable notice and to continue the servant in his employment. If the servant was dismissed without reasonable notice he was entitled to the damage that flowed from the failure to observe this contractual obligation, which damage the servant was bound in law to mitigate to the best of his ability. ([1960] O.W.N. 253 at 254 (H.C.))

Notice period only — Only benefits that would have been received within the notice period are awardable, not those that would have accrued if the employee had continued in the job indefinitely. This is because the breach consists of the failure to give notice, not the termination itself. If an employee has received pay in lieu of notice, and would have received more if he had been given working notice, he will be entitled to the extra damages.

Loss must be shown — To be entitled to damages, an employee must have suffered an actual loss. The onus is on the employee to prove he has suffered a loss. For example:

- An employee who worked for the employer through the entire notice period was not entitled to damages.

- An employee who received a lesser amount due to a constructive dismissal was entitled to the difference between the amount paid and the amount owed under the contract.
- An employee who immediately obtained other work with equal pay was not entitled to damages, as he had mitigated his entire loss.
- An employee who received a benefit such as disability pay or maternity leave during the notice period may still be entitled to compensation in lieu of reasonable notice in some cases. See Chapter G-11, "Deductions from the Damage Award".
- An employee whose salary was continued throughout the notice period, without having to work, was still entitled to the value of benefits for the notice period.

Working notice vs. pay — The weight of judicial authority says that it is up to the employer to decide whether to give working notice or pay in lieu of notice, and that the employee is not entitled to demand one over the other. A few judges have expressed concern that it may be too much to expect a particular employee to work through a notice period, and that he should be given damages instead. Also, there may be concerns that working notice is not effective notice unless the employee is able to actively seek other work during that time.

Salary continuance vs. lump sum — An employee may not be entitled to decide whether payment is made by way of continuing regular payroll payments or by way of a lump-sum payment. However, in one case it was held that a 62-year-old employee with a lengthy notice period was entitled to "close the chapter" by receiving a lump sum rather than salary continuance. In another case, where a contract provided for periodic payments, a lump-sum payment was a breach of the contract.

Judge may select method of payment — Where an action is heard before the end of the notice period, some judges have ordered the award to be satisfied by salary and benefits continuation to the end of the notice period. In another case, however, an employer's request for periodic payments was refused; a lump sum award was "appropriate".

Discounts — Where damages are ordered before the end of the notice period, contractual damages period or fixed term contract, some judges have applied discount rates, deductions for contingencies or present value calculations. Others have imposed a trust in favour of the employer on any earnings received by the employee within the notice period. See also Chapter G-11, "Deductions from the Damage Award".

G-1.2 DAMAGES FOR BENEFITS

General principles — Fringe benefits are an important part of most employment contracts and they must be taken into account in assessing dismissal damages unless the employee is dismissed under a contract providing for a set termination or severance payment. Damages are based on the benefits being received by the employee at the time of dismissal, and will cover the part of the notice period during which actual benefits coverage was not provided by the employer. Courts usually do not have the power to order that benefits be reinstated.

No damages — Damages for benefits may be refused where there was no contractual obligation to provide them, they were not yet being provided, or where the employee paid for them himself. In a few cases, damages were refused for expenses that would have been reimbursed under group health insurance, as this was said to be a matter between the employee and the insurer; but these cases seem to be an aberration.

Damages depend on type of benefit — The courts' treatment of damages depends on the type of benefit being considered. Generally, there is a distinction between fringe benefits, which represent a personal or take-home benefit, and benefits that merely reimburse an employee for work-related expenses. Fringe benefits are generally compensable, while reimbursement benefits are not, since no expenses would be incurred if the employee did not work through the notice period. A distinction is also made between insurance-type benefits and other benefits, as discussed in Chapter G-5, "Insured Benefits, Sick Leave and Disability Benefits" and Chapter G-6, "Employment Insurance and Pension Benefits".

Entitlement to be proven — Entitlement to each benefit must generally be proven individually. Damages may be refused if they are not pleaded, or if there is a total lack of evidence about the benefits provided, or their value. The employer is not required to make a lump-sum payment in lieu of benefits, for example, a percentage of salary. Sometimes, however, judges lump benefits together in a single benefits award; or include them with other damages; or compensate for benefits by increasing the notice period.

Vesting within notice period — Where entitlement to a benefit such as long-term disability pay or life insurance vests within the notice period, the employee may be entitled to full damages for the lost benefit. See Chapter G-5, "Insured Benefits, Sick Leave and Disability Benefits".

Duty to mitigate benefits loss — The duty to mitigate applies to benefits as well as salary:

- The value of benefits obtained in a new job that starts during the notice period should be deducted from the damages payable by the old employer for lost benefits.
- The employee will still be entitled to compensation for any difference in benefits between the old and the new jobs.
- The value of benefits provided by the dismissing employer during the notice period should be deducted from damages for lost benefits.

G-1.3 TIME FROM WHICH DAMAGES RUN

General principles — Normally, damages will be computed from the time of breach. This is usually the time that notice of termination is given, as long as the notice has been clear and unequivocal. Where the employer continues to pay the employee in lieu of notice but the employee has been told he or she is dismissed, the payments do not prolong the employment and damages run from the date the employee was told of the dismissal, so that the employer receives credit for all paid notice it has given. Damages may be computed from the date of dismissal, rather than from the date of notice, where ongoing negotiations prevent certainty until actually dismissed. Other examples include:

- An employee who was given notice of a fundamental change but was not sure when it would take effect. His damages were said to run from the actual termination date.
- An employee who accepted a temporary assignment during his notice period. The start of damages was not delayed, even where the temporary assignment was extended several times, as it was always clear that he would be terminated at the end of the assignment.

Constructive dismissal — In constructive dismissal situations, the notice period generally will run from the time of the unilateral change, even if the employee did not elect to treat the change as a dismissal until a few weeks later. In some cases, where the changes are not fundamental or are not immediately treated as a constructive dismissal, however, damages may run from the time of actual termination rather than the time of the change. For example, where an employee was reasonable in trying to resolve the situation before he finally resigned, his damages ran from the date of his resignation, not from the date of the change, which was not clear and definitive in any event.

Anticipatory breach — Where an employee is terminated before actually starting work, damages will run from the date of notice. In one case, where notice was given very close to the start date, damages ran from the day the employee would have started work. Where an employee would have been on probation for the first three months of her employment, she was awarded damages for the entire probationary period.

Exceptions — There are a few exceptions in the case law to the principle that damages start from the date notice is given:

- Where an employee was working outside Canada, damages did not start to run until he returned to Canada, since the purpose of notice is to allow the employee to seek other work and he could not do that until he returned.
- Damages of a teacher dismissed at the end of the school year did not start to run until the beginning of the next school year, although the teacher was paid through the summer under the terms of her hiring.
- Where an employee had worked for the employer for one week after termination at his own suggestion and for the employer's benefit, the termination date was delayed by one week so that the employee's earnings in that week would not be deducted from his damages.
- Where an employee took his earned vacation immediately after removal from his job, his damages did not start to run until the end of his vacation.
- Where an employee had surgery shortly after receiving four months' notice of termination, the court held that his damages should not start to run until the end of the 16-week rehabilitation period to which he was entitled under his disability plan.

In other cases, however, the fact that an employee was disabled at the time of termination has not been held to affect commencement of the notice period; see Chapter G-11, "Deductions from the Damage Award".

G-1.4 TIME AT WHICH DAMAGES END

General principles — Normally, damages continue to the end of the notice period. Any event occurring after dismissal and before the end of the notice period may affect damages, although it should not affect the notice period itself.

New job — Some judges routinely cut off damages at the point when the employee obtains an equal-paying or higher-paying new job, but this is improper in principle.

Failure to mitigate — Damages may be cut off at the point when the employee should have accepted a new job or made proper efforts to find a new job, but did not. See Chapter H-1, "Mitigation of Damages".

Death — An employee's death within the notice period may stop damages from running. In one case, it was said that the cause of action survived the employee's death, and therefore the severance pay offer made but not yet accepted at the time of her death survived, and her estate was awarded the full amount of the offer.

Retirement — The fact that an employee has reached age 65 or other normal retirement age may end damages, if the employee had agreed to mandatory retirement at age 65. If there was no such agreement, reaching age 65 will not normally affect the damage award.

Planned resignation — If an employee had already announced plans to resign, but was terminated before resigning, damages will be cut off as of the planned resignation date. Similarly, an employee who resigned part way through a period of working notice had his damages cut off at that point, except for a sum the employer had offered to pay which did not depend on the employee remaining at work.

Repudiation — If an employee otherwise repudiates the contract after receiving notice but before termination, damages may be cut off. For example, an employee who sued within the period of working notice was found to have repudiated the contract in one case.

Disability — Where an employee becomes totally disabled within the notice period, damages may be cut off as of the date he could no longer have worked.

Employer's bankruptcy — The fact that an employer becomes bankrupt several months after an employee's dismissal, and within the employee's notice period, does not limit the employee's right to or amount of damages.

G-1.5 EARLY TERMINATION OF FIXED-TERM CONTRACTS

General principles — In the absence of an industry custom, statute or contractual limit on termination pay, damages for dismissal before the end of a fixed term are based on the unexpired portion of the contract, rather than reasonable notice. Thus, the employee will normally be entitled to damages equal to the compensation due under the entire balance of the contract. The damages payable are limited to the amount due under the unexpired portion of the contract and may not exceed that amount even if the employee would have been entitled to a greater amount of reasonable notice.

Reduction in damages — The amount of reasonable notice to which the employee would have been entitled is normally not considered. In a few cases, where the remaining contract period is very lengthy, however, damages have been reduced based on a comparison with the reasonable notice that would have applied. For example, where an employee was dismissed less than six months into a five-year contract, he was awarded damages for only half the remaining term of the contract. Damages may also be reduced to reflect expected mitigation or other contingencies; see the discussion under Section G-11.4, "Future Contingencies" in Chapter G-11, "Deductions from the Damage Award".

Anticipatory breach — Where there was anticipatory breach of a fixed-term contract, the court found that the plaintiff had never become an employee but was entitled to reasonable notice of termination, to run from the date of notice, not the date on which employment would have started.

Renewal option — Where the contract that was breached contained a renewal option, damages have been mixed. For example:

- Where a contract contained an option for a five-year renewal, no damages were awarded for this period. Dismissal during the first five-year period, although wrongful, was effective notice under the contract that it would not be renewed.
- Where the employer breached its duty to use its best efforts to obtain an employee's reappointment but the appointment was not certain even if the employer had met its duty, damages were awarded based on the loss of a chance for the one-year reappointment.
- Where an employee almost certainly would have exercised his option to extend the contract for a further three years, he was awarded two-thirds of the present value of the future pay and benefits, with the deduction reflecting contingencies and a failure to mitigate.

Unenforceable fixed term — Where a fixed-term contract is intended but the contract is unenforceable, an employee may receive damages based on reasonable notice instead. The expectation of a fixed term may be taken into account in setting the notice period.

Additional damages — In a few cases, where early termination of a fixed-term contract caused other harm to the employee, additional damages have been awarded. For example:

- An employee who would have qualified for unemployment insurance benefits at the end of his four-month contract but did not qualify when dismissed after three months was awarded the amount of the benefits which had been forfeited by the employer's actions.
- An employee who suffered income tax disadvantages because of the dismissal had his damages "grossed up" to adjust for the income tax difference.

Nonrenewal — An employee's rights upon nonrenewal of a fixed-term contract are discussed in Chapter A-2, "Employment Status and Types of Employment Contract".

Increased damages — Although an employer's bad faith can increase the reasonable notice period, this principle would not seem to apply to damages for breach of a fixed-term contract, where damages are not based on reasonable notice.

G-1.6 CONTRACTUAL NOTICE PROVISIONS

General principle — Where a contract provides for a specified amount of notice, its terms pre-empt the right to reasonable notice, and the employee will be entitled only to damages based on the contractual provision. See Chapter E-6, "Express Termination Provisions". An employee entitled to a contractual notice period may also be entitled to a period of notice required by statute.

Exceptions — Where the employer breaches the contract, the courts may or may not apply the contractual notice period. For example:

- Where a contract contemplated dismissal with cause or without cause, but the employer wrongly dismissed the employee on the basis of cause that did not exist, the contractual notice period was considered but not followed.
- Where a contract for a fixed term of employment also included a severance pay clause that was breached by the employer, the employee became entitled to payment under the severance clause plus damages for the remainder of the fixed term.

Benefits — Where a contract provides for the employee to receive a certain amount of pay, or uses language that does not specify the amounts to be included in the damages, it may or may not be interpreted to include benefits. In one case, damages for lost benefits were refused, except for vacation pay.

Duty to mitigate — Sums earned in mitigation may not be deductible from contractually-required termination pay. However, where a trial takes place before expiry of the notice or severance pay period, damages may be subject to a deduction for contingencies.

Chapter G-2

SALARY, WAGES AND ALLOWANCES

TABLE OF CONTENTS

G-2.1   General Principles
G-2.2   Salary and Wages
G-2.3   Rate of Pay
G-2.4   Raises During Notice Period
G-2.5   Overtime Pay
G-2.6   Other Remuneration

G-2.1 GENERAL PRINCIPLES

Lost earnings — A wrongfully dismissed employee is entitled to damages based on the amount that he would have earned if working notice had been given. His lost remuneration — the salary, wages, commissions or bonuses he was paid — is usually the largest segment of his damages. Damages are to be based on the amount paid to the employee, not the amount charged to customers for the employee's services. For a discussion concerning commissions and bonuses, see Chapter G-3, "Commissions and Bonuses" and Chapter G-4, "Profit Sharing and Stock Options".

Other remuneration — An employee will be entitled to all remuneration he or she normally received, including special cost of living and location supplements, or other allowances, as discussed later in this chapter.

Circumstances during notice period — Damages are based on what the employee would have earned during the notice period. For example:

- An employee who would only have been able to work half-time through most of the notice period was only awarded half pay.
- An employee who would have been on an unpaid bereavement leave for several weeks during the notice period did not receive damages for those weeks.
- An employee who only worked when the employer had contracts had his damages reduced from one year's pay to 10 weeks' pay, the length of the contract work that would have been available to him during the one-year notice period.

- A part-time employee was only entitled to damages based on her part-time earnings.
- An employee was awarded damages based on his annual earnings, even though the notice period would have occurred during a season when there would have been less work available.
- An employee whose pay was reduced for several months before his termination due to the employer's financial problems was awarded damages based on his previous pay rate.

G-2.2 SALARY AND WAGES

Salary — Where remuneration is by salary, the calculation of damages is usually straightforward, based on the gross salary that would have been payable during the notice period. Damages are based on the employee's gross pay, not net, although occasional awards have included additional damages for income tax liability.

T4 slips — While some judges base damages on the employee's T4 slips, including amounts such as lump-sum vacation payments, others have said that taxable benefits, overtime pay and vacation pay should not be included in salary, but should be dealt with separately.

Hourly wages — Hourly wages will generally be calculated by applying the number of work hours in the notice period. Where an employee's hours would have varied over the notice period or over the course of employment, courts have based damages on:

- Average figures.
- Evidence of how much work was available during the notice period.
- An employee's earnings in the most recent months or the year before dismissal, excluding special payments that would not ordinarily have been received.

G-2.3 RATE OF PAY

Official pay rate governs — The pay rate for damages is normally the rate to which the employee is contractually entitled. For example:

- Where the employer was gratuitously paying more than it had agreed to pay in the last few months before termination, damages were calculated at the official salary rate.
- Where an employee had received a raise shortly before the termination, he was entitled to damages at the increased rate.

- Where an employer had recently added duties and agreed to increase the employee's pay, he was entitled to the surcharge the employer had agreed to pay.
- Where training had been imposed unilaterally and without justification on a long-term employee, the employer was not entitled to reduce the employee's damages to reflect the training period.

Unilateral change — Where an employer has unilaterally changed an employee's pay before termination, the employee is usually entitled to damages based on the original rate. The exception is where the employee's conduct shows he or she has accepted the change, or it was not a breach of contract by the employer.

Calculation methods — Where the rate of pay is in dispute, various methods have been used to calculate it. The rate of pay may be assessed on the balance of probabilities where it had not yet been agreed to. For example:

- A seasonal employee's damages were not based on the previous season where that rate had been exceptionally high, and it would not have been as high during the notice period due to the employer's financial situation.
- Where the parties had agreed on a standard, such as the league average, it was applied even though they had never agreed to an actual dollar figure.

Quantum meruit — Where a pay rate was never agreed to, an employee may be awarded damages based on what the work was worth, considering what is reasonable, what similar employees were earning at the time, what the plaintiff had earned in the past, and any representations made to the plaintiff about earnings. For example, a farm hand who had performed general labour, repairs and maintenance plus special projects for the farm owner in return for free housing was awarded the value of his work, including the value of renovations he had done to the house, less the value of the free rent provided.

G-2.4 RAISES DURING NOTICE PERIOD

General principle — Generally, an employee is not entitled to increases that were scheduled or were given to other employees within the notice period, on the basis that an employer is only required to maintain the same terms of employment during the notice period. It is usually unrealistic to think an employee given working notice would receive an increase, since the incentive basis of a wage increase is removed by the notice of dismissal. Increases were not granted where:

- Increases were purely discretionary and there was no contractual right to a raise.
- Increases were based on performance and the employer was dissatisfied with the employee's performance.
- An employee had been offered a raise but had declined it until the end of the year. The promise of a retroactive increase at a later date was found to be gratuitous.
- An employee had been told he would get a salary increase but it was never forthcoming and he was then dismissed. The increase had been deferred, and it was said the court could not rewrite the terms of the agreement.
- A raise had been promised conditionally.
- An employee's wage rate for the coming year had not yet been set. His damages were assessed on the basis of the previous year's rate.
- An employee had twice been granted an annual raise. This did not create an implied term that she would always receive an annual raise, especially where her pay was already at the top of the scale for her position.
- An employee's replacement was paid a higher rate, as there was no contractual obligation to increase his pay.
- Employers were imposing wage restraints or cutbacks at the time or were experiencing financial problems or business uncertainties.
- An employee's pay was red-circled at the time of dismissal.

Raise granted — Occasionally, however, raises are included in damages. Grounds for awarding a raise have included:

- The employee was wrongfully deprived of a raise prior to the start of the notice period.
- Increases were an express term, or an implied term, of the contract based on past practice, as long as there is evidence of the amount of such an increase. For example, the fact that all other employees were given a non-discretionary, uniform increase, such as a cost of living increase, may be evidence of a contractual right.
- An employee was in a management trainee program and would have been promoted within the notice period if he had not been dismissed.
- A retroactive raise was given to other employees effective as of a date before the notice period began. However, an increase from a statutory pay equity process was awarded to an employee who had been dismissed before the date of the retroactive increase.

Amount of damages — Where damages have been awarded, they have been based on the average of past increases, the amount of increases to others within the notice period, or on the amount paid to an employee's replacement. Even where a raise should be included in damages, it will be refused if the evidence as to amount is too vague.

G-2.5 OVERTIME PAY

Entitlement — An employee may be entitled to damages for overtime pay if it likely would have been received within the notice period, or if it was regularly worked by the employee in the past. Damages will likely not be payable where there was no contractual right to work overtime. Where damages are awarded, they may be based on an average of overtime pay received before termination. Damages may also be awarded for overtime worked but not paid before dismissal.

Examples — overtime pay awarded — For example, damages for overtime pay were awarded where:

- An employee had regularly worked overtime but had not been paid for it, contrary to the applicable employment standards statute. Damages included overtime based on the amount of overtime he had worked in the past.
- The employee's replacement did not work overtime but the employee had regularly worked it without complaint from the employer.

Examples — no award — No damages for overtime pay were awarded where:

- It was unlikely that overtime would have been offered to the employee.
- The employee would not have been able to work overtime during the notice period for personal reasons.
- The employee would likely have worked overtime during the notice period, but the amount of damages was too hard to quantify.
- Salaried management employees were not paid extra for overtime worked.

Lieu time — Employees who work overtime are sometimes compensated by paid time off in lieu of overtime pay. Compensating these employees becomes an issue where they are dismissed before being given the time off. Whether the employee will be compensated may depend on whether there is a contractual entitlement to the lieu time. For example, the fact that an employer had informally allowed an employee to take time off in exchange for overtime did not amount to an agreement that she could bank her overtime, and she was not entitled to extra damages. Loss of credit time, which entitled an employee to time off in lieu of overtime worked, was refused where it was said the employee would have received the same pay as had already been awarded, simply working fewer hours.

Damages for lieu time — Where compensation has been awarded, courts have:

- Awarded monetary damages to compensate employees for the time off they would not be able to take.

- Awarded partial compensation for employees' accumulated lieu time, where it was clear that they never would have been able to take the full time off or receive the full payment, even if they had remained employed.

G-2.6 OTHER REMUNERATION

Extra fees for extra services — In some cases, employees who were entitled to earn extra fees for extra services as part of their regular employment have been entitled to damages based on the average fees per month earned during their employment. In other cases, no damages were awarded for extra fees. No damages were awarded where:

- Fees were earned from third parties for a separate, though related, position.
- An employee was paid a salary plus additional sitting fees for each meeting, but the contract was breached early in its term before an activity level had been established.

Shift premiums — Shift premiums were denied in one case on the basis that they were too hard to quantify, but they have been awarded in other cases; for example, where:

- An employee commonly received shift premiums, and likely would have been entitled to them if he had worked through the notice period.
- An employee would have worked and received payment for after-hours calls. He was awarded damages for that loss.

Tips or gratuities — An employee may also be entitled to damages for tips or gratuities that would have been received within the notice period, although damages are not always awarded on this ground. Damages were awarded in one case on the basis of actual past earnings, not on the basis of the amount claimed for income tax purposes.

Incentives — No damages were awarded for the value of an incentive trip for which the employee would have qualified if he had worked through the notice period, as the employer had no obligation to make such a payment.

Directors' fees — Directors' fees have been granted in some cases, but not in others. Directors' fees have been granted where they had been a regular part of an employee's pay. A chairman of the board was held to be entitled only to payment for the months of the year he served, not to the full amount of an "annual" retainer. Directors' fees were denied where:

- An employee had no contractual entitlement to them. The fact that other directors had been paid did not entitle the employee to payment.

- The employee probably would have been removed as a director during the notice period.

Expenses — Expenses that would have been incurred by the employee in performing his or her job should not be deducted from damages where the employer normally reimbursed the employee for the expenses. Personal expenses generally will not be deductible either. See Chapter G-11, "Deductions from the Damage Award". Business expenses normally deducted from commission earnings may be deducted from damages, as discussed in Chapter G-3, "Commissions and Bonuses".

Advances — Where an employee has already received advances that exceed the amount to which he is entitled upon dismissal, the employer will have a valid counterclaim or even a free-standing claim for the excess, or will be entitled to deduct the overpayment from other damages owed.

Chapter G-3

COMMISSIONS AND BONUSES

TABLE OF CONTENTS

G-3.1   Contractual Entitlement to Commissions
G-3.2   Evidence Commissions Would Have Been Earned
G-3.3   Calculating Damages for Commissions
G-3.4   Deductions from Commission Damages
G-3.5   Bonuses Generally
G-3.6   Bonus Entitlement
G-3.7   Calculating Damages for Bonuses

G-3.1 CONTRACTUAL ENTITLEMENT TO COMMISSIONS

General rule — Dismissed employees who were paid partly or wholly by commission are entitled to damages for the commissions they would have earned during the notice period, if

(1)   contractual entitlement is established;
(2)   there is evidence that the commissions would have been earned; and
(3)   there is evidence to allow the court to estimate the amount.

Of course, damages can also be awarded for outstanding commissions that were earned before termination. Where an employee received more in a draw against commissions than he actually earned before termination, the employer had a valid claim or counterclaim for the excess.

Contractual entitlement — Issues may arise as to whether an employee was to receive a particular commission, both before and after termination. For example:

- Where it was not clear whether a General Sales Manager was to receive commission on all sales or only on all car sales, the court found he should receive commission only on car sales, as this was his area of responsibility.
- Where an employee had made a proposal and the employer had accepted it, but later read the proposal more carefully and refused it, the employer was held to its original acceptance, and the employee was

awarded commissions on that basis both before and after the notice period.
- An employer who changed an employee's entitlement to commissions in mid-employment, without notice, was required to pay damages based on the original agreement made with the employee.

Commissions on gross sales — Where an employee's commission is based on the employer's gross sales rather than just the employee's own sales, some employees have argued that damages should be based on a time period prior to the notice period, since the gross sales would have been higher if their services had been retained. This argument was unsuccessful in two cases where economic conditions in the industry were generally poor; instead, the actual figures during the notice period were used as the basis for calculating damages. However, the argument has succeeded in a few cases:

- Where an employee-manager was to receive a share of profits and the company had not declared any profits, the court said it was entitled to estimate damages based on reasonable probabilities, since the employee was entitled to a share of the profits which might have been earned under his own management, not those earned under someone else's guidance.
- One employee was awarded damages based on his previous performance, on the assumption that he would have worked hard during the notice period to prove to the employer it had made a mistake in firing him.

Particular entitlement — Courts are sometimes asked to assess whether employees are entitled to particular commissions:

- A salesman entitled to commissions on all sales was entitled to be paid for goods sold before his termination but shipped after termination, because the commissions had already been earned and only the time of payment was delayed. An employee in a similar situation was entitled to the commissions, because it was said he had done everything to be done by him prior to his dismissal.
- Where the contract provided for a commission on all sales effected prior to termination, commission was payable on a sale completed before termination, even though delivery was later refused.
- Where the contract stated that the employee was entitled to a commission upon shipment and invoicing, this applied to product shipped and invoiced during the notice period, not just before termination.
- An employee was held to be entitled to a major commission on a sale during the notice period when he had been responsible for the earlier sale on which the subsequent sale was based.

- An employee was not entitled to a commission on sales after dismissal where there was no evidence that they were a result of her specific efforts.
- Where short-term leases sold by the employee were converted to full sales agreements after dismissal, the employee was not entitled to a commission, as he was not the effective cause of the sales.
- Where a commission was meant purely as an incentive to encourage an employee to collect on delinquent accounts, there was no entitlement once employment ceased.
- An employee was neither entitled to the projected value of a contract he negotiated, nor to the future value of contracts he negotiated. He was a salesman, not a business partner.

Contract ending entitlement — Contracts cutting off commissions as of the termination date are often strictly enforced. Sometimes, however, they have been more liberally interpreted:

- A contract that said payment of earned commissions was at a company's discretion once an employee "ceased to work" for the company was held to apply only to voluntary terminations, not to dismissals.
- Where an employee at the start of employment had received the benefit of commissions on sales he had not caused, he was not entitled to commissions not payable until after his termination, even though they were for sales before his termination.

G-3.2 EVIDENCE COMMISSIONS WOULD HAVE BEEN EARNED

Likelihood of earnings — Judges look at the likelihood that an employee would have earned commissions if he had worked through the reasonable notice period. This can involve looking at business factors, the employee's personal factors, the employee's past history of earning commissions, and the parties' expectations. For instance, judges have considered:

- The percentage increase or decrease in the employer's business.
- General economic conditions affecting the industry.
- The trend in the employee's earnings over the history of his employment.
- The unlikeliness of an increase in earnings during the notice period.
- The employee's projected income, as estimated by the employer.
- The amount earned by an employee's successor, although this will not always be appropriate.

Combination of factors — A damages assessment usually involves considering many of these factors in combination, and making a best guess at what the employee would have earned during the notice period. For example:

- Where an employee's service was very short so there was no commission history, and there were no comparable employees earning commissions, a judge estimated commissions by considering the parties' expectations. Additional considerations were the various positive and negative contingencies and the fact that the job was expected to be developmental for the first few months so that earnings would have been lower at the beginning rather than later on.
- One employee was awarded damages based on the mid-point between his earnings in the past year and his projected earnings in the year of termination, because it had been the best year in the company's history to the date of termination, and the employee had a history of increasing his earnings each year.
- One case accepted an employee's evidence as to his likely sales level and concluded his earnings would have been as good as in the past.
- Where an employee paid by salary plus commissions had worked on straight commission during the notice period in an effort to mitigate his damages, he was awarded damages based on his minimum guaranteed income, and the amount earned in mitigation was deducted. Since the dismissal was due to lack of business, there was no evidence justifying an award for lost commissions.

G-3.3 CALCULATING DAMAGES FOR COMMISSIONS

Rate at time of dismissal — As with other types of remuneration, the rate at which damages will be calculated will be the rate in effect at the time of dismissal, not, for example, a lower rate adopted by the employer during the notice period.

Averaging — Sometimes judges simply estimate commission earnings during the notice period, but usually they use an average of past commission earnings to estimate earnings during the notice period, in addition to the factors discussed earlier. An average amount may be refused where it is inappropriate; for example, to even out seasonal fluctuations where the employee had only been employed for part of one season. Where averaging is not appropriate, judges may make a comparison with the same time period in the previous year. In one case, where the method of calculating commissions had been inconsistent, an average of the two methods was used.

Time period for averaging — The most common averaging period is probably one year. Often, the reason for choosing the time period over which earnings are averaged is not explained, although the following factors seem to have been considered:

- Where earnings varied widely over time or between seasons, or the compensation method had recently changed, a longer averaging period may be required.
- Where an employee's commission income had been artificially decreased due to changes in the employer's policies, a longer time window was justified, since choosing too narrow a window could encourage employers to cut back an employee's income just before a planned termination.
- Some judges seem to purposely endorse averaging periods that reflect an employee's best earnings. Where the circumstances make it hard to assess what would have happened during the notice period, however, last year's figures may be used, even where it was a "slow" year or a better than average year.

Personal factors — Judges may take into account personal factors that have affected earnings before dismissal. For example:

- The fact that an employee's earnings were starting to recover after a maternity leave was considered in basing her damages on a higher amount than that earned in the last year.
- Where an employee's sales in the year before dismissal had been lower than normal due to the fatal illness of his son, he was awarded a higher amount.

G-3.4 DEDUCTIONS FROM COMMISSION DAMAGES

Deductions from profits — Where items were unfairly charged against profits, the employee was entitled to a commission on the profit as properly calculated. Only half of a chargeback due to a cancelled sale was deducted from a plaintiff's commissions where there was a good chance the sale would not have been cancelled if the plaintiff had not been fired.

Expenses — Expenses that would have been incurred by the employee in earning the commissions are normally taken into account, on the theory that he should not be placed in a better position than he would have been in if he had continued working. Where deducted, the amount of the deduction may be based on the expenses accepted by Revenue Canada.

Expenses not deducted — Some judges, however, refuse to deduct the expenses an employee would have incurred. In some cases, the reason for refusing to deduct normal expenses is not clear. Expenses were not deducted where:

- It was said the employee would have been entitled to a greater period of notice if damages had been calculated on his net remuneration rather than his gross commissions.
- Gross commissions rather than net commissions were awarded where the employee incurred substantial out-of-pocket expenses in new employment taken to fulfill his duty to mitigate.

G-3.5 BONUSES GENERALLY

Similarities — Some commission plans and some profit-sharing plans are similar to some bonus plans in structure. The legal treatment also may be similar. Profit-sharing plans are discussed in Chapter G-4, "Profit Sharing and Stock Options".

Contractual entitlement — Where there is a contractual right to the bonus, it will be included in an employee's damages, even if it was intended as a performance incentive from the employer's point of view. This may include the right to a bonus at the end of a fixed-term contract. A contractual entitlement has been found where:

- The bonus was mentioned at the time of hiring.
- Removal of the bonus would be a serious downgrading of the employee's status, akin to a constructive dismissal.
- A bonus was standard in the industry and was a substantial part of an employee's income.

Discretionary amount — Even where the amount is discretionary, if entitlement to a bonus is an integral part of an employee's contract, a court may still award damages. Conversely, some judges have refused damages where the amount of the bonus, being discretionary, could have been minimal. One case has said that if there are conditions on an employee's entitlement to a bonus, these must be communicated to the employee by the employer. An employee who was guaranteed a bonus of "at least $5,000" had a contractual right to the bonus, and was awarded the guaranteed amount.

Entitlement created over time — Most judges accept the view that a contractual right can be created over time where a discretionary bonus is always paid over many years of employment. A contractual claim may be particularly strong if the bonus has been used by the employer as an adjustment for wages below the prevailing rate or has been an integral part of the pay package. In one case, where a bonus had been given to compensate for a low salary, entitlement to the bonus was eliminated by a substantial salary increase.

Bonus based on merit — Where performance, merit or other criteria affect bonus entitlement, the employer cannot act arbitrarily or Capriciously in refusing a bonus, and must act reasonably and honestly in assessing a discretionary amount. The court may consider an employee's entitlement to a bonus for the notice period based on his actions before termination and expected actions during a period of working notice. For example:

- Where the discretionary bonus was based on performance, the employee's performance was good and all other employees in his position received bonuses, the employee was awarded the bonus.
- Where a merit bonus was based on performance and the employee had been guilty of misconduct short of just cause for dismissal, it was unlikely he would have received a bonus that year, so no damages were awarded. Yet in another case, misconduct was held not to justify withholding an expected bonus.
- Where an employee had been denied the merit portion of his bonus for several years and was terminated due to dissatisfaction with his performance, no damages for the merit portion were justified, although he was still awarded the non-discretionary portion.
- A truck driver who was dismissed for unsafe driving was refused a safety bonus.

Purely discretionary bonuses — Where bonuses have been awarded in the past but only at the employer's complete discretion, with no contractual right arising expressly or by implication, they are generally treated as voluntary payments which are not compensable in damages. Damages have been refused where:

- A bonus was not an integral part of an employee's compensation, and his damages had included a substantial salary increase which he received one month before dismissal.
- An employee had received bonuses in the past but was terminated upon sale of the business. His claim for a bonus during the notice period was too speculative.
- An employee's contract had provided for a bonus in a particular year, which had been paid, but the contract said nothing about future bonuses.
- An employee received an incentive bonus plan while employed, but the incentive purpose of the bonus would have disappeared once notice was given.
- The employer had no contractual duty to pay the cash value of an incentive trip for which the employee would have qualified if he had worked through the notice period.

G-3.6 BONUS ENTITLEMENT

General principles — Once a bonus is announced to an employee, or he has met all eligibility requirements of a non-discretionary bonus before dismissal, it may be treated as a contractual term that cannot be revoked, even where the employee is terminated before the bonus has been paid. All contractual conditions must have been met before termination, or there must be evidence they would have been met within the notice period, to justify an award. For example:

- Damages were refused where the bonus depended on the employee remaining at a remote mining site and he had not remained there through the notice period.
- Where a condition had been met — for example, staying on until the end of the notice period — the employee did not lose entitlement to the bonus due to her refusal to accept a severance package offered by the employer.

Examples — bonus awarded — Damages were awarded for a bonus where:

- Money had already been allocated to an incentive bonus plan on the employee's behalf before dismissal. He was entitled to the bonus for that year, although not for the rest of the notice period, since the incentive purpose of the bonus would have disappeared once notice was given.
- A bonus plan was adopted retroactively just after an employee's constructive dismissal. He was entitled to a bonus for the period before dismissal, but not for the notice period, because he failed to mitigate by failing to stay on while looking for a new job.
- An employee was due to receive a bonus payment on the very day of dismissal.
- An employee who was entitled to a bonus had her position changed without mention of any effect on her bonus entitlement.
- The notice period encompassed two bonus payments but the employee had not worked at all during the notice period, the employee was awarded only one bonus. In another case, however, it was stressed that this will depend on the circumstances; where a bonus represented both a reward for past service and an incentive for future performance, at least partial compensation was appropriate in both years.

Examples — bonus denied — No damages for a bonus were awarded where:

- An employee had not met the contractual requirements or performance standards to be entitled to a bonus, and no bonus had been approved for him before his dismissal.

- An employer agreed to forgive a loan in lieu of a bonus. An employee may be entitled to the bonus or forgiveness of the loan, but not both, and perhaps neither.
- The employer had revoked the bonus several months before the employee's termination. By staying on the job rather than quitting at the time, the employee had earned more than the amount of the bonus and so had suffered no damages.
- An employee, whose contract was changed to eliminate his participation in a discretionary bonus plan several years before termination, did not object to the change. He was not entitled to damages for past bonuses after termination.

Conditional on employment — Some bonus plans may contain provisions that the employee must remain employed on the bonus payment date, or remain employed for an entire year, to be entitled to the bonus. Where the employee would have met this condition if he or she had received working notice of termination, damages will generally be allowed.

Partial entitlement? — A requirement that an employee remain employed through the end of the year may bar recovery where the time worked plus the length of the notice period still do not cover the full bonus period, although a *pro rata* bonus has been awarded in some cases, as discussed later in this chapter under G-3.7, "Calculating Damages for Bonuses".

Resignation after bonus payment — An employer was not entitled to repayment of a bonus paid to an employee just one week before he resigned.

Share of profits — Where a bonus was to be based on profits, and profits were unlikely or non-existent during the notice period due to the employer's financial situation or general business conditions, no damages will be awarded unless the bonus has been "guaranteed" or otherwise made part of the employee's basic compensation. For example, in one case, a profit figure was not reached so that a bonus was not payable by the terms of the contract; damages were refused even though the employer had paid a gratuitous bonus to all other members of the bonus plan. However, for the next year included in the notice period, the profit figure was reached, so the employee was entitled to the bonus for that period.

Employer profitable — The fact that the employer did well financially, leading to higher bonuses for other employees, has been considered in assessing damages. Where a bonus depended on reaching a profit target, proof of the target actually being reached within the time period may be required; where the trial occurs before the end of the period, the court may not be entitled to assume that the target will be reached. Where an employee's contract provided for a bonus based on profits to a certain date, the fact that an employer changed its year end did not change its obligation to pay the bonus.

G-3.7 CALCULATING DAMAGES FOR BONUSES

Determining bonus payments — A court may correct errors in bonus payments prior to dismissal where the employee had a contractual right to a certain payment. For instance, an amount improperly deducted from the bonus, or from the figures on which the bonus is based, may be rectified. A court may also settle the terms of the bonus where entitlement is clear but the formula for calculating the bonus is not.

Factors to consider — Where no formula for calculating a bonus has been agreed to, judges have used various approaches to assess the amount of damages, based on:

- An amount regarded as fair or reasonable, or a *quantum meruit* assessment.
- The bonuses paid to other employees.
- The amount paid to an employee's successor.
- The amount expected by the employee, particularly where the employee's expectations were reasonable and known to the employer.
- The amount the employee was likely to earn under the economic circumstances at the time, where the bonus depended on sales or profits.
- The amount promised to the employee's replacement as an annual minimum bonus.

Previous bonuses — Reliable evidence of the employer's actual performance or the actual amounts paid to others within the notice period may be preferred to evidence based on the past. However, damages are often based on an amount paid in the past (although not necessarily the highest amount paid in the past), or on an average of past amounts. Where nothing was paid in the past, that fact may also be taken into account. For example:

- Damages were based on a past amount where the employer had never accepted or rejected the employee's proposed formula, but the employee had been paid in accordance with it in the previous year.
- An employee, who claimed that she was entitled to a bonus based on a percentage of sales, had her claim dismissed. No mention was made of the entitlement in her hiring letter, and she had accepted bonuses on a different basis throughout her employment, without complaint.

Share of profits — The calculation of bonuses based on profits is similar to the calculation of commissions, as discussed earlier in this chapter.

***Pro rata* payments** — Employees who resign prior to the time of payment of a bonus sometimes seek a *pro rata* payment. These claims have met with mixed success.

Examples — *pro rata* **payment denied** — Some cases have refused payment because:

- The bonus was not due and payable at the time of the employee's resignation and there was no contractual provision for *pro rata* payments.
- The bonus was intended as a performance incentive and there was no motivational benefit once the employee quit.

Examples — *pro rata* **payment awarded** — *Pro rata* payments have been awarded where:

- The bonus was an important part of the employee's compensation.
- The employer never made clear to the employee that there would be no entitlement if the employee left before the end of the year.
- There was a contractual right that was neither discretionary nor dependent on the employee's performance.
- Other employees had been paid a *pro rata* bonus after resigning.
- An employee's resignation before the bonus qualification date was prompted by the employer's anticipatory breach.
- An employee's service plus the notice period totalled less than one year, but his contract provided for a minimum guaranteed bonus of $25,000 per year. It was proper to prorate the bonus from his hiring date until the end of the notice period.

Chapter G-4

PROFIT SHARING AND STOCK OPTIONS

TABLE OF CONTENTS

G-4.1   Profit-Sharing Plans
G-4.2   Stock Options and Stock Purchase Plans

G-4.1 PROFIT-SHARING PLANS

Discretionary plan — Some profit-sharing plans are similar to bonuses or even commissions, as discussed in Chapter G-3, "Commissions and Bonuses". As with bonuses, damages may be refused where a profit-sharing arrangement was completely discretionary. An employee who had been given equity participation in a project was denied damages for the lost chance to transfer that participation to a more profitable project, as his rights were entirely at the employer's discretion. Similarly, he was not entitled to damages for the lost chance to participate in an unspecified future project, as the claim was entirely too uncertain.

Contractual entitlement — Where a profit-sharing arrangement is an express or implied part of an employee's contract, the employee may be awarded damages for the benefit he would have received during the notice period, or a prorated amount as damages for the lost profit sharing.

Entitlement within notice period — Where a plan requires employment upon a certain date to be entitled to payment, courts may interpret the plan as applying as long as the date falls within the notice period. In one case, where the length of the notice period was not long enough to have entitled an employee to benefits under the terms of a Deferred Profit Sharing Plan (DPSP), he was not entitled to any damages for the part of the year he had been employed. Where the terms of a profit-sharing plan required employment at the end of the year to be entitled to payment and this term had been made clear to an employee, he could not claim damages when he resigned before the end of the year.

Part of compensation — In some circumstances, the profit-sharing arrangement may be such a vital part of an employee's compensation that he will be entitled to a *pro rata* share, even if he would not have become entitled to full payment within the notice period. Damages were awarded where an employer had started a profit-sharing program instead of giving an employee a raise. Even though the plan was not to vest for three years, the employer could not take away its value, once it was promised, by firing the employee.

No profit — There is a dispute about whether a court should consider the fact that no profit was made during the notice period and thus that no benefit was payable, or whether the value of the benefit should be assessed as of the date of dismissal.

Contributions — The amount of contributions that would have been made during the notice period to a combined DPSP/RRSP has been awarded in several cases.

G-4.2 STOCK OPTIONS AND STOCK PURCHASE PLANS

Terms of agreement — A number of cases have considered damages for the lost opportunity to buy shares under a stock option plan or for the premature forced resale of shares to the company on termination. Each case will depend on the interpretation of the agreement involved. An agreement that limited rights of "employees" used that term to mean all people entitled to participate in the stock option plan, so it was found to apply to a consultant who was not legally an employee. Where there was no share purchase agreement and there was only a discussion about the possibility of offering the employee the chance to buy shares, the employee was not entitled to damages; the conduct, however, was taken into account in setting the notice period. Courts will also enforce the terms of shareholder agreements, including enforcing transfers and setting the valuations of shares.

Limited rights upon "termination" — There may be no entitlement where there was a valid condition limiting the employee's rights upon termination for any reason, or upon termination for cause. Some cases have held that where an agreement was said to end upon "termination of employment," this should be taken to mean lawful termination, i.e. the end of the notice period. In other cases, however, the contract's wording has been interpreted to mean the dismissal date and not the end of the reasonable notice period.

Change during notice period — Where an employer changed its prospectus within the notice period to suggest that options which had not been vested now were vested, this new contractual right did not give the plaintiff employee additional rights over those that he had at the time of termination.

Option to purchase — Damages will generally be allowable based on the difference between the option price and the market value on the date within the notice period when the employee could have purchased, multiplied by the number of shares the employee would have purchased, as established by the evidence. Where the options did not specify a date, a judge in one case found that they should have been exercised when the employee's duty to mitigate arose, and damages were assessed as of the month following his termination.

Resale agreement — Damages generally will be the difference in price between the date the contract was wrongfully terminated and the date it would properly have been terminated. This is normally within or at the end of the notice period, but may be the date on which the employee took a new job. However, where it was found the agreement ceased as of the dismissal date, the dismissal date and the date of actual sale, rather than the end of the notice period, were used to assess the value of shares.

Option to purchase and resale agreement — Where both an option to purchase and a resale agreement are involved, damages will be the difference between the purchase price and the resale price.

Stock purchase plan — Where a stock purchase plan involved a purchase over time, damages will be the difference between the value at the subscription date and the value at the time the shares would have vested, without a deduction for contingencies. Where an employer would have contributed to a share purchase plan on the employee's behalf, she was awarded the amount of contributions that would have been made during the notice period.

Dividends — The employee will be entitled to any dividends payable during the period he was entitled to hold the shares. Where dividends were not payable until declared by the company, an employee was not entitled to a *pro rata* share of dividends for the notice period.

Share-purchase loan — A claim for both the loss of an interest-free share purchase loan and the shares themselves could not stand. The loan was not a separate benefit, but merely a means of facilitating the share purchase. Damages for loss of the shares and dividends would therefore compensate the employee fully.

Shares in place of other benefits — In one case where an employee had been promised shares to compensate him for pension benefits he had lost by giving up his former job, he was awarded the amount of the lost pension benefits. Where an employee had been promised shares to be purchased with his share of a profit-sharing plan, he was simply awarded the monetary value of the profit share.

Valuation date — In one case, an employee was to have received shares on a certain date, but the shares had still not been transferred to him by the time he was terminated. It was held that he was entitled to the value of the shares as of his termination date, since once he was terminated it was clear he was not going to receive the shares. A later valuation date was said not to be appropriate because the employee had not participated in the company's growth after his termination. In another case, an employee had been promised a certain percentage of the employer's shares, with an agreement that the employer would repurchase the shares. The employee was awarded the fair value of the shares in the month before termination.

Effect on notice period — One employee's notice period was increased slightly to allow him to participate in an initial public offering that occurred three days after the end of his original notice period. The employee was held to be entitled to purchase shares from the restricted stock portion of the offering.

Exceptions — The following situations have disentitled an employee to damages:

- His own breach of contract.
- Failure to object to a demand that he surrender his shares and options.
- Where the employer retained a discretion as to whether to offer stock options.
- Where the sale of shares upon termination of employment was required by an outside regulatory agency.
- The employee had never before taken advantage of a stock purchase plan and he had taken no steps to take advantage of the plan prior to termination, so there was no evidence he would have taken advantage of the benefit if he had been given reasonable notice.
- An employee would not likely have purchased shares during the notice period because of the high cost of obtaining a loan to do so.
- Where the shares would have been purchased from a bonus payment, but there were no bonuses paid during the notice period.
- Where an employee had sold his existing shares upon termination and there was no evidence the dividends during the notice period would have exceeded the interest on the resulting capital.
- Where the shares of a closely-held company were worth less than the employee had paid for them.
- Where the early forced resale actually left the employee better off than he would have been if he had sold the shares at the end of the notice period.

Sale before transfer — Where an employee sold his shares before being transferred to the United States, he was not entitled to damages for the additional profit he would have made if he had held the shares until termination, as he had voluntarily sold the shares on the basis of tax advice he had received.

Release — Where a shareholder agreement required the employee to give a release of all claims in order to be paid for his shares, this was interpreted not to include a release of employment claims.

Employer acting on employee's behalf — Where an employer acted as an employee's investment advisor and advised him to buy certain shares, and then refused to sell them for him when he requested it, the employer was liable for the employee's loss on the shares. The employer had breached its fiduciary duty to the employee. Similarly, where the employer had sold the employee shares improperly, it was liable to the employee for the loss.

Chapter G-5

INSURED BENEFITS, SICK LEAVE AND DISABILITY BENEFITS

TABLE OF CONTENTS

G-5.1   Damages for Insured Benefits Generally
G-5.2   Amount of Damages
G-5.3   Medical and Dental Insurance
G-5.4   Life Insurance
G-5.5   Sick Leave
G-5.6   Disability Benefits

G-5.1 DAMAGES FOR INSURED BENEFITS GENERALLY

Two views — Canadian courts do not agree about the treatment of damages for insured benefits. One group, which includes courts in British Columbia, takes the view that damages will not be awarded unless the employee can show he suffered an actual loss. The other group, including the Ontario courts, takes the view that damages should be awarded regardless of whether the employee can show a loss. The issue of a "loss" partly depends on whether you consider only monetary losses, or also consider the value of peace of mind created by insurance coverage. In addition, it depends on whether you consider the employee's position at the beginning or the end of the notice period, as explained by the British Columbia Court of Appeal:

> That difference in viewpoint may be significant in relation to certain fringes such as life insurance. At the beginning of the [notice] period, coverage must be seen to have value. At the end, if the risk did not materialize [i.e. if the employee did not die], its absence can be said to have caused no loss. (*Scott v. Lillooet School Dist. No. 29* (1991), 60 B.C.L.R. (2d) 273 at 279 (C.A.).) [Emphasis added]

No loss, no damages — In this view, an employee who received insurance coverage as a benefit of employment will receive no damages unless he suffers an insured loss within the notice period, in which event the insurer would have paid, or unless he replaces the insurance coverage at his own expense. Damages may be awarded where an employee has not yet replaced benefits but the judge believes he will do so when his current benefits run out. One judge handled this situation by stating that the employee was entitled to either benefits continuation for the notice period or reimbursement for the cost of replacing the insurance coverage. Otherwise, damages will be refused if the employer has already provided coverage for the notice period, or if the judge is not satisfied that the benefits will be replaced or claims incurred within the notice period. Damages may also be refused if no evidence of a benefit's value is tendered.

Damages regardless of loss — Damages are often awarded regardless of loss. This occurs in all provinces of Canada, depending on the individual judge, and has been sanctioned by the appeal courts of Alberta, Manitoba and Ontario.

Benefits upon retirement — One employee would have been entitled to elect early retirement if he had been given reasonable notice, and he then would have received benefits coverage throughout his retirement. He was awarded the expenses he incurred during the notice period, plus the future replacement costs for all benefits except those whose plan terms clearly stated they ceased upon retirement, even though he had not yet incurred the replacement costs.

G-5.2 AMOUNT OF DAMAGES

Damages regardless of loss — Where damages have been allowed despite the employee having suffered no loss (that is, the insurance not having been replaced and the insured event not occurring within the notice period), the amount to be awarded is usually based on the employer's cost of providing the benefit. In most cases, this measure seems to be used for ease of calculation more than logic, especially since replacement insurance on an individual basis is usually much more expensive than group insurance purchased by the employer. Damages have also been based on:
- A percentage of salary.
- The actuarial value of the benefits coverage.
- The employee's average claims in the last two years.
- The taxable benefits amount.
- The present value of the lost coverage, where the award was made within the notice period.
- The greater of the employer's costs, or the employee's actual replacement costs, or the employee's out-of-pocket expenses.

Employee's contribution — If coverage was provided on a cost-shared basis, with the employee's share being deducted from net pay, the employee's cost should also be deducted from damages based on the total cost of the insurance. In the alternative, damages should be based only on the employer's share of the cost.

Damages based on loss — Where damages are based on the employee's loss, the usual measure of damages is either the replacement cost, where the employee has replaced the insurance coverage on his own, or the amount of the claims incurred within the notice period that would have been covered if the insurance coverage had still been in place. Damages may be limited by the coverage limits under the previous insurance policy. Where the cost of replacement coverage is awarded, damages for incurred expenses will be denied, since these remedies are alternatives to each other. Note that occasionally, damages have been awarded for the employer's cost of coverage, even though the judge has purported to base damages on replacement cost.

Replacement through new job — Where damages have been allowed for a benefit, but the employee obtained a new job with coverage for that benefit within the notice period, damages should be adjusted to reflect the amount mitigated through the new employment. In one case, an employee obtained a new job but there was a gap in his medical coverage, and he was required to pay for the new coverage but had not been required to pay in the past. He was awarded the actual expenses incurred for the period of the gap, and the value based on the old employer's cost for the balance of the notice period. He was also awarded the cost of disability benefits provided by the old employer, plus the employer's cost of the higher coverage provided as compared to the coverage with the new employer.

Pretreatment authorization — Damages were allowed in one case where an employee had submitted a pretreatment authorization form and had been advised to wait until the next calendar year to have dental work done, but she was terminated before she could have the work done. Even though the work was not done within the notice period, she was still entitled to reimbursement under these circumstances.

Tax implications — In one case, an employee was awarded a gross up on the damages award to reflect the tax liability, presumably because the benefits themselves would not have been taxable, or at least not at the same rate as the lump-sum damages award. However, a tax gross up was refused in another case.

G-5.3 MEDICAL AND DENTAL INSURANCE

Government-sponsored insurance — Compensation for loss of government-sponsored medical plans is awarded fairly routinely, perhaps because its value is so easy to quantify and because it is assumed that every dismissed employee replaces this coverage. Compensation has been denied where the employee is already covered by a spouse's plan, and where the employee moved out of the country and so was no longer eligible.

Private insurance — Damages are also frequently awarded for loss of private insurance plans, although the amounts awarded vary, as discussed earlier in this chapter. Damages have been refused where an employee was no longer eligible for coverage under an employer's group plan due to health problems.

Life benefits — Where a dismissed employee had been entitled to lifetime benefits coverage, but shortly after his termination the employer changed its policy so that benefits ended at age 65, the employee was entitled to damages based on lifetime benefits. Specific performance was refused, and the employee was awarded damages based on actuarial evidence, the cost of a replacement plan, an amount to reflect the reduced coverage available, and a gross up to cover income tax liability.

G-5.4 LIFE INSURANCE

General principles — Damages for lost life insurance plans have often been awarded. In some cases, however, damages have been refused. For instance, "key-man" life insurance was a benefit to the employer, not the employee, so damages were not payable. The same concerns can arise with life insurance as with other insured benefits, namely that if the employee has suffered no loss by the end of the notice period, some judges will not award damages. Where damages are awarded, they are generally based on replacement cost. One employee was awarded the replacement cost of life insurance coverage when he would have been entitled to retire at the end of the notice period and would then have been entitled to continued coverage. The employee could not otherwise afford the coverage and was awarded the replacement cost even though he had not contracted for replacement coverage.

Group coverage — Where an employee replaces group life insurance coverage, damages may be appropriate only for the cost of term insurance, not for the cost of a policy that accumulates an asset value. The employer was not held liable for the amount of insurance benefits that would have been payable where:

- The employee had been given the chance to convert his group coverage into individual coverage but had chosen not to do so, and the group coverage had ended upon termination by the terms of the insurance contract.
- An employer failed to warn an employee about the necessity to convert his life insurance coverage within 30 days, but the employee had

consulted counsel within the 30 days, and he must have known about this requirement due to his own job responsibilities.
- An employer failed to specifically tell an employee that he had to convert his group coverage to individual coverage within 31 days of his termination, since the employer had told the employee that all his benefits would cease. This put the onus on the employee to review his coverage, and he could not hold the employer liable for his failure to convert his coverage, or the fact that he was uninsurable by the time of trial.

Death during notice period — Where an employee's group life insurance coverage was not continued through the notice period and the employee died within that time, results have varied. However, employers have been held liable for damages where:

- The employer had never told the employee about the coverage or that he had to choose to convert it upon termination. If the employee had remained employed through the notice period, his widow would have received the benefit, and so it was granted to her.
- The policy was effective until 31 days after termination. The court held that this entitled the employee to coverage until 31 days after the end of the notice period. Where he died within that time, but the coverage had already lapsed due to his earlier termination without working notice, the employer was itself liable in warranty to the employee's widow.

Ownership — An employee who was to receive ownership of a life insurance policy on a sliding scale, with full ownership after 10 years, was awarded ownership of the policy even though he had resigned after seven years. His resignation had been justified due to reasonable fears about job security. The employee had become a trustee of the plan and was entitled to ownership upon reimbursing the employer for the premiums it had paid after the resignation, as well as the cash surrender value of the policy at the time the employee began paying the premiums himself.

G-5.5 SICK LEAVE

Sick leave and disability leave — Some employers do not provide paid sick leave, particularly for short-term illnesses. Others provide paid leave for illness, either short-term or long-term or both. Often, short-term sick leave is financed directly by the employer, while long-term disability leave is financed through insurance. The type of benefit provided, either insured or uninsured, should always be checked, as it may affect entitlement to damages.

Sick leave damages — An employee paid full salary for the notice period has been fully compensated for the right to take paid sick leave, and no extra damages are payable. Where an employee was sick within the notice period but paid sick leave was not normally provided, the period of illness was deducted from his wrongful dismissal damages. An employee who was sick during the notice period and who was entitled to sick leave with pay was awarded damages. A woman, who was ill within the notice period due to the stress caused by her termination and who was not entitled to sick pay from her new employer, was awarded damages for the period of her illness when she was unable to work.

Sick leave credits — Mere entitlement to accumulate sick leave credits does not create a right to compensation in the absence of an agreement to compensate. However, where an employee *is* contractually entitled to be compensated for unused sick time, this benefit can be awarded as damages, either in full or in part, depending on the circumstances. Where accumulated sick credits would have been payable upon a voluntary termination, some judges have held that they should also be payable upon an involuntary termination, although others have upheld the contract's strict wording. An employee entitled to a payout of accumulated sick leave was entitled to damages for the additional days he would have accumulated during the notice period, less the average number of sick days he usually took off in that time period.

G-5.6 DISABILITY BENEFITS

Disability insurance — Damages for lost disability insurance plans are often dealt with in the same way as claims for other insured benefits. As a result, damages may be refused where the employee did not become disabled before the end of the notice period and replacement coverage was not purchased, although some judges award damages for the lost coverage based on the employer's cost of providing it. Damages may also be based on the replacement cost, particularly where the employee actually replaced the benefit.

Contractual termination of coverage — Damages have been refused where:

- The policy stated that benefits cease upon termination, extended coverage was unavailable, and the employee did not replace the coverage.
- A disability benefits plan provided for termination of coverage after 31 days of absence from work due to layoff or leave of absence, and an employee did not become disabled until more than 31 days after termination without notice. Even if the employee had been given notice, the employer had no work for him, so his disability coverage would have terminated before he became disabled.

Duty to explain — In one case, it was held that an employer had a duty to pay an employee long-term disability benefits, despite her resignation, because the employer had failed in its obligation to explain the benefits plan to her when she resigned.

Damages for disability benefits — Damages for the actual benefits, as opposed to coverage, may be awarded where an employee qualified for benefits before dismissal or before the end of the notice period, but the coverage was not continued; or where the employer self-insured for long-term disability. However, an employee must comply with all requirements to claim the benefits, including applying within any time limit. Damages were awarded where:

- The decision to dismiss an employee was made while he was off work due to a disability, but he was not dismissed until he had recovered and returned to work. Damages were nevertheless awarded due to the chance of relapse.
- An employee suffered an injury while employed that was not diagnosed as disabling until after his coverage had ended. He was held to be entitled to long-term disability benefits, as he was insured at the time of the accident.
- A woman who immediately mitigated her damages, but then was ill within the notice period and received no pay from the new employer, was awarded damages for the period of illness during which she was unable to work. She was unable to mitigate this part of her loss from the dismissal.

Dismissal for just cause — The fact that an employee is dismissed for just cause will not affect the right to disability benefits if the employee had qualified for benefits before the termination. This is also true where the employee was fired for misconduct or performance problems caused by mental illness.

Disability during notice period — For a discussion of whether disability benefits for the notice period should be deducted from pay in lieu of reasonable notice, see Chapter G-11, "Deductions from the Damage Award".

Workers' compensation coverage — Damages for lost workers' compensation coverage have been refused where the employees had suffered no loss.

Chapter G-6

EMPLOYMENT INSURANCE AND PENSION BENEFITS

TABLE OF CONTENTS

G-6.1   Employment Insurance
G-6.2   Canada Pension Plan
G-6.3   Registered Retirement Savings Plans (RRSPs)
G-6.4   Private Pension Plans
    G-6.4.1   Entitlement to Damages
    G-6.4.2   Calculation of Damages
    G-6.4.3   Effect of Retirement
    G-6.4.4   Other Pension Issues

G-6.1   EMPLOYMENT INSURANCE

Contributions for notice period — Some cases have allowed damages for Employment Insurance (EI) contributions during the notice period, although it is questionable whether such an award is proper. In view of the fact that the Employment Insurance Regulations provide for severance pay and damages to be treated as earnings subject to contributions, a specific award for contributions would provide a windfall for the employee, unless the amounts are contributed to the Employment Insurance Commission on the employee's behalf, which may be what is intended by these awards.

No loss, no damages — A number of cases have refused damages for EI contributions where there was no proof the loss of contributions caused the employee harm, or on the basis that they are not a recoverable item of damages. For example:

- Where an employee still qualified for full EI benefits after dismissal, he had suffered no loss, and awarding the premiums for the notice period would not therefore benefit him.
- Where a long-time seasonal employee lost insurable hours of earning due to his wrongful dismissal, which affected his EI entitlement during the following off-season, he was compensated in damages for the lost EI benefits rather than the contributions.

Deduction for benefits received — With regard to a deduction from damages for EI benefits received, see Chapter G-11, "Deductions from the Damage Award".

G-6.2 CANADA PENSION PLAN

Contributions for notice period — Although some judges have refused damages for Canada Pension Plan (CPP) contributions that the employer would have made during the notice period, many other judges have compensated a dismissed employee for this loss. Presumably, the employee can remit these additional contributions directly to the Plan to increase the eventual pension entitlement, or invest them in a private pension plan.

New employer's contributions — Damages for CPP contributions should be offset by the amount of any contributions paid by a new employer within the notice period.

Calculating the damages — Damages are generally based on the amount of the employer's contributions for the notice period, rather than an actuarial study to determine the real loss in terms of pension entitlement. A lump-sum award for the value of the employer contributions has been said to be the preferable award, rather than a direction that the contributions be remitted to the Plan, where there was no evidence about the ability to repurchase coverage after the fact.

Loss of benefits — In the event that the employee does not obtain other employment before age 65, termination of employment may decrease the employee's CPP pension benefits upon retirement. This loss, however, is not compensable. The employer is not prohibited from dismissing an employee as long as reasonable notice is given.

G-6.3 REGISTERED RETIREMENT SAVINGS PLANS (RRSPs)

Employer contributions — Where an employer has made contributions to an individual or group RRSP on the employee's behalf, as a benefit of employment, the majority of cases hold that the value of the employer's contributions is a compensable fringe benefit upon dismissal. An employee is entitled to damages for the lost contributions whether or not he chooses to put the damages into an RRSP. For example, the employer was liable where:

- It had agreed to contribute a certain amount to an employee's RRSP, but the plan's terms did not permit payment of that amount. The employer was still bound to pay the amount to the employee in damages.
- It had agreed to match the employee's contributions and the employee quit contributing after dismissal. Damages were still awarded for the matching contribution.

RRSP damage claims arising from dismissal — Various claims have been made regarding the impact of a wrongful termination on the employee's RRSP. For example:

- An employee was not entitled to damages for the decrease in his RRSP limit due to having been terminated, as this was too remote.
- One employee claimed for the lost chance to contribute to an RRSP and the interest lost due to the employer's failure to pay her in lieu of reasonable notice at the time of dismissal. A judge ruled that the claim had not been sufficiently proved, given the complexities of the RRSP rules and the difficulties of computing damages.

RRSP withdrawal after termination — An employee who had to borrow money from his RRSP to support himself after dismissal was not entitled to lost interest on the RRSP funds, because he had already been awarded damages for lost salary. Another employee's claim for his tax loss upon collapsing his RRSP was also dismissed.

G-6.4 PRIVATE PENSION PLANS

G-6.4.1 Entitlement to Damages

Contractual entitlement — Entitlement to private pension plan benefits upon termination depends, as with other benefits, on whether the pension was a contractual obligation of the employer. For example:

- Where a pension plan had been agreed to and approved in principle by the employer and the plan would have received final approval as a housekeeping matter, the pension was a term of the contract and damages were awarded for its loss.
- Where a plan was implemented for all employees during the dismissed employee's reasonable notice period, he was awarded damages for loss of that benefit.
- Where a contract provided for terms of a pension to be agreed upon, and this had not been done, the court ruled that the provision was too vague to be enforceable.

Contributions for notice period — Whether the employer's pension contributions for the notice period are compensable in damages generally depends on whether the employee's pension rights have "vested" — i.e. whether the contributions made on his behalf have become irrevocably dedicated to providing an eventual benefit for that employee. Vesting is controlled by the terms of the pension plan and/or by statute, and is normally based on length of service, with two years' service being a common vesting time.

Pension not vested — Where the pension was not vested and would not have vested within the notice period, damages are properly refused, as they would not have benefited the employee in any event. The only exception is if the pension plan or statute provided for portability or a refund of contributions to be made to the employee upon termination before vesting, in which case the damages should be awarded.

Vested pension — Where an employee's pension has already vested or would have vested during the notice period, damages for the contributions that should have been made during the notice period will generally be justified. However, they are not always awarded, perhaps because of a lack of understanding of how pension benefits work. At the same time, many judges routinely award damages for lost pension contributions even where it is not clear the pension would have vested or the employee would have been entitled to a refund of contributions.

Vesting within notice period — Where the pension would have vested during the notice period, several cases have held that the employee would be entitled to the present value of the pension to which he would have become entitled at the end of the notice period. In that case, damages should not also be allowed for contributions during the notice period, as this would be a duplication.

Pension portability — Where a pension is portable — that is, it can be transferred to a new employer's plan within certain industries or within certain time limits, or it can be transferred to an RRSP — damages have sometimes been awarded even where the pension had not vested, while in other cases, they have been refused. For example:

- Damages were refused in one case where the employee could either transfer his contributions to a new employer, withdraw them or defer them and there was no evidence of any loss.
- Damages were awarded for the notice period where the pension contributions were returnable to the employee.
- A claim for the return of contributions was denied where they could only be rolled over into another plan and the employee had not taken the steps to do so.

G-6.4.2 Calculation of Damages

Vested pension — The method of calculation of damages varies where the pension has already vested. Employees have been entitled to:

- Damages for the employer's contributions that would have been paid within the notice period; this may include the employee's contributions where the employee would have contributed during the notice period or the employee's contributions would have been waived.
- The present value of the difference between the value of the pension at the time of termination and its value at the end of the notice period; this type of award has been made even if the employee already elected to receive a refund of contributions.

Other measures of damages — In other cases where damages have been awarded, whether or not the pension had vested, damage awards have consisted of:

- The contributions made during the notice period.
- The cost of a replacement plan for the period of notice.
- The difference between the amount of the benefit in new employment and the amount paid by the terminating employer.
- In some cases, a direction may be issued that the contributions be made and the time be treated as pensionable service.

Actuarial calculation — Since pension plan contributions are made in order to accrue a long-term benefit, the better view would seem to be that damages should consist of the capital value of the additional pension benefits which would have accrued during the notice period, or the lump sum required to purchase an annuity that will yield the amount of additional benefits the employee would have received with the additional service, less the employee's required contributions, if any. This practice is not always followed, however, likely because of the cost and complexity of obtaining an actuarial valuation. At least one judge has said that complex actuarial evidence may not be necessary where only a small amount is involved; in that case, it may be simpler to just award the amount of lost contributions.

Commuted value — In one case where the employee was entitled to a refund of the pension's commuted value, the court ruled that he was entitled to the commuted value based on the contributions that would have been made during the notice period.

Pension Adjustment Factor — In one case, the Pension Adjustment Factor for income tax purposes was used as the basis for calculating the pension's value.

Pension indexing — Where an employer had a policy of indexing pensioners' payments to account for inflation, this was part of the employee's contractual benefit and his damages for pension loss were to include indexing in the calculation of his damages.

G-6.4.3 Effect of Retirement

Early retirement option — Where the employee would have been entitled to opt for early retirement within the notice period, and would have done so if given working notice, he may be entitled to damages for the pension benefits (payments) he would have received during the notice period. Orders may also be made declaring an employee to have elected to retire as of a certain date. For example:

- A judge awarded an employee's pension entitlement at the end of the notice period, but the employee's reasonable notice damages were reduced by the pension contributions he would have made if he had worked through the notice period.
- Where the employee was entitled to elect early retirement retroactively, the judge said he should so elect as of the end of the notice period, or the last possible date within the notice period, and he should also receive damages for the amount he lost by not being able to retire on that date before, including the cost of an annuity to replace any reduction in future benefits.

Early retirement elected — Some judges have held that an employee who elects early retirement after dismissal should have the amount of the pension payments during the notice period deducted from his damages, but not the amount of the contributions he would have paid, as it would be unfair to deduct both. Damages could also reflect the difference in the capitalized value of the pension due to electing to retire at an earlier time because of the lack of working or paid notice. This will require proper evidence of the differential in value caused by the termination. For instance:

- Where an employee claimed his early retirement was due to constructive dismissal, the pension benefits paid were deductible from his damages in lieu of reasonable notice.
- Where an employee had elected to begin receiving a pension after dismissal, but the value of the pension was severely reduced due to the failure to give pensionable credit for the notice period, the employee was awarded damages reflecting the yearly difference in benefits for the balance of the employee's life expectancy.

No deduction — The common approach now is that pension benefits received by employees during the notice period will not be deducted from their reasonable notice damages. However, the contributions they would otherwise have paid during the notice period may be deducted. In one case, it was said that the fact the employee had reinvested his benefits did not guarantee that he would suffer no loss, and so he should still receive full damages. In another case, it was pointed out that the early retirement benefits were offset by the fact that the employee's later entitlement would be reduced. Furthermore, the pension funds belong to the employee, not the employer, even where the pension plan is fully funded by the employer; they are a separate right from the employee's wrongful dismissal rights, so they should not be deducted.

Gratuitous pension benefits — Where the employer gratuitously provides pension benefits to which the employee would not otherwise have been entitled, however, they may be deductible from wrongful dismissal damages. For example:

- Where an employee was forced to accept a credit for enhanced pension benefits rather than additional termination pay, only 50 per cent of the benefits was deducted from his dismissal damages, since it was not an immediate economic benefit and therefore was of more limited use than termination pay.
- Bridging benefits provided by way of annuity were deducted, despite the employee's lack of choice in the matter, because it was a voluntary payment by the employer. However, the proper amount to deduct was the cost of the annuity, not the total amount of benefits it would provide, nor the amount of benefits within the notice period. This was fair given the fact that the annuity was forced upon the employee.

G-6.4.4 Other Pension Issues

Refund of pension contributions — Where a refund of pension contributions was required upon termination by the terms of the pension contract, the amount refunded to the employee was not deductible from the other damages payable to him.

Transfer of refund into RRSP — In one case, an employer was ordered to transfer the employee's pension benefits into a locked-in RRSP of the employee's choice. In another case, the employee was allowed to pay part of the damages award into an RRSP.

Impending vesting's effect on notice period — It may be proper to extend a notice period slightly to include the pension's vesting in some circumstances, as discussed in Chapter F-3, "Reasonable Notice Factors: Age and Service Length".

Mistake — Employees have both received and been denied the benefit of amounts to which they were mistakenly told they would be entitled. For example:

- An employee had no claim based on an employer's mistaken estimate of the amount to be paid to him under a pension-bridging arrangement between the time of dismissal and the time he could elect early retirement.
- An employee was not entitled to a mistaken amount told to him at an information session, as no early retirement offer had been made at that point and the amount was corrected before the offer was made and accepted.
- Where an employer offered payouts based on a specific valuation date to induce employees to retire early, even though it knew the date was based on an improper valuation formula, it was liable to the employees for the amounts based on the valuation date promised.

Method of paying damages — In one case, a 53-year-old employee was offered a choice between salary continuance or a lump-sum severance payment. The employer told him to get legal advice, but did not advise him that choosing the lump sum would drastically affect the amount of his monthly pension payment upon early retirement at age 55. The employee chose the lump-sum payment and only learned of its pension effect when he reached age 55. The employer was held liable for negligent misrepresentation, on the ground that it had an obligation to disclose the highly relevant information about pension effects, and that the independent legal advice could not be competent without that information.

Survivor's benefit — A dismissed employee's widow was entitled to a survivor's pension under the pension plan where the employee was wrongly denied long-term disability benefits and the pension plan defined "service" to include any period during which the employee received disability benefits.

Post-retirement benefits — An employee who retired early at a time beneficial to the employer was entitled to continuation of the post-retirement benefits offered at that time, without subsequent reduction. His entire employment was consideration for those post-retirement benefits.

Chapter G-7

AUTOMOBILE BENEFITS, VACATIONS, STATUTORY HOLIDAY PAY AND OTHER BENEFITS

TABLE OF CONTENTS

G-7.1   Car Allowances
G-7.2   Company Vehicles
G-7.3   Other Automobile Benefits
G-7.4   Vacations
G-7.5   Statutory Holiday Pay
G-7.6   Living Allowances and Housing Benefits
G-7.7   Professional and Membership Fees and Club Dues
G-7.8   Loans and Discounts
G-7.9   Other Benefits

G-7.1 CAR ALLOWANCE

General principle — Damages for a car allowance, mileage allowance or parking allowance have been allowed in many cases without analysis. However, where the situation has been examined, damages are often denied on the basis that, because the employee has not had to use the vehicle for business purposes since the termination, he or she has suffered no loss. Even where the amount of the allowance was more than ample to cover business use, one judge refused damages, since the allowance had been intended only to cover business use.

Car allowance as remuneration — Some judges would limit damages to an amount representing the personal use or the taxable portion of the allowance. Others have not limited damages, particularly where the allowance was intended more as a fringe benefit than as reimbursement for actual business use. Damages have been awarded where:

- The parties anticipated personal use of the vehicle.
- The allowance was negotiated as a form of remuneration.
- The allowance was in the nature of a car rental.

Damages were denied where a car and gas allowance was provided as a fringe benefit, but it was a fiction because the employee never used his car for business. The court would not countenance the parties' arrangement, which was intended to allow the employee to escape paying income tax on part of his remuneration.

New job's effect — In a few cases, damages have been awarded where an employee needed his car for the new job he obtained within the notice period, but the new employer did not pay a car allowance. Damages have also been allowed for the difference in car allowance amounts where the allowance in the new job was less than the allowance in the old job.

G-7.2 COMPANY VEHICLES

Personal benefit intended — Most recent cases have recognized that employers usually intend the provision of a car to benefit the employee personally, and have awarded damages accordingly. One judge has distinguished situations where the employer allows personal use of a company car from situations where personal use is recognized by both parties as a benefit of employment; those in the second category would be entitled to compensation, but those in the first would not.

Examples — damages awarded — Damages awarded have included:

- $500 per month for the loss of unrestricted personal use of a company-provided vehicle plus availability of the vehicle at all times.
- Damages for loss of use of a second car where an employee had two cars in his old job but only one in his new job.
- Damages for loss of personal use of a company car, even though the employee had a car of his own.

Examples — damages refused — Damages have been refused where:

- No personal benefit was intended from the provision of a company car.
- A fleet of cars was to be shared by all employees and the cars were mainly intended for business use.

Replacement — Some judges only grant damages where a car has been replaced during the notice period; others reduce damages or refuse certain damages where it has not been replaced. Still others have said that where a personal benefit was intended, the employee has still suffered a loss, so replacement should be irrelevant. One employee who did not replace the car was allowed to claim his out-of-pocket expenses for alternate transportation, including trains, taxis and use of his wife's car.

Vehicle retained — If an employee was allowed to keep the company vehicle for part or all of the notice period, the employee would not be entitled to damages for that time. In one case, no damages were payable at all, because an employee was allowed to retain the vehicle for most of the notice period without tax liability, so that the benefit he received offset the benefit lost for the balance of the notice period.

Fleet vehicle — One employee who was allowed to use whatever car was available from the lot, but who had no designated company car, was nevertheless awarded damages for loss of the benefit. However, another employee in a similar situation was refused damages.

Income tax value — Some cases have awarded damages based on the income tax value of the company vehicle, as a realistic and convenient amount. Other cases, however, have disagreed; it has been said that the income tax value is not definitive, as it does not necessarily reflect the true value, especially where the amount of personal use is small but the intended convenience benefit is great. Where the benefit has not been declared for income tax purposes, the employee may not be entitled to any damages; it has been said that an employee should not receive more in damages than the amount on which he is willing to pay income tax.

Other valuation bases — Although the basis for valuing this benefit is rarely discussed, damages have been awarded based on:

- The employer's cost of providing the benefit. In one case, the value of a car provided by the new employer was deducted. In another case, damages were based on the "fair value" of the leased car.
- The estimated value of the employee's personal use. In one case, where the amount of personal use was small, however, this was said to be an inadequate remedy as it would not replace the benefit, and so the employee was awarded the full value.
- A true measure of the value of the employee's personal use. In one case, the employee was awarded less than the Revenue Canada amount, but more than the amount he had been required to pay the employer for his personal use, as this was considered a true measure of his damages.
- Replacement cost of a rental or leased vehicle, or the monthly cost of a purchased car. Only the replacement cost of the vehicle, not the operating costs, should be awarded, unless operating costs were also paid by the employer under the terms of the contract. Note, however, that other cases have refused damages on these bases, because the employee should be compensated only for lost personal use.
- Other replacement costs such as licensing, fuel, insurance and repairs of a personal vehicle.
- Parking expenses may or may not be awarded.

G-7.3 OTHER AUTOMOBILE BENEFITS

Lease cancellation — When termination of employment results in the employee having to cancel a vehicle lease, there is often a question as to who should bear the cost. The answer usually depends on who was contractually liable to the leasing company, the employee or employer, although this is not always the sole determinant. The employee was liable to pay the cost of a car lease cancellation where:

- He leased a car in his own name and received a car allowance from the employer rather than having the employer lease the vehicle directly.
- It was clear that providing a car was the employee's responsibility and the loss was neither foreseeable nor attributable to the breach. The fact that the employee was required to have a car for the job did not make the employer liable for the loss upon cancellation of the car lease. However, in another case, where the lease was entered into for purposes of employment and with the employer's full knowledge, damages were awarded for the cost of cancelling the lease upon dismissal.

Repossession — Where an employee's vehicle was repossessed after termination, results have varied:

- No damages were awarded where the employee was in arrears on his payments even before the termination.
- Where the employee was required to have a car for the job and bought the car outright, but the employment was short-lived, he was awarded the amount of the downpayment he lost when the car was repossessed after dismissal, as well as the amount he had to pay upon repossession.

Loss on resale — In some cases, a loss upon resale of a car was said to be a purely capital loss that was not reasonably foreseeable as flowing from the breach of contract. However, in another case, damages were awarded to an employee who had to sell his car at a loss after his termination.

Repairs — An employee who had undertaken expensive car repairs in reliance on his employment, because he would need his car for his job, was awarded 75 per cent of the cost of the repairs when he was dismissed after three days on the job.

G-7.4 VACATIONS

Vacation earned before dismissal — A number of cases have allowed damages for vacation entitlement accumulated before dismissal. One employee's claim was allowed even though company policy forbade banking of unused vacation days, because his supervisor had told him he could bank the unused days and receive a pay-out upon retirement.

However, an employee may not be able to claim for accumulated vacation from past years where that is against company policy or a limitations statute. The fact that an employee may not have to work during the notice period does not affect his entitlement to vacation pay earned before termination. The employer cannot deduct vacation pay for the period before dismissal from damages for the notice period, as these are separate entitlements.

Overpayment — In one case, where an employee resigned before earning entitlement to the paid vacation he had already taken, the employer was entitled to recover the overpayment.

Vacation pay for notice period — Many cases have compensated employees for vacation pay lost during the notice period. However, others have denied damages, or have limited them. There are a number of different approaches to vacation pay damages.

Pay vs. time off — One case said that if an employee commonly opted to receive vacation pay rather than paid time off, he should be awarded vacation pay damages. For instance, where a commissioned salesman received vacation pay as a lump sum, it was an income benefit to him, so it was included in his income for the purpose of calculating his damages.

Full compensation — Many judges, including most of those in Ontario, award full vacation pay entitlement for the notice period, unless it can be shown that the employee would not have taken the additional vacation pay rather than taking a paid vacation during the notice period.

Qualitative difference — Another view is that people who have been dismissed do not enjoy their time off, and the reasonable notice period cannot be considered to be like a vacation, since the time is spent searching for a new job and most people are unlikely to spend money on an actual vacation while unemployed. Therefore, vacation pay damages should be awarded in addition to other damages for the notice period. This view has been endorsed by the British Columbia Court of Appeal.

No loss, no damages — Many other cases have denied damages for vacation pay during the notice period, since an employee kept on during the notice period would generally be entitled to vacation with normal pay or to compensation in lieu. An award of salary during the notice period would include any paid vacation, and there is normally no indication that the employee would not have been allowed to take his or her vacation. Similarly, an employee who received commissions on sales during his vacations would have suffered no loss. Damages were denied where it was said that the employee had a history of taking time off with pay, rather than taking pay in lieu of vacation. If he had worked through the notice period, he would likely have taken time off within the notice period and would not have been entitled to any additional pay.

Presumption of no loss — Another approach would deny damages unless the employee could demonstrate an actual loss due to the loss of vacation entitlement, or proof that he was entitled to receive pay in lieu of vacation. For example:

- An employee who claimed he would have worked throughout the notice period rather than taking vacation had his claim for vacation pay denied, on the ground that there was no proof as to what vacation arrangements he would have made.
- An employee was compensated for unused vacation days based on the number of days unused in previous years.
- Where there was no evidence of the employee having been compelled to take his vacation time on a regular basis, the judge concluded he would have chosen to work straight through the notice period and take vacation pay instead of paid vacation.

Differing entitlement — In some cases, employees have been compensated for the difference in vacation pay entitlement between the old job and the new job for the duration of the notice period. In another case, vacation pay for the notice period was decreased by the vacation pay which would be paid for that period by the new employer. Where an employee's entitlement was higher than required by statute, but was only calculated on base pay instead of gross pay as required by statute, he was awarded the higher rate on his base pay plus the statutory rate on the remaining wage amounts.

Vacation bonus — Where the employee would have been entitled to a vacation bonus if he took his vacation within certain months of the year and there was evidence he would have done so, the bonus amount was awarded.

Dismissal before resignation — Where an employee had already given notice of his resignation but was dismissed before his resignation date, he was awarded vacation pay to the end of the notice period he had given, since he had been prepared to work and would have received the pay upon his resignation.

Gratuitous days off — An employee who was always given extra days off with pay in the summer, but who had no contractual entitlement to those days off, was refused damages for those gratuitous days off.

G-7.5 STATUTORY HOLIDAY PAY

Past entitlement — A claim for statutory holiday pay for past holidays worked was not allowed where the employer had not required the work. Nor was an employee entitled to pay for statutory holidays when she was on disability. Another employee's claim for six years' worth of statutory holidays was allowed, even though neither he nor the employer had kept a record of the statutory holidays he had worked; but his claim was limited by the two-year limitation period in the employment standards statute.

Holidays during notice period — A claim for pay for statutory holidays during the notice period was not allowed, even where the employee had routinely worked holidays in the past, since it was speculative whether he would have worked them during the notice period, and since he had received damages for his full salary for the notice period and therefore had suffered no loss.

G-7.6 LIVING ALLOWANCES AND HOUSING BENEFITS

Allowances generally — Most judges take the view that an allowance can be compensated for in damages if it involved a personal benefit, but not if it was solely work-related. Allowances will only be allowed in damages if they were an entitlement at the time of dismissal; where the entitlement had expired earlier, no damages will be owing.

Employer-provided benefits generally — Damages may be limited to the amount representing a personal benefit, or to reasonable amounts within the terms of the employer's policy and in accordance with the parties' past practice.

Clothing allowance — A clothing allowance and cleaning allowance for plain clothes were allowed as damages, but a uniform issue entitlement was not allowed, since it was entirely work-related. Similarly, a boot-and-clothing allowance that was akin to providing tools for the job was not compensable. A clothing salesman was denied damages for loss of free use of the products. An employee was denied damages for free uniforms where she had refused to accept employment with a new employer under the same terms as before. The value of free haircuts was awarded in one case.

Meal allowance — Damages for meal allowances or room-and-board allowances have been awarded in several cases. Damages for the value of free meals provided by the employer have also been allowed. However, damages were refused where an allowance was only to cover out-of-pocket expenses when the employee travelled out of town on business.

Room-and-board allowance — The value of a room in a room-and-board allowance was not awarded where the employee had his own home and had not required the room during the notice period. Where damages were awarded for a room-and-board allowance, they were based on the employer's cost, not on the retail value, since the employee returned home when the job ended.

Employer-provided housing — Employees who were provided with free housing or room-and-board but who were forced to move upon dismissal have been awarded damages based either on the value of the free housing or the employee's replacement costs during the notice period. An employee who received subsidized housing was awarded damages based on the difference between the market value and the amount he had paid.

No loss — Some cases have awarded damages even where an employee did not incur replacement housing expenses, perhaps for the inconvenience and disruption of being forced to move. In one case, damages were awarded for the entire notice period where an employee had been forced to move his family into a single room of a relative's house for several months. In other cases, however, damages have been refused where an employee was not out-of-pocket for replacement housing expenses.

No double compensation — An employee who was awarded damages for lost housing benefits for the notice period was not also entitled to the cost of storing his household goods for the notice period.

Mortgage subsidy — An employee was refused damages for a promised mortgage subsidy where he did not incur mortgage costs because construction of the house did not proceed.

Purchase of home — Where the employee would have been entitled within the notice period to enter into an agreement for the employer to purchase his home, he was entitled to that relief upon his action for wrongful dismissal.

Location supplements — Employees will generally be entitled to any location supplements normally received, at least where they remained in the location throughout the notice period. One employee was awarded isolation pay for the entire notice period, even though he relocated right after dismissal, because he would have received this amount if he had been given reasonable notice. Where a fixed-term contract had been breached, damages for the lost location supplement were awarded for the entire term of the contract. However, another employee was awarded a foreign service allowance, property management allowance, cost of storage of goods, housing allowance and house insurance costs only for the time during the notice period in which he actually resided overseas. Damages were refused in another case where airfares, free housing and subsidized groceries were benefits dependent on the employee remaining at an isolated mining site and he had not done so. Damages for an overseas spending allowance and store credits were refused where the employee returned to Canada after dismissal and he had not incurred similar expenses during the notice period.

G-7.7 PROFESSIONAL AND MEMBERSHIP FEES AND CLUB DUES

Professional fees — Professional fees have been allowed in some cases, but not in others. Damages were refused where the fees would not have been payable within the notice period. Where the employer's refusal to pay the employee's professional fees as agreed was a constructive dismissal, damages for the fees were awarded.

Professional education — Conference fees that would have been paid had employment continued have been awarded in several cases. However, in one case, damages were denied for professional courses and seminars.

Club fees — Club dues and association membership fees that have been paid by the employer during employment have sometimes been allowed as damages, but sometimes have not, either because they were said not to be expenses incurred on behalf of or in the interest of the employer, or because no personal benefit was intended. Damages were refused where it was not clear what time period was covered by the fees or whether fees fell due during the notice period. However, in one case, damages for annual fees were awarded even though the notice period was less than a year long. Where a club membership was a commitment by an employer that was not made just for the employee's benefit, he was awarded 50 per cent of the cost to represent his personal benefit. Damages were refused where the employee had not joined the clubs after dismissal and so had incurred no personal costs.

G-7.8 LOANS AND DISCOUNTS

Employee discounts — While some cases have refused damages for employee discounts, others have awarded damages even though valuation can be difficult. Damages may be awarded as long as there is evidence that the employee would have used the benefit during the notice period. Several cases have based damages on the employee's past use of the discount. Damages were allowed for the value of reduced-rate electricity used in the employee's home, based on the difference between the flat rate charged by the employer and the amount actually paid after dismissal. One employee who had been entitled to free dental work was refused damages for its loss, since she had declined a new job where she would have had the same benefit, and had thereby failed to mitigate her damages.

Loans, etc. — Many employees have been awarded damages for reduced-rate loans, credit cards and mortgages that were a benefit of employment.

The existence of a reduced-rate mortgage also may be a factor in setting an employee's reasonable notice period.

Damages refused — No damages were awarded where the prevailing interest rate at termination was the same as the employee's rate, and only nominal damages were awarded for loss of a loan at a preferable rate that the employer voluntarily carried for most of the notice period, even though by its terms it was payable upon termination. An employee was refused damages for a promised mortgage subsidy where he did not incur mortgage costs because construction of the house did not proceed. Where a mortgage provided for the balance to be due in full upon termination for any reason, the employee was not entitled to damages for the difference between the mortgage rate and the market rate. Even where the mortgage did not so provide, it has been held that an employer's obligations cease upon expiry of the notice period or dismissal for just cause.

Repayment — An employee was liable to repay a loan from the employer even though the employer had said it would forgive the loan in lieu of a bonus. The employer never took steps to cancel the promissory note or attribute the loan to the plaintiff's income, so the loan was still outstanding and payable when the employee was dismissed. Where a mortgage provided for immediate repayment upon termination of employment for any reason, the employee was required to repay the loan upon termination even though it had been intended that the mortgage would be repaid out of profits. Where an employee had signed a promissory note stating that payment was due upon cessation of employment, he was liable for the balance immediately upon his dismissal for just cause.

Loan forgiveness — Where an employer advanced an employee a loan to allow him to relocate for the job, and part of the loan was forgiven each month of employment, the employee was credited with loan deductions for the notice period. However, as there was no agreement that the loan would be completely forgiven upon wrongful dismissal, the employee was still liable for the balance of the loan.

G-7.9 OTHER BENEFITS

Expense accounts — Damages have sometimes been allowed for a lost expense account or "out-of-pocket" allowance. In other cases, however, damages have been refused, since there was no business need to incur expenses after dismissal and the amount of personal benefit was not proved. Of course, amounts owing for the time before dismissal can be claimed.

Subscriptions, tickets — Damages for lost newspaper and magazine subscriptions were refused since it was not clear what time period they covered, when payments were due or whether the employee had continued to receive them after dismissal. Damages for sports tickets were refused, as these had not been provided in the past as a personal benefit.

Computer allowance — Where the employer paid the employee a monthly amount toward a computer he had purchased, one judge found an implied contract that the employer was to pay the employee the balance of the computer's cost and was then entitled to keep the computer. In another case, however, the employer's program stated that if an employee was terminated before reimbursement was complete, there would be no further payments, but the employee would be entitled to keep the computer.

Office space and equipment — A doctor who had been provided with office space and staff was not compensated for their loss upon his wrongful dismissal. However, a university professor who had made personal use of the employer's computers to earn extra income was awarded damages for the loss of that income.

Travel benefits — The value of annual airfares to travel out of a remote location have been awarded. An employee who had received free travel benefits was awarded damages for their loss. Damages for personal use of travel points acquired through business travel were not allowed, as there was not enough evidence to prove entitlement as between the employee and employer, and because the employee was not required to travel in the course of business during the notice period. In one case, damages were awarded for lost travel insurance, without analysis.

Incentive prizes — A lost opportunity to earn sales prizes has also been compensated in some cases, but in other cases, damages have been refused as too remote or as not part of the employee's legal entitlement. In one case, where the employer had offered to compensate the employee for a lost trip the employee would have been entitled to take during the notice period, damages were awarded in the offered amount. In another case, however, damages were refused as the employee was said to have no contractual entitlement to the trip and the employer's offer was not binding. Where an employer provided an annual trip for employees and their spouses, but the employee's spouse had never gone on the trips in the past, he was awarded damages only for the value of his own trip. An employee was awarded damages for lost performance points that were convertible to merchandise, and for a trip for which he had already qualified before his resignation, where they were an integral part of his compensation. An employee who would have won a $3,000 prize from the employer's supplier if he had worked through the notice period was awarded damages for its loss.

Savings plan contributions — The amount of an employer's contributions to a savings plan which would have been made during the notice period have been awarded. However, damages were refused where the employee would not have been eligible to participate in the plan during the notice period, and where it was not clear whether or when the payments would have vested in the employee.

Education benefits — An employee who had taken an educational course upon the understanding that he would be reimbursed was entitled to reimbursement, even though the dismissal had intervened between the employer's approval and completion of the course. Damages have also been awarded for courses started after dismissal but within the notice period, where tuition reimbursement was an employment benefit. In one case, damages were refused even though the employer had paid for university courses in the past, because taking courses seemed to be a hobby of the employee that was not business-related. Damages for French lessons were refused, as these had not been provided as a personal benefit, but only for business purposes.

Financial counselling — Damages for loss of employer-provided financial counselling were refused where the employee, who had a background in economics, law and business, did not actually need the benefit. Nor were they awarded where the employee had not replaced the benefit. In another case, however, they were awarded.

Retiring allowance — An employee was not entitled to a lump-sum retiring allowance where he did not fall within the contract's strict wording providing for entitlement.

Miscellaneous — Damages have been awarded for the lost use of a cell phone. One employee was awarded damages for the loss of free boarding for her horse. Another was awarded the value of a hog he had been promised before termination.

Chapter G-8

JOB SEARCH EXPENSES, MOVING EXPENSES AND COSTS OF MITIGATION

TABLE OF CONTENTS

G-8.1   Costs of the New Job Search
G-8.2   Moving Expenses
G-8.3   Mitigation Expenses

G-8.1 COSTS OF THE NEW JOB SEARCH

General principles — Dismissed employees are usually awarded their reasonable costs of searching for new employment, as expenses incurred in mitigation of damages. Some judges have denied damages, on the basis that the expenses would have been incurred even if the employer had given reasonable notice. However, others have rejected that argument, pointing out that the expenses might not have been incurred if reasonable notice had been given, and that an employee should not be left in a worse position for having met the duty to mitigate than he or she would have been in by breaching the duty. Some judges have taken the view that job search costs should be compensated only where there are earnings from a new job to deduct in mitigation. However, this is not the common view. In Quebec, damages for job-search expenses may not be proper in the absence of malice or abuse of right.

Amount of damages — Based on the arguments noted above, one judge allowed only 50 per cent of the expenses incurred. However, most judges allow 100 per cent of expenses, as long as they are legitimate and not excessive.

Expenses within notice period — Despite the general trend to compensate for job-search expenses, many judges have limited damages to expenses incurred within the notice period.

Standard costs reimbursed — Damages have included the cost of:

- Long-distance telephone calls.
- Clerical work and résumé preparation.
- Postage and courier fees.

- Newspaper ads.
- Career counselling and travel to attend career counselling.
- Gas or mileage, and parking.
- Business lunches or other meals.
- Necessary professional fees, including the cost of registering with an industry employment service.

Out-of-town interviews — The costs of travel to out-of-town interviews have been awarded. Results have varied where the trip was undertaken before specific job interviews were set up and the effort was unsuccessful. Some cases have allowed the costs where the trip was a reasonable effort to mitigate the employee's loss; other cases have denied damages. It has been said that the test is whether the trip was reasonably likely to result in any meaningful job contacts. One case allowed only $1,000 of the $5,000 claimed since there would have been some expenses even if the employee had received reasonable notice. Damages have been denied where the major reason for a trip was a holiday or a family visit, even if the employee also investigated employment possibilities.

Job-related expenses — Other job-related expenses for which dismissed employees have been compensated include:

- Legal fees for negotiating an employment contract with a new employer.
- An hourly reimbursement for time spent filling out job applications, although the basis for this seems questionable where the employee was already being compensated for lost salary.
- Day care expenses while an employee looked for a new job.
- Travel costs for the employee and his family to visit the new city to which they were considering moving.
- Some or all of a former employee's costs of setting up business in an attempt to mitigate his damages, as discussed in Chapter H-3, "Career Changes and Relocating", under H-3.4, "Starting a Business".

Proof of expenses — Expense claims for items like mileage for travel to job interviews may have to be strictly proved, and expense claims may be refused where they are not documented. On the other hand, some claims have been allowed with little or no supporting evidence. One case stated that it is unreasonable to expect an employee to maintain comprehensive records during a prolonged job search.

Examples — expenses disallowed — Expenses that have been disallowed have included:

- Expenses which were "overkill".
- A consultant's fee of over $4,000, as it was unreasonably high, especially where no receipts or details of services were provided.

- The costs of computer hardware, software and training, as they were unnecessary to the mitigation effort.
- Relocation counselling where the judge was not satisfied it had been necessary. However, even a very high fee for outplacement was reimbursed where it was found to be reasonable and necessary.

G-8.2 MOVING EXPENSES

General principles — Reasonable expenses for moving to a new location to accept other employment have often been awarded. Some judges refuse damages unless relocation was reasonable and resulted in a new job; yet sometimes damages are awarded even where it is not clear they were incurred in order to mitigate. To be reimbursed, the expenses may need to have been incurred within the notice period, although not all judges follow this rule.

No loss or avoidable loss — Moving expenses were not reimbursed where they had already been borne by the new employer, although the difference between actual expenses and the amount paid by the new employer may be allowed. Where moving costs were paid by the new employer but that "benefit" had been reflected in a lower salary, an employee was properly awarded damages for the moving costs. An employee may need to prove the costs, and damages may be refused where there was a lack of documentation of expenses. Avoidable losses may be refused, such as damages for an early lease termination penalty and for a forfeited deposit.

Reasonableness of move — Moving must be reasonable in the circumstances. To be entitled to damages, an employee may need to prove that he could not have found a replacement job without moving. An employee who had relocated to take a job in an isolated community with no other jobs was reasonable in relocating after dismissal. However, an employee who moved to take a temporary job did not act reasonably. Damages were justified where an employee was forced to leave the community due to the employer's actionable slander of him, which made re-employment impossible in that location.

Dismissal must cause move — The move must be a result of the wrongful dismissal, not caused by other factors. The claim of an employee whose husband requested a transfer after her dismissal was too remote to attribute to the employee's dismissal, since her husband had been seeking a new job even before her termination. Damages have been refused where the move was motivated by other factors, such as a desire to be near family or a pre-existing desire to move, as in the case where the employee had listed his house for sale prior to his termination.

Returning to original location — Where an employee had changed locations at the employer's request, some judges have awarded damages for the cost of returning to the employee's original location, although other judges have refused damages on this basis. Damages may be refused where the employee does not intend to relocate back to the original location, or where the employee relocates to a different location. Damages would not be appropriate where an employee had already been given mobilization and demobilization expenses at the time of the first move. Where the move was voluntary, it may be appropriate that the employee bear at least part of the cost of relocation. For example, an employee who voluntarily moved closer to his job was awarded $150 moving expenses to return to his permanent home after termination, but he was not awarded the six weeks' extra rental on his apartment for the period after the dismissal.

Types of costs awarded — Damages have been allowed for:

- Moving and travel costs.
- Storage fees.
- Lost apartment rental or rent differential.
- A differential in utility costs.
- Living expenses while two houses were being maintained.

Moving or sale of specific items — Damages have been refused for:

- Loss upon forced sale of an employee's boat.
- The potential cost of moving a boat.
- Forfeited customs duties, as these could have been avoided if the employee had moved her possessions back to the United States instead of selling them in Canada.

Damages were allowed for an employee's loss of the sale of his computer, which he could not afford to ship back to his home in England.

Exceptions — Damages have been refused where:

- The amount was speculative because the employee had not yet relocated.
- The employee had received severance pay under a policy which stated that it was paid to assist the employee in establishing other employment.
- An employee did some of his own moving work. He was not compensated, as he was said to be simply mitigating his damages by doing so.

Sale of home — The issue of the costs and/or loss on the resale of a house is still in flux. Damages have been denied where it is not clear the sale was caused by the breach of contract; where there was no express or implied contractual term that the employer would be responsible for the expenses; and where neither the acquisition nor the sale of the house were tied to employment or termination.

Sale damages allowed — The following types of costs have been reimbursed, although the same types of damages have often been refused, as well, particularly if an employee did not suffer an overall loss upon the sale:

- Carrying charges on a home throughout the notice period.
- The real estate commission expenses of sale.
- Legal fees.
- A mortgage penalty for early termination.

Capital loss on resale — damages refused — Damages for a capital loss on resale have generally been disallowed, where:

- The employee had made a substantial profit upon moving to accept the job with the employer.
- It was unreasonable to buy a house so soon after accepting a new job, given that the contract was only for a year and provided for earlier dismissal upon one month's notice.

Capital loss on resale — damages allowed — However, damages for a capital loss have been permitted:

- In claims based on negligent misrepresentation upon hiring and on defamation, rather than breach of contract.
- On a reliance basis where the employer acted in bad faith toward the employee.

Capital profit — Where an employee had made a substantial profit on the resale of his house, the court refused to offset the profit against his moving expenses, for which the employer was responsible, since the profit or loss was said to be unrelated to the breach of contract.

House-related claims — damages allowed — House-related claims for which damages have been awarded include:

- Mortgage and maintenance costs of an employee's out-of-town home after he had relocated to accept new employment.
- Costs of buying a replacement home, where the employee relocated from England to take the job and returned to England after dismissal.

House-related claims — damages refused — House-related claims for which damages have not been awarded include:

- Capital expenditures on a new home.
- Lost appreciation on a house an employee sold in order to move at the defendant's request.
- Loss due to foreclosure, as there was no contractual requirement that the employee buy a home in the area.
- The claim of an employee who sold his home in order to buy a cheaper one, since this was too remote from the breach.

- The claim of an employee who had to abort his intended house purchase due to dismissal, since his employer had no special knowledge of his plans.

Costs of previous relocation at employer's request — Relocation expenses incurred to take the job with the dismissing employer generally will not be compensable, even where there is an element of enticement, unless there was an express agreement to that effect. Even where there is an agreement, such as an agreement to pay a bridge mortgage and expenses of the old home, these duties will generally cease at the end of the notice period, or upon dismissal for just cause. Where there is an agreement to compensate, the employee must have actually moved in order to receive damages. In one case the fact that the employee had sold his home, incurring legal and real estate costs, was sufficient to justify damages, even though he had not yet moved to the new location before he was terminated.

G-8.3 MITIGATION EXPENSES

Generally — Some judges refuse damages for expenses of mitigation unless the employee had actual earnings in mitigation — in other words, unless the mitigation was successful. Other judges, however, award damages as long as the mitigation attempt was reasonable. See also the discussion of mitigation in Chapter H-3.

Costs of new job — Where an employee has not relocated, the costs of commuting to a new job have been awarded. So have the costs of restaurant meals where the employee had to stay out of town all week for the new job. One judge disallowed such expenses, but allowed the cost of long-distance phone calls home. In one case, an employee was denied damages for the cost of clothing and equipment needed for his new job.

Retraining costs — The results of claims for damages for training costs are mixed. Where incurred as a legitimate attempt to mitigate they have been allowed in some cases, although in other instances they have not been allowed. Retraining costs incurred after the notice period ended have been refused. Approaches used include:
- Reimbursing the employee for the cost of courses taken to improve his ability to mitigate.
- Limiting recovery if there was no realistic prospect of earnings within the notice period, or if there were no actual earnings within the notice period.
- Refusing retraining costs, even where there were some earnings in mitigation, because the costs were said to be due to the decision to change occupations, which did not flow from the breach of contract.

- Refusing retraining costs, even where there were some earnings in mitigation, because the value of the education was greater than its cost, and the employee did not have a contractual right to better herself at her former employer's expense.

New business expenses allowed — An employee who starts his or her own business after dismissal may be entitled to reimbursement for the expenses of organizing the business, including legal costs, as long as these expenses are incurred within the notice period. For example, expenses were allowed where the employer had offered to pay them and where it seemed to be customary in the securities industry to reimburse an ex-employee for the costs of relocating his business.

New business expenses not allowed — Expenses were not allowed where:

- Damages were for the costs of setting up a professional practice, since these costs would be recovered in the course of the practice and there was no proven loss. Advertising costs, however, were allowed. In another case, these costs were allowed, including professional fees and a portion of capital expenses, although the employee might have to account for any capital assets acquired.
- It was unreasonable for the employee to start his own business because he could have easily found a similar job.
- There would be double recovery because the employee had already been compensated for his wage losses.
- The business had been set up before termination, the employee had made unnecessary purchases and at the time of the purchases he had not even attempted to obtain alternate employment.
- Expenses were incurred unreasonably. At least one judge has ruled that the onus is on the employer to prove that expenses claimed by the employee are unreasonable or improper.
- Expenses were incurred outside the notice period.

New business losses — Employees who start their own business but suffer a business loss may be entitled to compensation for the loss where they made a reasonable attempt to mitigate. For example, losses from an investment in a franchise were allowed in one case.

Chapter G-9

AGGRAVATED AND PUNITIVE DAMAGES

TABLE OF CONTENTS

G-9.1   General Principles
G-9.2   Mental Distress Damages
G-9.3   Damages for Loss of Reputation or Opportunity
G-9.4   Punitive Damages

G-9.1 GENERAL PRINCIPLES

Use of aggravated and punitive damages — Aggravated and punitive damages claims were common before the Supreme Court of Canada's decision in *Wallace v. United Grain Growers Ltd. (c.o.b. Public Press)*, [1995] 9 W.W.R. 153 (Man. C.A.). However, in *Wallace* the Supreme Court stated that many of the factors previously dealt with through aggravated and punitive damages should be taken into account in increasing the notice period. Since then, the use of aggravated and punitive damages has declined sharply, as it is much easier to meet the *Wallace* "bad faith" test and increase the notice period than to meet the legal tests for aggravated or punitive damages. Nevertheless, these types of damages do still arise from time to time.

Aggravated damages — The purpose of aggravated damages, such as mental distress and loss of reputation damages, is to compensate the employee for an intangible loss. The Supreme Court of Canada has stressed that aggravated damages can only be awarded where the damage arises out of the breach of contract itself.

Punitive damages — The purpose of punitive damages is to punish an employer whose conduct has been extremely harsh, vindictive, malicious or reprehensible. It should be noted that the Supreme Court has said that courts should award punitive damages cautiously.

Definition of terms — Note that some people tend to confuse aggravated, punitive, exemplary and mental distress damages. They may treat all four terms as being different from each other, whereas the proper view would seem to be that punitive and exemplary damages are the same thing, and mental distress damages are a type of aggravated damages. All these types of awards are sometimes called "general damages" in a wrongful dismissal context.

Exceptional remedy — Aggravated and punitive damages are intended to be exceptional remedies. As stated by the British Columbia Court of Appeal:

> A damage award for wrongful dismissal is not a fund of money to make the plaintiff feel better or to compensate him for his injured feelings or disappointment but is merely to compensate him for a breach of contract. (*Husson v. Alumet Manufacturing* (1991), 37 C.C.E.L. 252 (B.C.C.A.).)

Need for separate, actionable wrong — To justify an award of aggravated or punitive damages, there must be a separate, actionable wrong in addition to the dismissal. This requirement has been waived by statute in New Brunswick and some other judges continue to ignore this requirement. At least one judge has indicated that a statutory breach, such as discrimination under a human rights law, may support an aggravated and punitive damages claim, even if the employee could not directly sue for breach of the statute. The requirement for a separate actionable wrong has led to an explosion in claims based on little-known torts, which are discussed in Appendix 2, "Related Actions that are Commonly Joined with Wrongful Dismissal Actions".

Foreseeability — Foreseeability, usually a requirement of a successful tort action, has been said to be irrelevant in considering whether there was an independent actionable wrong, although there is some disagreement on the issue.

Damages vs. increased notice periods — The different facts that should lead a court to award one type of damages rather than another are unclear. A number of courts seem to use the concepts of aggravated damages, punitive damages, solicitor-and-client costs and tort damages almost interchangeably. Factors that might lead some judges to award aggravated or punitive damages may lead other judges to increase the period of notice instead. In fact, the Supreme Court of Canada said in *Wallace* that it is appropriate to lengthen the notice period, rather than award aggravated damages, where there is no separate actionable wrong.

Behaviour leading to damages — Where general damages have been awarded, there is great variety in the type of behaviour and extent of effects that will justify an award. Claims are often dismissed where the employer's behaviour, although cold, was not intended to cause distress or injury; where there was a legitimate basis for dispute; or where there was no objective unfairness or mistreatment of the employee. Damages were said to be inappropriate where the employee asked for his job back. An apology may mitigate an employee's damages in some circumstances.

Quebec cases — In Quebec, this kind of conduct may result in an award of moral damages. Damages can be awarded on the theory of abuse of right in contractual matters where the employer has acted maliciously or in bad faith. Damages have been refused in some cases where there was no maliciousness on the employer's part. As with mental distress damages in the rest of Canada, it may be necessary to prove a delict due to the manner of dismissal, and damages may be limited to those flowing from the failure to give notice. Recently, the Quebec Court of Appeal has said that the theory of abuse of right should be exercised with caution. Nevertheless, moral damages seem to be awarded fairly routinely in Quebec.

Pleadings — Claims may be denied if they have not been specifically pleaded, and a pleading of one type may be insufficient to support an award of another type of aggravated or punitive damages, as the employer must know the case it has to meet. Rules of pleading applying to defamation claims do not necessarily apply where defamatory statements are alleged as part of an aggravated or punitive damages claim in a wrongful dismissal action.

Procedural effects — Aggravated and punitive damages issues may make a matter unsuitable for summary trial procedures. They also may make a case inappropriate for a jury trial. In one case, the fact that an employee sued within the period of working notice and claimed aggravated and punitive damages was said to repudiate the contract, and her damages were cut off as of the date she sued.

G-9.2 MENTAL DISTRESS DAMAGES

General principles — Although not all judges seem to apply these standards, the Supreme Court of Canada has said that mental distress damages can only be awarded if:

(1) the damages arise from the dismissal itself, not from pre- or post-dismissal conduct;
(2) there is a separate, actionable wrong apart from the dismissal; and
(3) there was an intention to harm or to inflict mental distress.

Tort vs. mental distress damages — Even where mental distress damages have been refused, some judges have awarded tort damages instead, often on the basis of negligent or intentional infliction of mental suffering. Where tort damages are awarded, aggravated or punitive damages may be duplicative.

Degree of distress — Although the occasional judge still awards damages for distress that does not appear out of the ordinary, and may not even be the result of independently actionable conduct, most take the view that to justify an award, the dismissed employee must have suffered mental distress above and beyond the expected level of someone who loses their job. Even stress such as an employee's attempted suicide after losing his job and having to relocate for the first time in his life may not be sufficient to justify an award. Mental distress damages were said not to be justified where:

- There was mere upset and counselling, the use of sleeping pills, or an increase in the number of headaches. In one case, however, the fact that an employee broke out in a rash requiring medical treatment justified an award.
- There was a lack of medical evidence of distress, or medical evidence of causation.
- The employee suffered no compelling or long-term physical or emotional consequences.

Cause of distress — It must be clear that the distress was due to the lack of notice or other circumstances of dismissal, not the fact of dismissal itself, as it is not a breach of contract merely to terminate employment. Most judges say the distress must not have been caused by outside or pre-existing problems, although some judges will award damages as long as the circumstances of dismissal caused a major share of the distress or clearly aggravated a pre-existing condition. Mental distress damages were denied where:

- There had been no breach of contract.
- A liquidated damages clause in a contract already took mental distress into account.
- The distress was from the loss of job, not the lack of proper notice or other breach.
- There was no proof that an employee's marriage breakdown was due to her dismissal.

Conduct justifying damages — Much seems to depend on the trial judge's view of the severity of the employer's actions. The same type of conduct may be found to justify an award in one case but not in another. For example, mental distress damages have been awarded for:

- Untrue allegations of theft or other improper conduct such as fraud or bribery.
- Allegations of incompetence or poor performance, especially where the allegations become known to others.
- Failure to investigate thoroughly, particularly when allegations of dishonesty or moral turpitude are involved.
- Setting unreasonable performance standards, accompanied by failure to give an employee a reasonable chance to demonstrate his abilities.

- Breached promises of job security.
- Harassment, intimidation or assault of employees.
- Withholding of an employee's funds and property.
- An employer's refusal to pay to return an employee to his country of origin, as he was required to do by law, when the employer wrongfully dismissed him.
- Dismissal of an employee only a month after his son had died.
- Dismissal of an employee for a relatively trivial reason, such as a short-term illness or a single incident of poor judgment in a long career.
- Undue financial pressure or pressure to forego legal advice.
- Humiliation of an employee in front of his co-workers.
- An unjustified poor reference, given when the long-term employee had never been made aware of any dissatisfaction with his performance.

Just cause allegations — Some cases have awarded damages where groundless allegations of just cause were maintained long after the employer should have known they were false. Other judges have disagreed, however, stating that allegations in pleadings and other judicial utterances are protected by absolute privilege, and therefore cannot support an award. Note that misconduct short of just cause may be a factor against an aggravated damages award.

Failure to explain or give chance to respond — Some judges have based damages on a failure to give reasons and give the employee a chance to respond. Others, however, have said there is neither an obligation to give reasons for dismissal nor any common-law duty to fairly investigate allegations of wrongdoing, so this kind of conduct cannot support an award.

Conduct not justifying damages — Much of the conduct found not to justify damages is similar to conduct that has supported damages; it depends on the degree of bad treatment, or on the "reasonableness" or "fairness" of the employer's actions. For instance, mental distress damages were not awarded for:

- False allegations of theft or other improprieties.
- Unjustified, embarrassing allegations, even where the employer was out to get the employee.
- A failure to follow the employer's own discipline policy; it was high-handed, but not malicious.
- Dismissal of an employee on sick leave, or refusal to allow an employee to return from sick leave or to support a claim for long-term disability benefits.
- Unjustified allegations of poor performance, at least where there was some cause for dissatisfaction, even if it did not legally amount to just cause.

- Callousness, insensitivity, suddenness or coldness of the termination, as long as there was no public humiliation, malice or other reprehensible behaviour.
- Withholding funds or exerting undue financial pressure on the employee.
- The use of an employee's facsimile signature long after his dismissal.
- Dismissal of an employee in a legitimate reorganization or downsizing.
- Using a secret video camera to videotape an employee suspected of sleeping on the job.
- Failure to remedy problems between employees.
- Escorting the employee off the premises or calling in the police, as long as the employer acted reasonably and in good faith.
- Bad faith conduct and harassment, where they fell short of an independent actionable wrong.

G-9.3 DAMAGES FOR LOSS OF REPUTATION OR OPPORTUNITY

General principles — The effects of employers' actions on employees' reputations now seem to be a more accepted consideration in assessing their entitlement to aggravated damages. Claims of slander and defamation in the employment context are also arising more frequently, often as an independent cause of action said to justify aggravated or punitive damages. In some cases, loss of reputation considerations may be included in awards for mental distress or punitive damages.

Need for actual harm — Damages will be refused where there is no evidence of actual harm to an employee's reputation or opportunities. Resistance remains to the concept of loss of reputation damages, so the evidence may need to be compelling before an award will be justified. As with damages for libel or slander, truth of allegations will generally be a defence; accusations which were true were not cause for aggravated damages, even though they were not serious enough to amount to just cause for dismissal.

Unfavourable job references — Providing unfavourable job references may lead to an award of aggravated damages, either directly for loss of reputation or otherwise. Unjustified bad references also may be considered in increasing the notice period.

Lost opportunity to enhance one's reputation — Damages for lost opportunity to enhance one's reputation have been awarded, although these awards are traditionally limited to public performers.

Examples — damages awarded — Loss of reputation damages have been awarded for:

- False allegations of theft or other dishonesty or impropriety which become known to others; in one case, $75,000 in damages was awarded for untrue allegations against a senior official that resulted in his "public humiliation".
- False allegations about an employee's performance, made unreasonably and publicly or without an honest belief in their truth.
- Unfair performance criticisms which were made known to others, even where they were made with an honest belief in their truth.
- Public embarrassment and humiliation, plus a public perception of incompetence or worse due to the way an employer handled a termination. In a similar case, however, damages were not awarded.

Examples — damages not awarded — Loss of reputation damages were denied where:

- The allegations amounted to slander, since the tortious conduct was not a breach of contract; substantial slander damages, however, were awarded.
- The employer refused to discuss with others the reason for an employee's termination; this was not conduct injuring the employee's reputation.
- Any damage to reputation was due to the employee's own actions in holding a press conference about the termination.
- Press reports raised suspicions about an employee's honesty but the employer never provided any critical information to the press.
- An employee's termination merely became public knowledge.
- An accusation was made that the employee abused cocaine but it was not related to the dismissal and was not communicated to anyone outside the immediate workplace.
- Allegations of impropriety or incompetence were made, but they were not made public or otherwise spread by the employer. The employer did not go beyond its duty to report or to explain the employee's termination.
- Police were called in, where the employer had acted in good faith.

G-9.4 PUNITIVE DAMAGES

General principles — Extreme situations justifying punitive damages should be very unusual and occur only where there is exceptionally harsh, vindictive, reprehensible or malicious conduct that is deserving of the court's condemnation. Where the only conduct complained of involves the manner of dismissal and there is no independent cause of action, damages may be refused, even where the conduct is reprehensible. For example, punitive damages were refused against a non-profit employer, as well as a co-worker who had already been held personally, jointly and severally liable for a dismissed employee's damages. Courts rarely award punitive damages in the context of a commercial, non-employment contract.

Employee's conduct — Punitive damages have often been refused where the employee's conduct has been less than proper, even if falling short of just cause or where there has been blame on both sides.

Relationship to other damages — Some cases have refused punitive damages where an employee has already been awarded aggravated damages or tort damages, particularly if the conduct is intertwined in the other claims. Similarly, punitive damages have been refused where the improper conduct has already been taken into account in lengthening the notice period. Many other examples, however, exist where punitive damages have been awarded on top of other aggravated or tort damages, or in addition to increasing the notice period due to the employer's bad faith.

Conduct not justifying damages — Most cases which have considered the issue of punitive damages have denied damages. Yet damages have been allowed for many of the same types of conduct where damages have been refused in other cases. In general, abrupt or insensitive conduct, and even constructive dismissal situations, will not support a punitive damages claim in the absence of malicious or reprehensible conduct. Damages were not justified for:

- Sudden termination or termination at an insensitive time, especially where the employer tried to soften the blow by having a human resources representative attend the termination interview or by providing immediate outside relocation counselling.
- Insensitivity, carelessness, and even giving a false reason for dismissal.
- Refusing to allow an employee to return to work after a sick leave.
- Firing an employee after she requested an extension to an unpaid leave of absence.
- Dismissal due to a *bona fide* reorganization or downsizing.
- Constructive dismissal one year after the employer enticed an employee to relocate, and his wife gave up her job to accompany him.

Conduct justifying damages — Damages have been awarded where:

- Employees had been lured away from secure jobs through misrepresentations and then were abruptly terminated after only a few weeks' work.
- An employee was aggressively recruited and then constructively dismissed after he had quit his old job.

- An employee was subjected to humiliation in the workplace to try to pressure him to resign.
- An employer abused its fiduciary duties in a "power dependency" relationship.
- Employees were dismissed for improper or abusive motives, such as because they were pregnant or were about to earn a large commission.
- The employer gave repeated assurances of job security, which proved to be untrue.

Untrue cause allegations — A number of cases have said that false allegations of just cause justify punitive damages, particularly where the allegations involve theft or other dishonesty, they are unreasonable, or they are made known to others. More often, however, false allegations of just cause, failure to give a chance to explain, an incomplete investigation and poor job references have not justified damages where an employers' actions were imprudent but not malicious. The fact that an employer chose to believe other employees' tales of misconduct rather than to believe the dismissed employee did not warrant damages. Note that many of these types of conduct have led to an increase in the notice period; however, punitive damages were refused where an employer:

- Dismissed an employee charged with a criminal offence even though the employer believed he was innocent, because it feared bad publicity.
- Dismissed an employee under the cloud of a police investigation and concertedly tried to damage her reputation due to a love affair gone wrong.
- Made false allegations of theft or other dishonesty, or called in the police.
- Made intemperate but brief allegations in front of others, and they were not so loud as to involve other people.
- Made continued, unjustified allegations of cause.
- Dismissed an employee after giving assurances of security.
- Acted precipitously on the basis of rumours of conflict of interest.

Poor performance allegations — Similarly, unfounded allegations of poor performance and a lack of warnings have been found not to justify punitive damages, particularly where the allegations were not made known to others or there was no intention to embarrass or injure the employee. In other cases, however, false allegations have been found to justify an award where they were made without an honest belief in their truth, where they were publicized, or where the employer had set an unreasonable standard of performance. Persisting in groundless cause allegations to the eve of trial, despite having given the employee a glowing letter of reference, helped support a punitive damages award in one case.

Harassment and retaliation — Although some cases have refused punitive damages for harassment by the employer, harassment of an ill employee was cause for punitive damages in one case. Vindictive, harassing treatment of an ex-employee and his family members justified substantial punitive damages in another case. Claims of retaliatory discharge have had mixed results. An employee who was dismissed in retaliation for his threat to file a statutory health and safety complaint was awarded punitive damages. However, where an employee claimed she was dismissed in retaliation for complaints about management, punitive damages were not found to be justified.

Conduct following dismissal — Insensitive behaviour following termination generally has not attracted punitive damages where it was not motivated by malice. For instance, damages were not justified for:

- "Shabby" treatment, where the employer led the employee to expect a settlement but then forced him to sue, with attendant bad publicity.
- Failure to promptly provide the correct documents for Unemployment Insurance, benefits conversion or income tax purposes.
- Mere notification to others of the fact of termination, without libellous statements.
- Statements made to the Unemployment Insurance Commission regarding the reason for termination.
- Failure to find a new position for an employee, particularly where the employee had himself put limits on the positions he would consider.
- Non-compliance with employment standards obligations.
- Withholding payment in order to pressure the employee to settle; while not desirable, it was not high-handed enough to justify punitive damages.

Post-dismissal conduct justifying damages — Punitive damages have been awarded where:

- An employer dismissed an employee without paying him statutory severance pay to which he was clearly entitled.
- An employer refused to release an employee's property and research funds, making it nearly impossible for her to carry on with her research; she was awarded aggravated damages, although not punitive damages.
- An employer refused to pay for a transferred employee to return home to the United Kingdom, even though he was required to do so by law, and who then accused the employee of failing to mitigate for not reporting to work in the United Kingdom.
- An employer had breached its fiduciary duties by withholding wages for several months before termination.
- An employer dismissed an employee with a patently unreasonable severance offer and demanded that she sign a release to get any of it.
- An employer discriminated against the employee's family members after the employee's dismissal.

Chapter G-10

OTHER DAMAGES AND REMEDIES

TABLE OF CONTENTS

G-10.1 Other Damages and Remedies Generally
G-10.2 Losses in Reliance on Employment
G-10.3 Loss of Seniority
G-10.4 Lost Opportunities
G-10.5 Post-dismissal Financial Decisions
G-10.6 Income Tax Consequences
G-10.7 Cost of Professional Advice
G-10.8 Compensation for Proprietary Information
G-10.9 Damages for Spouses
G-10.10 Reinstatement
G-10.11 Other Specific Performance

G-10.1 OTHER DAMAGES AND REMEDIES GENERALLY

Introduction — Employees have sought a number of other damages and remedies. In general, to be compensable, a loss must have been caused by the dismissal without notice or other breach of contract.

Equitable remedies — Sometimes, employees seek a remedy other than monetary compensation. For example, employees may seek reinstatement, a court order that the employer provide a reference or the return of certain property. These equitable remedies are discussed at the end of this chapter.

Cross-references — Note that a number of atypical losses are dealt with in other chapters, particularly Chapters G-7 and G-8. Expenses incurred in seeking new employment or in starting a new business after dismissal are discussed in Chapter H-3, "Career Changes and Relocating".

G-10.2 LOSSES IN RELIANCE ON EMPLOYMENT

General principles — Employers may or may not be held liable for expenses incurred by the employee in reliance on his employment. The treatment of a particular expense will depend on how connected it is to the job or the dismissal, as employers are not generally responsible for the ways in which employees choose to spend their earnings. Costs for leased cars or cell phones that were required for the job have sometimes been reimbursed, as discussed respectively in Chapter G-7 under G-7.3, "Other Automobile Benefits" and G-7.9 "Other Benefits".

Losses from previous jobs — An employee who gave up a previous job to take a job with a new employer but was dismissed after a short time, was not entitled to the commissions that he would have made in his former job. The loss was due to the employee's choice and was not causally connected to the dismissal. An employee was not entitled to lost severance benefits which he failed to claim from the previous employer.

Salary lost while on leave — An employee, who was dismissed just after returning from a lengthy leave of absence to attend university, was not entitled to the salary he had lost while attending school, as full pay while at school was not a term of his contract. An employee in a similar situation was not entitled to damages for loss of opportunity during the leave.

Repairs to employer property — One employee who made extensive repairs to his company-owned residence was not entitled to reimbursement as there was no express or implied contract to indemnify him. Another employee, however, was awarded damages on a *quantum meruit* basis.

Living expenses — An employee was not entitled to compensation for his living expenses during his employment, as he had not been induced to relocate by the employer's promises. An employee who had rented an apartment closer to his job was not entitled to be reimbursed for rent he paid after his dismissal.

G-10.3 LOSS OF SENIORITY

Loss of seniority generally — Damages were refused where the employee had become re-employed in a much better position and there was no evidence of any lasting harm from the dismissal.

Failure to return to bargaining unit — Where an employee had a right to return to a more secure bargaining unit position, damages have been awarded for failure to allow the return. In one case, a judge found that a management employee had an implied right to be returned to the bargaining unit rather than to be terminated. He awarded damages for the anticipated balance of the employee's working life, subject to a discount rate and a 50 per cent discount for the contingencies of either earlier plant shutdown or termination for cause.

G-10.4 LOST OPPORTUNITIES

Training program — An employer who unjustifiably criticized an employee in the Record of Employment, resulting in denial of entry into a special EI program, was held liable to the employee for the loss due to not being in the program.

Certification — An employee was denied damages for the lost opportunity to obtain professional certification, since he had a history of failing the exams and had not passed the first exam until well after termination.

G-10.5 POST-DISMISSAL FINANCIAL DECISIONS

Loan interest claims — An employee's claim for the interest paid on a personal loan needed to cover his expenses while he was in between jobs was disallowed in several cases but allowed in another. Loan consolidation costs were disallowed where the employee had some severance pay available to him but chose not to apply it to the loans.

Property sold after dismissal — Employers are generally not responsible for losses on the sale of personal property after dismissal:

- An employee was not compensated for lost dividends on shares that he sold after dismissal.
- An employee's loss on the sale of his computer, which he could not afford to ship back to his home in England, was allowed.
- An employee who sold his own business when relocating after termination was refused damages for the buyer's subsequent default, because the sale was neither connected to the termination nor foreseeable by the employer.

Cancellation of vacation — An employee, who lost a non-refundable deposit on a vacation because he could not take the vacation after being dismissed, was awarded the lost deposit as part of his damages due to the employer's bad faith.

G-10.6 INCOME TAX CONSEQUENCES

Income tax damages awarded — Cases in this area are mixed. Successful employee claims have included:

- A ruling that an increase in income tax due to the damages being paid in a later year would be compensable in damages where a loss is proved.
- An employee, who suffered income tax consequences through loss of his nonresident status due to his dismissal, was compensated by "grossing up" his award so that his after-tax position would be the same as if he had worked through the notice period.
- An employer, who had undertaken to file the employee's income tax returns in the past and to remit the tax owing, was held liable for outstanding taxes.
- Increased tax liability on reimbursement of moving expenses was properly payable by the employer in one case.

Income tax damages not awarded — Claims that were not successful include:

- An employee, whose RRSP contribution limit decreased due to his termination before the end of the year, was not compensated because this damage was too remote.
- An employee was not entitled to damages for her increased tax liability because she was paid a lump-sum severance payment rather than periodic payments.
- Increased tax liability on a capital gain was the employee's and not the employer's responsibility.
- A claim for foreign income taxes was refused, on the basis that the parties' contract did not provide for the salary payments to be net of taxes.

G-10.7 COST OF PROFESSIONAL ADVICE

Accounting and tax advice — Again, the results are mixed. For example:

- An employee's claim for accounting advice on an offered severance package was allowed. However, his claim for general advice on the income tax aspects of termination was not allowed, as this cost would have been incurred regardless of whether he received reasonable notice of dismissal.
- Damages for tax advice and tax return preparation were allowed where the employee's need for advice upon repatriation was foreseeable.

Legal advice — A claim for legal expenses due to termination was disallowed in one case. In another case, legal expenses incurred to defend against an unjustified assault charge related to false sexual harassment accusations were allowed.

Public relations expenses — An employee's public relations firm costs were not allowed as damages, because there was no evidence that they were necessary due to the employer's behaviour.

Treatment costs — Out-of-pocket treatment costs and part of an employee's lost earnings after the notice period were awarded to an employee who suffered severe depression and was unable to seek other work as a result of her emotional problems caused by the way she was dismissed. This cost was in addition to general damages for mental distress. Even where the employee's symptoms were less extreme and the employee had been attending counselling before dismissal, another employee was awarded damages where the bulk of the treatment costs were incurred after dismissal.

G-10.8 COMPENSATION FOR PROPRIETARY INFORMATION

Patents — Compensation for patents for the employee's inventions was refused in one case, since it was not part of the employment contract and did not flow from breach of the contract.

Value of insurance agent's "book" — Where an insurance salesman had a vested right to buy back his "book of business" but he was unable to exercise his right due to the employer's sudden dismissal without adequate notice, he was compensated for the book's value.

Client lists — A broker, who would have been able to sell his client accounts if he had not been precipitously dismissed, was entitled to damages for the value of the accounts and his interest in the commissions which the accounts would have generated in the first year after sale.

G-10.9 DAMAGES FOR SPOUSES

Generally — Several spouses have attempted to claim damages for loss of care, guidance and companionship of the dismissed spouse under applicable provincial legislation, but no awards have yet been made.

Spouse's transfer — Nominal damages were awarded to one spouse where the employer had encouraged her to assist her husband with his management style. The employer knew that she was employed and should have foreseen that she would lose her job if the employer transferred the husband and then withdrew the transfer. In other cases:

- Where an employee's husband requested a transfer after her dismissal but was later laid off from the new position, the wife's employer was

not liable for his lost wages as this claim was too remote from the wife's dismissal.
- In one unusual case, an employer had breached its relocation policy but the employee's claim in the courts was barred due to the existence of a grievance procedure. However, the employee's wife, who was co-owner of the house, was allowed to continue her action against the employer.

Subcontractor — Where an employee hired his wife to perform occasional administrative work, he could not claim for her lost income in his wrongful dismissal action, as her loss was not a loss to the employee himself.

Business partner — A wife, who was a part owner of her husband's joint venture with the employer, was entitled to damages for the loss in the value of shares due to a breach of the joint venture agreement, as was the corporation of which she was a shareholder.

G-10.10 REINSTATEMENT

Definition — Reinstatement is an order requiring an employer to allow the employee to return to the job. It is a type of specific performance order — a court order that requires a party to do something or not do something, other than pay money damages.

General principle — Although the occasional case has expressed doubt, most have held that reinstatement is not available at common law, since it would breach the long-standing rule against ordering specific performance of a personal services contract.

Reinstatement is exceptional remedy — Reinstatement is an exceptional, discretionary remedy, which will only be justified in special circumstances. It may properly be refused where the issue of just cause is before the courts, or where damages would be more appropriate.

Quashing dismissal — Where an employee is dismissed in breach of a statutory procedure or provision or is dismissed without the required degree of administrative fairness, as discussed in Chapter D-2, "Duty to Warn and Duty of Fairness", the termination may be quashed, which has the same effect as a reinstatement order. Some judges have said that an employee in this situation can be awarded damages, at least if he does not seek reinstatement. Another judge has said that damages are not a proper remedy, since they do not give the employee the right to be heard. Therefore, quashing the dismissal is the only proper remedy.

Reinstatement will be ordered — Reinstatement may be ordered where:

- Statutory or contractual provisions governing an employee's termination have not been complied with.
- A statute specifically gives the power.
- The parties had agreed to resolve disputes through arbitration under a provincial arbitration statute that allowed for reinstatement.

Reinstatement will not be ordered — One judge has said that it is difficult to conceive of any circumstances that would justify reinstatement to a management job. An order of reinstatement would also be improper where:

- The employee had already accepted another job.
- The employment relationship had been irreparably damaged. For example, damage due to the employee's exaggerated pleadings.
- A fixed-term appointment had already expired.
- The position had already been filled.
- A minister had not shown a strong case for reinstatement or the likelihood of irreparable harm if the court did not grant an injunction forbidding his removal from the church rolls.

Examples — reinstatement ordered — Despite the general rule against reinstatement, reinstatement has been ordered in the following cases:

- A Quebec case that involved a fixed-term contract and a unique chance to enhance the employee's reputation.
- A minister's status was wrongfully revoked in breach of the church's by-laws. Damages for wrongful dismissal were not an adequate remedy; the termination was declared null and void and the minister's name was ordered restored to the rolls.

Failure to obey reinstatement order — Where reinstatement is an order, the employer is required to provide guidance, information, work tools, and the assignment of work requiring physical and/or mental effort. However, the penalties for failing to do so are not severe. For example:

- Where an employer breached its own procedures in dismissing an employee, the court merely awarded an extra $5,000 in damages for the failure to provide a hearing as required by contract.
- An employer who had failed to truly reinstate an employee was not fined for contempt of court, as that would not assist the parties' future relationship.

G-10.11 OTHER SPECIFIC PERFORMANCE

Definition — As discussed earlier under G-10.10 "Reinstatement", specific performance is a court order that requires a party to do something or not do something, other than pay money damages. Courts prefer to award damages rather than specific performance, as specific performance awards can be hard to supervise. However, courts will award specific performance where damages are not an adequate remedy.

Payment of offer — An employee, who was wrongfully dismissed after failing to accept a buyout offer, was granted a declaration that his termination was void and he was entitled to the offered severance package. In another case, the judge concluded that an employer's termination offer was fair and more generous than the employee would receive in court. The judge declared the offer open to be accepted by the employee.

Lifetime benefits — Specific performance was not ordered for the breach of a contractual obligation to provide lifetime medical and dental benefits; damages were awarded instead.

Employee's employment record — At least one case has ordered deletions from an employee's employment record of complaints or infractions used to justify dismissal which the court found to be invalid.

Letter of reference — Several cases have ordered employers to issue a letter of reference.

News release — One case ordered an employer to issue a news release absolving the employee from allegations of wrongdoing and announcing his reinstatement.

Pensions — Orders regarding pension entitlements have included the cases of:

- An employee who was unfairly dismissed for misconduct due to early Alzheimer's disease, thereby losing his pension entitlement. He was deemed to have applied for the pension as of the date of dismissal and consent to his early retirement was deemed granted. He was also awarded damages for back pension benefits.
- An employee whose contract promised pension credits for past service. The employee was awarded a declaration of entitlement to a pension based on the contract's terms, and the successor employer was ordered to assume all pension obligations to the employee.
- An employee who was entitled by statute to "fair compensation" for breach of his fixed-term contract. It was ordered that the compensation period be treated as employment for all pension purposes.
- An employer ordered to transfer the amount of an employee's pension benefits to a locked-in RRSP of the employee's choice.

Restrictive covenants — A declaration that a restrictive covenant was of no force or effect was refused where it was not specifically pleaded in the statement of claim. However, where a claim was properly pleaded, a restrictive covenant was declared to be no longer binding.

Employer's policies — A policy that breached employees' contractual rights was declared to be void in one case.

Rectification — Where a written contract did not reflect the actual agreement between the parties, rectification — a forced correction of the document — could be ordered.

Orders regarding property — Where the employee and employer retained each other's property, an order was made requiring both of them to release each other's property. Since the employee had kept much more than the employer, he was ordered to compensate the employer for the wrongful withholding.

Chapter G-11

DEDUCTIONS FROM THE DAMAGE AWARD

TABLE OF CONTENTS

G-11.1 Deductions from Damages Generally
G-11.2 Notice, Severance Pay and Termination Pay
G-11.3 Benefits
G-11.4 Future Contingencies
G-11.5 Other Deductions

G-11.1 DEDUCTIONS FROM DAMAGES GENERALLY

Introduction — In calculating overall damages for wrongful dismissal, certain amounts must be deducted from the initial calculation of damages based on the reasonable notice period. For example, amounts already paid toward salary and benefits for the notice period, and amounts earned by the employee within the notice period, will be taken into account. This chapter discusses all deductions from damages other than deductions due to the employee's mitigation efforts, which are discussed in Chapter H-5, "Deduction of Earnings in Mitigation".

Deductions in excess of damages — Where an employee has already received more in working notice and termination pay, or in termination pay plus amounts earned in mitigation, than the reasonable notice to which he or she was entitled, the wrongful dismissal action will be dismissed.

G-11.2 NOTICE, SEVERANCE PAY AND TERMINATION PAY

Working notice — The amount of any working notice given is normally deducted from the damages award. The occasional case has refused to deduct the amount of notice provided, however, perhaps to reflect bad faith or other unfair circumstances of dismissal.

Termination payment or salary continuance — Any payment upon termination that has been made by the employer in lieu of notice will also be credited against the damages payable, as will payments made by salary continuance. In most cases, payments of statutory termination notice or severance pay are credited against the damages payable.

Payment must be for termination — To be deducted, a payment must have been made in lieu of notice or because of the termination. For example, a payment after termination for work done before termination is not deductible from damages. Similarly, a deduction will be denied where the employee had a contractual right to the payment, separate and apart from the right to reasonable notice.

Contractual severance payment — Deduction may be denied where the payment is a contractual severance payment rather than a termination payment — that is, the payment was a reward for past service rather than in lieu of notice. See Chapter E-6, "Express Termination Provisions". Payments that were found to be a separate entitlement and which were not deducted from damages include:

- A severance payment under a collective agreement that related to an earlier period of employment, as it was not made in lieu of notice.
- Four weeks' pay at the end of an overseas assignment, as provided in the employee's contract.
- A lump-sum payment of severance pay offered in addition to termination pay by way of salary continuance. Only the termination pay was deductible from the employee's common-law entitlement.
- A bonus paid to an employee dismissed upon the sale of a business, where his contract provided for a special bonus upon sale.

In another case, however, the employer made a large payment, described as a bonus. The court found that the payment was much larger than the bonus to which the employee was entitled and that it had been described as a bonus to allow the employee to qualify earlier for unemployment insurance benefits. It was really pay in lieu of notice, and the court subtracted it from the damages payable.

Voluntary payment for relocation counselling — In some cases, an employer's voluntary payment for relocation counselling has been deducted from damages, but in others it has not. In one case, no deduction was made because it was found that the employee had been given no choice in the matter, and the employer had provided the payments for its own benefit in the hope that the employee would quickly obtain a new job.

Vacation pay, banked sick pay — The results of cases dealing with vacation pay and payment in lieu of sick leave are mixed. Whether they should be deducted from damages will depend on the contract's terms and the relevant statute law, as well as the period to which the payments relate. One case has said that pay for vacation accrued before dismissal should not be deducted from wrongful dismissal damages, as it was an earned benefit. The fact that the employee may not have to work during the notice period is irrelevant to the right to be paid for vacation earned before termination. Similarly, a payment for accrued overtime and holiday pay was not deducted from damages.

Payment in kind — Where an employee accepted some furniture in lieu of wages, its value was deducted from her damages for reasonable notice.

Income tax — The gross amount of a termination payment should be deducted, not the net amount of income tax and other statutory deductions, since those deductions are required by statute and are paid on the employee's behalf.

G-11.3 BENEFITS

General principle — Payments for benefits being compensated by damages should be deducted from the damages award. For example, if an employer has continued certain benefits for part of the notice period, and the full value of the benefit has been included in damages, the part that was already received through continued coverage should be deducted.

Pension benefits — Damages for pension benefits are discussed in Chapter G-6, "Employment Insurance and Pension Benefits". In some cases, payments related to pensions are deducted from wrongful dismissal damages; in other cases they are not. For example:
- A refund of pension contributions that was required by contract was not deducted.
- Where the employee elects to retire and start receiving pension benefits, the payments have generally not been deducted from wrongful dismissal damages.
- Where an employee claimed his election of early retirement was a constructive dismissal, the court said the pension benefits received would be deductible from any damages owed.
- Although it may not be appropriate in many cases, where a judge orders that the employee is to be given credit for pension purposes for the period of reasonable notice, it may be proper to deduct from his or her damages the amount of any pension premiums or contributions he or she would have had to make to have acquired the same benefit.

Voluntary or enhanced pension benefits — Where the employer has voluntarily provided pension benefits to which the employee was not otherwise entitled, they may be deducted from wrongful dismissal damages, at least in part. For example:

- One employee who received enhanced pension benefits upon his forced early retirement had only 50 per cent of them deducted from his wrongful dismissal damages, since they were not an immediate economic benefit, as termination pay would have been.
- In one case, only 75 per cent of the benefits were deducted, to reflect the tax disadvantages to the employee of receiving the enhanced pension rather than an immediate payment.
- In one case, however, the full amount of the enhancement was deducted.
- Where an employer purchased an annuity for the employee, only the cost of the annuity was deducted, not the amount of benefits the annuity would pay.

Workers' compensation benefits — Workers' compensation benefits may or may not be deducted from wrongful dismissal damages. Benefits were deducted in one case where an employee was injured on the job and received workers' compensation benefits for two months after his dismissal; the appeal court said the employer was entitled to the benefit of the fund to which it had contributed. In other cases, courts have refused a deduction, however, saying workers' compensation benefits are a separate, integral part of the employment contract unrelated to dismissal. For example, workers' compensation benefits were not deducted where the worker was receiving short-term disability benefits and the plan did not provide for deduction, but once the employee would have been receiving long-term disability benefits, a deduction was allowed since that plan provided for it.

Disability benefits — Where an employee is entitled to receive disability benefits for part or all of the notice period, some cases have upheld the employee's right to receive both disability payments and pay in lieu of notice, ruling that the period of disability postpones the start of the notice period, or that the two types of payments are for different purposes. However, the Supreme Court of Canada has ruled that the matter depends on the terms of the employment contract and the parties' intentions. Where the disability plan was an integral part of the employee's compensation, and was paid for by the employer, the benefits will be deductible. Disability benefits that are more like private insurance plans funded by the employee would not be deductible. Despite this principle, decisions have continued to be inconsistent. For example:

- Where an employee contributed directly to a sick leave bank through a trade-off in salary and benefits, and also contributed directly to a private group disability plan, the sick leave and disability benefits were not deducted from the employee's dismissal damages.

- An employee, who had contributed to premiums for a mandatory long-term disability (LTD) plan, was not entitled to reasonable notice damages as well, because the judge reasoned that the LTD benefits were intended to substitute for the employee's regular pay.

CPP disability payments — Similarly, Canada Pension Plan disability benefits received during the notice period would have been deducted from damages for reasonable notice, where they were deductible from LTD benefits under the terms of the LTD plan.

Maternity and parental leave — Some cases have suspended the notice period for the duration of a statutory leave, because it was said not to be equitable to include the leave period within the notice period since an employee would not be able to use that time for a new job search. Deduction has also been refused on the basis that the right to a paid leave arose by statute rather than from the terms of the employment contract. In another case, however, maternity and parental leave benefits have been deducted from wrongful dismissal damages.

Employment insurance — Although court decisions over the years have been inconsistent, legislation makes employers liable for repaying the Employment Insurance Commission when a settlement or damages are paid. Thus, the statutory deduction will be deducted upon payment, and does not need to be taken into account in the damages award itself. Note that a few judges continue to deduct EI benefits from the damages award; this is proper, as long as they order that the amount be deducted and remitted to the Commission as a means of satisfying the judgment.

G-11.4 FUTURE CONTINGENCIES

General principles — Where a trial takes place before the notice period is over, an issue may arise as to whether an amount should be deducted for the contingency of re-employment, or for any other contingency that might reduce an employee's entitlement for the rest of the notice period. Some judges refuse to make a deduction; others refuse to make them where the order is for salary continuance rather than a lump sum; but many have applied a deduction for contingencies or for anticipated mitigation. In other cases, judges have adjusted the notice period or damages awarded, although the manner of adjustment is not always made clear. The likelihood of an employee obtaining a new job within the notice period may be taken into account in setting the amount of any contingency to be deducted; the deduction may be modest if the evidence indicates only a small chance of the employee finding a new job.

Examples — no deduction — No deduction or discount was made where:

- The positive and negative contingencies of re-employment within the notice period balanced each other out.
- A deduction for contingencies should be refused for the sake of bringing finality to the proceedings.
- On the evidence, re-employment within the notice period seemed unlikely.
- The employee was setting up his own business, and would be unlikely to earn much within the notice period.

Examples — deduction made — In other cases, judges have dealt with the matter of contingencies in various ways. For example:

- Damages were refused for benefits or out-of-pocket expenses in lieu of a deduction for the contingency of future employment within the notice period.
- It has been left to the parties to agree on the deduction to be made if the employee got a new job.
- A judge ordered a case to be referred back to court for an assessment if necessary.
- Some judges have imposed a trust in favour of the employer on any future earnings received by the employee within the notice period; others have rejected this approach.
- Where damages were based on the employer's offer, some judges have continued a condition in the offer that damages would be reduced by 50 per cent for any time remaining in the notice period after the employee obtained a new job. In another case, however, this was rejected as unworkable and undesirable, because it would require the employee to report to the former employer on his mitigation efforts regularly for the rest of the notice period.
- Where a lump-sum damages award was being ordered before the damages period had expired, one judge ordered a discount rate to reflect the future difference between the investment rate of interest and the rate of general price inflation.

Other contingency situations — Contingencies other than re-employment before expiry of the notice period have also been considered:

- An employee was awarded the present value of his earnings for 11 years until retirement, and that amount was further discounted to allow for the contingencies of life.
- Where an amount was awarded for loss of a future bonus, it was discounted by 15 per cent to reflect the negative contingencies that could have affected payment of the bonus.
- Where damages were awarded for a two-year contractual period but there was a chance that the contract would not have been extended that long even if the employer had not breached it, a 20 per cent discount was applied.

G-11.5 OTHER DEDUCTIONS

Deductions for expenses of working — An employer was not entitled to deduct $800 per month from the employee's damages to represent the amount she would have spent on child care if she had worked through the notice period. An employer must pay an employee her earnings and is not entitled to look at how she would have spent them. Similarly, the fact that an employee ceased to maintain a second residence after dismissal was not to be taken into account in assessing damages.

Counterclaim — Of course, the amount of any counterclaim by the employer can be set off against damages, such as a claim for a pay advance or a loan repayment. Damages may also be subject to orders as to third-party claims or payments by jointly and severally liable parties.

Defamation damages — Defamation damages received from officers of the union due to statements made about the employee's performance were not deducted from his wrongful dismissal damages as against the employer, as they involved a separate claim against a separate party. Defamation damages as against the employer may or may not be treated as a separate entitlement, depending on the circumstances.

Chapter H-1

MITIGATION OF DAMAGES

TABLE OF CONTENTS

H-1.1 The Duty to Mitigate
H-1.2 Fixed-Term Contracts and Contractual Notice Periods
H-1.3 Effect of Failure to Mitigate

H-1.1 THE DUTY TO MITIGATE

General principles — In any breach of contract action, the innocent party has a duty to take all reasonable steps to lessen his or her damages. In a wrongful dismissal context, this means that the dismissed employee must do everything reasonable to reduce the amount payable by the employer. This duty applies whether the employer provides working notice, pay in lieu of notice, or no pay or notice. If an employee takes reasonable steps and lessens his loss, for example by earning income in a new job within the notice period, the amount earned will be deducted from the amount payable by the old employer for the dismissal. If an employee fails to take reasonable steps and could have lessened the loss, then some or all of his damages may be cut off. The duty to mitigate may also apply to a dismissed employee's claim for certain lost benefits.

Reasonable steps only — Dismissed employees are only required to take steps which a reasonable and prudent person would ordinarily take in the course of business.

Statutory employment schemes — Employees covered by statutory employment rules will generally still be subject to the duty to mitigate, unless the statute expressly exempts them from the common-law expectation of mitigation or otherwise indicates in clear language that they are not bound by the common-law rule. The obligation to mitigate may not apply to statutory severance pay or termination pay, depending on the statute's wording.

No duty to settle — While an employee is under a duty to mitigate his or her damages, there is no duty to negotiate a settlement with the employer.

Continuing duty — The fact that a damage award or settlement is issued before the end of the notice period may not absolve an employee from the duty to mitigate.

Death or disability during notice period — In some cases, damages are cut off if an employee dies within the notice period, due to the fact that the employee was no longer capable of mitigating his damages. However, an employee who is unable to fulfill his duty to mitigate due to disability may still entitled to damages. See Chapter G-1, "Damages: General Principles" under G-1.4 regarding the time at which damages end.

Efforts and likely results — An employer arguing that an employee has failed to mitigate his or her damages usually must be able to show both that the employee's efforts were insufficient, and that sufficient efforts would have lessened the employee's damages. It is not usually enough that the employee's conduct was unreasonable in one respect; the employer must show that it was unreasonable as a whole.

Total lack of effort — Some cases have reduced damages due to a total lack of effort to find new work, but in most cases lack of effort alone has not been enough to reduce damages. A total lack of effort may be explainable by other circumstances, particularly if the employee reasonably believed that there was no use in seeking work because none would be available. However, if an employee has clearly removed himself from the work force, for example by deciding to retire, this will generally cut off damages.

Onus to prove mitigation efforts — Most cases have said that the employer has the onus to prove that the employee could have avoided all or part of the loss if he or she had made sufficient mitigation efforts. A few cases say that the employee must initially show that he made reasonable efforts to mitigate, and it is then up to the employer to prove that the employee could have gotten another job.

Acceptable evidence — Evidence to prove the availability of similar work has included:

- Expert evidence, such as the evidence of a relocation counsellor or human resources consultant. However, one judge has pointed out that the job search standards of a professional may not be reasonable to expect from employees left on their own to find new work.
- The fact that the employer had great difficulty replacing the employee due to a shortage of qualified people in the area. This was taken in one case as evidence that jobs were available if the employee's efforts had been sufficient.

Insufficient evidence — The following evidence has not been enough to prove that other work was available:

- Copies of newspaper ads without expert testimony on the nature of the jobs and the employee's chance of getting a job.
- The fact that most employees laid off at the same time quickly found new jobs. This is not proof that every employee could have found a new job.
- The employer's opinion that other jobs were available, in the absence of proof of specific opportunities, with particulars. Even where there is evidence that similar jobs were available, the plaintiff's own job search experience may carry more weight where the court is satisfied that the employee was making reasonable efforts to find new work.

H-1.2 FIXED-TERM CONTRACTS AND CONTRACTUAL NOTICE PERIODS

General principles — The Supreme Court of Canada has confirmed that employees whose fixed-term contracts are breached have a duty to mitigate their damages. Any sums which the employee earns within the balance of the contractual term must be deducted from the damages for dismissal. This is, of course, subject to the contract's terms, and where the contract indicates that earnings should not be deducted, no deduction will be required.

Contractual notice period — duty to mitigate — Unless a contract is very specifically worded, or the payment is required within a very short time after termination so that it can be implied there is no duty to mitigate, it may be assumed that an employee is required to mitigate, even where a contractual payment is required. For example:

- A contract guaranteed a two-year minimum term of employment, plus a 12-month severance payment if the employee was terminated after the two years. The employee was terminated four and a half months before the end of the two-year term, with 12 months' salary and benefits continuance. He got a new job shortly after the end of the 12 months. While the judge held that he was not required to mitigate for the 12 months represented by the payment, he was held to have a duty to mitigate for the balance of the fixed term. Damages were calculated by subtracting his earnings in the first four and a half months of his new job from the amount that was owing to him under contract.
- Where an employee's contract provided for benefits continuation for six months after termination and the employer did not meet its obligation, its breach of covenant obligated the employee to mitigate her damages by seeking replacement coverage.

Contractual notice period — no duty to mitigate — However, if the contract classifies the payment as severance pay rather than pay in lieu of notice, and no duty to mitigate is stated in the contract, no duty may be imposed by the courts. For example, no duty to mitigate was found where a contract provided for payment of severance pay within 30 days of termination. It was clear that mitigation was not intended to be taken into account.

Severance policy — In some cases, an employer's severance policy that is silent on the issue of mitigation has been treated as a guaranteed amount. This is especially likely where the full amount has always been paid to other employees in the past, regardless of circumstances.

H-1.3 EFFECT OF FAILURE TO MITIGATE

General principles — Courts have accounted for an employee's failure to mitigate in a number of ways:

- In extreme cases, where an alternative offer at the same salary was refused, the employee's action for pay in lieu of notice may be dismissed.
- Amounts that the employee could have earned in mitigation during the notice period may be deducted from the damages.
- The notice period may be reduced.

Examples — reduced damages — Situations in which amounts have been deducted from damage awards for failure to mitigate have included:

- An employee who refused an alternative job that paid only $500 less per year. He was awarded only the $500 difference in salary between the two jobs.
- In another extreme case, only nominal damages of $500 were awarded.
- An unfairly dismissed professor who was entitled to a percentage of his income as if he had worked until normal retirement age had his damages reduced by 30 per cent for failure to mitigate after the first year of unemployment.
- An employee, who entered a Ph.D. program and received a small amount as a research assistant, rather than looking for a similar job with similar pay, had his damages reduced by the amount earned plus an additional $200 per month for the personal benefit of the education.
- An employee, who was laid off in breach of his contract, but who wrongly refused to return when recalled, was awarded damages only for the period prior to the recall.
- An employee, who initially attempted to mitigate but then decided to withdraw from the workforce, had his damages cut off as of the date he effectively retired from working.
- An employee, who had failed to mitigate by refusing an alternate job with the same employer, was not entitled to damages at all, except for a potential bonus payable in the old job.

- In some cases, interest is awarded only from the date the employee began fulfilling the duty to mitigate.

Reduced notice period — A common response is to reduce the notice period by cutting it off at the point when the employee could have found a new job with proper efforts, or by excluding damages for the time during which the employee made insufficient efforts to mitigate. However, one case has held that it is improper to consider the failure to mitigate in setting the notice period and then cut off damages as of the date the employee could have found a new job, which in effect penalizes the employee twice for the same lack of effort.

Chapter H-2

REASONABLE MITIGATION EFFORTS

TABLE OF CONTENTS

H-2.1   Standard of Reasonableness
H-2.2   Timing of Job Search Efforts
H-2.3   Quality of Job Search Efforts
H-2.4   Effect of Refusing Assistance

H-2.1 STANDARD OF REASONABLENESS

General principles — An employee seeking damages for wrongful dismissal is only required to make reasonable efforts to mitigate his or her damages. The standard of reasonableness may not be exacting. Even efforts that were not as assiduous as they might have been will not be a failure to mitigate unless they were unreasonable.

Act in own interests — An employee is not required to act in the employer's best interests to the detriment of his or her own interests. An employee is certainly not required to take risky or unsavoury steps, or even be held to the standard of making the best possible decisions.

Factors — The reasonableness of an employee's job search efforts should be judged with regard to the employee's individual circumstances: age, skills, background, health, and likelihood of finding another job. For example:

- Even a total failure to seek other work may not be a failure to mitigate if there was no realistic chance of finding other work.
- The fact that an employee was bound by a stringent non-competition agreement was a factor to be considered when deciding whether efforts to mitigate were reasonable.
- The effect of an employer's proprietary rights in hampering an employee's job search has also been mentioned as a factor to be considered.

H-2.2 TIMING OF JOB SEARCH EFFORTS

General principle — The employee should be allowed an appropriate amount of time to adjust to his or her situation and plan for the future before strictly imposing the obligation of mitigation. For example, there was no failure to mitigate where:

- A man, who was returning to his native England after dismissal, refused to leave his family behind and rush to England within weeks in order to seek short-term employment.
- An employee completed a planned move before seeking other work, even where this delayed her job search for three months.

Vacation before job hunt — no failure to mitigate — Where an employee takes a few months off for a vacation before starting to look for work, a number of cases have said there is no failure to mitigate, especially where the vacation was already arranged or where the employee had not had a vacation recently. The following examples were not failures to mitigate:

- Taking a normal vacation period within the notice period.
- Travelling overseas for family reasons.
- A woman fired two months before she had planned to take time off for her wedding had not failed to mitigate by not looking for a job until after the honeymoon, since it was unlikely she would have been able to get time off right away.

Vacation before job hunt — failure to mitigate — However, other cases have held that taking a vacation rather than starting a job search is a failure to mitigate. For example, an extended vacation was taken or an employee turned down possible job opportunities in favour of time off. In one case, there was a failure to mitigate where an employee went to the cottage for the first three months after his dismissal.

Pregnancy or parental leave — Some judges have held that a woman who was pregnant when dismissed was entitled to wait until several months after the birth to look for a job. Another judge, however, held that a woman dismissed early in her pregnancy should have tried at least to get part-time or temporary work. An employee dismissed during a maternity leave may have an immediate duty to mitigate.

Illness and disability — The employee's physical condition, mental condition and age must be taken into account, as well as his specific efforts to find a new job and the general availability of work in the area. For example, there was no failure to mitigate where:

- An employee was unable to look for work for several months due to illness.

- An employee delayed his job search because his wife became seriously ill at the time of his termination.
- A handicapped employee would have needed to change his residence to take other jobs within the same city. He was not required to do so and was entitled to wait until he found a suitable job within a reasonable distance to his home.

Initial inaction — no failure to mitigate — In some cases, initial inaction has been overlooked even where there is no real justification given. For example, there was no failure to mitigate where:

- An employee's failure to seek work for the first few months after termination was due to distress caused by the termination.
- The employee reasonably expected to be recalled from layoff.

Initial inaction — failure to mitigate — However, in other cases, vague claims of stress or depression that are not substantiated by medical evidence have been found not to justify a failure to look for new work. For example, an employee who did not look for work for nine months, until her Employment Insurance had run out, had failed to mitigate.

Time of year — The timing of a dismissal may affect the timing of efforts to mitigate, and may therefore excuse a delay. For example:

- In cases where an employee was dismissed shortly before Christmas, judges have considered the fact that a job search at that time of year probably would not have been successful.
- Teachers dismissed after the start of the school year have been treated leniently for not looking for work until the next school year, given the unlikelihood of finding new work in the middle of the year.

Criminal charges — A delay in mitigating occasioned by pending criminal charges seems to be justified. For example, there was no failure to mitigate where:

- An employee's job search was impeded by work-related criminal charges laid while he was in the employer's service. He had not failed to mitigate by not finding a job until the charges were dropped.
- An employee faced criminal charges that were not work-related. He did not fail to mitigate by not looking for a job until after his trial, since the charges would have hampered his job search to the point that re-employment would have been highly unlikely. However, the employee was only entitled to damages for the reasonable notice period, not the entire time spent awaiting trial, given his total lack of effort.

Attempts before termination — Several employers have argued that employees should have started looking for new jobs even before termination, as they should have known their jobs were in jeopardy. This argument has not succeeded. One judge said that while an employee "perhaps" should have started a job search earlier, even if he had done so it would not have helped him find a job within the notice period.

Premature end to job search — Ceasing the job search prematurely may be a failure to mitigate where similar jobs would have been available if the employee had continued to look. However, removing oneself from the job market at the end of the regular notice period, but before expiry of the increased notice period due to bad faith, was not held to be a failure to mitigate in one case.

H-2.3 QUALITY OF JOB SEARCH EFFORTS

General principles — The type of effort that will be considered reasonable depends on the nature of the job, the market and how one would normally seek a job in that field.

Examples — reasonable search efforts — For example, the following efforts have been found to be reasonable:

- Seeking a job in the same way an employee had obtained previous jobs.
- Registering with headhunters and reviewing ads. Given the nature of her position, the employee was not required to register with Canada Manpower.
- Mailing out résumés without personally attending at prospective employers' premises.
- Visiting Canada Manpower every few weeks and spreading the word through friends that the employee was seeking a new job.

Examples — unreasonable search efforts — The following search efforts were not adequate and amounted to a failure to mitigate:

- Failing to approach all similar employers, and merely relying on contacts within the industry where jobs were available, although this may not always be the case.
- Doing nothing except reviewing newspaper ads.
- Registering with Canada Manpower and calling potential employers without sending out résumés or following up more than sporadically.
- Waiting until the employee's Employment Insurance ran out, then sending out a bulk mailing of résumés without further contacts. The employee was said to have made it clear to potential employers that she was not seriously seeking work.
- Doing nothing while hoping unreasonably to get the old job back.
- Failing to register with a union for a work assignment if there was work available during the notice period.
- Failing to register with a centralized industry employment service, especially since the employee had used it in the past.

Restricted efforts — An employee who restricts his efforts and makes very few contacts may also have failed to mitigate, although this may not be enough to reduce damages unless it is shown that suitable jobs were available. Some judges have ruled that it is unreasonable to refuse to approach similar employers or follow up on known possibilities. However, several judges have ruled that this is not enough to prove a failure to mitigate, particularly where the employee had a valid reason for not approaching the employer.

Sufficient time — While an employee is not required to spend his full time looking for a new job, there may be a failure to mitigate where he spends most of his time on other interests and very little time on the job search.

Volunteer work — One judge viewed spending a substantial amount of time on volunteer work as a failure to mitigate. However, another judge said that there was no failure to mitigate, since the employee had made contacts and sustained his profile in the volunteer work. There was no evidence that paying work was available in any event.

Résumés — The number of résumés an employee sends out is not the only measure of his attempts at mitigation. The quality also matters, and a handful of applications may be enough where they are "thoughtful and sufficient". For example:

- In one case, using relocation services provided by the employer and sending out 75 résumés was said to be an insufficient effort.
- Where there was a relatively small employment community and few jobs available, it was appropriate to send only a few letters.
- A bulk mailing of résumés was criticized where the employee had waited until her Employment Insurance had run out. She had thereby made it clear to potential employers that she was not seriously seeking work.
- There was a failure to mitigate where an employee did not know how to prepare a proper résumé or conduct a proper job search and did not get help. However, another employee who made a lot of good faith but misguided efforts did not fail to mitigate, as the 30-year employee did not know how best to look for a job and the employer should have provided relocation counselling for him.
- A misleading résumé was not a failure to mitigate, as there was no proof that it was so misleading as to jeopardize the employee's chance of new employment, or that a potential employer had in fact been put off by the puffery.

Jobs with equal pay — Restricting a job search to jobs with equal pay is not necessarily a failure to mitigate. See Chapter H-3, "Career Changes and Relocating" for more information on similar or dissimilar jobs.

Part-time or consulting work — Where the employee had already been seeking other work as a consultant, he fulfilled his obligation to mitigate by continuing to do so. Similarly, an employee who had reasonably continued his part-time work had not failed to mitigate.

H-2.4 EFFECT OF REFUSING ASSISTANCE

Failure to seek assistance or reference from employer — The fact that an employee does not seek assistance from the former employer or ask for a reference will not necessarily be held against him. For example, there was no failure to mitigate where an employee refused to use a letter of recommendation from her employer because she had never been given any explanation for the dismissal and was unsure of how the employer would respond to telephone inquiries.

Employer's behaviour — The employee's lack of efforts to find similar work may be less culpable where the employer:

- Failed to provide a reference.
- Failed to provide a reason for dismissal.
- Dismissed the employee for untrue allegations of just cause.
- Has otherwise harmed the employee's reputation.

Refusal of outplacement counselling — Refusing to use the services of a placement firm provided by the employer may or may not be an unreasonable failure to mitigate. For example, there was no failure to mitigate where:

- The employee was herself a qualified relocation counsellor, and the offer of relocation counselling was part of an unacceptable settlement package.
- An employee failed to co-operate with an outplacement counsellor where he had good reason to be suspicious due to the counsellor's participation in the termination meeting.
- There was a delay of a few months before using the services, especially where the employee was contacting a former employer during that time.
- An employee failed to apply for jobs for which he had a priority rating, because no one had told him his priority status had been extended.

Other jobs with same employer — The employee is not required to seek out other opportunities with the dismissing employer. Rather, the onus is on the employer to present any other job offers to the employee. However, an employee may not be entitled to refuse an offer of another job with the dismissing employer, as discussed in Chapter H-4, "Rejecting an Offer and Other Failures to Mitigate".

Chapter H-3

CAREER CHANGES AND RELOCATING

TABLE OF CONTENTS

H-3.1   Similar or Dissimilar Job
H-3.2   Retraining
H-3.3   Relocating
H-3.4   Starting a Business

H-3.1 SIMILAR OR DISSIMILAR JOB

General principles — Questions about similar and dissimilar jobs arise in several contexts. On the one hand, an employer may challenge the employee's exclusion of certain jobs from the job search, or even a refusal of an offer. On the other hand, employers sometimes argue that accepting a dissimilar job is a breach of the employee's duty to mitigate. Generally speaking, while personal preferences and career objectives are a consideration in deciding whether an employee's efforts are appropriate, they are not the controlling factors. The employee must still act reasonably. This is a particular concern where an employee turns down a job offer, as is discussed later in this chapter.

Obligation to seek similar employment — Generally, the employee will only be obligated to look for similar employment in mitigation of his loss. Refusing a materially dissimilar job will not be a failure to mitigate. An employee usually will not be required to accept employment that is of a much lower status or that is beneath his skills and training. An employee is not required to apply for jobs for which he appears to be unqualified. Even where the employee is unemployed for a long time, he may be entitled to keep looking for similar work instead of looking for a different kind of job, although a great deal depends on the judge's assessment of the circumstances, as discussed below.

Looking for dissimilar work — In fact, looking for dissimilar work may be a breach of the duty to mitigate, although allowance is often made for the employee's interests and career objectives. Judges may look at the employee's subjective reasons for seeking different work, and decide whether they are reasonable. One judge said that an employee is entitled to look for a job in his current field of expertise and in all areas in which he is qualified. Another judge said that an employee can deviate from the kind of work he had with the employer, as long as the income from the new type of work approaches the income level of the old work.

Different work environment — An employee is not required to accept substantially different work conditions, such as shirt work that was not required in the old job. However, purposely looking for the same type of job in a different kind of environment or with different working conditions is not necessarily a failure to mitigate. In fact, there was a failure to mitigate where a salesman refused to look for other sales jobs involving different products, even though he had sold one type of product for virtually his entire career.

Different pay — Restricting a job search to jobs with equal pay is not necessarily a failure to mitigate, although restricting efforts to find jobs paying higher than the old job may be improper. Refusing a job that pays substantially less will not necessarily be a failure to mitigate. Refusing a job that pays somewhat less may not be reasonable if the pay differential is not too great, or if the old job's pay was unduly high.

Similar work unavailable — Looking for dissimilar work is permissible when similar work is essentially unavailable, or where the employer's unfair treatment has harmed the employee's re-employment prospects. For example, where similar work was not available, employees met their duty to mitigate where they accepted:

- Work of a different calibre, such as temporary, part-time or seasonal work.
- Employment paying only half as much.
- A new, dissimilar job or a job in a different industry.
- A job with no income within the notice period.

Similar work available — However, accepting a lower-paying job in a different industry was a breach of the duty to mitigate where an equivalent job in the same industry had been offered. The employer should not be burdened by the employee's decision to change careers.

Lower status job — It is often argued that an employee should mitigate by accepting a lower job, particularly a job he had held in the past. This argument has met with mixed results. Employees were not required to seek another or previous type of work in these cases:

- An employee had worked for 34 years in a type of employment that was no longer available to him.
- An employee had been trained in one area but had not worked in that area for many years.
- A salesman had worked as a sales manager for many years; he was not required to seek jobs as a salesman.

- A management employee was offered a bargaining-unit position.
- A former farmer was not required to return to farming where there was no evidence that doing so would decrease his loss.
- A hockey coach was not required to accept a job as a trainer, as this would have harmed his potential to find a new coaching job.

Lower status job required — Some recent judgments, however, have been less sympathetic towards unemployed employees. A failure to mitigate was found where:

- A real estate agent nominee refused to work as a real estate salesman and earn more money.
- A car dealer's business manager failed to take a job as a commissioned salesman, at least temporarily, given his recent history as a very successful salesman.
- A stenographic supervisor could have sold her skills at some lower level if she had been willing to do so.
- An employee should have reconsidered accepting a junior job after 16 months of unemployment.

Different job required — An employee who insisted on looking for a job involving declining technology, even though she was trained in the newer technology that was more in demand, had not met her duty to mitigate.

Effect of new employment — Once an employee accepts a different type of employment or a lower-paying job, the usual practice is to deduct his new earnings from the damages owing by the previous employer, even if the employee could not have been faulted for passing up the dissimilar work.

H-3.2 RETRAINING

General principles — The effect of retraining on the duty to mitigate is another area where decisions conflict. The issue is whether the time and cost of retraining increase the employee's damages by creating a delay in becoming re-employed, or whether they are justified because they facilitate re-employment. It has been held that retraining in order to enter a field with better job prospects is not a failure to mitigate, even where the employee does not become successfully re-employed. The focus seems to be on whether the retraining was reasonable under the circumstances. Note that where retraining was reasonable, the employee may be entitled to compensation for the costs of the retraining, as discussed in Chapter G-8 under G-8.3, "Mitigation Expenses".

Retraining acceptable — For example, the upgrading of skills was acceptable where:

- An employee earning $14 per hour was able to get a new job paying $15 per hour.
- An employee retrained in two different areas.

Retraining not acceptable — Retraining was unreasonable where:

- Jobs were available but the employee ceased to seek work once he had begun upgrading his education.
- An employee turned down a similar job to complete upgrading that could have been completed in the evening while continuing to work during the day.
- An employee had to wait 15 months to start a retraining program, but jobs for which she was already trained were available.

Training required — Some employers have argued that where there are no realistic employment prospects in the employee's old field, it is a failure to mitigate for the employee to refuse training. Again, however, the question is whether the employee's actions were reasonable. The failure to retrain was reasonable where:

- The employee reasonably believed that he was still employable in his field.
- Even six months' retraining would not give the specialized skill needed for a new type of job, and there was no guarantee a job would be available anyway.

Accounting for retraining costs — A final issue is how to account for the benefit of retraining in mitigation of damages. For example, where:

- There were no actual earnings within the notice period. The value of the employee's newly-acquired real estate licence was set off against his damages, since he had acquired a prospective benefit during the notice period. Presumably, these efforts could have been expended in looking for work.
- The value of the education exceeded its cost, the excess was deducted in mitigation, as well as the employee's part-time earnings during his re-education.

H-3.3 RELOCATING

General principles — Whether an employee should be required to relocate to obtain a new job in mitigation of damages is a matter of dispute. Some cases seem to accept that restricting a job search to a specific area is not necessarily a failure to mitigate, regardless of the circumstances; other cases do not. Where an employee does relocate in order to accept a new job, he may be entitled to damages for his moving costs, as discussed in Chapter G-8 under G-8.2, "Moving Expenses".

Relocation not required — Relocation was not required where:

- Employees had long-standing roots in the community.
- The employee's wife would lose her job.
- The employee had recently transferred at the employer's request, at great personal sacrifice, and had only recently re-established his family.
- An employee's custody and access arrangements would make relocation difficult.
- The employee was handicapped and would have had to relocate his residence within the same city in order to mitigate.
- The employee was caring for elderly parents at home. Restricting a job search to jobs within 40 minutes of home was reasonable.
- The employee's wife was diagnosed with cancer shortly after his termination. He was said to have a valid reason for not seeking similar employment in other locations.
- The employee was an older woman who did not have a driver's licence. She reasonably restricted her job search to places in her city accessible by public transit.

Relocation required — Failure to relocate was a failure to mitigate where:

- An employee did not seek employment outside the town where she had spent her whole life.
- A young employee's skills were marketable in other locations but not in the one in which he had chosen to stay.
- An employee accepted retraining knowing that it would likely require him to relocate and he thereby led the employer to believe he would accept relocation. His refusal to move after eight months of retraining was essentially a failure to mitigate.

Long-distance relocation — Relocation out of the province or across the country may not be required, unless the employee has a history of such moves. There was no failure to mitigate where:

- An overseas move would interfere with a job search at home, and there were reasonable prospects for the employee in Canada.
- An employee's earnings within the notice period would have been offset by his moving costs. It was held that he was reasonable in staying put and starting his own business.

Industry custom — A failure to mitigate has been found where relocation was customary in the industry. For example, where an employee knew chances for re-employment were poor in his present location and relocation was common in the industry, there was a failure to mitigate when he did not seek employment outside that location.

Need to commute — Failure to relocate may also be unreasonable where the employee could have commuted to the new location, although this will not always be the case. For example, an employee who had legitimate concerns about a long commute on poor roads had not failed to mitigate by refusing a transfer.

Voluntary relocation unacceptable — Choosing to relocate when it may not be necessary may lead to a finding of failure to mitigate. There was a failure to mitigate where an employee restricted his job search to another province because he wanted to move there, as the employer should not be required to subsidize his move. Once the employee's wife got a job in that location, however, it was reasonable for him to restrict his search to that area.

Voluntary relocation acceptable — However, a voluntary relocation will not necessarily be a failure to mitigate. For example, relocation was acceptable where:

- An employee chose to relocate to his country of origin, even though he remained out of work. There was no proof that he intended to retire by moving away.
- An employee relocated to an area with better job opportunities, even though it took him several months to find a comparable job.

H-3.4 STARTING A BUSINESS

General principles — An employee in some cases may fulfill the duty to mitigate by starting a business. Some cases have said that it is necessary for the employee to exhaust other job-search opportunities first. The question seems to be whether it is reasonable for the employee to start his own business, given his age, circumstances and prospects for re-employment. Reasonableness is assessed as of the time the employee made the decision, not as of the time of trial.

Business not successful — Starting a business may have been reasonable even where it did not succeed. Even where a business generates no net income or shareholder dividends within the notice period, starting it may not be unreasonable.

Starting a business reasonable — For example, starting a business was not a failure to mitigate where:

- An employee would have had to relocate to find a new job and his moving expenses would have offset any earnings within the notice period.
- An employee's chances of re-employment were limited by a non-competition clause.

- The employer failed to provide a reference.
- The employee became "enthralled" with the idea of starting his own business in part due to the counselling of a relocation counsellor provided by the employer. The employer could not complain that he had failed to mitigate his damages.

Starting a business not reasonable — Starting a business was a failure to mitigate where:

- The employee made no effort to find a comparable job, especially where jobs were available.
- The employee's job-search efforts were lessened by her efforts to start her own business. One judge seemed to take this into account in setting the reasonable notice period.

Indemnification for start-up costs — Where start-up costs are incurred or the new company suffers a loss, the employee may be entitled to indemnity for sums reasonably expended in an attempt to mitigate. See Chapter G-8, "Job Search Expenses, Moving Expenses and Costs of Mitigation".

Treatment of earnings in new business — Where an employee earns income in the new business, the income will be deducted from his or her damages as income earned in mitigation, as discussed in Chapter H-5 "Deduction of Earnings in Mitigation".

Chapter H-4

REJECTING AN OFFER AND OTHER FAILURES TO MITIGATE

TABLE OF CONTENTS

H-4.1 Offer from New Employer
H-4.2 Offer from Dismissing Employer
H-4.3 Offer of Working Notice
H-4.4 Other Offers
H-4.5 Other Failures to Mitigate

H-4.1 OFFER FROM NEW EMPLOYER

General principles — As discussed in Chapter H-3, "Career Changes and Relocating", the duty of mitigation only obligates an employee to act reasonably in his own interests and not to act in the employer's interest by taking any job that comes along in order to lessen the damages to be paid by the employer. Personal preferences and career objectives are a consideration in deciding whether an employee is entitled to turn down another job, but the employee must still act reasonably, and he may be required to accept positions that are substantially similar, even if they are not identical to the old job in type, terms or location.

Judged as of time decision made — A decision to refuse a job offer must be judged as of the time it was made. The fact that the employee had preferable opportunities at the time which later fell through will usually not be held against him. An employee is entitled to take a reasonable amount of time to consider an offer and is not to be faulted if the job is no longer available. For example, where an employee refused an offer and later obtained a better job with a higher salary, there was no failure to mitigate.

Test similar to constructive dismissal — The test of whether refusing an offer was a failure to mitigate is similar to the constructive dismissal test of whether a new job would be a demotion, including considerations about the nature of the work, the job's status, the working conditions, and the pay. There was no failure to mitigate where an employee refused:

- A part-time job.

- Evening and night work where the employee had formerly worked days only.
- Junior-level jobs in the employee's field, although he should have reconsidered accepting such jobs once he had been unemployed for 16 months.
- A job that involved travel, when the previous job did not.

Refusal unreasonable — The following job refusals were found to be an unreasonable failure to mitigate:

- Refusal of a job in the employee's accustomed type of work.
- A salesman's refusal of a job selling a different product, particularly since the job would have paid more than his old job. In another case, however, a salesman's refusal of jobs involving different products and lower pay was reasonable.
- A sales manager's refusal of a sales job on straight commission, although other judges might view this as a lower status job that the employee would not be required to accept.
- An employee's acceptance of a new job at a lower salary and in a different industry, even though an equivalent job in the same industry had been offered.
- Refusal of a similar but lower-paying job without attempting to negotiate for better pay and conditions.
- Refusal of two jobs with a base salary plus commissions by an employee who had previously been paid by straight commission. While total earnings would not have been as high as the old job, the offers were reasonable in the limited and very competitive market in the employee's particular field.

Refusal reasonable — There was no failure to mitigate where:

- Employees attempted in good faith to negotiate a better deal and the potential employer abruptly withdrew the offer.
- An employee would have been required to bear a major expense that had not been required at the previous job.

Nominal change of employer — Refusing the same job under the employment of a new legal entity may be a failure to mitigate, even when forcing that change upon an employee may be a constructive dismissal.

Reasonable concerns about new job — An employee is entitled to rely on his experience and is not required to accept a job where he has reasonable concerns that make the job offer unacceptable, such as concerns that a venture will fail, or concerns about a company's organizational structure, plans to reorganize, or job security. However, concerns about a prospective employer's legal battle with a minority shareholder and about drug charges against the employer were not said to be sufficient concerns in one case.

Financial investment — An employee was entitled to refuse a job offer where he would have been required to make a financial investment in the venture.

Confidential information — An employee is not obligated to take a job by way of mitigation where he would be required to divulge confidential information.

H-4.2 OFFER FROM DISMISSING EMPLOYER

General principles — The question often arises whether a dismissed employee is required to accept an alternative offer of employment from the employer, or a related employer. Refusing to return to the original job under the original conditions will be a failure to mitigate in most cases. Refusing another job with the employer may be a failure to mitigate, depending on the circumstances. In most cases, the courts have said that an employee cannot be required by the duty of mitigation to accept an offer that:

- Constitutes constructive dismissal or a demotion, as discussed in Part C, "Constructive Dismissal".
- Involves a job that he is incapable of doing.
- Involves bad faith, for example, where the employer had no true intention of rehiring the employee. There will be a failure to mitigate, however, when a recall is made in good faith, even though the layoff was a breach of contract.
- Involves a recall after the employee had raised allegations of discrimination which were never dealt with by the employer.
- Involves an offer of short-term, temporary work or part-time work, although cases are mixed in this area.
- Does not clearly set out the offered job's terms and conditions.
- Does not give the employee a reasonable time to consider it.
- Does not make clear that the employee will be terminated if the alternative offer is not accepted.

Refusal unreasonable — Refusing another job with the employer may be unreasonable where:

- An employee had worked his way up through the ranks. He may be in a different position than a person hired for a specific position, and may have to accept an offer of another job.
- The offered job involved a good faith lateral transfer for reasonable business objectives, without demotion or other humiliating treatment.
- An employee was unlikely to find new employment due to his age and inability to relocate, as long as there was no humiliating treatment.

- An employee's job would not have changed significantly for several months. He should have stayed on until it substantially changed.

Job and personal circumstances — The reasonableness of expecting an employee to continue in another job with the dismissing employer will depend on the employee's personal circumstances, work history, the nature of the job and the workplace. It was not unreasonable for an employee to refuse another job with the employer where:

- An older employee who had been away from his trade for 20 years was asked to go back to work on the shop floor.
- The workplace contained only two people who had to work closely together. It was not reasonable to expect the dismissed employee to continue in order to mitigate her damages.
- Equivalent employment was nonexistent and the employee's only option was to start his own business.
- The employee has other prospects at the time.
- The offer would require relocation, with or without the loss of a spouse's job or separation from the employee's family.
- The offered job would require an unreasonable, onerous commute.

Relationship unfeasible — An employee will not be required to accept an offer if a continued employment relationship would be impossible due to acrimony, improper behaviour by the employer, a loss of respect or prestige, embarrassment or humiliation. Where the employer's workforce is particularly small or the working relationship would be particularly close, it may not be reasonable to expect the employee to continue with the employer in order to mitigate damages. The question is whether the employment relationship is sufficiently frayed that a reasonable person would not think the employee could work in harmony with the employer or other employees. This is often the case in situations where the offered job would amount to a constructive dismissal. Where dismissal was for neutral reasons such as economic conditions or reorganization, a sale of the employer, or circumstances beyond the employer's control, there will not likely be humiliation justifying the refusal of an offer. Dismissal because the employee was unable to properly handle the job he had may also require an employee to accept another offer from the employer.

Examples — relationship unfeasible — The following factors entitle an employee to refuse an offer:

- A demotion or other loss of status, profile or prestige due to the offered job's diminished scope, lesser character or reduced pay.
- Substantially less favourable working conditions.
- Unfair treatment by the employer, including untrue allegations of just cause, lack of honesty or good faith, or insensitive or unreasonable treatment upon termination.

- A generally acrimonious, uncooperative or unreasonable atmosphere.
- The fact that the employee had complained about his boss to the boss's superiors.
- A contractual change that leaves the employee uncertain of his compensation or working conditions in the new position
- The fact that the employee was specifically hired for a particular position.
- The fact that an employee paid by commission would have had to lose income in order to seek a comparable job while continuing in the new position.

Objective test — Most judges say that the reasonableness of a continuing relationship should be judged on an objective basis, although some judges say the employee's view of the offered job may be a factor in deciding whether it is reasonable for him to refuse the job. In one case, the fact that an employee offered to stay on until his severance package was finalized was proof that there was no humiliation justifying his refusal of the alternative job.

Effect on wrongful dismissal claim — Cases differ on whether an employee is entitled to consider the effect that accepting an alternate offer would have on his wrongful dismissal claim. Some judges have said that considering the effect on a wrongful dismissal claim was an improper consideration. The employee, however, may be entitled to time to discuss the offer with his lawyer. Other judges have said that employees were justified in refusing an offer where:

- It would have been too humiliating for the employee to return to work while suing the employer.
- It would be unreasonable to expect an employee to accept an offer made during the course of litigation.
- A re-employment offer was conditional on the employee dropping her wrongful dismissal suit.

H-4.3 OFFER OF WORKING NOTICE

Refusal to work through notice period — A refusal to work through the notice period given by the employer may be a failure to mitigate, unless it would be humiliating or otherwise unreasonable to expect the employee to stay at work.

Examples — failure to mitigate — For example, there was a failure to mitigate where:

- An employee refused to even discuss the settlement of a dispute, and instead claimed constructive dismissal.

- An employee refused to accept a generous severance package and make the best of his situation.

Examples — no failure to mitigate — There was no failure to mitigate where:

- An employer breached an employee's contract by giving less working notice than was required by statute. It could not complain about the employee's failure to work through the notice period.
- An employee wrote a letter attempting to clarify matters and the employer took it as an ultimatum. There had been no failure to mitigate, as the employee was not actually refusing to work through the notice period.
- An employer purported to terminate the employee but then tried to force the employee to work through a notice period after negotiations failed.
- An employee refused an unspecified amount of additional notice because he already had another job prospect, although at lower pay.
- An offer — even an offer to keep the employee on the payroll through the notice period — contained onerous conditions which included reporting on job-search efforts or cutting off benefits when a new job was found.
- The employer refused to let the employee stay on once he raised a claim of constructive dismissal.

Repudiation by employee — In some cases, employees who sue during the period of working notice have been found to repudiate the contract by filing suit at that time. See Chapter B-5, "Repudiation by Employee".

H-4.4 OTHER OFFERS

Salary continuation — Some employers offer to pay for the notice period by keeping employees on the payroll, without requiring them to work. Employers have argued that refusing a reasonable offer of salary continuation should bar a wrongful dismissal action because it is a failure to mitigate. However, judges most often simply award damages in the amount of the offer, rather than refusing damages altogether. Onerous conditions attached to an offer may make an offer unreasonable. For example, the following conditions are onerous: a condition that salary continuance would cease upon the acceptance of a new job, regardless of how much it paid and a condition that the employee must file biweekly reports on job-search efforts.

Relocation counselling — Refusing an offer of relocation counselling provided by the employer may be a failure to mitigate, as discussed in Chapter H-2, "Reasonable Mitigation Efforts".

Early retirement — Unless there is a contractual obligation to retire at a certain point, an employee is usually not required to elect early retirement in order to mitigate damages.

Return to bargaining unit — An employee who is entitled to return to a bargaining unit, but elects not to, may have failed to mitigate. For example, an employee had the right to elect to return to the bargaining unit within six months of a promotion, but he did not do so. This was said to be a failure to mitigate because he knew that his management position was being eliminated. However, on appeal, it was said to be the employer's responsibility to return the employee to the bargaining unit within the allowable time, and the employee was not penalized for failing to take steps on his own to return.

Leave of absence — An employee did not refuse to mitigate by refusing an offer of a leave of absence without pay, especially since he was legitimately ill and unable to lessen his damages by working for any other employer at the time.

H-4.5 OTHER FAILURES TO MITIGATE

No duty to inquire — An employee is not required to inquire about other job opportunities with the dismissing employer; it is up to the employer to make the offer.

Employment Insurance benefits — An employee is not required to apply for Employment Insurance (EI) benefits to fulfill his duty to mitigate. Where an employee chooses to collect EI benefits, his failure to take a minimum wage job instead of staying on EI may not be a failure to mitigate, depending on the circumstances. For example:

- Where the employee quit an hourly-paid job as soon as she requalified for EI benefits, she was found to have failed to mitigate by failing to continue in the lower-paid job.
- There was a failure to mitigate where an employee collected EI while starting his own business and making few inquiries about jobs.

Regarding the deductibility of EI benefits from damages, see Chapter G-11, "Deductions from the Damage Award".

Failure to seek professional help — In one case, an employee sued an employer on the basis of negligence and intentional infliction of nervous shock. Her failure to seek professional help for her depression, which was said not to be a failure to mitigate, was nevertheless a factor considered in assessing her damages.

Conflict resolution — There was a failure to mitigate in one case where an employee failed to discuss a conflict with the employer. Instead, the employee stormed out and claimed constructive dismissal.

Chapter H-5

DEDUCTION OF EARNINGS IN MITIGATION

TABLE OF CONTENTS

H-5.1   Mitigation Earnings Generally
H-5.2   Higher-Paying New Job
H-5.3   Different Type of Job
H-5.4   Employee's Own Business
H-5.5   Business Expenses
H-5.6   Mitigation Expenses

H-5.1 MITIGATION EARNINGS GENERALLY

General principle — Any sums that are earned during the notice period in alternative employment will be deducted from the employee's damages for wrongful dismissal. The only exception is where there is a special provision guaranteeing a specific amount of notice or pay, as discussed in Chapter H-1, "Mitigation of Damages". Even sums earned in further work with the employer will be deducted. While a few judges simply cut off damages as of the time the employee finds a new job, this is a shortcut that is not strictly in accordance with the law.

Failure to deduct — Occasionally, a court may refuse to deduct sums earned in mitigation, perhaps in lieu of interest, or to bring finality to the proceedings, but this is rare. For example, a deduction was refused where:

- The amount earned was small and the large expenses of mitigation were non-compensable.
- The monies were earned for short-term, casual employment.
- There was a brief period of temporary employment at the end of the notice period, but the notice period had been increased due to the employer's misconduct, and deducting the earnings would have nullified the penalty to the employer.

Constructive dismissal — Where an employee has been constructively dismissed but has stayed on to mitigate damages, the measure of damages will be the difference between the salary and benefits he would have received before the change and the salary and benefits he received after the change.

Employment earnings — Only amounts earned in new employment or self-employment are to be deducted from the damages otherwise awarded. Unrelated income will not be deducted, such as:

- An employee's investment income.
- Claims staked by an employee during his employment, which were later sold to his new employer in exchange for shares in the new employer. They did not represent compensation for services and they were not a profit earned during the notice period.

Sums not otherwise earned — Only sums that would not have been earned but for the dismissal will be deductible. Where an employee had other earnings before dismissal and they continued after dismissal, they have not been applied to offset damages for the wrongful dismissal. For example:

- Private practice earnings of a psychologist who had always carried on a private practice in addition to his employment.
- Teaching income of an employee who could have taught a university night class even if he had still been employed.
- Earnings from part-time employment by an employee who had always had a part-time job in addition to her regular job. This was the case even where her part-time work had increased somewhat, because it was not clear whether the increased work would have impinged on her job with the employer if she had continued to be employed.
- Earnings from an independent venture undertaken before dismissal.
- Earnings within the bounds that the parties had agreed could be pursued by the employee during his employment.
- Earnings of an employee who had always had his own business on the side. The business was found to be a separate entity from the employee himself. Note, too, that there was no evidence that the increase in business earnings was related to the termination, since the employee went on to obtain another full-time job.

Earnings within notice period — Only sums earned within the notice period are to be deducted. For example, there was no deduction where an employee:

- Started new employment within the notice period but did not earn anything.
- Received a sum within the notice period representing work to be done both within and after the notice period. The amount was apportioned over the time period and the portion relating to the post-notice period was not deducted.

Draw against future earnings — A draw against earnings was not deducted in one case, because there were no actual earnings within the notice period, and the employee ended up having to repay the draw. In another case, however, an employee's draws from his own company were treated as his actual earnings.

Notice period not over — Where a trial takes place before expiry of the notice period, evidence of earnings in mitigation may be considered at a later assessment hearing. If the employee has already started a new job, it may be assumed that his earnings during the rest of the notice period will follow the same pattern as has already occurred in the new job. See also the discussion under G-11.4, "Future Contingencies" in Chapter G-11, "Deductions from the Damage Award".

Overtime earnings — Whether an employee's overtime earnings in a new job should be set off against damages for dismissal from a job that did not require overtime is a matter of dispute. A deduction has been ordered in some cases, but the practice has been strongly criticized in other cases. A deduction was properly allowed, however, where the employee was also claiming for loss of overtime earnings from the dismissing employer.

New job ending before notice period — Where the employee accepts a new job but it does not last to the end of the notice period, he will generally still be entitled to damages for the balance of the notice period. For example, damages for the balance of the notice period were awarded where:

- A firing during the notice period arose out of the tensions of the original constructive dismissal, and the employee had tried to work through the notice period but failed.
- An employee was fired from a new job because of untrue rumours spread by the old employer.
- The employee provided a reasonable explanation for leaving the new job — even the fact that he did not like the new type of work.
- An employee left a new job because he was making very little money at it.
- An employee was working in a temporary job by the end of the notice period. Her damages were reduced by only part of her earnings in order to reflect the contingency that the job would not last.

Reason for new job loss — However, one judge has said that the court should consider the reason for the new termination, to see whether it shows a failure to mitigate. There was a failure to mitigate where an employee quit a new job without acceptable explanation. His damages were reduced by the amount he could have earned in mitigation if he had not quit.

Determining amounts earned in mitigation — In one case, where it was known the plaintiffs had found new jobs, the plaintiffs and their former solicitor were ordered to provide proper evidence of their earnings in mitigation.

Benefits earned in new job — The value of a new job's benefits may also be deducted from a damage award, particularly when damages for lost benefits are being awarded.

Calculating deduction — Gross earnings should be deducted from gross damages, as far as income tax goes. However, the earned sum to be deducted may be net of any expenses incurred in mitigating, as discussed later in this chapter. In one case, net earnings were deducted from net damages.

Different currencies — An employee who became re-employed in the United States had his earnings converted to Canadian dollars at the average exchange rate for each month of employment, before deduction from his Canadian-dollar damages.

H-5.2 HIGHER-PAYING NEW JOB

General principle — Where an employee's attempts at mitigation have been too successful and he has obtained a higher-paying job, the court often sets the notice period as the exact period of unemployment, or simply fails to deduct the extra amount earned in mitigation. Some cases have stated outright that these extra earnings are a windfall and are not to be deducted from the employee's damages. However, other cases have held that the full earnings within the notice period are deductible in mitigation, and that there is no justification for treating wrongful dismissal damages any differently from other breach of contract damages. For example:

- Where the employee not only got a higher-paying job but received a large signing bonus from the new employer that completely offset his losses, the employee's wrongful dismissal action was dismissed.
- One employee's higher-paying new job was taken into account by reducing the damages she was awarded for defamation upon her dismissal.

Strategic litigation — Sometimes parties get around having the pay from the new job deducted by:

- Asking the court to award damages in an agreed amount representing the period of unemployment.
- Only suing for damages for the period of unemployment.

- Bringing an action in a lower court and seeking damages only for the period of unemployment. The court may be prohibited by restrictions on its monetary jurisdiction from inquiring further, and the employee can obtain his full damages.

H-5.3 DIFFERENT TYPE OF JOB

Different type of job — Generally, earnings from a new job are to be deducted whether it is a similar or a different type of job. Even if the employee would not have been required by the duty of mitigation to accept the new job, once the employee does accept, the new earnings will usually be deducted from damages.

Part-time employment — The earnings from part-time, new employment may be set off against damages, as long as they would not have been earned but for the dismissal. Where an employee continued to work part-time at night for his old employer even after finding a new full-time job, his night earnings were not deducted, as this would have been his free time if he had continued to work full-time for the dismissing employer.

Temporary or casual employment — The earnings from temporary or casual employment are also generally deducted. However, a deduction of earnings from brief casual employment has been refused in a few cases.

H-5.4 EMPLOYEE'S OWN BUSINESS

General principle — Where the employee starts his own business, his income during the notice period must be deducted in mitigation from his damages. However, calculating the appropriate amount to deduct can be complicated. Common issues are the income of a new start-up business, and how to calculate an employee's income separate and apart from that of the business. Various methods have been used. For example:
- Where financial statements were inadequate, but the judge was satisfied that there was no intent to mislead, only a nominal amount of earnings was deducted.
- The profit of a new company was not treated as the employee's income, but a reasonable amount was designated as his or her income.
- Where the employee has taken an income but the business was in a deficit position, the company's finances may be treated as if they were the employee's finances, and nothing may be deducted in mitigation.
- Where the new venture was in a deficit situation, only $100 a week was attributed to the employee as income.

- Where an employee had never received the salary to which he was entitled under a shareholders' agreement, and there was a chance he might never receive it if the company did not become profitable, no earnings were deducted in mitigation.
- Where only a small amount of earnings was retained in the company, it was not deducted in mitigation but where an employee had retained all the earnings in the business and had paid himself nothing, they were attributed as his income and deducted in full.
- After-tax income was used as the amount of earnings to deduct in one case, even though the income tax paid by the employee's company was unclear.
- Where proper expenses such as depreciation had not been deducted, and only a small profit was made, one judge declined to deduct anything, as he was not satisfied any real gain had been made.

Pre-existing business — In one case, where an employee had started a business before dismissal and worked full-time in it after dismissal, the court said the business might have earned just as much even if he had remained employed, and declined to deduct any earnings from his dismissal damages. In other cases, however, it has been said that where the employee spends time and ability that were previously devoted to the employer on new ventures to earn income, that income is properly deducted in mitigation. For example:

- Where an employee had started his own business in the month before dismissal and he had not yet had significant earnings before being dismissed, his earnings after dismissal were all deductible in mitigation.
- Even where an employee's earnings were paid to his own numbered company, they were deducted from his damages.

Proportionate calculation possible — Sometimes the amount to be deducted may be a proportion of the earnings of an expanded side-line, or an estimate of prospective earnings. For example, where an employee had retrained as a real estate agent during the notice period, an amount was deducted to reflect the value of the licence which he had spent his time obtaining.

Award during notice period — Where the award is made within the notice period, the estimated amount of anticipated profits may be deducted, based on the judge's assessment of the business's likely growth. In one case heard before the end of the notice period, the judge ordered the employee to account to the employer for any net income received within the notice period, in essence by imposing a trust. See also Chapter G-11, "Deductions from the Damage Award".

Work in progress — In one case, where the employee started a professional practice, the value of work in progress was deducted.

Business equity and income attribution — A deduction from damages reflecting equity built up in a company may not be appropriate where it is still in a deficit position. However, a deduction is sometimes made based on a business's equity. For example:

- Where an employee's company had paid $16,500 to his family members during the notice period and built up $23,000 equity, yet he paid himself only $100, the court determined that he had enjoyed benefits or income of $10,000 during the notice period.
- Another case focused on whether the employee was getting a "concealed remuneration" by keeping profits in the company rather than taking a proper salary. It was said that the trial judge should be given the company's full financial details in order to make this determination.
- In one case, a company's whole income was attributed to an employee, without reduction for the portion of the company owned by the employee's spouse.
- Attributing some of a company's income from its second fiscal year to the first fiscal year, which was within the employee's notice period, was refused where the court was satisfied that there had been no intentional or improper attempt to defer salary payments or distribution of profits.
- A share of a related company's profits may properly be attributed to the employee's company in some cases.

Capital gain — A capital gain made from selling shares in the new company was not treated as earnings in mitigation.

Business losses — The amount of start-up costs or business losses in a venture entered into in mitigation may be awarded as damages, as discussed in Chapter G-8, "Job Search Expenses, Moving Expenses and Costs of Mitigation".

H-5.5 BUSINESS EXPENSES

General principles — In determining the business income to be deducted in mitigation, the employee may first reduce his business income by his reasonable business expenses. Reasonable business expenses can include, among other things:

- Depreciation.
- The cost or value of an office in his home.
- Interest paid on funds invested in the business.

Proper expenses — Issues often arise as to whether particular expenses were proper. For example:

- A deduction from earnings for the capital cost of a club membership was refused in one case, as were the capital costs of office equipment and other unreasonable, undocumented expenses.
- A deduction for an excessive amount paid to a spouse for bookkeeping services was refused.
- In one case, it was said that a loan to the employee's new business should not be considered his income earned in mitigation, but the earnings he applied to reduce the loan should be.
- An employee who had deducted car expenses from his earnings could not also receive damages for a lost car allowance, as this would be double compensation.
- Where an employee had paid substantial amounts to family members but there was no evidence that they did sufficient work to earn those amounts, he was not allowed to deduct them as expenses against his earnings.

Method of calculating business expenses — A number of methods have been used to calculate allowable business expenses. For example, it has been held that:

- The amount to be deducted should be calculated based on Generally Accepted Accounting Principles.
- The expenses to be used are those accepted as business deductions by Revenue Canada for income tax purposes.
- The amount should be in current dollars, since that is the basis used for damages based on salary; a claim based on the present value of the economic impact of termination was disallowed.
- One case said that a former employee could deduct business expenses incurred, but he would have to account to the former employer for the value of any assets he acquired as a result of those expenses.

H-5.6 MITIGATION EXPENSES

Expenses of mitigation — Expenses of mitigation can often be deducted from earnings in mitigation, before the earnings are deducted from damages. See also Chapter G-8, "Job Search Expenses, Moving Expenses and Costs of Mitigation". Expenses have been dealt with in various ways. For example:

- Income tax-deductible costs of travelling to the new job were not compensated in one case, but actual costs incurred were allowed in another case.
- In a further case, a number of expenses were allowed in deduction from earnings where they had been accepted by Revenue Canada.

- An employee who was required to stay out of town all week for his new job was awarded the cost of his restaurant meals during the notice period.
- Expenses were not allowable deductions from earnings where they had already been reimbursed by the new employer.
- An employee was not entitled to damages for clothing and equipment needed for the new job which he obtained during the mitigation period.
- Where an employee claimed his expenses were 85 per cent of his income, but some of the expenses were questionable and others were undocumented, less than half of the claimed expenses were allowed to be deducted from his earnings.
- Where an employee would have been unable to work for part of the notice period and he was not entitled to paid sick leave, his wages for the period of disability were deducted from the damages to be paid by the employer.

Retraining costs — Where retraining is accepted as a legitimate mitigation of damages, a final issue is how to account for the benefit of the retraining. For example:

- There were no actual earnings within the notice period. The value of the employee's newly-acquired real estate licence was set off against his damages, since he had acquired a prospective benefit during the notice period and these efforts could have been expended in looking for work.
- The value of the education exceeded its cost. The excess was deducted in mitigation, as well as the employee's part-time earnings during his re-education.

Expenses greater than earnings — Note that if expenses incurred in mitigation are greater than the amount earned in mitigation, some cases have said that the loss is not recoverable, as it is only proper to decrease damages due to an employee's efforts to mitigate, not increase them. However, in other cases, expenses have been awarded. See Chapter G-8, "Job Search Expenses, Moving Expenses and Costs of Mitigation".

Appendix 1

STATUTORY TERMINATION NOTICE PROVISIONS

Individual Termination Notice

Jurisdiction & Statute	Service Length	Required Notice
Federal (*Canada Labour Code*, R.S.C. 1985, c. L-2, as amended)	3 months+	2 weeks
Alberta (*Employment Standards Code*, R.S.A. 2000, c. E-9, as amended)	3 months – 2 years 2 – 4 years 4 – 6 years 6 – 8 years 8 – 10 years 10 years+	1 week 2 weeks 4 weeks 5 weeks 6 weeks 8 weeks
British Columbia (*Employment Standards Act*, R.S.B.C. 1996, c. 113, as amended)	3 – 12 months 12 months – 3 years 3 – 4 years 4 – 5 years 5 – 6 years 6 – 7 years 7 – 8 years 8 years+	1 week 2 weeks 3 weeks 4 weeks 5 weeks 6 weeks 7 weeks 8 weeks
Manitoba (*Employment Standards Code*, C.C.S.M., c. E110, as amended)	pay period monthly or more often pay period less often than monthly	at least 1 pay period at least 30 days
New Brunswick (*Employment Standards Act*, S.N.B. 1982, c. E-7.2, as amended)	6 months – 5 years 5 years+	2 weeks 4 weeks
Newfoundland and Labrador (*Labour Standards Act*, R.S.N.L. 1990, c. L-2, as amended)	3 months – 2 years 2 – 5 years 5 – 10 years 10 – 15 years 15 years+	1 week 2 weeks 3 weeks 4 weeks 6 weeks
Northwest Territories and Nunavut (*Labour Standards Act*, R.S.N.W.T. 1988, c. L-1, as amended)	90 days – 3 years 3 – 4 years 4 – 5 years 5 – 6 years 6 – 7 years 7 – 8 years 8 years+	2 weeks 3 weeks 4 weeks 5 weeks 6 weeks 7 weeks 8 weeks

Jurisdiction & Statute	Service Length	Required Notice
Nova Scotia (*Labour Standards Code*, R.S.N.S. 1989, c. 246, as amended)	3 months – 2 years 2 – 5 years 5 – 10 years 10 years+	1 week 2 weeks 4 weeks 8 weeks
Ontario (*Employment Standards Act, 2000*, S.O. 2000, c. 41, as amended)	3 months – 1 year 1 – 3 years 3 – 4 years 4 – 5 years 5 – 6 years 6 – 7 years 7 – 8 years 8 years+	1 week 2 weeks 3 weeks 4 weeks 5 weeks 6 weeks 7 weeks 8 weeks
Prince Edward Island (*Employment Standards Act*, R.S.P.E.I. 1998, c. E-6.2, as amended)	6 months – 5 years 5 – 10 years 10 – 15 years 15 years+	2 weeks 4 weeks 6 weeks 8 weeks
Quebec (*Labour Standards Act*, R.S.Q., c. N-1.1, as amended)	3 months – 1 year 1 – 5 years 5 – 10 years 10 years+	1 week 2 weeks 4 weeks 8 weeks
Saskatchewan (*The Labour Standards Act*, R.S.S. 1978, c. L-1, as amended)	3 months – 1 year 1 – 3 years 3 – 5 years 5 – 10 years 10 years+	1 week 2 weeks 4 weeks 6 weeks 8 weeks
Yukon (*Employment Standards Act*, R.S.Y. 1986, c. 54, as amended)	6 months – 1 year 1 – 3 years 3 – 4 years 4 – 5 years 5 – 6 years 6 – 7 years 7 – 8 years 8 years+	1 week 2 weeks 3 weeks 4 weeks 5 weeks 6 weeks 7 weeks 8 weeks

Group Termination Notice*

Jurisdiction	Number of Employees	Terminated within:	Notice Period
Federal	50+	4 weeks	16 weeks
Alberta	50+	4 weeks	4 weeks
British Columbia	50 – 100 101 – 300 301+	2 months	8 weeks 12 weeks 16 weeks
Manitoba	50 – 100 101 – 299 300+	4 weeks	10 weeks 14 weeks 18 weeks
New Brunswick	10+ if at least 25% of workforce	4 weeks	6 weeks
Newfoundland and Labrador	50 – 199 200 – 499 500+	4 weeks	8 weeks 12 weeks 16 weeks
Northwest Territories and Nunavut	25 – 49 50 – 99 100 – 299 300+	4 weeks	4 weeks 8 weeks 12 weeks 16 weeks
Nova Scotia	10 – 99 100 – 299 300+	4 weeks	8 weeks 12 weeks 16 weeks
Ontario	50 – 199 200 – 499 500+	4 weeks	8 weeks 12 weeks 16 weeks
Prince Edward Island	—	—	—
Quebec	10 – 99 100 – 299 300+	2 months	8 weeks 12 weeks 16 weeks
Saskatchewan	10 – 49 50 – 99 100+	4 weeks	4 weeks 8 weeks 12 weeks
Yukon	25 – 49 50 – 99 100 – 299 300+	4 weeks	4 weeks 8 weeks 12 weeks 16 weeks

*Note that these provisions typically require giving notice to a specified government authority, but do not necessarily require giving notice to the affected employees.

Appendix 2

RELATED ACTIONS THAT ARE COMMONLY JOINED WITH WRONGFUL DISMISSAL ACTIONS

CONTRACT OR STATUTORY CLAIMS BY EMPLOYEES

Outstanding wages, overtime pay, vacation pay — Claims may be based on an express or implied contractual term, or on a statutory term. Claims based on employment standards statutes may or may not be enforceable in court; in some jurisdictions, employees must file a claim under the statute to enforce those rights, but filing a claim can in some cases affect an employee's common-law rights. Wage claims may also be filed against corporate directors under most business corporations statutes. Directors are often personally liable for a certain amount of wages per employee.

Benefits — Employees may also claim amounts based on benefit plans or employer-provided insurance policies, such as sick leave pay, disability pay, life insurance or pension benefits. Travel and sales incentives, employee loans and relocation benefits have also been joined with wrongful dismissal claims. These claims can be for benefits before termination, or after the end of the notice period, although the latter is uncommon. Benefits for the notice period are generally a normal part of a wrongful dismissal claim.

Breach of pre-employment contract, collateral agreement or warranty — Several cases have dealt with the situation where there has been a pre-employment misrepresentation, usually about the expected length of employment. In cases where there was no negligence — because the statements were based on honest beliefs that turned out to be wrong — several employers have been found liable on the basis of breach of a pre-hiring contract that employment would continue for a certain minimum time. Another employer was found liable on the basis of a pre-employment contract to pay a certain rate of pay, where the rate had been promised to induce the employee to accept a transfer.

Other Claims — Other claims have included: enforcement of other contractual agreements; enforcement of termination agreements; an implied right to return to the bargaining unit rather than be dismissed; and shareholder issues, where an employee was also a shareholder in the employer corporation.

TORT CLAIMS BY EMPLOYEES

Negligent misrepresentation and negligence — Negligent misrepresentation actions in the employment context are often based on representations made during the hiring process which turn out to be inaccurate. The Supreme Court of Canada has said that there are five general requirements for a negligent misrepresentation claim:

(1) a duty of care based on a special relationship;
(2) a representation that is untrue, inaccurate or misleading;
(3) the misrepresentation must have been made negligently;
(4) the employee must have reasonably relied on the misrepresentation;
(5) the reliance must have been detrimental, in that it caused damages.

The fact that a negligent misrepresentation is made in a pre-contractual setting such as negotiations or an employment interview, and the fact that a contract is subsequently entered into, do not in themselves bar an action for negligent misrepresentation.

Inducing breach of contract and interference with contractual relations — The tort of negligently or intentionally inducing breach of contract involves a duty of care arising from the proximity of a relationship and the foreseeability of harm. The facts of the tort must be independent of the breach of contract itself. The cause of action requires a valid contract, a breach by the defendant, that the breach was effected by wrongful interference, and that the plaintiff suffered damages. This tort has met with only limited success in the usual wrongful dismissal context, due to the fact that most dismissed employees wish to sue a fellow employee or corporate officer or director. However, a person who was acting in good faith within his capacity as an officer or employee, and within the scope of his authority, will not generally be liable for inducing a breach of contract. Nevertheless, individuals and corporate directors and shareholders have been held personally liable where their intent was fraudulent, or where they acted in bad faith or outside the scope of their authority as servants of the corporation.

Conspiracy — Civil conspiracy requires an agreement between two or more persons in the sense of a joint plan or common design. A conspiracy can be established where the predominant purpose of the agreement is to injure the plaintiff or where the conspirators use unlawful means to achieve their end, even though they know or should know that the plaintiff may be injured. Individuals who were acting within the scope of their authority, or were acting in the course of their employment, generally will not be held personally liable for conspiracy.

Retaliatory, bad faith or abusive discharge — The tort of retaliatory discharge is recognized in the United States; however, the United States employment law context is quite different from the Canadian context. Although several Canadian plaintiffs have attempted to claim on the basis of this tort, none have succeeded so far. The Supreme Court of Canada has refused to recognize the existence of a tort of bad faith discharge, but has said that a lack of good faith and fair dealing by an employer is a relevant consideration in setting an employee's notice period.

Defamation — Defamation claims can arise in the employment context based on statements made after termination or even based on statements made at the time of termination, if the statements bring a person's occupation or calling into question. The test is whether the words used would tend to lower the employee in the estimation of right-thinking members of society. Truth (or justification, as it is known in the law of defamation) is a valid defence. As with other employment-related tort claims, individuals who act within the scope of their own employment or authority may not be personally liable for defamatory statements. A defence of qualified privilege is available where a report is made to another party by virtue of a duty to report. However, the defence of qualified privilege can be defeated by malice.

Wrongful referencing — At least one case has stated emphatically that an employer has no legal duty to provide references, and damages for failure to provide references were refused. However, another case allowed damages for the employer's failure to provide references to the dismissed employee, without explaining the basis for the award. Failure to provide references has also been a factor in lengthening the reasonable notice period, and in aggravated and punitive damages claims.

Intentional or negligent infliction of mental suffering — This tort goes by several names — infliction of mental suffering, infliction of mental distress, wilful infliction of mental distress, intentional infliction of nervous shock, etc. — but the essence is the same. The cause of the victim's upset can be either intentional or due to the perpetrator's negligence. It has been said that, to be actionable, the claimant must have a recognizable physical or psychiatric illness, and it must be proved that this illness was caused by the impugned conduct and not by some other cause.

Harassment — Several employees have successfully sued for harassing conduct throughout their employment. Most cases say there is no common-law action of harassment, and employees have generally not been allowed to sue civilly based on human rights laws against harassment. However, the same type of conduct may be actionable if it is extreme enough to fall within the tort of intentional infliction of mental distress. Liability may also be claimed on the basis of constructive dismissal, loss of reputation, breach of fiduciary duty, negligence, or breach of privacy. Sexual assault is another possible cause of action, where the harassment is sexual and has progressed beyond verbal harassment.

Breach of fiduciary duty — One case has said that there is no authority for an action based on breach of fiduciary duty of an employer to an employee. However, in another case, the employer was said to have a fiduciary duty to act in the employee's best interests, and the employee was awarded substantial damages. In yet another case, a judge ruled that an employer had a duty of fairness toward its employees in a promotion situation; however, no breach of the duty was found. Other cases have refused to strike out actions based on breach of fiduciary duty; these have included a claim based on an alleged breach of a health and safety statute, and a sexual harassment claim.

CLAIMS BY EMPLOYERS

Overpayments and loans — Employers have successfully claimed or set off claims for recovery of a wage overpayment, commissions paid by advance draw but not earned before termination, and an amount advanced on account of a bonus which was not subsequently earned. Where an employee who resigns has been substantially overpaid, the employer may have to initiate its own action to recover the amount owing. Employers have also been allowed to counterclaim or set off claims for repayment of employee loans that had not been forgiven before termination. Employers have successfully claimed repayment of an employee purchase account, repayment of unauthorized expense claims or personal expenses, and for the value of a company car or other property retained by the employee after dismissal.

Employee misconduct — Costs incurred by an employer due to an employee's misconduct or poor performance prior to dismissal generally have not been recoverable, especially where that very conduct led to termination. Even where employees acted fraudulently, the employer's claim against them failed, as no damages had been proven. Damages have been allowed in only a few cases, and many other similar cases exist which did not allow damages.

Breach of fiduciary duty — A number of recent cases have involved claims by employers for breach of fiduciary duty. Breach of a non-competition clause has been compensated under a claim for breach of fiduciary duty, as has a misuse of confidential information. However, awards to employers under this category are still fairly rare.

Wrongful resignation — Cases where the employer sues the employee for terminating employment without adequate notice have been dubbed "wrongful resignation" cases. Note, however, that if the employer has attempted to limit its duty to give notice to the employee, the same limits may apply to the employee's duty to give notice to the employer. Where an employee leaves in response to a constructive dismissal, an employer may be disentitled to damages for lack of notice. Damages may be refused unless the employer can prove it suffered a loss because of the lack of notice. The employer may also have a duty to mitigate its loss. One case allowed damages both for extra costs and for loss of the increased business the employer had expected from an employee's employment. To date, the amount of damages awarded has often followed statutory termination notice amounts rather than the much greater notice required at common law. One case has stated that reasonable notice in such cases is generally less than the amount of notice required for the employer to dismiss the employee.

Appendix 3

PRECEDENTS

WARNING LETTER: MISCONDUCT – FIRST INSTANCE

Dear [*employee*]:

I am writing about your conduct at work and specifically about [*specify misconduct*]. I learned of this incident on [*date*]. Your explanation at that time was [*detail explanation*]. As I explained at the time, this is not satisfactory.

I view your conduct in this matter as totally unacceptable. [*Type of conduct*] is prohibited by our company rules as set out in [*location, if applicable*]. Furthermore, as our [*job title*], you had the clear responsibility to [*do whatever the employee should have done*].

I regard your conduct as proper cause for discipline. I consider appropriate discipline in this case to be this written warning, which shall remain in your permanent employee file [*or details of other discipline, such as suspension*].

Any repetition of this conduct will lead to further discipline. However, we trust that you will in future [*abide by the rules, or detail conduct expected*]. If you remain uncertain about the standard expected of you, please seek clarification from your manager or from myself so that we may avoid further discipline.

WARNING LETTER: MISCONDUCT – FINAL WARNING

Dear [*employee*]:

I am writing about your conduct at work and specifically about [*specify misconduct*].

I learned of this incident on [*date*]. Your explanation at that time was [*detail explanation*]. As I explained at the time, this is not satisfactory.

I viewed your conduct in this matter as totally unacceptable. [*Type of conduct*] is prohibited by our company rules as set out in [*location, if applicable*]. Furthermore, as our [*job title*], you had the clear responsibility to [*do whatever the employee should have done*]. I regard your conduct as proper cause for discipline. Serious discipline is called for in this case because of your record of unsatisfactory conduct, which has not shown improvement, despite warnings dated [*dates of all previous warnings for similar misconduct*]. Because of these past warnings, there can be no doubt that you were aware of the conduct expected of you.

For all these reasons, I have decided that appropriate discipline in these circumstances is [*state details of discipline — final warning or suspension and final warning, etc.*].

You must recognize that this is your final warning. I will consider any further incidents of misconduct to be grounds for your immediate dismissal without notice or pay in place of notice. A copy of this letter will remain in your permanent employee file.

To repeat, this is your last chance. Please govern yourself accordingly.

WARNING LETTER: POOR PERFORMANCE

Dear [*employee*]:

I am writing to confirm our discussion on [*date*] that we are not satisfied with your performance as [*job title*] over the past [*time period*].

In particular, you have failed to maintain reasonable performance objectives for the position of [*job title*] in these respects:

[*detail shortcomings*]

We wish to assist you in improving your performance to an acceptable level. For this purpose, [*name of persons*] are available to assist you [*over the next number of months*]. Your performance objectives [*for this time period, if desired*] are:

[*detail objectives*]

We sincerely hope that you will be able to improve your performance to meet these reasonable objectives. However, if you fail to meet these objectives without a satisfactory reason, we will consider your continued poor performance to be cause for termination of your employment.

TERMINATION NOTICE: JUST CAUSE

Dear [*employee*]:

This letter will confirm that you are being dismissed as of [*date*] for just cause, due to [*type of misconduct*].

[*optional summary of previous misconduct or poor performance reviews and warnings*]

A cheque for outstanding salary and vacation pay in the amount of [*amount*] is enclosed. In view of the fact that we are dismissing you for just cause, it is our position that we are not required to provide you with termination notice or pay in lieu of notice. However, in recognition of your past service and to assist you in the future, without prejudice and without in any way contradicting our position that you are being dismissed for just cause, we are offering you a gratuitous payment of [*amount*].

This payment will be available to you upon our receipt of a signed copy of the attached release by [*insert date*].

TERMINATION NOTICE: NO JUST CAUSE

Dear [*employee*]:

As discussed, your employment with [*employer*] will end on [*date*]. [*If dismissal is due to workforce reduction or other reason unrelated to the employee's performance, this can be stated here.*]

As this dismissal is without just cause, we are prepared to offer you the following financial settlement.

Your salary will be continued for a maximum of [*number of weeks or months*] or for such shorter period as you require to find a new job with equivalent remuneration or commence self-employment. Your benefits coverage, except for [*list exceptions, if any*], shall also be continued for this time. This amount shall include all statutory termination notice to which you are entitled under the [*name of Act*]. In addition, we will pay you [*amount*] representing your statutory severance pay entitlement.

You agree that it is a condition of this salary continuation that you will use your best efforts to find alternate employment as soon as you reasonably can, and that you will advise us as soon as you have done so.

In the alternative, you may elect on or before [*date*] to receive an immediate lump sum payment of [*amount*], which shall include statutory termination pay [*and statutory severance pay, if applicable*]. If you elect to receive the lump sum, your benefits entitlement will cease as of the date of payment of the lump sum.

Please note that your group life insurance coverage will cease [*number of days*] days after your termination. However, you can elect within [*number of days*] days to convert your coverage to personal coverage. If you require assistance in converting your coverage, please contact [*name*] in Personnel.

Under the terms of the Pension Plan of which you are a member, you may elect to receive repayment of your contributions to the plan, transfer your contributions to a new plan or leave them in the plan and receive a pension benefit upon reaching retirement age. We will require you to advise us of your election [*or other details of pension benefits*].

We propose to allow you to keep your company-provided motor vehicle for the duration of the salary payment period. In the alternative, if you elect to receive a lump sum payment, you can elect to receive a further [*amount*] as compensation for the immediate return of the motor vehicle. [*If vehicle can be purchased by employee, set out details here.*]

We will require the immediate return of your company keys and company credit card, and removal of your personal possessions by [*date*].

In order to assist you in finding future employment, the services of [*relocation counsellor*] will be available to you from now until [*date*]. [*Set out other details as necessary.*]

In order to finalize our financial arrangements, we require that you sign the attached Election Form and Release [*if desired*] by [*date*]. If we do not receive a signed copy of the Election Form and Release by [*date*], we will assume that you have elected [*to continue salary payments, or whichever option the employer wishes to assume*]. We recommend that you obtain independent legal advice before signing the Election Form and Release.

We thank you for your past service and wish you the best in the future.

RELEASE

In consideration of the payment of [*amount*], less deductions as required by law, I [*employee*], do hereby release and forever discharge [*employer*] and its officers, directors and employees (and all related and affiliated companies, their officers, directors and employees) from any and all claims and causes of action related to my employment and the termination of my employment with [*employer*].

I also acknowledge that the aforesaid sum of [*amount*] includes any and all amounts to which I am entitled under [*name of employment standards statute*].

I confirm that I have obtained independent legal advice with respect to the payments made to me and the execution of this release.

Or: I confirm that [*employer*] has advised me to obtain independent legal advice with respect to the payments made to me and the execution of this release, but that I have declined to do so.

I also confirm that I am executing this release freely and voluntarily.

Dated this [*date*] day of [*month*], [*year*].

Witness:

```
                              )
                              )
_____ )   _____
                              )
                              )                 [employee's name]
```

Appendix 4

REASONABLE NOTICE CHARTS

In the following reasonable notice charts, an attempt has been made to classify employees in various categories. This process is necessarily subjective and may not account for factors such as size of establishment, which can greatly affect an employee's responsibility level.

There may be some overlap between charts, and users are encouraged to review all charts that might be relevant, without strict regard to category. For example, substantial overlap may occur between the categories of Senior Executives and Upper Management, and between Lower Management and Foremen and Supervisors.

Cases are in chronological order by year within each chart. Case names and citations are available in the *Butterworths Wrongful Dismissal Practice Manual*.

A. REASONABLE NOTICE PERIODS — SENIOR EXECUTIVES: 1987 – PRESENT

Position	Age	Length of Service	Period of Notice
1987			
President	51	8 yrs.	18 mos.*
Vice President	40	18 mos.	12 mos.
Vice President, Individual & Association Services Division	37	13.5 yrs.	5 mos.*
Vice President, Marketing	—	11 mos.	3 mos.
President	42	7 yrs.	16 mos.
Vice President	46	3 yrs.	6 mos.
Senior Position, Director	—	2.5 yrs.	3 mos.
1988			
Vice President, Sales	—	4 yrs.	12 mos.
President and Chief Operating Officer	40	11 yrs.	1 yr.

* Provisional assessment only.

Position	Age	Length of Service	Period of Notice
President, General Manager	40	6 yrs.	10 mos.
Vice President, General Manager	44	8 yrs.	14 mos.
Principal & Director	53	28.5 yrs.	21 mos.
Vice President	57	8 yrs.	7 mos.
Senior Executive	—	—	12 mos.
1989			
Vice President	40	22 yrs.	10 mos.[*]
Vice President	45	3.5 yrs.	14 mos.[**]
Vice President, Operations	61	24 yrs.	15 mos.[*]
Vice President	52	8 yrs.	15 mos.
Vice President, Industrial Products	54	17 yrs.	18 mos.
Vice President, Canadian Sales Manager	38	11 yrs.	12 mos.
Vice President	42	9 yrs.	12 mos.
1990			
Vice President, Operations/Maintenance	55	8 yrs.	15 mos.
President, Chief Operating Officer	39	4 yrs.	12 mos.
1991			
President	60	40 yrs.	2 yrs.
President, General Manager	32	3.5 yrs.	3 mos.[*]
Vice President	49	8.5 yrs.	15 mos.
Chief Executive Officer, Secretary, Director	44	21 yrs.	12 mos.
Vice President	37	9 yrs.	12 mos.
1992			
Senior Vice President, Director	46	10 yrs.	12 mos.
Senior Vice President, Alta.	56	18 mos.	12 mos.
Vice President, Marketing	46	5 mos.	16 wks.
President & CEO	47	10 yrs.	18 mos.

[*] Provisional assessment only.
[**] Notice reduced due to "near cause" or failure to mitigate.

APPENDIX 4   445

Position	Age	Length of Service	Period of Notice
1993			
Vice President, Development & Construction	42	21 mos.	8 mos.
Division President	43	7 yrs.	9-12 mos.*
Senior Vice President & Director of Research	51	21 mos.	9 mos.
Vice President, Internal Audit	44	16 mos.	13 wks.*
Vice President & Director	—	31 yrs.	14 mos.**
Vice President, Sales	—	2.5 yrs.	12 mos.
Senior Vice President	35	10 yrs.	12 mos.*
Treasurer, Director, Inside Sales	54	25 yrs.	20 mos.
1994			
Vice President, Finance & Administration	48	9.5 yrs.	15 mos.
Vice President, Finance	—	6 yrs.	12 mos.
Vice President, Public Affairs	—	—	6 mos.
1995			
Vice President, Operations	49	23 yrs.	18 mos.
Vice President, Leasing & Franchising	39	2 yrs.	5 mos.*
President & General Manager	—	10 yrs.	15 mos.
Regional Vice President	—	15 yrs.	15 mos.
Vice President & General Manager	41	8 yrs.	15 mos.
President & CEO	43	7.5 mos.	14 mos.
Vice President	—	7 mos.	6 mos.
Vice President, Equities & Investment Strategy	44	12 yrs.	15 mos.
1996			
Vice President, Sales Manager & Director	40's	6 yrs.	15 mos.
President & CEO	45	10 yrs	18 mos.

*   Provisional assessment only.
** Notice reduced due to "near cause" or failure to mitigate.

Position	Age	Length of Service	Period of Notice
1997			
Vice President, Corporate Finance	41	6 yrs.	12 mos.
Vice President, Business Development	61	40 yrs	24 mos.
Vice President		22 mos.	3 mos.
1998			
Chief Executive Officer	60	5.5 yrs.	30 mos.***
Chief Executive Officer		2 yrs.	6 mos.
President & Director	46	9 yrs.	9.5 mos.
Vice President, Finance & Administration	51	8 mos.	12 mos.
1999			
Director	40	18 yrs.	12.5mos.
2000			
President	54	29 yrs.	30 mos.+ 6 mos.***
Senior Vice President, Finance		18 yrs.	18 mos.
President	59	24 yrs.	24 mos.+ 2 mos.***
Chief Executive Officer		3 yrs.	18 mos.
2001			
Vice President, Sales & General Manager		21 yrs.	21 mos.+ 3 mos.
Vice President, Finance; CFO	54	9 yrs.	15 mos.+ 3 mos.***
Vice President, Operations	43	16.5yrs.	16 mos.*
President	54	23 yrs.	30 mos.***
2002			
Vice President, Sales & Marketing		13 yrs.	18 mos.
Vice President, Sales & Marketing	43	5.5 yrs.	8 mos.

* Provisional assessment only.
*** Notice increased due to employer's conduct.

B. REASONABLE NOTICE PERIODS — UPPER MANAGEMENT: 1987 – PRESENT

Position	Age	Length of Service	Period of Notice
1987			
Pulp Mill Superintendent	44	20 yrs.	17 mos.
General Manager	52	5.5 yrs.	9 mos.
Plant Manager	46	18 yrs.	15 mos.
Operations Manager	36	16 yrs.	12 mos.
Senior Manager and Officer	—	10 mos.	9 mos.
General Manger	61	10 yrs.	16 mos.
General Manager	—	1 yr.	3 mos.
Assistant Regional V.P., Marketing	47	21 yrs.	18 mos.
1988			
Credit Manager, Office Manager, Director	—	8 yrs.	9 mos.
Plant Manager	—	20 yrs.	18 mos.
Executive Director	47	5.5 yrs.	12 mos.
Director of Management Information Services	46	22 mos.	10 mos.
Assistant Vice President, Traffic Safety	—	10 yrs.	12 mos.
Director of Operations	42	2.5 mos.	3 mos.
General Manager	40's or 50's	23 days	6 mos.*
Town Manager	—	5 yrs.	15 mos.*
1989			
Manager, Long Range Planning	55	2.5 yrs.	1 yr.
Director of Meat Merchandising	53	15 yrs.	14 mos.
Deputy Minister, Fisheries	46	9 yrs.	1 yr.
Deputy Minister, Justice; Deputy Attorney General	49	16 yrs.	18 mos.
Executive Director	61	11.5 yrs.	18 mos.
General Manager	48	17 yrs.	18 mos.
Plant Manager	38	"short"	8 mos.

* Provisional assessment only.

Position	Age	Length of Service	Period of Notice
Operation Manager	50	9 mos.	5 mos.
General Director	34	2 mos.	9 mos.
1990			
Plant Manager	56	18 yrs.	18 mos.
1991			
General Manger	44	11 mos.	3 mos.
General Manger	46	19 yrs.	22 mos.
Superintendent of Utilities	62	38 yrs.	24 mos.
Director of Nursing	47	16 yrs.	18 mos.
General Manager	—	13 yrs.	1 yr.*
Controller	40	2.5 yrs.	8 mos.
Consultant, former President & General Manager	61	18 yrs.	22 mos.
1992			
Managing Editor	46	24 yrs.	21 mos.
General Sales Manager	66	20 yrs.	20 mos.
Manager, Construction Sales	41	4 yrs.	14 mos.
General Sales	—	5 yrs.	8 mos.
Tax Manager	55	20 mos.	5 mos.
General Manager	—	20 yrs.	15 mos.
Deputy Fire Chief/Acting Chief	48	17 yrs.	24 mos.
Director, Marketing Services	41	6 yrs.	12 mos.
1993			
Assistant V.P., Network Services	—	19 mos.	15 mos.*
Fire Chief	60	9 yrs.	12 mos.
Senior Management	63	13 yrs.	12 mos.
Key Executive	—	18 mos.	18 mos.
Director of Production	41	21 yrs.	14 mos.
Eastern Region Director	52	31 yrs.	12 mos.
Senior Engineer, Acting General Manager	—	27 yrs.	24 mos.*
1994			
Plant Manager	—	13 mos.	4 mos.

* Provisional assessment only.

APPENDIX 4   449

Position	Age	Length of Service	Period of Notice
1995			
Regional Manager	56	28 yrs.	24 mos.
Zone Manager	55	37 yrs.	20 mos.
Controller	37	4 yrs.	7 mos.
President & General Manager	—	10 yrs.	15 mos.
Plant Superintendent	50	35 yrs.	21 mos.
Plant Manager	44	13 yrs.	20 mos.
Comptroller	50	18 mos.	7 mos.
National Marketing Development Manager	54	8 yrs.	9 mos.
1996			
Director of Engineering	46	23 yrs.	18 mos.
General Manager, Director	56	15 yrs.	20 mos.
Chief Financial Officer	52	3 yrs.	9 mos.
Comptroller	51	4 yrs.	6 mos.
Senior Manager, Corporate Banking		10 yrs.	12 mos.
1997			
Director of Security	14 yrs.		15 mos. (9 mos. at trial)**
Regional Manager		18 yrs.	12 mos.
Vice Chairman	39	11 yrs.	13 mos.
Director of Operations	42	16.5 yrs.	18 mos.
Plant Manager	41	12 yrs.	13 mos.
Plant Superintendent	58	25 yrs.	18 mos.
Controller	54	22 yrs.	14 mos.
General Manager/ Salesperson	71	30 yrs.	16 mos.
1998			
Senior Manager	40	6 yrs.	12 mos. (6 mos. at trial)
General Manager	51	32 yrs.	24 mos.
Manager	46	9 mos.	9 mos.***
Regional Executive Director, Mental Heath		17 yrs.	17 mos.
1999			
Executive Director	mid 40's	4 yrs.	12 mos.+ 6 mos.

** Notice reduced due to "near cause" or failure to mitigate.
*** Notice increased due to employer's conduct.

Position	Age	Length of Service	Period of Notice
Sales Manager	51	28.5 yrs.	22 mos.
Senior Sales Representative	54	30 yrs.	24 mos. reduced to 22 mos.**
Senior Management	60	35 yrs.	27 mos.
General Manager	52	13 yrs.	18 mos. + 6 mos.***
General Manager	59	9-10 yrs.	14 mos.
Director, Engineering & Works	50	25.5 yrs.	25.5 mos.
2000			
General Manager	51	4 yrs.	10 mos.
Claims Manager, Canada	45	21 yrs.	18 mos.**
General Manager	mid-50's	2.5 mos.	18 mos.
Human Resources Director	56	24 yrs.	16 mos.
2001			
National Operations Manager		19 yrs.	20 mos. + 4 mos.***
Controller, Treasurer	49	17 yrs.	22 mos. + 4 mos.***
2002			
Human Resources Manager		19 yrs.	18 mos.***

C. REASONABLE NOTICE PERIODS — MIDDLE MANAGEMENT: 1987 - PRESENT

Position	Age	Length of Service	Period of Notice
1987			
Production Manager	55	9 mos.	3 mos.
Construction Project Manager	52	9 mos.	6 mos.
National Underwriting Manager	39	1.5 yrs.	4 mos.
Branch Manager	56	1 yr.	4 mos.
Branch Manager	40	15 yrs.	15 mos.

** Notice reduced due to "near cause" or failure to mitigate.
*** Notice increased due to employer's conduct.

APPENDIX 4   451

Position	Age	Length of Service	Period of Notice
Store Manager	36	3.5 yrs.	4 mos.*
Manager	55	20 yrs.	15 mos.
Director of Personnel & Purchasing	—	9 mos.	5 mos.
District Manager	52	17 yrs.	12 mos.
Commercial Loans Manager	—	10 yrs.	12 mos.
1988			
Hotel Co-Manager	—	3 yrs.	6 mos.
Senior Psychologist, Forensic Services	53	27.5 yrs.	2 yrs.
Branch Manager	53	18 yrs.	9 mos.*
Manager, Purchasing	34	9 yrs.	10 mos.
Government Agent	38	15 yrs.	1 yr.
Grocery Store Manager	—	23 yrs.	14 mos.
Systems Manager	47	22 yrs.	15 mos.
Business Economic Advisor	52	22 yrs.	12 mos.
Branch Manager	35	under 1 yr. (7 prev. yrs.)	6 mos.*
Branch Manager	56	16 yrs.	12 mos.
Service Superintendent	43	15 yrs.	8 mos.
1989			
Branch Manager	47	2 yrs.	4 mos.
Construction Project Superintendent	43	2.5 yrs.	6 mos.
Personal Trust Dept. Manager	40	19 yrs.	12 mos.
Regional Manager	mid-50's	13 yrs.	15 mos.*
Manager of Human Resources	—	5 yrs.	10 mos.
Station Manager	—	31 yrs.	15 mos.
Branch Manager/ Collections Manager	35	7.5 yrs.	12 mos.
Quality Assurance Manager	59	33 yrs.	20 mos.
Terminal Manager	53	11.5 yrs.	16 mos.
Advertising Manager	—	21 yrs.	12 mos.*
Business Manager & Sales Manager	45	11.5 yrs.	12 mos.

* Provisional assessment only.

Position	Age	Length of Service	Period of Notice
General Manager, Canadian Subsidiary	61	6 yrs.	12 mos.
1990			
Store Manager	—	1 yr.	6 mos.
Motel Manager	53	10 mos.	6 mos.
Director, Vocational Educational Services	39	10 yrs.	12 mos.*
Area Manager, Lending	46	20 yrs.	18 mos.
Ship's Master	68	8 yrs.	8 mos.
Naval Surveyor & Office Manger	49	12 yrs.	18 mos.
Store Merchandiser	early middle age	21 yrs.	18 mos.
Terminal Manager	60	21 yrs.	24 mos.
Store Manager	51	5 yrs.	1 yr.
Program Manager	54	22 yrs.	18 mos.
Restaurant Manager	27	4 yrs.	4 mos.
Regional Manager	39	2 yrs.	12 mos.
Terminal Manager	50	8 yrs.	9 mos.*
1991			
Business Manager	37	2 yrs.	3 mos.**
Plant Production Manager	—	25 yrs.	15 mos.*
Operations Manager	55	25 yrs.	18 mos.
Restaurant Manager	—	3 yrs.	3 mos.
Store Manager	44	15 yrs.	18 mos.
Maintenance Shop Supervisor	—	12 yrs.	14 mos.
Regional Manager	—	21 yrs.	15 mos.
Woodlands Manager	47	over 10 yrs.	15 mos.
Service Manger	50	29.5 yrs.	18 mos.
Human Resources Manager	52	7.5 yrs.	12 mos.
Manager, Cdn. Drilling Operations	41	—	12 mos.
Parts Manager	—	over 4 yrs.	6 mos.
Chief Producer	54	30 yrs.	12 mos.
Senior Warranty Administrator	43	7.5 yrs.	9 mos.

* Provisional assessment only.
** Notice reduced due to "near cause" or failure to mitigate.

APPENDIX 4 453

Position	Age	Length of Service	Period of Notice
1992			
Branch Manager	48	4 yrs.	9 mos.
Branch Manager	41	8.5 yrs.	12 mos.
Manager	45	almost 7 yrs.	13 mos.
Director, Social Development	35	17 yrs.	15 mos.
Director of Nursing	59	25 yrs.	22 mos.
Production Manager/Music	41	20 yrs.	12 mos.
Store Sales Manager	40	18 yrs.	12 mos.
Business Manager	45	19 yrs.	12 mos.
Estimator/Manager	61	3 mos.	1 mo.
Manager, Real Estate Division	37	11 yrs.	12 mos.
Business Manager/Salesman	—	5 yrs.	4 mos.
Director of Education	54	10 yrs.	12 mos.
Director of Operations	37	3 mos.	9 mos.
Restaurant Managers	—	4 & 5 mos.	6 mos.
Store Operations Manager	57	23 yrs.	20 mos.
Retail Marketing Representative	56	23 yrs.	20 mos.
Store Manager	30	11 mos.	6 mos.
Vice President, Marketing	46	5 mos.	16 wks.
Branch Manager	—	18 yrs.	8 wks.[*]
Branch Manager	53	10 mos.	5 mos.
Division Manager	53	13 yrs.	12 mos.
Store Manager	30	4 yrs.	6 mos.
Labour Relations	51	10.5 yrs.	9 mos.
Office Manager/Bookkeeper	35	2 yrs. p/t, 2 yrs. f/t	8 mos.
Store Manager	32	7 yrs.	6 mos.
Director, Student Affairs	—	9 yrs.	9 mos.
Branch Manager	59	33 yrs.	20 mos.
1993			
Manager, Administrative Services	50	16 yrs.	11 mos.
Managing Partner, Tax Sheltered Services	45	26 yrs.	18 mos.

[*] Provisional assessment only.

454   THE WRONGFUL DISMISSAL HANDBOOK

Position	Age	Length of Service	Period of Notice
Construction Manager	52	20 mos.	4 mos.
Branch Manager	50	6 yrs.	13-½mos.
Vice President, Production	46	15 yrs.	15 mos.
Branch Manager	62	20 mos.	6 mos.
Route Operations Manager	54	30 yrs.	18 mos.
Department & Section Manager	42	24 yrs.	12 mos.
Quality Assurance Department Head	46	20.5 yrs.	22 mos.
Garage Manager	50	20 yrs.	16 mos.
Superintendent, Fire & Security	48	7 yrs.	11 mos.**
General Manager	—	9 mos.	5 mos.**
Manager, Electrical Utilities	59	23 yrs.	24 mos.
Assistant Manager, Electrical Utilities	60	22 yrs.	24 mos.
General Superintendent, Planer Mill	36	5.5 yrs.	11 mos.
Branch Manager	37	3 yrs.	8 mos.
Branch Manager	43	1 yr.	3 mos.*
1994			
Director of Development	—	2.5 yrs.	4 mos.
Branch Manager	41	20 yrs.	12 mos. (0 on appeal)**
Grocery Industry Manager	51	7 yrs.	7 mos.
Middle Manager	37	approx. 20 yrs.	12 mos.
Manager	45	3 yrs.	12 mos.
Manager	—	7 yrs.	5 mos.
Engineering Department Manager	59	2 yrs.	4 mos.
Zone Manager	44	23 yrs.	18 mos.*
Store Manager	43	8 yrs.	12 mos.
Unit Manager, Obstetrics Ward	57	37 yrs.	21 mos.
Branch Manager	—	2.75 yrs.	8 mos.
Business Manager, Regional Operations Group	43	15 yrs.	15 mos.

*   Provisional assessment only.
**   Notice reduced due to "near cause" or failure to mitigate.

APPENDIX 4   455

Position	Age	Length of Service	Period of Notice
Manager, Microwave and Outside Plant	54	34 yrs.	24 mos.
Mechanical Superintendent	45	14 yrs.	12 mos.*
Branch Manager	—	24 yrs.	18 mos.
Food & Beverage Manager	52	6 yrs.	8 mos.
Manager	—	4 yrs.	6 mos.*
Operations Manager	51	15 yrs.	17 mos.
Executive Director	44	8 yrs.	6 mos.
Executive Director	44	1 yr.	9 wks.
Distribution Centre Manager	44	6.5 yrs.	10 mos.
Middle Manager	55	15 yrs.	12 mos.
Nursing Home Administrator	54	22 yrs.	8 mos.
Business Manager	—	4 mos.	3 mos.*
Mechanical Engineer	56	35 yrs.	18 mos.
Manager, Respiratory Services	55	32 yrs.	18 mos.
1995			
Operations Supervisor	41	15 yrs.	12 mos.
Manager of Administration	52	1 yr.	6 mos.
Distribution Manager	50	22 yrs.	16 mos.
Director, Child Guidance Services	—	6 yrs.	5 mos.
Radio Station News Director	41	3.5 yrs.	7 mos.
Sales Manager, Catalogue Desk	55	27 yrs.	75 wks.
Bank Manager	42	25 yrs.	12 mos.*
Branch Store Manager	—	2 yrs.	1-2 mos.
Superintendent, Human Resources, Woodlands Operation	56	30 yrs.	20 mos.
Service Manager	47	12 yrs.	12 mos.
Merchandise Manager	—	21 yrs.	1 yr.
Director, Human Resources	—	38 mos.	7 mos.
Store Manager	44	23 yrs.	12 mos.
Supervising Engineer,	48	2.5 yrs.	6 mos.

* Provisional assessment only.

Position	Age	Length of Service	Period of Notice
Science Workshops			
Superintendent, Public Works	50	18 yrs.	18 mos.*
Business Development Manager	43	4.5 yrs.	10 mos.
Section Head, Financial Analysis	—	26 mos.	4 mos.
Branch Manager	53	8 mos.	7 mos.
Works Supervisor	—	25 yrs.	6 mos.*
Manager	—	4.5 mos.	5 mos.
Business Manager	—	1 yr.	2 mos.
1996			
Restaurant Manager	31	9 yrs.	10 mos.
Inn Manager (seasonal)	68	20 yrs.	6 mos. (1 season)
Head of Security	47	5 yrs.	10 mos.
Senior Systems Analyst		17 yrs.	18 mos.
Area Farm Supply	32	11 yrs.	10 mos.
Manager		6 mos.	6 mos.
Ship's Captain	57	2.5 yrs.	3 mos.
Equipment Procurement Manager	62	24 yrs.	18 mos.
Project Manager	46	20 yrs.	16 mos.*
Store Manager		16 yrs.	12 mos.
Store Manager	29	10 yrs.	18 mos.
City Manager		16 mos.	4 mos.
Assistant Plant Manager	33	17 yrs.	14 mos.
1997			
Store Manager	48	26 yrs.	22 mos.
Operations Manager		3 mos.	6 mos.
Manager	50	32 yrs.	21 mos.
Property Manager	43	20 yrs.	20 mos.
Fleet and Lease Manager	58	19 yrs.	8 mos.**
Store Manager	34	6 yrs.	6 mos.***
Truck Stop Manager		12.5 yrs.	11 mos.
1998			
Store Manager	51	14 yrs.	12 mos.

---

* Provisional assessment only.
** Notice reduced due to "near cause" or failure to mitigate.
*** Notice increased due to employer's conduct.

APPENDIX 4   457

Position	Age	Length of Service	Period of Notice
Superintendent	55	11 yrs.	14 mos.
Store Manager	58	33 yrs.	24 mos.***
Manager	43	13 yrs.	14 mos.+4 mos.***
Administrator, Manager	43	3 yrs.	8 mos.***
Operations Manager	32	5.5yrs.	8 mos.
Manager	40	22 yrs.	12 mos.
Hotel Manager/ Administrator	41	4 yrs.	12 mos.***
Computer Program	45	19 yrs.	14 mos.+6 mos. – 4 mos.***, **
1999			
Accounting Employee	33	4.5 yrs.	6.5 mos.
Operations Manager		19 yrs.	15 mos.*
Branch Manager, Insurance Claims Adjuster	57	2 yrs.	8 mos.
Assistant General Manager, Vancouver Office	38	9 yrs.	8 mos.
Branch Manager	38	3 yrs.	4 mos.
Theatre Manager	25	9 yrs.	1 yr. (approx.)
2000			
Branch Manager	67	20 yrs.	18 mos.
Controller/Office Manager		7 yrs.	7 mos.
Purchasing Manager, Western Division	57	28 yrs.	24 mos.+3 mos.***
Store Manager		17 yrs.	17 mos.+12 mos.***
Manager, Internal Audit	35	22 mos.	5 mos.*
Controller		20 mos.	3 mos.
Store Manager	42	24 yrs.	16 mos.
2001			
Manager, Security Services		5 yrs.	10 mos.
District Manager	53	2.5 yrs.	4 mos.
Restaurant Manager	34	4 yrs. Full-time +5.5 yrs. Part-time	8 mos.

*   Provisional assessment only.
**   Notice reduced due to "near cause" or failure to mitigate.
*** Notice increased due to employer's conduct.

Position	Age	Length of Service	Period of Notice
2002			
Manager & Professional Engineer		20 yrs.	116 weeks (80 weeks on appeal)
Branch Manager/ Salesman	52	5 yrs.	8 mos.***
2003			
Bartender/Manager, Part Owner		6 yrs.	16 mos.
Industrial Engineering Manager	47	17 yrs.	18 mos.
Terminal Manager	44	20 yrs.	15 mos.

D. REASONABLE NOTICE PERIODS — LOWER MANAGEMENT: 1987 – PRESENT

Position	Age	Length of Service	Period of Notice
1987			
Service Manager	40	6 yrs.	9 mos.
Assistant Store Manager	26	8.5 yrs.	5 mos.**
Plant Manager	—	17 yrs.	6 mos.
Stores Manager	49	23.5 yrs.	47 wks.
1988			
Golf Course Superintendent	—	5.5 mos.	2 mos.
Safety Coordinator	56	24 yrs.	18 mos.
Technical Supervisor	—	6 yrs.	10 mos.
Approving Officer, Subdivision Applications	—	9 yrs.	10 mos.
Purchasing Manager	—	8 yrs.	6 mos.
1989			
Resource Economist	43	2 yrs.	6 mos.
Manager, Building Management	41	14 yrs.	12 mos.
Project Controller	49	9 yrs.	12 mos.

** Notice reduced due to "near cause" or failure to mitigate.
*** Notice increased due to employer's conduct.

Position	Age	Length of Service	Period of Notice
Assistant Manager, Customer Service	36	4 yrs.	6 mos.
Territory Manager	—	26 yrs.	9 mos.*
Hotel Promotions Manager	—	3 yrs.	5 mos.
Regional Comptroller/ Assistant Manager, Credit	—	13 yrs.	12 mos.*
Hotel Assistant Manager	39	11 mos.	5 mos.
Assistant Branch Manager, Documentation & Records	41	13 yrs.	10 mos.
1990			
Farm Manager	38	2 yrs.+	6 mos.
Fleet & Lease Manager	59	6.5 yrs.	6 mos.
Assistant Divisional Manager, Beauty Products	27	7 yrs.	3 mos.*
Used Car Manager	59	31 yrs.	20 mos.
1991			
Maitre'd	—	25 yrs.	14 mos.
Room Service Captain	—	11 yrs.	10 mos.
Room Service Captain	—	14 yrs.	10 mos.
Room Service Manager	—	21 yrs.	14 mos.
Manager/Supervisor	45	22 yrs.	16 mos.
Manager	32	12 yrs.	18 mos.
Service Manager	"relatively young"	10.5 mos.	4 wks.
Manager, Tow Truck Repairs	58	11 yrs.	7 mos.
1992			
Credit Manager	48	22 yrs.	16 mos.
Production Manager	—	21 yrs.	15-18 mos.*
Manager	61	4.5 mos.	6 mos.
Materials Control Manager	47	12 yrs.	9 mos.
District Service Manager	52	26 yrs.	18 mos.
Service Manager	—	7 yrs.	8 mos.

* Provisional assessment only.

460 THE WRONGFUL DISMISSAL HANDBOOK

Position	Age	Length of Service	Period of Notice
1993			
Captain, Morning Room Service	38	5 yrs.	4.5 mos.**
Assistant Manager, Composing Room Supervisor	43	17 yrs.	12 mos.
Branch Manager	46	6.5 yrs.	6 mos.
Business Manager	46	1 yr.	4 mos.
Realty Manager	45	16 yrs.	12.5 mos.
1994			
Technical Support/ Customer Service Manager	29	4 yrs.	15 mos.
Parts Manager	57	14 yrs.	14 mos.
Service Manager	—	4 yrs.	6 mos.*
Building Administrator	45	2 yrs.	4 mos.
Buyer, Inventory Controller	—	20 yrs.	9.5 mos.
1995			
Manager Level 04	55	19 yrs.	20 mos.
Group Representative	37	16 yrs.	14 mos.
Senior Transit Planner, Operations	50	21 yrs.	18 mos.
Assistant Store Manager	48	21 yrs.	18 mos.
Assistant Manager	35	more than 10 yrs.	6 mos.**
Sales & Service Manager, Accounts Receivable Clerk	27	3 yrs.	15 wks.*
Maintenance Manager	—	1 yr.	7 mos.
"Managerial"	—	12.5 yrs.	10 mos.
1996			
"Lower-level Manager"	—	13 yrs.	11 mos.
Engineering Manager	42	16 yrs.	15 mos.
Senior Equipment Technician	38	17 yrs.	16 mos.
Accounts Receivable Manager	51	22 yrs.	17 mos.
Data Systems Manager	65	12 yrs.	10 mos.

*   Provisional assessment only.
** Notice reduced due to "near cause" or failure to mitigate.

APPENDIX 4 461

Position	Age	Length of Service	Period of Notice
Head of Security	47	5 yrs.	10 mos.
Operations Manager	—	19 yrs.	15 mos.*
Senior Systems Analyst	—	17 yrs.	18 mos.
Farm Supply Manager	32	11 yrs.	10 mos.
Manager	—	6 mos.	6 mos.
Ship's Captain	57	2.5 yrs.	3 mos.
Equipment Procurement Manager	62	24 yrs.	18 mos.
Project Manager	46	24 yrs.	18 mos.
Service Manager	32	16 mos.	6 mos.
Administrative Co-ordinator	48	10 yrs.	10 mos.
Auto Body Shop Manager		5 mos.	5 mos.
Service Manager	52	15 yrs.	12 mos.
Bakery Hygiene Manager	51	22 yrs.	16 mos.
1997			
Production Manager	34	17 yrs.	12 mos.*
Information Systems Manager	32	9 mos.	5 mos.
Administration Manager	35	4 yrs. 11 mos.	7 mos.
Cashier Supervisor	48	14.5 yrs.	34.8 wks
1998			
Safety & Compliance Director	35	4 yrs.	4 mos. (0 on appeal)
Credit Manager	55	15.5 yrs.	12 mos.
Superintendent, Sales Equipment Services	55	32.5 yrs.	18 mos.
Manager, Permits Department	62	41 yrs.	21 mos.
Building Material Sales Coordinator		22 yrs.	15 mos.+5 mos.***
Assistant Spa Manager		5.5 yrs.	5 mos. + 3 mos.***
Assistant Banquet Manager		12 yrs.	16 mos.***
Assistant Manager	49	13 yrs.	12 mos. increased to 16 mos.***
1999			
Promotions Manager		10 yrs.	10 mos.+2 mos.***

* Provisional assessment only.
*** Notice increased due to employer's conduct.

Position	Age	Length of Service	Period of Notice
Office Manager	41	16 yrs.	19.4 mos. (16 mos.+E.S.A. serverance pay)
Promotions Manager		10 yrs.	10 mos. increased to 12 mos.***
2000			
Yard Supervisor/ Operations Manager	45	9 yrs.	18 mos.***
Geologist/Junior Manager		5 yrs.	7 mos.
Manufacturing Manager	45	19 yrs.	22 mos.***
Assistant Manager		5.5 yrs.	5 mos.
Service Manager		9 yrs.	12 mos.
Secretary/Manager	52	14 yrs.	18 mos.
Manager, Engineering & Procurement	55	31 yrs.	20 mos.
2001			
Purchasing Manager	35	14 mos.	6 mos.
Building Manager	62	5.5 yrs.	9-12 mos. + 2 mos.***
2002			
Hairdressing Shop Manager	52	17 yrs.	12 mos. (18 mos. at trial)
Project Manager	43	9 mos.	5 mos.+2 mos.***
2003			
Small Group	40	21 yrs	12 mos.
Property Manager, Exec. Assistant to Administrator	46	15 yrs.+10 yrs.	24 mos.

*** Notice increased due to employer's conduct.

E. REASONABLE NOTICE PERIODS — FOREMEN AND SUPERVISORS: 1987 – PRESENT

Position	Age	Length of Service	Period of Notice
1987			
Area Supervisor	—	6 yrs. plus 8 yrs.	8 mos.
Maintenance Supervisor & Dispatcher	—	7 yrs.	4 mos.
Shift Superintendent	43	18 yrs.	10 mos.
Clean-up Foreman	40	21 yrs.	9 mos.**
District Claims Adjuster	44	4 yrs.	9 mos.
Area Supervisor	56	5.5 yrs.	9 mos.
Shift Foreman, Maintenance Crew	41	23 yrs.	12 mos.
Garage Foreman	51	10 yrs.	10 mos.
Mine Shift Boss	—	3 yrs.	4 mos.**
Dispatcher-Supervisor	35	15 yrs.	6 mos.
Hardware Supervisor	30	5 yrs.	12 wks.*
Planning Forester	—	9 yrs.	10 mos.
Management Security Captain	—	20 yrs.	17 mos.
Warehouse Supervisor	—	4 yrs.	18 wks.
1988			
Supervisor of Office Services	37	17.5 yrs.	15 mos.
Cosmetics Supervisor	38	4 yrs.	3 mos.
Cosmetics Supervisor	40	3 yrs.	3 mos.
Cosmetics Supervisor	24	4 yrs.	3 mos.
Distribution Supervisor	40	6.5 mos.	4 mos.
Supervisor, Account Regulation	36	4.5 yrs.	10 mos.
Design Engineering Supervisor	60	24 yrs.	15 mos.
Head Cashier	47	7 yrs.	3 mos.*
Geomechanics Supervisor	34	4 yrs.	9 mos.
Accounting Supervisor	35	12.5 yrs.	9 mos.

* Provisional assessment only.
** Notice reduced due to "near cause" or failure to mitigate.

Position	Age	Length of Service	Period of Notice
1989			
Residence Installation Foreman	39	11 yrs.	12 mos.*
Foreman	37	16 yrs.	14 mos.
Foreman	48	23 yrs.	24 mos.
Planer Shift Supervisor	52	21 yrs.	14 mos.
Executive Secretary	—	3.5 yrs.	6 mos.
Sales & Service Supervisor	61	9 yrs.	11 mos.
1990			
Mining Shift Boss	54	10 yrs.	9 mos.
Probationary Shift Supervisor	30	less than 90 days	2 wks.
Pickle Department Foreman	59	24 yrs.	18 mos.
Forestry Area Supervisor	—	4 yrs.	8 mos.*
Maintenance Supervisor	60	31 yrs.	20 mos.
1991			
Farm Supply Supervisor	50ish	8 yrs.	8 wks.*
Maintenance Supervisor	—	10 yrs.	15 mos.
Stockroom Supervisor	59	40 yrs.	22 mos.
Electrical Supervisor	58	34 yrs.	20 mos.
Human Resources Supervisor	31	11 yrs.	6 mos.
Field Engineer	50	31 yrs.	15 mos.
Plant Maintenance Supervisor	54	4 mos.	1 mo.
Leadhand, Receiving Dept.	50	32 yrs.	18 mos.
Mill Foreman	30	2 yrs.	9 mos.
1992			
Land Supervisor	48	20 yrs.	18 mos.
Quality Control Supervisor	54	12 yrs.	12 mos.
Pipeline Stringing Foreman	—	18 yrs.	10 wks.
Mill Shift Supervisor	53	16 yrs.	15 mos.
Supervisor, Stenography	—	11 yrs.	5 mos.
Foreperson, Laundry Division	52	18 yrs.	12 mos.
Power Engineer/Comptroller	—	5 yrs.	12 mos.*
Supervisor, Shipping	57	36 yrs.	18 mos.

* Provisional assessment only.

APPENDIX 4   465

Position	Age	Length of Service	Period of Notice
1993			
Foreman	33	14 yrs.	8 mos.
Composing Room Supervisor, Assistant Manager	43	17 yrs.	12 mos.
Supervisor/Machine Operator	—	9 yrs.	9 mos.*
Quality Control Supervisor	—	11 yrs.	9 mos.
Supervisor, Credit Office	58	29.9 yrs.	47 wks.
Shift Supervisor	62	32 yrs.	22 mos.
Assistant Supervisor, Sales Support	—	14 yrs.	10 mos.
Warehouse Foreman	54	8 yrs.	8 mos.
Regional Credit Manager	44	10 yrs.	12 mos.
Maintenance Supervisor	—	24.5 yrs.	12 mos.*
1994			
Supervisor, Human Resources, Shipping, Warehousing & Quality Assurance	54	34 yrs.	18 mos.
Classified Supervisor	46	15.5 yrs.	15 mos.
Mill Shift Supervisor	54	22 yrs.	16 mos.
Foreman	40	11 mos.	2 mos.
Supervisor	—	9 yrs.	12 mos.
Security Supervisor	46	3 yrs.	4 mos.
Certified Welding Supervisor	60	33.5 yrs.	18 mos.
Security Supervisor	—	23 yrs.	21 mos.
Foreman	41	20 yrs.	10 mos.
1995			
Electrical Supervisor	57	35 yrs.	24 mos.
Store Supervisor	42	19 yrs.	12 mos.*
Foreman	56	19 yrs.	10 mos.
Joist Line Foreman	34	6 yrs.	7 mos.
Foreman/Supervisor	56	31 yrs.	14 mos.
Evening Nursing Coordinator	—	23 yrs.	20 mos.
Mill Foreman	45	14 yrs.	14 mos.
Supervisors	—	26-27 yrs.	22 mos.

* Provisional assessment only.

Position	Age	Length of Service	Period of Notice
Carpenter/Supervisor	45	5 yrs.	6 mos.
Restaurant Supervisor		5.5 mos.	6 wks.*
1996			
Service Manager	32	16 mos.	6 mos.
Administrative Coordinator	48	10 yrs.	10 mos.
Warehouse Supervisor	53	29 yrs.	18 mos.
Public Works Foreman	58	25 yrs.	14 mos.
Labour Relations Supervisor		14 yrs.	10 mos. (0 on appeal)
Foreman, Material Stores	44	24 yrs.	12 mos.
Supervisor	64	40 yrs.	24 mos.
Shift Supervisor	39	17 yrs.	12 mos.*
Assistant Chief Revenue Collector	40	20 yrs.	15 mos.
Van Foreman	48	19 yrs.	12 mos.
Mechanic Group Leader	60	22 yrs.	16 mos. (14 mos. originally)
Sales Supervisor	63	19 yrs.	7 mos.
Office Supervisor	50	15 yrs.	3 mos.*
1997			
Supervisor		21 yrs.	18 mos.
Lead hand, material handling	32	8 yrs.	6 mos.
Mechanical Supervisor, Project Employee	65	3 yrs.	0 (12 mos. at trial)
Assistant to Department Head	35	6 wks.	4.5 mos.
Shift Supervisor	35	15 yrs.	12 mos.
Office Supervisor	36	16 yrs.	12 mos.
Maintenance Planner (Millwright)	47	15 yrs.	15 mos.
1999			
Foreman	47	21 yrs.	15 mos.*
Seasonal Superintendent & Head Greenskeeper		11 yrs.	6 mos.
Yard Foreman		6 yrs.	5 mos.

---

* Provisional assessment only.

APPENDIX 4   467

Position	Age	Length of Service	Period of Notice
Body Shop Foreman/Assistant Manager	35	6 yrs.	7 mos.
Probationary Production Supervisor		6 mos.	5 mos.***
Assistant Warehouse Manager	38	14 yrs.	12 mos.
2000			
Child Care Supervisor	54	10 yrs.	11 mos.***
Yard Supervisor/ Operations Manager	45	9 yrs.	18 mos.***
Foreman	42	20 yrs.	14 mos.
2001			
Technical Maintenance Supervisor	49	22.5 yrs.	15 mos.+8 mos.***
Warehouse Supervisor		22 yrs.	12 mos.
2002			
Mail Room Supervisor		19 yrs.	20.5 mos.+6.5 mos.***
Waitress/Restaurant Supervisor	59	13.5 yrs.	16 mos.***
2003			
Welder, Supervisor	39	16 yrs.	13 mos.*
Maintenance Supervisor	51	31 yrs.	28 mos.
Shift Supervisor	52	32 yrs.	28 mos.

F. REASONABLE NOTICE PERIODS — PROFESSIONALS: 1987 – PRESENT

Position	Age	Length of Service	Period of Notice
1987			
Engineer	46	12 yrs.	12 mos.
Mechanical Engineer	44	3.5 yrs.	10 mos.
Assistant Controller	—	2 wks.	6 mos.
Planner	—	6 yrs.	3 mos.
Engineer	45	10 yrs.	6 mos.

* Provisional assessment only.
*** Notice increased due to employer's conduct.

Position	Age	Length of Service	Period of Notice
Dealership Accountant	46	10 yrs.	12 mos.
Estimating Engineer	58	8 yrs.	10.5 mos.
Planning Forester	—	9 yrs.	10 mos.
Project Engineer	54	6 yrs.	7.5 mos.
Financial Planner	—	2.5 yrs.	3 mos.
Lawyer	—	4 mos.	6 mos.
Chemical Engineer	38	18 mos.	3 mos.
1988			
Forestry Engineer	61	10 yrs.	20 mos.
Senior Psychologist, Forensic Services	53	27.5 yrs.	2 yrs.
Project Engineer	39	4.5 yrs.	6 mos.*
Specifications Engineer	41	15 yrs.	14 mos.
Geomechanics Supervisor	34	4 yrs.	9 mos.
Architect	54	4 yrs.	20 mos.
Design Engineering Supervisor	60	24 yrs.	15 mos.
Corporate Counsel	—	13 mos.	5 mos.
Veterinarian	—	6 mos.	2 mos.
1989			
Resource Economist	43	2 yrs.	6 mos.
Engineer, Construction Project Superintendent	43	2.5 yrs.	6 mos.
Engineer	45	13 yrs.	15 mos.
Plant Engineer	49	15 yrs.	9 mos.**
Actuary Pension Consultant	—	4 yrs.	12 mos.
"Skilled Professional"	37	2 yrs.	4 mos.
Engineer, Divisional Vice President	47	15 yrs.	12 mos.
1990			
Engineer, Manager of Engineering	43	13 yrs.	10 mos.
Engineer, Project Manager	33	9 yrs.	8 mos.
Specialist Engineer	33	10 yrs.	9 mos.
Engineer, Supervisor	51	13 yrs.	10 mos.
Design Engineer	29	8 yrs.	7 mos.
Pharmacist	—	2-½ yrs.	3 mos.

* Provisional assessment only.
** Notice reduced due to "near cause" or failure to mitigate.

Position	Age	Length of Service	Period of Notice
Senior Engineer	—	21 yrs.	24 mos.*
1991			
Lease Administrator, In-house Counsel	36	3 yrs.	8 mos.
Controller	—	11 yrs.	15 mos.
Director of Nursing	47	16 yrs.	18 mos.
Doctor	—	5 mos.	4 mos.
Controller	40	2.5 yrs.	8 mos.
Senior Economist	"young"	4 yrs.	6 mos.
Registered Nurse	57	27 yrs.	12 mos.
1992			
Land Supervisor	48	20 yrs.	18 mos.
Director of Pharmacy	43	7 yrs.	12 mos.
Director of Nursing	59	25 yrs.	22 mos.
Comptroller	64	5 yrs.	6 mos.**
1993			
Chemical Engineer	45	22 yrs.	18 mos.
Controller	—	4 mos.	1 mo.
Engineer/Salesman	42	25 yrs.	16 mos.*
1994			
Mechanical Engineer/Manager	59	2 yrs.	4 mos.
Mining Engineer/ Mill Shift Supervisor	54	22 yrs.	16 mos.
Nurse/Unit Manager, Obstetrics Ward	57	37 yrs.	21 mos.
Mechanical Engineer	early 30's	4 yrs.	6 mos.*
Engineer	47	17 yrs.	15 mos.**
Medical Director, Transfusion Centre	53	14 yrs.	20 mos.**
Controller/Office Manager	47	20 mos.	4 mos.
Mechanical Engineer	56	35 yrs.	18 mos.
1995			
Controller	42	6.5 mos.	5 mos.
Geologist	38	9 yrs.	12 mos.
Controller	37	4 yrs.	7 mos.

* Provisional assessment only.
** Notice reduced due to "near cause" or failure to mitigate.

Position	Age	Length of Service	Period of Notice
Director, Nursing & Support Services	49	21 yrs.	18 mos.
Comptroller	50	18 mos.	7 mos.
Engineering Manager	42	16 yrs.	15 mos.
Research Economist	—	10 mos.	9 mos.
1996			
Design Engineer	34	6 yrs.	7 mos.
Warehouse Supervisor	53	29 yrs.	18 mos.
Public Works Foreman	58	25 yrs.	14 mos.
Labour Relations Supervisor	—	14 yrs.	10 mos.
Foreman	44	24 yrs.	12 mos.
Supervisor	64	40 yrs.	24 mos.
Shift Supervisor	39	17 yrs.	12 mos.*
Assistant Chief Revenue Collector	40	20 yrs.	15 mos.
Comptroller	51	4 yrs.	6 mos.
Doctor			18 mos.
Electrical Engineer		10 yrs.	12 mos.
Electrical Engineer		26 yrs.	12 mos.
Assistant Director of Nursing	53	28 yrs.	24 mos.
1997			
Mechanical Engineer	44	16 yrs.	15 mos.
Chartered Accountant	51	7.5 yrs.	8 mos.
1998			
Lawyer	35	4 yrs.	8 mos.
Survey Engineer	56	32 yrs.	24 mos.***
1999			
Computer Analyst & Engineer	39	7.5 yrs.	7.5 mos. + 1.5 mos.***
Psychiatrist	53	21 yrs.	20 mos.
2000			
Electrical Engineer	52	6 yrs.	15 mos.
Geological/Junior Manager		5 yrs.	7 mos.
Manager, Internal Audit (Chartered Accountant)	35	22 mos.	5 mos.*

* Provisional assessment only.
*** Notice increased due to employer's conduct.

APPENDIX 4   471

Position	Age	Length of Service	Period of Notice
Controller		20 mos.	3 mos.
2001			
Financial Advisor, Preferred Shares	49	4 yrs.	17 mos.
Therapist		7 yrs.	8 mos.
Actuary	60	9 yrs.	12 mos.
2002			
Manager & Professional Engineer		20 yrs.	116 weeks (80 weeks on appeal)
2003			
Senior Staff Engineer	47	19 yrs.	15 mos.

G. REASONABLE NOTICE PERIODS — EDUCATION EMPLOYEES: 1987 – PRESENT

Position	Age	Length of Service	Period of Notice
1988			
Teacher	—	4 yrs.	12 mos.
1991			
Resident Counselor	45	13 yrs.	15 mos. (0 on appeal)
1992			
Director of Education	54	10 yrs.	12 mos.
1994			
Educational Administrator	50	2 yrs.	8 mos.
Director of Education		6 yrs.	5 mos.
Teacher's Assistant		8 yrs.	7 mos.
1997			
Probationary Overseas Ditching Instructor		4 yrs.	2 wks.[*]
1998			
Adjunct Professor		14 yrs.	18 mos.
2000			
Registrar		6 yrs.	12 mos.[***]

[*] Provisional assessment only.
[***] Notice increased due to employer's conduct.

Position	Age	Length of Service	Period of Notice
2001			
Dean		8 yrs.	9 mos.
2002			
Part-time Teacher		5.5 mos.	1 mo.

H. REASONABLE NOTICE PERIODS — ADMINISTRATORS: 1987 – PRESENT

Position	Age	Length of Service	Period of Notice
1987			
Chief Estimator	54	12 yrs.	15 mos.
Director of Personnel & Purchasing	—	9 mos.	5 mos.
1988			
Office Manager	53	5 yrs.	8 mos.
Town Manager	—	5 yrs.	15 mos.[*]
Head of Accounting	—	3 yrs.	6 mos.
Clerk/Administrator	44	2.5 yrs.	6 mos.
Bookkeeper	36	12 yrs.	9 mos.
Approving Officer, Subdivision Applications	—	9 yrs.	10 mos.
Deputy Minister of Fisheries	46	9 yrs.	1 yr.
Purchasing Manager	—	8 yrs.	6 mos.
1989			
Regional Manager	—	13 yrs.	15 mos.[*]
Deputy Minister of Justice, Deputy Attorney General	49	16 yrs.	18 mos.
Insurance Claims Manager	66	5.5 yrs.	8 mos.
Manager of Human Resources	—	5 yrs.	10 mos.
Municipal Clerk	—	9 yrs.	9 mos.[*]
Personnel Coordinator	—	0	6 mos.
Wholesale Lumber Trader	42	6.5 mos.	3 mos.
Office Manager	54	13 yrs.	8 mos.

[*] Provisional assessment only.

Position	Age	Length of Service	Period of Notice
1990			
Nursing Home Administrator	—	2 yrs.	4 mos.
Office Manager	—	5 yrs.	6 mos.
1991			
Senior Buyer	—	11 yrs.	10 mos. (0 on appeal)
Director of Nursing	47	16 yrs.	18 mos.
Human Resources Supervisor	31	11 yrs.	6 mos.
Human Resources Manager	52	7.5 yrs.	12 mos.
Senior Warranty Administrator	43	7.5 yrs.	9 mos.
Assistant Buyer	—	15 yrs.	6 mos.
1992			
Director of Pharmacy	43	7 yrs.	12 mos.
Director of Nursing	59	25 yrs.	22 mos.
Residential Property Supervisor	25	13 mos.	4 mos.
Estimator/Manager	61	3 mos.	1 mo.
Office & Personnel Manager	—	2 yrs.	6 mos.
Human Resources Coordinator	36	10 yrs.	8 mos.
Operations Analyst	—	8.5 yrs.	8 mos.
Director, Student Affairs	—	9 yrs.	8 mos.
Office Manager/ Bookkeeper	35	2 yrs. p/t, 2 yrs. f/t	8 mos.
1993			
Director, Corporate Communications	36	3.5 yrs.	6 mos.
Manager, Administration	—	16 yrs.	11 mos.
Quality Assurance Representative	—	5 yrs.	6 mos.*
Mutual Funds Administrator	50	12 yrs.	9 mos.
Quality Assurance Department Head	46	20.5 yrs.	22 mos.
Quality Control Engineer	45	21 yrs.	8.5 mos.

* Provisional assessment only.

Position	Age	Length of Service	Period of Notice
Coordinator, National Systems Audit	—	5 yrs.	12 mos.
Loans Officer	36	3 yrs.	3 mos.
Major Loss Litigation Specialist	55	21 yrs.	18 mos.
Senior Claims Adjuster	57	13 yrs.	16 mos.
1994			
Supervisor, Human Resources, Shipping, Warehousing & Quality Assurance	54	34 yrs.	18 mos.
Purchasing Agent	62	11 yrs.	12 mos.
Quality Control Inspector	—	5.25 yrs.	4 mos.
Director, Computer Services	—	10 yrs.	8 mos.
Office Supervisor	31	10 yrs.	5 mos.*
Banker	43	2 wks.	1 mo.*
Controller/Office Manager	47	20 mos.	4 mos.
Nursing Home Administrator	54	22 yrs.	8 mos.
Band Manager & Educational Administrator	50	2 yrs.	8 mos.
Manager, Respiratory Services	55	32 yrs.	18 mos.
1995			
Manager of Administration	52	1 yr.	6 mos.
Quality Control Analyst	43	17 yrs.	13 mos.
Buyer	39	5 yrs.	6 mos.
Chief Building Official/ By-Law Enforcement	47	7.5 yrs.	6 mos.
Senior Business Analyst	41	14.5 mos.	12 wks.
Technical Representative	—	10 yrs.	10 mos.
Government Services Underwriter	40	11 yrs.	12 mos.
Group Representative	37	16 yrs.	14 mos.
Superintendent, Human Resources, Woodlands Operation	56	30 yrs.	20 mos.
Payroll Accountant	—	19 yrs.	14 mos.

* Provisional assessment only.

APPENDIX 4 475

Position	Age	Length of Service	Period of Notice
Insurance Adjuster	53	18 yrs.	24 mos.
Director, Human Resources	—	38 mos.	7 mos.
Sales & Service Manager, Accounts Receivable Clerk	27	3 yrs.	15 wks.*
Director, Nursing & Support Services	49	21 yrs.	18 mos.
Administrative Assistant	—	6 yrs.	9 mos.
Purchaser	52	24 yrs.	18 mos.
1996			
Accounts Receivable Manager	51	22 yrs.	17 mos.
Financial Director & Office Manager	59	22 yrs.	20 mos.
Comptroller	51	4 yrs.	10 mos.
Doctor	—	—	18 mos.
Electrical Engineer	—	10 yrs.	12 mos.
Electrical Engineer	—	26 yrs.	12 mos.
Assistant Director of Nursing	53	28 yrs.	24 mos.
Accounts Receivable Manager	51	22 yrs.	17 mos.
Office Supervisor	50	15 yrs.	3 mos.*
1997			
Office Manager	45	6 yrs.	12 mos.
Insurance Appraiser		6 yrs.	6 mos.*
Purchasing Agent	43	16 yrs.	12 mos.
Administrator		10 yrs.	16 mos.
Assistant Administrator		10 yrs.	8 mos.
Executive Assistant to CEO	34	7.5 mos.	5 mos.
Administrator	62	10.5 yrs.	12 mos.
1998			
Financial Director & Office Manager	59	22 yrs.	20 mos. (0 on appeal)
Credit Manager	55	15.5 yrs.	12 mos.
Manager, Permits Department	62	41 yrs.	21 mos.

* Provisional assessment only.

Position	Age	Length of Service	Period of Notice
Administrator, Manager	43	3 yrs.	8 mos.****
International Banker		approx. 3 days	3 mos. (12 mos. at trial)
Hotel Manager/ Administrator	41	4 yrs.	12 mos.***

1999

Position	Age	Length of Service	Period of Notice
Administrative Director	41	15 yrs.	16 mos. reduced to 12 mos.**
Probationary Town Manager & Town Clerk	34	9 mos.	9 mos.
Quality Assurance Consultant	40	15 mos.	5 mos.

2000

Position	Age	Length of Service	Period of Notice
Senior Mortgage Collections	33	10 yrs.	6 mos.

2001

Position	Age	Length of Service	Period of Notice
Financial Advisor, Preferred Shares	49	4 yrs.	17 mos.
Actuary	60	9 yrs.	12 mos.
Town Clerk		16 yrs.	16 mos.
Town Treasurer		8 yrs.	8 mos.
Part-time Service Representative		20 mos.	10 wks.
Administrator		6 yrs.	8 mos.*

2002

Position	Age	Length of Service	Period of Notice
Communications Consultant		1 yr.	9 mos.+3 mos.***
Placement Agent		7.5 yrs.	8 mos.

---

*   Provisional assessment only.
** Notice reduced due to "near cause" or failure to mitigate.
*** Notice increased due to employer's conduct.

APPENDIX 4   477

I. REASONABLE NOTICE PERIODS — SALES/MARKETING EMPLOYEES AND MANAGERS: 1987 – PRESENT

Position	Age	Length of Service	Period of Notice
1987			
Regional Sales Manager	55	18 yrs.	16 mos.
Real Estate Agent	—	3 yrs.	2 mos.
Commercial Real Estate Salesman	—	3.5 yrs.	7 mos.
District Sales Representative	34	10 yrs.	12 mos.
Probationary Sales Supervisor	34	3 mos.	1 mo.[*]
Sales Manager	29	7.5 yrs.	7.5 mos.
Lumber Salesman	32	2 yrs.	4 mos.
Assistant Regional Marketing V.P.	47	21 yrs.	18 mos.
Senior Salesman	42	7 yrs.	2.5 mos.
Sales Manager	49	18 yrs.	3 mos.
1988			
Regional Sales Manager	—	18 yrs.	12 mos. (0 on appeal)
Sales Manager	51	9 yrs.	12 mos.
Sales Manager	40	5 wks.	4 mos.
Salesman	—	8 yrs.	8 mos. (3 mos. on appeal settlement)
Senior Salesman	57	6 mos.	4 mos.
Salesman	34	5 yrs.	4 mos.
Salesman	53	2 yrs.	3 mos.
Sales-Secretary	29	1.5 yrs.	7 wks.
Business Economic Advisor, Marketing Group	52	22 yrs.	12 mos.
Marketing Vice President	—	3 yrs.	4 mos.
1989			
Merchandising Coordinator	—	17 yrs.	8 mos.
Salesman	—	1 yr.	2 wks.
Manager, Govt. Accounts	57	13 yrs.	12 mos.

[*] Provisional assessment only.

Position	Age	Length of Service	Period of Notice
Salesman	—	35 yrs.	12 mos.
Real Estate Agent Nominee	42	2.5 yrs.	3 mos.
Marketing Manager	41	4.5 mos.	6 mos.
Sales Manager/ Business Manager	45	11.5 yrs.	12 mos.
Sales Manager	37	18 mos.	2 mos.
Probationary Salesman	—	8 wks.	2 wks.
Division Sales Manager	41	10 mos.	2 mos.
Western District Sales Manager	39	20 mos.	3 mos.**
Regional Sales Manager	50's	21 yrs.	21 mos.
General Sales Manager	53	4.5 mos.	7 wks.
Marketing Manager	42	11 yrs.	12 mos.*
Canadian Sales Manager & V.P.	38	11 yrs.	12 mos.*
Sales Manager	—	6.5 mos.	3-4 mos.
Salesman	40	1 yr.	4 mos.
Sales Employee	52	9 mos. prev. 10 yrs.	6 mos.
Salesman	—	2 yrs.	3 mos.**
Salesman	37	8 yrs.	7 mos.
1990			
Salesman	52	6 yrs.	6 mos.
Car Salesman	—	13 mos.	1 mo.
District Sales Representative	52	20 yrs.	12 mos.
Sales Manager	—	3.5 yrs.	12 mos.
Commercial Printing Salesman	61	11.5 yrs.	12 mos.
District Sales Manager	45	5 yrs.	8 mos.
Marketing Manager	38	13 days	10.5 mos.
Lumber Salesman	56	31 yrs.	10 mos.
Marketing Manager	—	22 mos.	4 mos.*
Lumber Trader	60	24 yrs.	12 mos.
1991			
Sales Agent	—	15 yrs.	8 mos.*
Sales Representative	42	3 yrs.	4 mos.

*   Provisional assessment only.
**   Notice reduced due to "near cause" or failure to mitigate.

APPENDIX 4   479

Position	Age	Length of Service	Period of Notice
Sales Manager	36	9.5 yrs.	13 mos.*
Regional Sales Manager	41	8 yrs.	9 mos.
Salesman/Sales Manager	40	2 wks.	1 mo.
District Sales Manager	34	13 yrs.	1 yr.
Division Sales Manager	51	28 yrs.	18 mos.
Manager, Account Executive, Sales	44	12 yrs.	10 mos.
Sales Manager	34	16 mos.	8 mos.
Vice President, Sales	37	9 yrs.	12 mos.
Salesman	50's	8 yrs.	8 mos.
Salesman	42	3.5 yrs.	2.5 mos.
Store Sales Manager	40	18 yrs.	12 mos.
Computer Salesman	42	5 mos.	6 mos.
Manager, Construction Sales	41	4 yrs.	14 mos.
1992			
Sales Representative	49	21 mos.	5 mos.
District Sales Manager	41	11.5 yrs.	12 mos.
General Sales Manager	66	20 yrs.	20 mos.
Sales Representative	—	12.5 yrs.	12 mos.*
Salesman/Business Manager	—	5 yrs.	4 mos.
General Sales Manager	—	5 yrs.	8 mos.
Sales Manager	40	12 yrs.	15 mos.
Canadian Marketing Manager	41	22 yrs.	22 mos.
New Car Sales	—	2 yrs.	3 mos.*
Retail Marketing Representative	56	23 yrs.	20 mos.
Sales Manager	56	4 yrs.	12 mos.
Design Consultant	"young"	16 mos.	5 mos.
Vice President, Marketing	46	5 mos.	16 wks.
Senior Marketing Rep.	—	29 yrs.	12 mos.*
Salesman	37	10 yrs.	6 mos.
Sales Rep.	—	5 yrs.	5 mos.
Contractor Sales Representative	37	10 yrs.	4 mos.*
Salesman	37	22 mos.	3 mos.

* Provisional assessment only.

Position	Age	Length of Service	Period of Notice
Regional Sales Manager	—	11 yrs.	12 mos.*
1993			
Sales Rep.	41	2.5 mos.	3 mos.
Branch Sales Manager	45	26.5 yrs.	17 mos.
Supervisory Salesman	32	12 yrs.	30 wks.
Salesman	—	12.5 yrs.	12 mos.*
Regional Sales Manager	—	13 yrs.	15 mos.*
Sales Manager	52	3 yrs.	6 mos.
Sales Director	—	9 mos.	5 mos.
Account Executive	34	8-9 yrs.	8 mos.
Insurance Broker	48	4 yrs.	8 mos.
National Sales Manager	—	9 mos.	6 mos.
Sales Representative	59	21.5 yrs.	18 mos.
Territory Manager	48	11.5 yrs.	9 mos.
Branch Manager	43	1 yr.	3 mos.*
Treasurer, Director, Inside Sales	54	25 yrs.	20 mos.
Senior Sales Manager	46	26 yrs.	15 mos.
Salesman	39	8.5 yrs.	9.5 mos.*
Engineer/Salesman	42	25 yrs.	16 mos.*
1994			
Salesman	51	9 yrs.	6 mos.
Area Manager	43	7 yrs.	12 mos.
Sales Manager	48	8.5 yrs.	12 mos.
District Sales Manager	39	6 yrs.	10 mos.
Advertising Salesperson	50	10 yrs.	15 wks.
Salesman	—	4 yrs.	5 mos.**
Perfume Demonstrator	49	18 mos.	10 wks.
Sales Manager, Postal Automation	58	4 yrs.	5 mos.*
Territorial Sales Manager	63	17 yrs.	12 mos.
Regional Sales Director	40	4.5 yrs.	3.5 mos.
Advertising Salesperson	36	13 yrs.	12 mos.
Salesperson	35	4 yrs.	5 mos.
Regional Marketing Manager	42	6.5 yrs.	12 mos.

* Provisional assessment only.
** Notice reduced due to "near cause" or failure to mitigate.

APPENDIX 4   481

Position	Age	Length of Service	Period of Notice
Heavy Equipment Salesperson	65	8 yrs.	12 mos.
Leasing Representative	56	10 yrs.	8 mos.
Salesman	—	16 yrs.	9 mos.
Marketing & Sales Manager	—	0	1 yr.
Regional Account Manager	28	6 yrs.	6 mos.
Marketing Representative	—	3 yrs.	4 mos.
Sales Manager	61	30 yrs.	24 mos.
Technical Service Rep/Salesman	60	22 yrs.	12 mos.
Life Insurance Salesman	53	18 yrs.	18 mos.
Sales Manager	52	5 yrs.	12 mos.
1995			
Salesman	59	14 yrs.	15 mos.
Sales	36	5 wks.	30 days
Sales	38	3.5 wks.	30 days
Sales	32	3.5 wks.	30 days
Senior Sales Rep	40	14.5 yrs.	15 mos.
Sales Manager, Catalogue Desk	55	27 yrs.	75 wks.
Negotiator	—	8 yrs.	6 mos.
Salesperson	55	8 yrs.	8 mos.
Regional Sales Manager	46	9 yrs.	15 mos.
Business Development Manager	43	4.5 yrs.	10 mos.
Sales Manager	—	5 yrs.	9 mos.
Salesperson	—	5 yrs.	5 mos.
Sales Rep.	—	4 mos.	6 mos.
Senior Sales Executive	59	27 yrs.	22 mos. plus 2 mos.
National Marketing Development Manager	54	8 yrs.	9 mos.
Sales Supervisor	—	8 yrs.	12 mos.
Marketing Representative	37	9 yrs.	12 mos.
Sales Executive	—	25 yrs.	18 mos.
Regional Sales Manager	57	3.5 yrs.	12 mos.
Salesperson	47	2.5 yrs.	8 mos.
Sales Agent		26 yrs.	14 mos.
1996			
Senior Sales Person	57	7 yrs.	10 mos.

Position	Age	Length of Service	Period of Notice
Sales Representative	62	31 yrs.	16 mos.
Sales Manager	46	4 yrs.	6 mos.
Equipment Procurement Manager	62	24 yrs.	18 mos.
Sales Supervisor	63	19 yrs.	7 mos.
Salesman	52	22 yr.s	20 mos.
Market Analyst/ Salesperson		3 yrs.	6 mos.
Director, Sales & Marketing	47	18 yrs.	15 mos.
1997			
Regional Sales Manager	44	5.5 mos.	12 mos.
Account Manager		4 yrs.	6 mos.
Commission Salesperson		25 yrs.	18 mos.
Salesperson	36	4 yrs.	5 mos.
Marketing Manager	56	14 yrs.	15 mos.
Salesperson	31	9 yrs.	7 mos.
Sales Manager	39	10 mos.	5 mos.
General Sales Manager/ Salesperson	71	30 yrs.	16 mos.
1998			
Sales Agent	34	8 yrs.	8 mos.[*]
Junior Sales Representative		2.5 mos.	11 mos.[***]
Sales Manager	37	13 yrs.	13 mos. increased to 19 mos.[***]
National Sales Manager	39	almost 3 yrs.	8 mos.
1999			
Sales/Distribution Agent		11 yrs.	9 mos.(15 mos. at trial)
Regional Sales Manager	40	17 yrs.	10 mos.
Regional Sales	47	10.5 yrs.	12 mos.
Customer Service Representative		34 mos.	4 mos.
National Sales Manager	57	28 yrs.	24 mos.
Sales Manager	51	28.5 yrs.	22 mos.
Senior Sales Representative	54	30 yrs.	24 mos. reduced to 22 mos.[**]

[*] Provisional assessment only.
[**] Notice reduced due to "near cause" or failure to mitigate.
[***] Notice increased due to employer's conduct.

Position	Age	Length of Service	Period of Notice
National Sales Manager, US subsidiary		4 yrs.	6 mos.
Sales Representative	54	27 yrs.	17 mos.
Promotions Manager		10 yrs.	10 mos. increased to 12 mos.***
Derivatives Salesman	41	16 yrs.	12 mos.*
Real Estate Agent		6 yrs.	6 mos.
2000			
Office Manager, Insurance Broker		6 yrs.	12 mos. (42 mos. at trial)***
Leasing Manager	45 (approx.)	16 mos.	12 mos.
Head, Construction Contract Sales		5 yrs.	2 mos.*
Investment Dealer/Broker	30's	4 yrs.	16 mos.***
Investment Advisor		18 yrs.	18 mos.*
Sales Agent		19 mos. (non-employee)	5 mos. (on appeal)
2001			
Bond Salesman		5 yrs.	13 mos. (12 mos. at trial)
Marketing Employee	44	39 mos.	8 mos. (10 mos. at trial)
Vice President, Sales & Marketing		13 yrs.	18 mos.*
Regional Sales Manager		13 yrs.	16 mos.
Salesperson	48	1 yr.	24 mos.***
Sales Manager	52	18 yrs.	18 mos.
Salesperson	57	1 yr.	9 mos.***
District Sales Representative	48	17 yrs.	15 mos.
Auto Salesperson		4 yrs.	4.5 mos.
Salesman	53	3 wks.	7.5 mos.***
2002			
Branch Manager/Salesman	52	5 yrs.	8 mos.***
New car sales manager		4 yrs.	2.5 mos.
Insurance Sales Representative	36	1.5 yrs.	6 mos.

---

* Provisional assessment only.
*** Notice increased due to employer's conduct.

Position	Age	Length of Service	Period of Notice
Sales Administrator	28	6 mos.	1 mo.*
Insurance Broker		2 yrs.	6 mos.
Salesman	65	36 yrs.	2 yrs.
2003			
Salesman	48	24 yrs.	15 mos.

J. REASONABLE NOTICE PERIODS — TECHNICAL AND SKILLED EMPLOYEES: 1987 – PRESENT

Position	Age	Length of Service	Period of Notice
1987			
Dental Assistant	—	4 yrs.	4 mos.
Chef	—	1.5 yrs.	7 wks.**
Apprentice Millwright	—	11 mos.	4 wks.
Assistant Research Technician	29	17 mos.	12 wks.
Marine Electronic Technician	55	20 yrs.	15 mos.
Design Draftsman	61	8 yrs.	12 mos.
Sales Forecaster	45	16 yrs.	4 mos.
Management Security Captain	—	20 yrs.	17 mos.
1988			
Senior Land Supervisor	49	28 yrs.	18 mos.
Diesel Mechanic	—	1 yr.	1 mo.
Meat Cutter	—	10.5 yrs.	9 mos.
Solder Operator/ Senior Assembler	29	6 yrs.	8 mos.
Diesel Mechanic/ Branch Manager	56	16 yrs.	12 mos.
1989			
Technologist	—	6 yrs.	8.5 mos.
Baker	62	18 yrs.	12 mos.*

---

* Provisional assessment only.
** Notice reduced due to "near cause" or failure to mitigate.

Position	Age	Length of Service	Period of Notice
Gas Field Operator	—	7 yrs.	6 mos.*
Auto Body Mechanic	40	10 yrs.	8 mos.
1990			
Senior Research & Development Technician	53	8 yrs.	9 mos.
Architectural Coordinator	—	6 mos.	4 mos.
Dental Assistant	—	13 yrs.	6 mos.
Ship's Master	—	11 yrs.	12 mos.
Radio Technician	27	4.5 yrs.	5 wks.
1991			
Maitre'd	—	25 yrs.	14 mos.
Boilerroom Operator/Watchman	58	17 mos.	2 mos., 9 days
Field Engineer	50	31 yrs.	15 mos.
Spray Painter	62	7 yrs.	18 wks.
1992			
Receptionist/Dental Assistant	—	25 yrs.	7.5 mos.
Stringing Foreman	—	18 yrs.	10 wks.
Drafting Project Coordinator	48	27 yrs.	16 mos.
Mechanic	33	2 yrs.	9 wks.
Programmer Analyst	53	13 yrs.	12 mos.
Boiler-room Power Engineer	—	5 yrs.	12 mos.*
Oil Furnace Technician	—	7 mos.	1 mo.
1993			
Engineering Assistant Technician	53	10 yrs.	10 mos.
Technician	53	3 yrs.	4 mos.
Machinery Designer	50	31 yrs.	18 mos.
Electrician	53	1 yr.	1 mo.*
Chef	45	8 mos.	3 mos.
Vice President, Production	46	15 yrs.	15 mos.
Senior Oilfield Operator	47	12 yrs.	10 mos.
Journeyman Litho-Stripper	50	18 mos.	4 mos.
Small Engine Mechanic	29	4 yrs.	3 mos.

* Provisional assessment only.

Position	Age	Length of Service	Period of Notice
1994			
Technical Support/ Customer Service Manager	29	4 yrs.	15 mos.
Chief Pilot	—	4 yrs.	6 mos.
Head, Technical Services	—	27 yrs.	18 mos.
Chief Technician	36	5 yrs.	6 mos.
Head Cook/ Kitchen Manager	—	7 yrs.	5 mos.
Heavy Duty Mechanic	—	9 yrs.	8 mos.**
Chef	—	2.5 yrs.	8 mos.*
Furniture Maker	65	20 yrs.	6-7 mos.
Lab Technician	48	8.25 yrs.	5 mos.
Colour Computer Operator	49	10.3 yrs.	6 mos.
Batch Maker	40	15 yrs.	9 mos.
1995			
Meter Technician	—	15 yrs.	6 mos.
Compositor	51	29 yrs.	6 mos.
Electrical Technician	—	14 yrs.	15 mos.
Auto Mechanic	56	16 yrs.	9 mos.
Auto Mechanic	59	26 yrs.	10 mos.*
Pilot	36	3.5 yrs.	5 mos.
Consumer Service Rep.	57	39 yrs.	20 mos.
Carpenter/Supervisor	45	5 yrs.	6 mos.
Carpenter	—	—	3 mos.
Salesperson	—	26 yrs.	14 mos.
1996			
Senior Equipment Technician	38	17 yrs.	16 mos.
Site Representative Surveyor	41	21 yrs.	19 mos.
Data Systems Manager	65	12 yrs.	10 mos.
Senior Salesperson	57	7 yrs.	10 mos.
Sales Representative	62	31 yrs.	16 mos.
Sales Manager	46	4 yrs.	6 mos.
Senior Technician	—	14.5 yrs.	10 mos.
Auto Mechanic	42	9 yrs.	7 mos.

* Provisional assessment only.
** Notice reduced due to "near cause" or failure to mitigate.

APPENDIX 4   487

Position	Age	Length of Service	Period of Notice
Senior Draughtsman		16 yrs.	11 mos.
Systems Engineer	51	33 yrs.	24 mos. (20 mos. on appeal)
Senior Systems Analyst		17 yrs.	18 mos.
Physical Plant Manager	40	12 yrs.	8 mos.
Cartographer		15 yrs.	5 mos.**
Manufacturing Engineering	46	22 yrs.	24 mos.
Light Tunnel Operator	58	5 yrs.	6 mos.
Repair Coordinator		15 yrs.	10 mos.
Senior Draftsman	55	17 yrs. Less 5 yrs.	15 mos.
Chief Stationary Engineer	61	29 yrs.	21 mos.
Probationary Pilot	47	4 mos.	2 mos.
1997			
Regional Sales Manager	44	5.5 mos.	12 mos.
Senior Architectural Technician	45	6 yrs.	8 mos.
Information Systems Manager	32	9 mos.	5 mos.
Carpenter	62	9 mos.	10 mos.*
Welder	50	7.5 yrs.	7 mos.
Head Chef	50	20 yrs.	18 mos.
Maintenance Planner/ Millwright	47	15 yrs.	15 mos.
Mechanical Welder		30 yrs.	12 mos. reduced to 6 mos.**
Computer Service Representative	34	3.25 yrs.	6 mos.
Electrician	44	10 yrs.	10 mos.
1998			
Electronics Technician	54	29 yrs.	20 mos.
Lead Hand Film Stripper	53	11 yrs.	11 mos.
Lab Technologist		19 yrs.	18 mos.*
Technical Support Analyst		12.5 yrs.	12 mos.
Computer Program Manager	45	19 yrs.	14 mos.+6 mos. – 4 mos.***,**

*   Provisional assessment only.
** Notice reduced due to "near cause" or failure to mitigate.
*** Notice increased due to employer's conduct.

Position	Age	Length of Service	Period of Notice
Computer Consultant	53	11 mos.	5 mos.
1999			
Computer Analyst & Engineer	39	7.5 yrs.	7.5 mos.+1.5 mos.
Computer Analyst	52	29.5mos.	7 mos.
Hairstylist	50	4 yrs+9 yrs.	6 mos.+6 mos.***
Cook	41	9 yrs.	8 mos.
Dental Assistant	55	18 yrs.	9 mos.
Body Shop Foreman/Assistant Manager	35	6 yrs.	7 mos.
2000			
Certified Dental Assistant		21 yrs.	12 mos.
Nurse/Receptionist		25 yrs.	18 mos.
Paste-Up Artist	38	18 yrs.	12 mos.*
Auto Body Technician		16 yrs.	12 mos.
2001			
Technical Consultant	53	31 yrs.	18 mos.
Welder	49	2 yrs.	2 mos. +1 mo.***
Draftsperson	52	22yrs.+3 yrs.	4 mos.
2002			
Temporary Dental Assistant		5 mos.	3 wks.
Systems Analyst	31	6 yrs.	5 mos.
Welder		14 yrs.	10 mos.
2003			
Welder, Supervisor	39	16 yrs.	13 mos.*
Marine Surveyor	48	19 yrs.	30 mos.***

---

* Provisional assessment only.
*** Notice increased due to employer's conduct.

K. REASONABLE NOTICE PERIODS — CLERICAL EMPLOYEES: 1987 – PRESENT

Position	Age	Length of Service	Period of Notice
1987			
Loans Clerk	44	2.25 yrs.	6 mos.
Keypunch Computer Operator	—	1 wk.	2 wks.
Senior Teller	34	7 yrs.	5 mos.
Assistant Controller	—	2 wks.	6 mos.
Part-time Cashier/Store Clerk	—	8 yrs.	8 wks.*
Senior Secretary	—	4 yrs.	3 mos.
Equipment Clerk	56	31 yrs.	12 mos.
Secretary/Office Manager	30	14 mos.	4 mos.
1988			
Senior Secretary	43	23 yrs.	18 mos. (0 on appeal)
Secretary	50	2.5 yrs.	3 mos.
Input Operator	—	8 yrs.	4 mos.*
Secretary/Salesperson	29	1.5 yrs.	7 wks.
Clerk	50	8.5 yrs.	6 mos.
Head of Accounting	—	3 yrs.	6 mos.
Bookkeeper	36	12 yrs.	9 mos.
Part-time Clerk	—	3 yrs.	17 wks.
Dental Receptionist	44	5 yrs.	6 mos.
Head Cashier	47	7 yrs.	3 mos.*
1989			
Consumer Loan Officer	—	6 yrs.	8 mos.*
Merchandising Coordinator	—	17 yrs.	8 mos.
Insurance Claims Adjuster	66	5.5 yrs.	8 mos.
RCMP Day Clerk	46	23 yrs.	12 mos.
Shift Clerk	27	7 mos.	3 mos.
Administrative Assistant	41	13.5 yrs.	8 mos.
Grocery Warehouse Costing Clerk	—	9 yrs.	6 mos.
Personnel Coordinator	—	0	6 mos.
Executive Secretary	39	1 mo.	4 mos.
Sales Secretary	41	13 yrs.	10 mos.

* Provisional assessment only.

Position	Age	Length of Service	Period of Notice
Senior Order Analyst	25	8 yrs.	4.5 mos.
Office Manager	54	13 yrs.	8 mos.
Data, Accounting & Payroll Clerk	—	15.5 yrs.	1 yr.
Personnel Services Assistant	53	15 yrs.	10 mos.
1990			
Clerical Worker	31	4 yrs.	8 wks.
Office Manager	—	5 yrs.	6 mos.
Accountant	—	3.5 mos.	2 wks.
1991			
Service Advisor	31	7 yrs.	18 mos.
Part-time Receptionist/Clerk	56	10 yrs.	5 mos.**
Service Advisor	—	20 yrs.	6 mos.*
Clerk IV	52	12 yrs.	9 mos.**
Cashier	—	21 mos.	8 wks.*
Grocery Clerk	34	12 yrs.	10 mos.
Service Manager	"young"	10.5 mos.	4 wks.
1992			
Receptionist/Dental Assistant	—	25 yrs.	7.5 mos.
Clerk Typist	65	43 yrs.	18 mos.
Human Resources Coordinator	36	10 yrs.	8 mos.
Supervisor, Stenography	—	11 yrs.	5 mos.
Office Manager/Bookkeeper	35	2 yrs. p/t, 2 yrs. f/t	8 mos.
1993			
Secretary	56	15 yrs.	4 mos.
Assistant Supervisor, Sales Support	—	15 yrs.	10 mos.
Supervisor, Credit Office	58	29.9 yrs.	47 wks.
Accounts Payable Clerk	—	4.5 yrs.	9 mos.**
Sales Secretary	51	6 yrs.	3 mos.
Loans Officer	36	3 yrs.	3 mos.
Order Clerk	44	4 yrs.	3 mos.
Senior Claims Adjuster	57	13 yrs.	16 mos.

* Provisional assessment only.
** Notice reduced due to "near cause" or failure to mitigate.

APPENDIX 4 491

Position	Age	Length of Service	Period of Notice
Major Loss Litigation Specialist	55	21 yrs.	18 mos.
1994			
Clerk-Typist	—	5 yrs.	4 mos.
Office Supervisor	31	10 yrs.	5 mos.[*]
Building Administrator	45	2 yrs.	4 mos.
Executive Secretary	36	8 yrs.	5.5 mos.
Junior Desk Trading Clerk	—	32 mos.	4 mos.
Part-time Cashier	—	11 yrs.	4 mos.
1995			
Assistant Underwriter	55	29 yrs.	12 mos.
Manager of Administration	52	1 yr.	6 mos.
Receptionist	53	16 yrs.	10 mos.[*]
Secretary	51	13 yrs.	8 mos.
Payroll Accountant	—	19 yrs.	14 mos.
Court Clerk	77	17.6 yrs.	12 mos.[*]
Sales & Service Manager, Accounts Receivable Clerk	27	3 yrs.	15 wks.[*]
Office Worker	53	27 yrs.	18 mos.
Senior Legal Secretary	—	3.5 yrs.	3 mos.
Office Person	—	7 yrs.	6 mos.
Preventive Dental Technician	—	8 mos.	5 wks.
1996			
Production Coordinator	50's	16 yrs.	16 mos.
Probationary Secretary	48	2.5 mos.	4 wks
Part-time Clerk/Bookkeeper	47	6 yrs.	5 mos.
Office Worker	25	33 mos.	1 mo.
Clerk	34	4 yrs.	10 wks.
1997			
Secretary	54	8 yrs.	7 mos.
Secretary	57	5 yrs. F/T, 3 yrs. P/T	5.5 mos.
Materials Purchasing Clerk	62	34 yrs.	18 mos.
Administrator		10 yrs.	16 mos.

[*] Provisional assessment only.

Position	Age	Length of Service	Period of Notice
Assistant Administrator		10 yrs.	8 mos.
Office Supervisor	36	16 yrs.	12 mos.
Payroll Clerk		1.5 yrs.	4 mos.
Secretary/Dispatcher	35	2 yrs.	8 wks.
Secretary		2.5 days	1 wk.
Clerical/Accounting	33	6.5 yrs.	8 mos.
Seasonal Clerk		20 yrs.	8 mos.
1998			
Office Manager		19 yrs.	9 mos.
Store Clerk	43	11 yrs.	10 mos.
Bookkeeper (Part-time)	62	18 yrs.	4 yrs.
Senior Deposit Account Clerk	47	20 yrs.	12 mos.
Office Manager	60	4 yrs.	10 mos. +3 mos.***
Law Clerk/Secretary/Immigration Consultant		18 mos.	4 mos. +3 mos.***
Bookkeeper	49	5 yrs.	7 mos.
1999			
Office Manager	41	16 yrs.	19.4 mos. (16 mos.+ E.S.A. severance pay)
Clerical Jobs	41	23 yrs.	18 mos.
Clerical Jobs	42	20 yrs.	16 mos.
Secretary	51	18 yrs.	13 mos.
Clerical Jobs	41	16 yrs.	13 mos.
Receptionist	27	2 yrs.	2 mos.
Office Manager		1 yr.	3 mos.
Office Manager/Bookkeeper		23 yrs	1 yr.
2000			
Accounts Receivable Clerk	60	18 yrs.	3 mos.+1 mo.***
Secretary/Clerical Assistant	54	12 yrs.	10 mos.
Nurse/Receptionist		25 yrs.	18 mos.
Paste-Up Artist	38	18 yrs.	12 mos.*
Teller	41	20 yrs.	15 mos.
Part-time Secretary	64	20 yrs.	18 mos.

* Provisional assessment only.
*** Notice increased due to employer's conduct.

Position	Age	Length of Service	Period of Notice
Office Manager		20 yrs.	14 mos.
2001			
Secretary	54	18 yrs.	9 mos.
Secretary/Office Manager	52	10 yrs.	7 mos. +5 mos.***
Legal Assistant	38	16.5 yrs.	10 mos.
Part-time Member Service Representative		20 mos.	10 wks.
2002			
Office Manager	41	12 yrs.	13 mos. +2 mos.***
2003			
Clerical Worker	45	19 yrs.	12 mos.*
Property Manager, Exec. Assistant to Administrator	46	15 yrs.+10 yrs.	24 mos.

L. REASONABLE NOTICE PERIODS —LABOURERS: 1987 – PRESENT

Position	Age	Length of Service	Period of Notice
1987			
Parking Lot Attendant	52	5 yrs.	6 mos.
Waitress	—	2 yrs.	10 weeks
1988			
Chamber Maid	—	6 yrs.	4 mos.
Waitress	27	1 mo.	3 wks.
1989			
Dye Department Worker	26	7 yrs.	6 mos.
General Office Worker/Bus Driver	56	38 yrs.	20 mos.
1990			
Probationary Security Shift Supervisor	30	less than 90 days	2 wks.
Maintenance Worker	54	23 yrs.	15 mos.
Security Guard & Last Employee	53	24 yrs.	3 mos.

* Provisional assessment only.
*** Notice increased due to employer's conduct.

Position	Age	Length of Service	Period of Notice
1991			
Machine Operator	—	6 yrs.	3 mos.*
Electroplater	—	2.5 yrs.	16 wks.*
Machine Operator	—	8.5 mos.	2 mos.*
Shipper/Receiver	20's	4 yrs.	4 wks.
1992			
Polisher Grinder	—	—	5 mos.
Labourer	—	0	3 mos.
Seasonal Road Worker	—	16 yrs.	6 mos.
Delivery Person/Stock Clerk	25	5.5 mos.	2 wks.*
1993			
Service Station Attendant	44	17 yrs.	8 mos.
Machine Operator/Supervisor	—	9 yrs.	9 mos.*
Labourer	47	7 yrs.	14 wks.
4 Drivers	40's	15-16 yrs.	34-36 wks.
Swamper	40	18 yrs.	40 wks.
Swamper	33	14.8 yrs.	31 wks.
Driver	43	10.65 yrs.	22 wks.
Roustabout	42	1 yr.	4 mos.
Lathe Operator	58	7 yrs.	9 mos.
Helper	—	2 yrs.	6 wks.
Technician	—	3 yrs.	8 wks.
Technician	—	3 yrs.	8 wks.
Senior Technician	—	7 yrs.	18 wks.
Senior Technician	—	8 yrs.	20 wks.
Bin Chaser (Lumber Sorter)	38	9 mos.	3 wks.
Hourly-rated Employee	51	3.5 yrs.	9 mos.
Assistant Counselor/Maintenance Worker	—	under 3 yrs.	2 wks.
1994			
Production Worker	51	19 yrs.	8.25 mos.
Seasonal Greenskeeper	63	30 yrs.	1 yr. (1 season)
Seasonal Greenskeeper	—	10 yrs.	6 wks.*
Batch Maker	40	15 yrs.	9 mos.

* Provisional assessment only.

APPENDIX 4   495

Position	Age	Length of Service	Period of Notice
1995			
Partsman	52	14 yrs.	5 mos.
Spare Bus Driver	52	4 yrs.	2 mos.
Bartender	45	14 yrs.	8 mos.
Farm Hand	—	—	1.5 mos.
Fabric Cutter	62	21 yrs.	2.5 mos.
Delivery Courier	—	4 yrs.	1 mo.
Security Guard	—	4 yrs.	2 mos.
Labourer	34	16 yrs.	6 mos.
1996			
Senior Technician	—	14.5 yrs.	10 mos.
Auto Mechanic	42	9 yrs.	7 mos.
Senior Draughtsman	—	16 yrs.	11 mos.
Systems Engineer	51	33 yrs.	24 mos.
Senior Systems Analyst	—	17 yrs.	18 mos.
Physical Plant Manager	40	12 yrs.	8 mos.
Cartographer	—	15 yrs.	5 mos.**
Manufacturing Engineering Technologist	46	22 yrs.	24 mos.
Light Tunnel Operator	58	5 yrs.	6 mos.
Repair Coordinator	—	15 yrs.	10 mos.
Chambermaid	—	4.5 yrs.	4.5 mos.
Lead Hand	43	21 yrs.	1 yr.
Truck Driver	47	5.5 yrs.	5 mos.
Cut Saw Operator	51	5 yrs.	20 wks.
Counter/Parts Person		12 yrs.	9 mos.*
Truck Driver	51	27 mos.	2 mos.
Technician		6 yrs.	24 wks.
Drywaller		20 mos.	6 mos.
1997			
Shipper/Receiver	40	28 mos.	4 mos.
Shipper	39	10 yrs.	10 mos.
Shipper/Receiver	63	19 yrs.	10 mos.
Forklift Operator/ Cycle Counter	45	20 yrs.	12 mos.
Restaurant Hostess	59	32 yrs.	16 mos.

---

*   Provisional assessment only.
** Notice reduced due to "near cause" or failure to mitigate.

Position	Age	Length of Service	Period of Notice
1998			
Parking Lot Attendant	55	14.5 yrs.	8 mos. (4 mos. at trial)
Mining Employee	49	13 yrs.	3 mos.
Shirt Repairer/Presser	61	23 yrs.	15 mos.
Production Line Worker (Seasonal)	48	2 yrs.+8 yrs.	4 mos.
1999			
Maintenance Worker	43	11 yrs.	13 mos.
Area Superintendent of Tenants		14 yrs.	12 mos.
Seasonal Superintendent & Head Greenskeeper		11 yrs.	6 mos.
Construction Worker (Seasonal)	33	6 yrs.	6 mos.***
Hairstylist	50	4 yrs.+9 yrs.	6 mos.+ 6 mos.***
Cook	41	9 yrs.	8 mos.
Forklift operator	53	34 yrs.	24 mos.
Forklift operator/truck driver	45	15 yrs.	13 mos.
Cleaner	41	4 yrs. 10 mos.	12 wks.
Cleaner	39	4 yrs. 10 mos.	12 wks.
Yard Foreman		6 yrs.	5 mos.
Production Worker	29	9.5 yrs.	6 mos.
Drywaller	50	8 yrs.	7 mos. reduced to 3.5 mos.**
Janitor	34	8.5 yrs.	8.5 mos.
Bartender	29	2 yrs.	10 wks
2000			
Ice Maker (seasonal)	62	15 yrs.	7 mos.
Assembly Line Worker	45	5 yrs.	6 mos.
Groundskeeper	36	11 yrs.	9 mos.
Weaver	32	5.5 yrs.	4 mos.
2001			
12 non-managerial, non-unionized employees		14-28 yrs.	7.3 -15 mos.
Warehouseman		25 yrs.	22 mos.+2 mos.***
Seasonal Grounds Keeper	67	27 yrs.	1 season

** Notice reduced due to "near cause" or failure to mitigate.
*** Notice increased due to employer's conduct.

Position	Age	Length of Service	Period of Notice
Janitor/Pool Maintenance	63		
2002			
Probationary Labourer	27	2 mos.	8 wks.(1 wk. at trial)
Waitress/Restaurant Supervisor	59	13.5 yrs.	16 mos.***
Punch Press Operator	63	25 yrs.	20 mos.
Assembly Line Worker		3.5 yrs.	4 mos.+2 mos.***

M. REASONABLE NOTICE PERIODS — MISCELLANEOUS EMPLOYEES: 1987 – PRESENT

Position	Age	Length of Service	Period of Notice
1987			
Dispatcher & Maintenance Supervisor	—	7 yrs.	mos.
Union Business Representative	—	4 yrs.	6 mos.*
Union Organizer	—	3.5 yrs.	6 mos.
Management Security Captain	—	20 yrs.	17 mos.
1988			
Union Representative	—	6 yrs.	12 mos.
Union Organizer	40	5 wks.	6 wks.
Editor	64	16 yrs.	12 mos.
Apartment Superintendent	40	6 yrs.	6 mos.
Head Cashier	47	7 yrs.	3 mos.*
Town Manager	—	5 yrs.	15 mos.*
Editor	62	8 yrs.	18 mos.
1989			
Deputy Minister of Justice/Deputy Attorney General	49	16 yrs.	18 mos.
Deputy Minister of Fisheries	46	9 yrs.	1 yr.

---

* Provisional assessment only.
*** Notice increased due to employer's conduct.

Position	Age	Length of Service	Period of Notice
Union Business Representative	53	10.5 yrs.	12 mos.
Counselor	48	10 yrs.	6 mos.
Social Worker	43	12 yrs.	7 mos.
Family Worker	45	3 yrs.	3 mos.
1990			
Advertising Creative Director	59	10 yrs.	10 mos.
Resident Apartment Building Manager	63	1 yr.	5 mos.
Probationary Security Shift Supervisor	30	less than 90 days	2 wks.
1991			
Resident Counselor	45	13 yrs.	15 mos.
Radio Announcer	32	7 mos.	3 mos.
Chief Producer	54	30 yrs.	1 yr.[*]
Consultant/former President	61	18 yrs.	22 mos.
Part-time Clerk	61	19 yrs.	3 yrs
1992			
Managing Editor	46	24 yrs.	21 mos.
Director, Social Development	35	17 yrs.	15 mos.
Residential Property Supervisor	25	13 mos.	4 mos.
Design Consultant	"young"	16 mos.	5 mos.
1993			
Tour Escort	29	3.5 yrs.	6 mos.[*]
Assistant Counselor/ Maintenance Worker	—	under 3 yrs.	2 wks.
1995			
Director, Child Guidance Services	—	6 yrs.	5 mos.
Radio Station News Director	41	3.5 yrs.	7 mos.
Chief Building Official/By-Law Enforcement	47	7.5 yrs.	6 mos.
Community Worker	49	21 yrs.	11 mos.[*]
—	47	26 yrs.	22 mos.
Pastor	—	4 yrs.	3 mos.

[*] Provisional assessment only.

APPENDIX 4 499

Position	Age	Length of Service	Period of Notice
Campground Leader	—	5.5 yrs.	7 mos.
Real Estate Appraiser	46	3.5 yrs.	4 mos.
1996			
Sports Editor	57	36 yrs.	28 mos. (18 mos. at trial)
Purchaser/Assignment Employee		2 yrs.	10 wks.
Trade Show Manager		10 mos.	5 mos.
Child Youth Care Counsellor		1 yr.	6 mos.
Ship's Captain	57	2.5 yrs.	3 mos.
Managing Editor		11 yrs.	12 mos.
International Development Workers		3 yrs.	6 mos.
1997			
Probationary Overseas Ditching Instructor		4 mos.	2 wks.[*]
After School Program Manager		4 yrs.	4 mos.
Interpreter		4 yrs.	8 mos. increased from 6 mos.[***]
Digest Writer	72	20 yrs.	16 mos.
1998			
Executive Analyst/ Management Consultant	44	4 yrs.	9 mos.
Nanny		4 yrs.	3 mos.[**]
1999			
Sales/Distribution Agent		11 yrs.	9 mos. (15 mos. at trial)
Area Superintendent of Tenants		14 yrs.	12 mos.
Rabbi	59	26 yrs.	30 mos.[***]
Social Worker	66	almost 5 yrs.	2-3 mos.[*]
2000			
Child Care Supervisor	54	10 yrs.	11 mos.[***]
Legal Information Worker	47	7 yrs.	7 mos.+ 6 mos.[***]
Sales Agent (non-employee)		19 mos.	5 mos. (on appeal)

[*] Provisional assessment only.
[**] Notice reduced due to "near cause" or failure to mitigate.
[***] Notice increased due to employer's conduct.

Position	Age	Length of Service	Period of Notice
2001			
Golf Pro	30	9.5 yrs.	29 wks.
Trucking Contractor (non-employee)		16 yrs.	9 mos.
Seasonal Worker (4 mos./yr)		3 yrs.	6 mos.[*]
2002			
Temporary Dental Assistant		5 mos.	3 wks.

---

[*] Provisional assessment only.

INDEX

A

Abandonment of claim, implied, 222
Absence from work
- generally
- - condonation, 190
- - examples where just cause, 191
- - examples where no just cause, 190-191
- - excusable absences, 191
- - general principles, 190
- - lying, 191
- - onus of proving authorization, 190
- illness
- - failure to return to work, 75, 193-194
- - general principles, 191-193
- - malingering, 193
- - mental illness, 193
- lateness, 195-197
- leave of absence
- - notice of termination, effective date of, 47-48
- - status as employee, 32
- repudiation
- - authorized absence, 75
- - failure to return after illness, 75
- - unauthorized absence, 75
- vacations, 194-195
- workplace safety issues, 194

Abuse of authority, 165-166
Abusive discharge, 433
Accidental breach, 83
Accord and satisfaction
- cheque cashing, 219
- examples, 219-220
- general principle, 218-219
- negotiations, effects of, 219
- pension payments, 219
- salary continuation, 220

Account changes, 96
Accounting advice, 374
Accumulated sick leave, 276
Actuarial calculation, 337
Addiction, 197-198
Administrators
- reasonable notice charts, 472-476

Advances, 304-305
After-acquired knowledge
- frustration, 60
- misconduct, of, 123
- revelation of character, 149

Age
- discrimination, 184
- employees in their 40s, 263-264
- employees in their 50s and up, 263
- employees over 65, 264
- employees under 40, 264
- general rule, 263
- pension and benefits vesting, 265
- planned retirement, 264-265
- service length, and, 264
- where age no hindrance to job search, 264

Agents
- just cause, 31
- notice of termination, 30-31
- sales agents. *See* **Salespersons or sales agents**
- status, reduced emphasis on, 30

Aggravated damages
- generally
- - aggravated damages, purpose of, 361
- - behaviour leading to damages, 362
- - definition of terms, 361-362
- - exceptional remedy, 362
- - foreseeability, 362
- - general principles, 361-363
- - increased notice periods, *vs.*, 362
- - pleadings, 363
- - procedural effects, 363
- - Quebec cases, 363
- - separate, actionable wrong, 362
- loss of reputation or opportunity, 366-367
- mental distress damages, 363-366

Agreements in principle, 218
Airing complaints, 177
Alcohol consumption, 197-198
Allegations of theft or fraud, 111
Alternative dispute mechanisms, 207
Ambiguous terms, 224
Angry words, 44-45
Anticipatory breaches
- actionable nature of, 82
- employer's intention, 83
- fixed-term contract, 297
- time from which damages run, 294
- warning, *vs.*, 82

Appeal procedures
- general principles
- - alternative dispute mechanisms, 207
- - choice of forum, 207
- - statutory procedure, 208-209

Application forms, 233-234
Arbitration procedures
- contractual procedure, 209
- exclusion, 3
- general principles
- - alternative dispute mechanisms, 207
- - choice of forum, 207

Assignment employees
- generally, 28-29
- just cause, and, 31

Assignment in bankruptcy, 56
Assignment of contract, 52-53
Assistance program, 143
Association membership fees, 349
Assurance of job security, 283-284
At-pleasure employment. *See* **At-will employment**
At-will employment
- consideration of all circumstances, 7
- constructive dismissal, 84
- definition, 6
- examples of, 7
- limited dismissal rights, 6
- presumption against
- • Crown employees, 21
- • municipal employees, 21
- • public employees, 21
- rarity of, 6
- rebuttals of
- • Crown employees, 22
- • municipal employees, 22
- • public employees, 22

Authorized absence, 75
Automatic renewal clause, 240
Automobile benefits
- car allowances, 341-342
- company vehicles, 342-343
- lease cancellation, 344
- loss on resale, 344
- repairs, 344
- repossession, 344

Availability of new job. *See* **Job availability**
Averaging, 310-311

B

Bad economy, 278-279
Bad faith
- breach of expectations, 286
- delay, 286
- employees' conduct in dismissing another, 38
- employers, of, 286-289
- government forms and agencies, 288
- harsh, callous or high-handed treatment, 287
- humiliating treatment, 110
- insensitivity, 287
- job search help, failure to give, 289
- malice, 288
- manner of dismissal, 285
- procedural failures, 287
- references, withholding of, 289
- severance arrangements, 288
- timing of dismissal, 287
- tort claim, 433
- unfair evaluation, 286
- untrue allegations, 287

Bankruptcy of employer
- after dismissal, 57
- assignment in bankruptcy, 56
- damages, 296
- involuntary assignment, 37
- petition into bankruptcy, 56
- statutory pay, 56
- unionized employees covered by collective agreement, 207

Bargaining unit. *See* **Unions**
Benefits
- association membership fees, 349
- automobile benefits. *See* **Automobile benefits**
- changes in
- • frequent flyer points, 94
- • multiple changes, 94
- • new policies, 93
- • significant value, 93-94
- • simple change, 94
- • where decrease found, 93
- club fees, 349
- computer allowance, 351
- damages for, 293-294
- deductions from damage award
- • CPP disability payments, 385
- • disability benefits, 384-385
- • Employment Insurance, 385
- • general principle, 383
- • maternity leave, 385
- • parental leave, 385
- • pension benefits, 383-384
- • workers' compensation benefits, 384
- education benefits, 352
- employee discounts, 349
- employer-provided benefits generally, 347
- expense accounts, 350
- financial counselling, 352
- housing benefits, 347-348
- incentive prizes, 351
- insured benefits
- • amount of damages, 326-327
- • dental insurance, 327-328
- • disability benefits, 330-331
- • generally, 326-327
- • life benefits, 328
- • life insurance, 328-329
- • medical insurance, 327-328
- level of, 275
- living allowances, 347-348
- loans, 349-350
- new job, in, 420
- office space and equipment, 351
- professional education, 349
- professional fees, 349
- related actions for, 431
- retiring allowance, 352
- savings plan contributions, 352

Benefits — *continued*
• statutory holiday pay, 346-347
• subscriptions and tickets, 351
• travel benefits, 351
• vacations, 344-346
• vesting within notice period, 293
Bonuses
• changes in, 92-93
• damages
• • calculation of damages, 316-317
• • contractual entitlement, 312
• • discretionary amount, 312
• • entitlement, 314-316
• • entitlement over time, 312-313
• • generally, 312-313
• • merit-based, 313
• • partial entitlement, 315
• • previous bonuses, 316
• • *pro rata* payments, 317
• • profitable employer, 315-316
• • purely discretionary, 313
• • share of profits, 315, 316
Breach of contract
• action, 41-42
• inducement, 432
Breach of expectations, 286
Breach of fiduciary duty, 434-435
Breach of rules
• communication of rule, 171
• examples where just cause, 171
• general principles, 171-172
• inconsistent application, 171
• intention, requirement of, 171
• just cause, 171
• non-enforcement by supervisor, 171
• reasonableness, 171
• specific rule required, 171
• wilfulness, requirement of, 171
Breach of settlement, 206, 218
Breaking chain of command, 173
Brochures, 235
Business expenses, 423-424

C

Callous treatment, 287
Canada Pension Plan
• contributions, 334
• deductions from damage award, 385
Cancellation of vacation, 373
Capital loss on resale, 357
Car allowances, 341-342
Career changes
• retraining, 403-404
• similar or dissimilar job, 401-403
Casual employees
• change of status, 29
• generally, 28-29
• just cause, and, 31
• mitigation earnings and, 421

Change in employment terms. *See* **Constructive dismissal**
Change of employer
• assignment of contract, 52-53
• bankruptcy
• • after dismissal, 57
• • assignment in bankruptcy, 56
• • petition into bankruptcy, 56
• • statutory pay, 56
• common law *vs.* statute, 51
• • employment standards law, 51
• • parallels between statute and common law, 51
• • statute law, effect of, 51
• general principles
• • duty to mitigate, 52
• • general rule, 52
• • implied term, 52
• • issues, 52
• • methods of change, 52
• length of service
• • agreement between employer, 54
• • circumstances showing non-continuous service, 53-54
• • statutory service length, 54
• • vendor's promise to terminate employment relationships, 54
• • where ownership changes, 53
• novation
• • factors to be considered, 53
• • forced resignation, 53
• • generally, 52-53
• • time to decide on acceptance, 53
• receivership, 56
• sale or transfer of business
• • both employers liable, 34
• • general principles, 54-55
• • issues, 33-34
• • new employer, liability of, 34
• • new employer's policies, 55
• • old employer, liability of, 34
• service length calculations, 269-270
• transfer of employee to related company
• • effect of, 55
• • statutory entitlement, test for, 55-56
• winding up, 56
Character of employment
• job status
• • hierarchy, questioning of, 256-257
• • higher level, more notice, 256
• • management functions, 257
• • non-management employees, 257
• • probationary employees, 257
• • seasonal employees, 257
• • supervisory duties, 257
• • time of assessment of, 261-262
• nature of industry and employer
• • cyclical industry, 260
• • employer size and sector, 260
• • small industry, 259

504   INDEX

Character of employment — *continued*
- • transferable skills, 260
- • unstable industry, 260
- nature of job
- • commission, 259
- • income level, 258
- • individual characteristics, 259
- • public visibility, 259
- • unstable job, 259
- precariousness, 260-261
- service length, and, 266
- significance of job character
- • actual duties *vs.* job title, 255
- • change in employment status, 256
- • employment status, 256
- • part-time employees, 256
- • traditional importance of, 255
- • weight given to job status, 255
- specialization, degree of, 258

Character of words or actions, 174
Charter of Rights and Freedoms, 206
Cheating, 152
Child care expenses, 387
Chronic performance problems
- chronic substandard work, 142
- condonation, 142
- poor performance after warnings, 142
- when warning not necessary, 142

Clear and unambiguous
- express termination, 44
- warnings, content, 127

Clerical employees
- reasonable notice charts, 489-493

Client lists, 375
Clothing allowance, 347
Club fees, 349
Collateral agreement, 431
Collective agreement
- bargaining unit. *See* **Unions**
- Crown employees, 23
- exclusion, 3
- existence of
- • bankrupt employer, claim against, 207
- • breach of settlement, 206
- • Charter of Rights and Freedoms, 206
- • general principle, 205
- • misrepresentations during hiring, 206
- • no peripheral actions, 205
- • non-unionized employees, 206-207
- • parties agreement as to outside matter, 206
- • probationary employees, 206
- • statute claims, 206
- • tort claims, 206
- • union employees without collective agreement, 207
- • where common law action permitted, 206
- municipal employees, 23
- notice period in, 249
- probationary employees, and, 20

- public employees, 23
- statute-governed employment, 24

Commissions
- calculation method, changes in, 95-96
- changes in, 91
- damages
- • averaging, 310-311
- • calculation of damages, 310-311
- • contractual entitlement to, 307-309
- • deductions from damages, 311-312
- • evidence of likely earned commissions, 309-310
- • gross sales, 308
- reasonable notice, and, 259
- withholding commissions, 96

Common law
- change of employer, 51
- collective agreements, where actions permitted, 206
- express termination
- • angry words, 44-45
- • clear and unambiguous, 44
- • effective notice, examples of, 45-46
- • employee's perception as one factor only, 45
- • examples, no use of express words, 43
- • form of notice, 43
- • "magic words," no need for, 43
- • notice must be received, 43
- • notice of termination, 42
- • notice with indeterminate date, 45
- • objective test, 45
- • on-going negotiations, 44
- • reasonable belief, 44
- • technical mistakes, 43
- • warnings not effective, 45
- principle
- • contract matter, 1
- • creation of common law, 1
- • express terms, 1
- • implied terms, 1
- • statute law, effect of, 2

Commuted value, 337
Company policy. *See* **Employer's policy**
Company vehicles
- examples, 342
- fleet vehicle, 343
- income tax value, 343
- personal benefit intended, 342
- replacement of, 342
- retention, 342-343
- valuation bases, 343

Competency test, 141
Competing duties, 177
Competition with employer, 157-158
Compulsory resignation. *See* **Forced resignation**
Computer allowance, 351
Conditional resignation, 64-65

Condonation
- absence from work, 190
- chronic performance problems, 142
- conflicts of interest, of, 156
- constructive dismissal, of
- • circumstances, 87
- • employee may need to wait, 87
- • express condonation, 85-86
- • finances no excuse, 87
- • generally, 85
- • if mitigating, 86
- • implied condonation, 85-86
- • inferior bargaining position no excuse, 87
- • knowledge of change, requirement of, 86
- • limits on reasonable time, 87
- • reasonable time to decide, 87-88
- • where employer's offer considered, 86
- • where no choice, 86
- • working under protest, 86
- harassment, of, 183
- insolence or insubordination, 174
- lateness, 195
- misconduct, of
- • behaviour constituting condonation
- • • acts of commission or omission, 136
- • • examples where misconduct condoned, 136
- • • examples where misconduct not condoned, 136-137
- • • failure to discipline where others aware of misconduct, 137
- • • personality conflicts, 137
- • dismissal
- • • non-cause explanation, 137-138
- • • with notice or pay, 137
- • general principles
- • • condonation defined, 133
- • • employer's knowledge, 133
- • • imputed knowledge, 134
- • • onus of proof, 134-135
- • • reasonable time to investigate and decide, 134
- • • relevant time, 134
- • • standard of conduct, 133
- • • supervisor's conduct, employer bound by, 134-135
- • revival of past misconduct, 138
- • summary dismissal, 121
- • warnings
- • • behaviour condoned in past, 135
- • • discipline, *vs.*, 135-136
- • • no condonation where warnings given, 135
- • • refute condonation, to, 125-126
- • • repeat of minor misconduct, 135
- • • where behaviour corrected, 135
- • • where warnings not acted on, 135

Confidential information, 164-165, 411
Conflict resolution, 416
Conflicting work, acceptance of, 75

Conflicts of interest
- competition with employer, 157-158
- corporate opportunities, 156-157
- employer's customers or suppliers, dealings with, 162-163
- family members' and friends' activities, 161-162
- fiduciary duties, 156-157
- general principles
- • condonation, 156
- • defences, 156
- • duty of fidelity, 155
- • duty to disclose conflict, 155
- • existence of real conflict, 155-156
- • standard for dismissal, 156
- incompatibility of outside activities, 159
- moonlighting, 158-159
- other employees, dealings with, 163-164
- outside business interests, 159
- personal interests, favouring, 159-160
- sales agents, 157
- shareholders, dealings with, 163-164

Considerate treatment, 285
Consideration
- for releases, 221
- for written contracts, 224

Conspiracy, 432-433
Constructive dismissal
- acceptance by employee
- • not repudiation or resignation, 76
- compulsory resignation, 117
- condonation
- • circumstances, 87
- • employee may need to wait, 87
- • express condonation, 85-86
- • finances no excuse, 87
- • generally, 85
- • if mitigating, 86
- • implied condonation, 85-86
- • inferior bargaining position no excuse, 87
- • knowledge of change, requirement of, 86
- • limits on reasonable time, 87
- • reasonable time to decide, 87-88
- • where employer's offer considered, 86
- • where no choice, 86
- • working under protest, 86
- contractual changes, 109
- described, 42
- discipline, 113
- duty to mitigate
- • example, 85
- • possibility of continued relationship, 85
- • unreasonable refusal to change, 85
- effective date of notice, 47
- employer's intention
- • accidental breach, 83
- • anticipatory breach, 83
- • examples where no intention to dismiss, 83-84
- • reasonable business decision, 83

Constructive dismissal — *continued*
- exceptions
  - at-will employees, 84
  - existence of agreement, 84-85
  - implied probationary period, 85
  - just cause, 84, 85
- factors to consider, 83
- failure to manage change, 83
- general principles
  - circumstances, importance of, 80
  - contract, effect of, 80
  - employee's options, 79
  - no repudiation where notice given, 80
  - no right to impose change, 79
  - past acceptance, 80
  - reasonable time to decide, 80
  - resignation triggers right to sue, 80
- geographical transfer
  - constructive dismissal after move, 116
  - employer's financial situation, 115
  - examples where constructive dismissal, 115-116
  - examples where no constructive dismissal, 116
  - failure to mitigate, 115
  - implied terms, 114
  - multi-location employers, 115
  - multiple changes, 114
  - reasonableness, test of, 114-115
- harassment, 110-111
- humiliating treatment, 110-111
- job content and status, changes in. *See* **Job content and status**
- layoffs, 113-114
- manner of imposing change, 83
- mitigation earnings and, 417-418
- objective question of fact, 82-83
- onus, 83
- pay in lieu of notice, 118
- remuneration changes. *See* **Remuneration**
- resignation following
  - allegations of constructive dismissal, 69
  - constructive dismissal must exist, 69
  - general principle, 69
  - hard bargaining, 69
- retirement, 116-117
- suspensions, 113
- termination, *vs.*, 84
- time from which damages run, 294
- unfair dealings by employer, 111-112
- unilateral and fundamental change
  - anticipatory breaches, 82
  - incorporation into new job description, 82
  - minor changes, 81
  - multiple changes, 81
  - repudiation without changing specific term, 82
  - requirement, 80
  - single change, 81
  - warning *vs.* anticipatory breach, 82
- where salary freeze, 90-91
- working conditions. *See* **Working conditions**

Contract claims, 431-432
Contractual notice provisions, 298
Contractual terms and restrictions. *See* **Employment contracts; Written contracts**
Corporate directors. *See* **Directors**
Corporate documents, 235-236
Corporate opportunities, 156-157
Counterclaims, 387
Criminal activity
- allegations of, 124
- job search, and, 397
- just cause, and, 145-146
- off-the-job conduct, 201-202
- pending criminal charges, 277

Crown employees
- abolition of position, 23
- at-will employment
  - presumption against, 21
  - rebuttals of, 22
- collective agreement coverage, 23
- discontinuance of position, 23
- exclusion, 3
- grievance schemes, 23
- narrow interpretation of statutes, 22
- notice of termination, statutory limit on, 22
- procedural fairness, right to, 23
- Saskatchewan statute, 22-23
- statutory dismissal procedure, 23
- statutory limitation, 21
- statutory protection of officers, 22

Custom of the trade. *See* **Industry custom**
Customer records, 164
Customer relations
- examples where just cause, 186
- examples where no just cause, 186-187
- general principle, 185
- prejudicial effect, need for, 185-186
- warnings, 186

Customers, personal dealings with, 162-163
Cyclical industry, 260

D

Damages
- aggravated damages
  - generally
    - aggravated damages, purpose of, 361
    - behaviour leading to damages, 362
    - definition of terms, 361-362
    - exceptional remedy, 362
    - foreseeability, 362
    - general principles, 361-363
    - increased notice periods, *vs.*, 362
    - pleadings, 363

Damages — *continued*
- • • procedural effects, 363
- • • Quebec cases, 363
- • • separate, actionable wrong, 362
- • loss of reputation or opportunity, 366-367
- • • mental distress damages, 363-366
- • automobile benefits
- • • car allowances, 341-342
- • • company vehicles, 342-343
- • • lease cancellation, 344
- • • loss on resale, 344
- • • repairs, 344
- • • repossession, 344
- • benefits
- • • association membership fees, 349
- • • club fees, 349
- • • computer allowance, 351
- • • discounts, 292
- • • education benefits, 352
- • • employee discounts, 349
- • • employer-provided benefits generally, 347
- • • Employment Insurance (EI), 333-334
- • • expense accounts, 350
- • • financial counselling, 352
- • • generally, 293-294
- • • house-related claims, 357-358
- • • housing benefits, 347-348
- • • insured benefits
- • • • amount of damages, 326-327
- • • • dental insurance, 327-328
- • • • disability benefits, 330-331
- • • • generally, 326-327
- • • • life insurance, 328-329
- • • • medical insurance, 327-328
- • • living allowances, 347-348
- • • moving expenses, 355-358
- • • office space and equipment, 351
- • • professional education, 349
- • • professional fees, 349
- • • savings plan contributions, 352
- • • subscriptions and tickets, 351
- • • travel benefits, 351
- • bonuses
- • • calculation of damages, 316-317
- • • entitlement, 314-316
- • • generally, 312-313
- • Canada Pension Plan contributions, 334
- • commissions
- • • averaging, 310-311
- • • calculation of damages, 310-311
- • • contractual entitlement to, 307-309
- • • deductions from damages, 311-312
- • • evidence of likely earned commissions, 309-310
- • • gross sales, 308
- • contractual notice provisions, 298
- • deductions from damage award
- • • benefits
- • • • CPP disability payments, 385
- • • • disability benefits, 384-385
- • • • Employment Insurance, 385
- • • • general principle, 383
- • • • maternity leave, 385
- • • • parental leave, 385
- • • • pension benefits, 383-384
- • • • workers' compensation benefits, 384
- • • child care expenses, 387
- • • contractual severance payment, 382
- • • counterclaims, 387
- • • defamation damages, 387
- • • excess of damages, in, 381
- • • future contingencies, 385-386
- • • generally, 381
- • • income tax, and, 383
- • • payment in kind, 383
- • • relocation counselling payments, 382
- • • salary continuation, 382
- • • sick pay, banked, 382-383
- • • termination pay, 382
- • • vacation pay, 382-383
- • • working expenses, 387
- • • working notice, 381
- • defamation damages, 387
- • definite-term employment, effect of, 8
- • disability leave, 329-330
- • early termination of definite term contract, 12, 296-298
- • general principles, 291-292
- • goal of, 291
- • gratuitous days off, 346
- • incentive prizes, 351
- • job-related expenses, 354
- • job search expenses, 353-355
- • loans, 349-350
- • loss must be shown, 291-292
- • mitigation. *See* **Mitigation of damages**
- • mitigation expenses, 358-359
- • notice period only, 291
- • other damages
- • • cancellation of vacation, 373
- • • generally, 371
- • • income tax consequences, 373-374
- • • living expenses, 372
- • • loan interest claims, 373
- • • lost opportunities, 373
- • • post-dismissal financial decisions, 373
- • • professional advice, costs of, 374-375
- • • property sold after dismissal, 373
- • • proprietary information, compensation for, 375
- • • reliance on employment, losses in, 371-372
- • • seniority, loss of, 372-373
- • • spouses, 375-376
- • private pension plans
- • • calculation of damages, 337-338
- • • early retirement option, 338-339
- • • entitlement to damages, 335-336
- • • method of paying damages, 339
- • • mistake, 339

Damages — *continued*
- • post-retirement benefits, 339
- • refund of pension contributions, 339
- • transfer of refund into RRSP, 339
- • vesting, and notice period, 339
- profit-sharing plans, 319-320
- punitive damages
- • conduct following dismissal, 370
- • conduct justifying damages, 368-369
- • conduct not justifying damages, 368
- • definition of terms, 362-363
- • employee's conduct, 368
- • general principles, 367-368
- • harassment, 370
- • poor performance allegations, 369
- • post-dismissal conduct justifying damages, 370
- • purpose of, 361
- • relationship to other damages, 368
- • retaliation, 370
- • untrue cause allegations, 369
- • use of, 361
- reduced damages, and failure to mitigate, 392-393
- remuneration
- • advances, 304-305
- • directors' fees, 304-305
- • expenses, 304-305
- • extra fees for extra services, 304
- • general principles, 299-300
- • incentives, 304
- • overtime pay, 303-304
- • pay rate, 300-301
- • *quantum meruit*, 301
- • raises during notice period, 301-302
- • salary and wages, 300
- • shift premiums, 304
- • tips or gratuities, 304
- renewal option in contract, 297
- retiring allowance, 352
- RRSP contributions, 334-335
- salary continuation *vs.* lump sum, 292
- sale of home, 356-357
- share-purchase loan, 321
- sick leave, 329-330
- statutory holiday pay, 346-347
- stock options, 320-323
- stock purchase plans, 321-322
- time at which damages end, 295-296
- time from which damages run, 294-295
- vacations, 344-346
- workers' compensation coverage, 331
- working notice *vs.* pay, 292

Death
- damages, and, 295
- notice period, during, 390

Deduction of earnings in mitigation. *See* **Mitigation earnings**

Deductions from damage award
- benefits
- • CPP disability payments, 385
- • disability benefits, 384-385
- • Employment Insurance, 385
- • general principle, 383
- • maternity leave, 385
- • parental leave, 385
- • pension benefits, 383-384
- • workers' compensation benefits, 384
- child care expenses, 387
- contractual severance payment, 382
- counterclaims, 387
- defamation damages, 387
- excess of damages, in, 381
- future contingencies, 385-386
- generally, 381
- income tax, and, 383
- payment in kind, 383
- relocation counselling payments, 382
- salary continuation, 382
- sick pay, banked, 382-383
- termination pay, 382
- vacation pay, 382-383
- working expenses, 387
- working notice, 381

Defamation, 433
Defamation damages, 387
Defence to conflicts of interest, 156
Definite-term employment
- automatic renewal clause, 240
- benefits, effect of, 9
- circumstances, effect of, 9
- common terms in, 8
- conditions, effect of, 9
- contractual changes during renewal, 240
- damages, effect on, 8, 296-298
- definition, 8
- dismissal rights, 8
- employment beyond end of term, 9
- examples
- • business, termination of, 10
- • date, term defined by, 10
- • employment until certain age, 11
- • event, term defined by, 10
- • expectations of project length, 10
- • explicit agreement required, 11
- • guaranteed employment until retirement, 11
- • project, term defined by, 10
- • special considerations for project employment, 10
- • time, term defined by, 10
- expectations, effect of, 8-9
- expiration, with continued employment, 239
- extension of, 239
- formal requirements, 9
- mitigation of damages, 391-392
- mutual commitment, 9
- notice where employment continues, 239
- other types of

Definite term employment — *continued*
- • examples, 13
- • intention of permanence, 12
- • long-term continuous employment, 13
- • seasonal employment, 12
- • series of term contracts, 12-13
- question of fact, 8
- termination clause, 9
- termination of
- • before end of term, 12
- • breach of contract, 12
- • damages for early termination, 12
- • end of contract, 11
- • exceptions, 11-12
- • just cause, 12
- • nonrenewal of contract, 11-12
- unenforceable, and damages, 297
- written contracts, 223

Degree of specialization, 258
Delay, 222, 286
Demotion
- downward change in status, 101
- express term, 101
- general principle, 100-101
- implied term, 101
- just cause, 101
- minor changes, 101
- office reassignment, 101
- surrounding circumstances, 101

Dental insurance, 327-328
Dependent contractors, 30-31
Depressed area, 278
Detrimental reliance, 283-284
Different type of job, 421
Direct competition with employer, 157
Director-employees, 25
Directors
- director-employees, *vs.*, 25
- fees, 304-305
- personal liability
- • other amounts, 36-37
- • other causes of action, 36
- • piercing the corporate veil, 36
- • statutory liability, 36
- • wages, 36

Disability
- arising after dismissal, 276
- damages, 296
- examples where frustration found, 61
- examples where frustration not found, 61-62
- job search, 396-397
- leave, 47-48, 329-330
- nature and length of employment, 61
- nature and length of illness, 60-61
- notice period, during, 390
- partial disability, 61
- prognosis, 60-61
- reasonable notice, determination of, 276
- sick leave, 61

- temporary illness, 61

Disability insurance, 330-331
Disability payments
- deductions from damage award, 384-385
- frustration and, 61
- generally, 330-331
- resignation and, 71

Disciplinary probation
- described, 15
- full period to show improvement, 20
- good faith and objectivity requirement, 20
- imposition of, 20
- timing of probation, 20

Discipline
- disciplinary suspensions, 113
- duty to warn policy, 126
- failure to discipline where others aware, 137
- unjustified discipline, 113
- warnings, *vs.*, 135-136
- where no constructive dismissal found, 113

Disclosure of information, 164-165, 218
Discounts, 292, 349
Discrimination
- age, 184
- failure to pay equally for equal work, 184-185
- pregnancy, 184

Dishonesty
- duty of frank disclosure, 152
- expense account abuse, 150
- failure to tell the truth, 151-152
- financial improprieties, 150-151
- general principles
- • balance of proof, 146
- • categories amounting to just cause, 145
- • criminal conduct, 145-146
- • duty of fairness, 146
- • employee's misconduct, 146
- • following orders, 146
- • intention required, 146
- • modern approach, 145
- • objective standard, 145
- • suspicion, 146
- • uncharacteristic act, 146
- intent to mislead, 151-152
- lies, 151-152
- prejudicial conduct
- • examples of seriously prejudicial conduct, 147-148
- • "minor" dishonesty, 147
- • serious prejudicial conduct required, 147
- professional qualifications, 152-153
- résumé disclosure, 152-153
- revelation of character
- • after-acquired knowledge, 149
- • examples, 149-150
- • general principles, 148
- • trust, special requirement of, 148-149

Disloyalty, 177

510   INDEX

Dismissal for cause. *See* **Just cause**
Disobedience
- breach of rules
- - communication of rule, 171
- - examples where just cause, 171
- - general principles, 171-172
- - inconsistent application, 171
- - intention, requirement of, 171
- - just cause, 171
- - non-enforcement by supervisor, 171
- - reasonableness, 171
- - specific rule required, 171
- - wilfulness, requirement of, 171
- generally
- - clear, lawful instructions, 168
- - contractual change, 168
- - different names, similar issues, 167
- - examples where just cause, 169
- - examples where no just cause, 169
- - excuses, 168-169
- - insolence, avoidance of, 168
- - passive rebellion, 167-168
- - reasonable requests, requirement of, 168
- - repeated or combined disobedience, 168
- - single act of disobedience, 167
- insolence and insubordination
- - general principles, 173-174
- neglect of duty, 170-171
- refusal to perform duties, 170-171

Dissimilar job, 401-403
Dissolution of employer, 56
Doctors. *See* **Statute-governed employment**
Double compensation, 212, 215
Draft contracts, 235
Drinking on the job, 197-198
Driving licence, loss of, 203
Driving of company vehicle, 203
Duress, 68, 224
Duty of departing employees, 158
Duty of disclosure, 218
Duty of fairness
- *see also* **Fairness**
- change of reason, 128-129
- dishonest conduct and, 147
- generalized duty, 128
- job content and status changes, 98
- office held at pleasure, 129
- office holders, 128-129
- opportunity to explain, 128-129
- proper investigation, 128-129
- reasons for dismissal, 128
- statute-governed employment, 24

Duty of fidelity, 155
Duty of frank disclosure, 152
Duty of good faith
- job content and status changes, 98
- warnings, 128

Duty to bargain in good faith, 76
Duty to communication, 192

Duty to disclose
- conflict of interest, 155
- job prospects, 243-244

Duty to inform, 99
Duty to mitigate
- *see also* **Mitigation of damages**
- benefits loss, 293-294
- change of employers, 52
- constructive dismissal situations, 85
- continuing duty, 390
- death or disability during notice period, 390
- efforts and likely results, 390
- evidence of availability of similar work, 390-391
- general principles, 389
- no duty to settle, 389
- onus to prove, 390
- reasonable steps only, 389
- statutory employment schemes, 389
- total lack of effort, 390

Duty to warn
- *see also* **Warnings**
- drinking on duty, 197
- employee relation problems, 181
- employer policy, 126
- form of warning, 126
- general principle, 125
- good faith requirement, 128
- job insecurity, of, 284
- multiple warnings, need for, 126
- new warning, need for, 126
- no duty to warn of investigation, 125
- onus, 125
- oral warning, risks of, 126
- warning to refute condonation, 125-126
- where no warning required, 125

E

Early retirement. *See* **Retirement**
Economic climate, 278-279
- job availability, and reasonable notice, 279-280

Economic problems
- geographical transfers, 115
- redundancy, 202-203
- statutes, effect of, 203

Education benefits, 352
Effective date of notice
- changes during notice period, 47
- constructive dismissal, 47
- disability or other leave, 47-48
- general principle, 46
- working notice, 46, 47

Elected officials, 31-32
Employee discounts, 349
Employee loans, 349-350
Employee relation problems. *See* **Workplace conflicts**

Employee transfers
- geographical transfer
  - constructive dismissal after move, 116
  - employer's financial situation, 115
  - examples where constructive dismissal, 115-116
  - examples where no constructive dismissal, 116
  - failure to mitigate, 115
  - implied terms, 114
  - multi-location employers, 115
  - multiple changes, 114
  - reasonableness, test of, 114-115
- need to relocate, 278
- previous relocation costs, 358
- refusal to relocate, 278
- service length calculations and, 271
- statutory entitlement, test for, 55-56
- transfer agreement, 236

Employees
- *see also* **specific types of employees**
- assignment employees, 28-29
- casual employees, 28-29
- change to, 268
- dealings with other employees, 163-164
- finances, 277
- financial burden imposed on, 107
- governed by statute. *See* **Statute-governed employment**
- independent contractors, *vs.*, 25
- managers as, 25
- merits of, 289-290
- moonlighting, 158-159
- near cause, 289
- outside business interests, 159
- perception of dismissal only one factor, 45
- personal liability
  - acting within authority, 38
  - bad faith, 38
  - denial of costs, 38
- personal use of employer's tools, 160
- on probation. *See* **Probationary employment**
- project employees, 28-29
- reasonable notice charts
  - clerical employees, 489-493
  - labourers, 493-497
  - miscellaneous employees, 497-500
  - skilled employees, 484-488
  - technical employees, 484-488
- repudiation. *See* **Repudiation**
- seasonal employees, 28-29
- status, reduced emphasis on, 30
- suing employer, 76-77, 177
- temporary employees, 28-29
- tort claims, 432-434

Employer brochure, 235
Employer-provided housing, 348
Employer records, 164

Employers
- bad faith of, 286-289
- bankrupt, 37-38
- change of. *See* **Change of employer**
- economic problems
  - geographical transfers, 115
  - redundancy, 202-203
- individual liability, 33
- leeway to alter job content, 98
- multi-location employers, 115
- multiple possible employers, 33
- other individuals
  - acting within authority, 38
- other jobs with same employer, 400
- partners as, 37
- policy. *See* **Employers' policy**
- purpose of determination, 33
- receivers and trustees, 37-38
- related entities
  - absence of payroll practices, 36
  - employee's consent to change, 34
  - employer, identification of, 34
  - employment standards, 36
  - multiple possible employers, 35
  - payroll practices and common control, 35
  - rebuttal of presumption, 35
  - services provided to multiple entities, 35
- repudiation, 41
- sector, 260
- size, 260
- suing, 76-77, 177
- tort claims, 434-435
- unfair dealings
  - allegations of theft or fraud, 111
  - examples where constructive dismissal, 111-112
  - examples where no constructive dismissal, 112
  - general principles, 111
- unincorporated associations, 37
- unions, 37

Employers' policy
- absence of, 232
- absenteeism, and medically justified absences, 194
- binding on employer, 233
- changes after hiring, 232
- duty to warn, 126
- employee conduct, 231
- example where policy enforced against employer, 233
- example where policy not binding, 233
- forms of, 229-230
- general principles, 229-230
- interplay between policy and contract, 231-232
- interpretation of, 231
- knowledge and agreement, 230
- proof of acceptance, 230
- reasonable notice, 250

Employers' policy — *continued*
- standard of conduct policies, 232
- termination pay policies, 232
- unilateral change, 232
- union policies, 232
- voiding of, 379
- warnings, reconciliation with, 127-128
- where binding due to employee conduct, 231
- where no knowledge or agreement, 230
- where policies upheld, 230-231

Employment contracts
- absence due to illness, 192
- agreement to permit changes, 80, 84-85
- arbitration procedure, 209
- at-will employment
  - consideration of all circumstances, 7
  - definition, 6
  - examples of, 7
  - limited dismissal rights, 6
  - rarity of, 6
- breach of contract, 41-42
- change to terms. *See* **Constructive dismissal**
- civil actions, restrictions on, 215-216
- contractual changes, and constructive dismissal, 109
- contractual notice provisions, 298
- definite-term employment
  - benefits, effect of, 9
  - circumstances, effect of, 9
  - common terms in, 8
  - conditions, effect of, 9
  - damages, effect on, 8
  - definition, 8
  - dismissal rights, 8
  - employment beyond end of term, 9
  - examples, 10-11
  - expectations, effect of, 8-9
  - formal requirements, 9
  - mutual commitment, 9
  - other types of, 12-13
  - question of fact, 8
  - seasonal employment, 12
  - series of term contracts, 12-13
  - termination clause, 9
  - termination of, 11-12
- draft contracts, 235
- express termination provisions
  - expiry of fixed-term contracts, 239-240
  - extension of fixed-term contracts, 239-240
  - lapse of time, effect of, 240-241
  - promotions, effect of, 240-241
  - severance clauses, 241-242
  - termination agreements, 242-244
  - termination clauses, 241-242
- frustration
  - general principles, 59-60
  - illness and disability, 60-62
  - labour disputes, 62
  - self-induced frustration, 60
- grievance procedure, 209
- indefinite employment
  - changes to term of hiring, 7
  - definition, 7
  - dismissal rights, 8
  - employment beyond end of definite term, 9
  - guaranteed term, 8
  - long-term continuous employment in series of term contracts, 13
  - norm, as, 6
  - presumption of, 7
- legal correspondence, exchange of, 235
- oral agreements, 223
- reassignment, permitted, 80
- right to negotiate employment terms, 160
- series of contracts, 240
- standard form contracts, 229
- substance abuse, 197
- summary dismissal, limit on, 121
- termination of contract, 41
- types of, 6
- unacceptable performance
  - agreed subjective standard, 143
  - contractual standards, 143
  - industry custom, 143
  - objective standard implied, 143
  - silent on issue, 143
- written contracts
  - ambiguous terms, interpretation of, 224
  - consideration, 224
  - definite-term contracts, 223
  - duress, 224
  - express agreements, 223
  - express agreements strictly interpreted, 223-224
  - failure to enter into, 226-227
  - form of contract, 225-226
  - illegality, 224
  - inequality of bargaining power, 224
  - *non est factum*, 224
  - normal contract rules, application of, 224
  - offer and acceptance, 224
  - parol evidence rule
    - defined, 224
    - examples, 224-225
    - exceptions, 224-225
  - unconscionability, 224
  - written *vs.* oral agreements, 223

Employment Insurance (EI)
- application not required, 415
- contributions, and damages, 333-334
- deductions from damage award, 385
- rulings, effect of, 214

Employment offers, 234-235
Employment relationship, 5
Employment standards legislation
- change of employment situations, 51

Employment standards legislation — *continued*
- effect of, 2
- notice of termination, 2
- related entities, 36
- rulings, and issue estoppel
- • application to both parties, 213
- • consent required, 213
- • examples where civil actions permitted, 213
- • issue estopped but not action, 212
- • multiple employment standards actions, 213
- • wording of statute, 212
- severance agreements, 244
- statutory notice period, effect of, 251
- summary dismissal, 121
- unacceptable performance, 139

Employment status
- *see also* **Employment contracts**
- broad range of employees, 6
- casual employees, and change of status, 29
- change in, and reasonable notice, 256
- changes, 105-106
- intermediate category, 6
- no longer definitive, 6
- reasonable notice, and, 256
- reduced emphasis on, 30
- service length calculations
- • business owner, change to, 269
- • employee, change to, 268, 269
- • exception, 268
- • full-time, change to, 268
- • non-union, change to, 269
- • part-time, change to, 268-269
- • parties' intentions, 268
- temporary employees, and change of status, 29

Enticement by employer, 270-271
Equal pay for equal work, failure to pay, 184-185
Evidence
- availability of similar work, 390
- extrinsic evidence, 224-225
- likely earned commissions, 309-310
- parol evidence rule
- • defined, 224
- • examples, 224-225
- • exceptions, 224-225

Exaggerated qualifications, 152
Exclusions from general principle
- described, 3
- employees with limited rights, 3
- office holders' rights, 3

Excusable absences, 191
Expense account abuse, 150
Expenses, 304-305
Experience, 273-274
Express termination
- by-law, contract or statute, under

- • compliance, lack of, 42
- • permissive language, 42
- • statutory requirement, 42
- common law, at
- • angry words, 44-45
- • clear and unambiguous, 44
- • effective notice, examples of, 45-46
- • employee's perception as one factor only, 45
- • examples, no use of express words, 43
- • form of notice, 43
- • "magic words," no need for, 43
- • notice must be received, 43
- • notice of termination, 42
- • notice with indeterminate date, 45
- • objective test, 45
- • on-going negotiations, 44
- • reasonable belief, 44
- • technical mistakes, 43
- • warnings not effective, 45
- provisions
- • fixed-term contracts
- • • automatic renewal clause, 240
- • • contractual changes during renewal, 240
- • • expiration, with continued employment, 239
- • • extension of, 239
- • • notice where employment continues, 239-240
- • lapse of time, effect of, 240-241
- • promotions, effect of, 240-241
- • series of contracts, 240
- • severance clauses, 241-242
- • termination agreements, 242-244
- • termination clauses, 241-242

Express terms
- demotion, 101
- generally, 1

Extrinsic evidence, 224-225

F

Failure to disclose information, 151-152
Failure to follow procedure
- probationary employment
- • failure to follow disciplinary procedure, 19
- statute-governed employees, 24

Failure to mitigate
- confidential information, refusal to divulge, 411
- conflict resolution, failure to participate in, 416
- dismissing employer's offer, rejection of, 411-413
- early retirement, refusal of, 415
- Employment Insurance, no requirement to apply, 415
- generally, 392-393

Failure to mitigate — *continued*
- leave of absence, refusal of, 415
- new employer's offer, rejection of, 409-411
- no duty to inquire, 415
- professional help, failure to seek, 415
- relocation counselling, refusal of, 414
- return to bargaining unit, failure to, 415
- salary continuation, refusal of, 414
- working notice, refusal of, 413-414

Failure to safeguard information, 164
Failure to tell the truth, 151-152
Fairness
- duty of fairness
- • change of reason, 128-129
- • generalized duty, 128
- • job content and status changes, 98
- • office held at pleasure, 129
- • office holders, 128-129
- • opportunity to explain, 128-129
- • proper investigation, 128-129
- • reasons for dismissal, 128
- • statute-governed employment, 24
- procedural fairness
- • examples where duty met, 130
- • examples where duty not met, 130-131
- • failure to comply with duty, 130-131
- • lack of hearing not significant, 130-131
- • natural justice, *vs.*, 129-130
- • right to be heard, 130
- • third-party decision, 130-131

Family members' activities, 161-162
Fiduciary duties, 156-157, 434-435
Financial burden imposed on employee, 107
Financial counselling, 352
Financial improprieties, 150-151
Firefighters, 3
- *see also* **Statute-governed employment**

First job in industry, 274
Fixed-term employment. *See* **Definite-term employment**
Fleet vehicle, 343
Following orders, 146
Forced resignation, 53, 117
Foreign government employees, 32
Foremen
- reasonable notice charts, 463-467

Foreseeability, 362
Form of contract, 225-226
Formal education, lack of, 273
Friends' activities, 161-162
Frustration
- general principles
- • after-acquired knowledge, 60
- • doctrine of frustration, 59
- • examples of, 59
- • impossibility of performance, 59
- • objective test, 60
- • unforeseen and without fault, 59
- illness and disability, 192

- • disability benefits, 61
- • examples where frustration found, 61
- • examples where frustration not found, 61-62
- • nature and length of employment, 61
- • nature and length of illness, 60-61
- • partial disability, 61
- • prognosis, 60-61
- • sick leave, 61
- • temporary illness, 61
- labour disputes
- • shutdown due to strike, 62
- self-induced
- • examples of self-induced frustration, 60
- • examples where no self-induced frustration, 60
- • generally, 60

Full-time employee status, change to, 268
Future contingencies, 385-386

G

Generalists, 273-274
Geographic location, 278
Geographical transfers
- constructive dismissal after move, 116
- employer's financial situation, 115
- examples where constructive dismissal, 115-116
- examples where no constructive dismissal, 116
- failure to mitigate, 115
- implied terms, 114
- multi-location employers, 115
- multiple changes, 114
- reasonableness, test of, 114-115

Good faith. *See* **Duty of good faith**
Government-funded training program, 39
Government-sponsored insurance, 327-328
Gratuities, 304
Gratuitous days off, 346
Grievance procedures, 207-209
Gross incompetence, 141
Group termination notice, 429
Guaranteed employment until retirement, 11

H

Harassment, 110-111, 182-184, 370
Harassment claim, 433-434
Harassment policy, 183
Hard bargaining, 69
Harsh treatment, 287
High-handed treatment, 287
High-level job, 274
Higher-paying new job, 420-421
Hiring terms. *See* **Employment contracts**
Home purchase, 348

House-related claims, 357-358
Housing benefits, 347-348
Human rights claims, 200, 221
Human rights complaints, 214-215
Humiliating treatment
- bad faith, 110
- change in working relationship, 110
- examples where constructive dismissal found, 110-111
- examples where no constructive dismissal, 110-111
- general principles, 110
- test for, 110

I

Illegal contracts
- minor illegalities, 4
- nonenforcement by courts, 3-4, 224

Illness
- absence from work
- • company policy, and, 194
- • duty to communication, 192
- • failure to communicate, 192
- • frustration, 192
- • inappropriate accommodation, 194
- • issue, 191
- • long-term illness, 191
- • permanently incapable, 191
- • statutory duties, 192
- • temporary illness, 191
- • time for assessment of permanence, 191-192
- • ultimatum, 194
- • workplace safety issues, 194
- • written agreement, 192
- failure to return after illness, 75, 193-194
- frustration
- • examples where frustration found, 61
- • examples where frustration not found, 61-62
- • just cause, *vs.*, 192
- job search, 396-397
- malingering, 193
- mental illness, 193
- • unacceptable performance, 139
- nature and length of employment, 61
- nature and length of illness, 60-61
- pregnancy, 184
- prognosis, 60-61
- reasonable notice, determination of, 276
- sick leave, 61
- temporary illness, 61

Implied terms
- change of employer, 52
- demotion, 101
- entitlement to, 5
- generally, 1
- geographical transfer, 114
- tests for, 5-6

Impossibility of performance, 59
Improper use of information, 164-165
Inappropriate accommodation, 194
Incentive prizes, 351
Incentives, 304
Income level, 258
Income tax damages, 373-374
Incompatibility
- outside activities, of, 159
- workplace conflicts, and, 180

Indefinite employment
- changes to term of hiring, 7
- definition, 7
- dismissal rights, 8
- employment beyond end of definite term, 9
- guaranteed term, 8
- long-term continuous employment in series of term contracts, 13
- norm, as, 6
- presumption of, 7

Indemnity agreements, 236
Independent contractors
- duty of, in not competing, 158
- employment status, and, 6
- just cause, and, 31
- managers as, 25
- notice of termination, 30-31
- salespersons or sales agents, 27-28
- status, reduced emphasis on, 30

Independent legal advice, 218
Individual characteristics, and notice, 259
Individual termination notice, 427-428
Inducing breach of contract, 432
Industry custom
- implied right to reassign, 102
- poor performance term in contract, 144
- reasonable notice period, 250-251
- relocation, and mitigation of damages, 405

Industry hiring practices, 275
Inequality of bargaining power, 217-218, 224
Initial probationary period, 15, 143
Insecure position, 260-261
Insensitivity, 287
Insolence
- avoidance of, in turning down unreasonable requests, 168
- character of words or actions, 174
- condonation of, 174
- context, importance of, 174
- contractual disputes, and, 174
- dispute outside of employment, 174
- examples where just cause, 176
- examples where no just cause, 176
- general principles, 173-174
- insubordination, *vs.*, 173
- private disagreements, 173
- profanity, 174
- provocation, 174
- public complaint, 173, 175-176

Insolence — *continued*
- single incidents, 173-174
- standard for just cause, 173
- vulgar language, 174

Insubordination
- after warning, 175
- breaking chain of command, 173
- character of words or actions, 174
- condonation of, 174
- context, importance of, 174
- examples where just cause, 175
- examples where no just cause, 175
- general principles, 173-174
- insolence, *vs.*, 173
- private disagreements, 173
- public complaint, 173, 175-176
- single incidents, 173-174
- standard for just cause, 173

Insured benefits
- amount of damages, 326-327
- dental insurance, 327-328
- disability benefits, 330-331
- generally, 326-327
- life benefits, 328
- life insurance, 328-329
- medical insurance, 327-328

Insurers, action against, 39
Intent to mislead, 151-152
Intention of permanence, 12
Intentional infliction of mental suffering, 433
Intentional interference with contractual relationships, 38
Interference with contractual relations, 432
Intermediate status
- generally, 6
- just cause, 31
- notice of termination, 30-31
- salespersons or sales agents, 28
- status, reduced emphasis on, 30

Intoxication, 197-198
Investigation
- criminal activity, allegations of, 124
- need for proper investigation, 128-129

Involuntary assignment in bankruptcy, 37
Involuntary resignation
- duress, 68
- examples of, 69
- severance pay, acceptance of, 68
- voluntary, *vs.*, 68

Issue estoppel
- contractual restrictions, 215-216
- Employment Insurance (EI) rulings, 214
- employment standards rulings, 212-214
- generally
- • double compensation, rule against, 212, 215
- • general principles, 211
- • judicial decision, test of, 211-212
- • judicial discretion, 212
- • onus, 212
- • requirements, 211
- human rights complaints, 214-215
- pay equity complaint, 215
- previous civil action, 216
- unjust dismissal adjudication, 215

J

Job abolishment by statute, 24
Job availability
- economic climate, 278-279
- employer's financial problems, 279-280
- evidence of, 390-391
- experience, 273-274
- geographic location, 278
- job characteristics, 274-275
- personal characteristics, 275-277
- proof of, 280-281
- qualifications, 273-274
- training, 273-274

Job characteristics, 274-275
Job content and status
- demotion
- • downward change in status, 101
- • express term, 101
- • general principle, 100-101
- • implied term, 101
- • just cause, 101
- • minor changes, 101
- • office reassignment, 101
- • surrounding circumstances, 101
- downward change in status
- • general principle, 103
- • objective standard, 103
- • return to job held previously, 103
- • work with former subordinates, 103-104
- employment status changes, 105-106
- general principles
- • duty of good faith and fairness, 98
- • duty to inform, 99
- • employer leeway, 98
- • express agreement, 98-99
- • hirings under definite capacity, 98
- • implied agreement, 98-99
- job duties
- • appropriation of duties, 99
- • examples where constructive dismissal found, 98-99
- • examples where no constructive dismissal, 99-100
- • general principles, 98
- • increase in duties, 100
- • minor change in scope, 99
- • new assignments, 100
- • removal of duties, 99
- • significant change in scope, 99
- • temporary assignments, 100
- job title
- • actual duties, *vs.*, 255

INDEX   517

Job content and status — *continued*
• • changes, 104
• • leaves of absence, right to, 105-106
• • reasonable notice, and
• • • hierarchy, questioning of, 256-257
• • • higher level, more notice, 256
• • • management functions, 257
• • • non-management employees, 257
• • • probationary employees, 257
• • • seasonal employees, 257
• • • significance of job character, 255
• • • supervisory duties, 257
• • • time of assessment of job status, 261-262
• • reassignment without demotion
• • • agreement to reassignment, 102
• • • custom of the trade, 102
• • • examples where constructive dismissal, 102-103
• • • examples where no constructive dismissal, 103
• • • express agreement, 102
• • • general principles, 102
• • • right *vs.* obligation, 102
• • • reporting level changes, 103-104
Job duties. *See* **Job content and status**
Job prospects, 243-244
Job reclassification, 90
Job-related expenses, 354
Job requirement changes, 107
Job search
• assistance with, 289
• attempted before termination, 397-398
• criminal charges, 397
• dissimilar pay, 402
• expenses, 353-355
• general principle, 396
• illness and disability, 396-397
• initial inaction, 397
• parental leave, 396
• pregnancy, 396
• premature end, 397-398
• quality of efforts
• • consulting work, 400
• • general principles, 398
• • jobs with equal pay, 399
• • part-time work, 400
• • reasonable search efforts, 398
• • restricted efforts, 399
• • résumé distribution, 399
• • sufficient time, 399
• • unreasonable search efforts, 398
• • volunteer work, 399
• similar *vs.* dissimilar work, 401-403
• time of year, 397
• timing of efforts, 395-398
• vacation before job hunt, 396
• working conditions, substantially different, 402
Job security assurances, 283-284

Job-sharing arrangements, 32
Job status. *See* **Job content and status**
Job title
• actual duties, *vs.*, 255
• changes, 104
Judicial decision, 211-212
Judicial review, 24
Just cause
• absence. *see* Absence from work
• abuse of authority, 165-166
• conflicts of interest. *See* **Conflicts of interest**
• constructive dismissal, 84, 85
• criminal activity, allegations of, 124
• customer relations, 185-187
• definite-term employment, 12
• demotion, 101
• disclosure of information, 164-165
• dishonesty
• • failure to tell the truth, 151-152
• • financial improprieties, 150-151
• • general principles, 145-146
• • lies, 151-152
• • prejudicial conduct, 147-148
• • professional qualifications, 152-153
• • résumé disclosure, 152-153
• • revelation of character, 148-150
• disloyalty, 177
• disobedience
• • breach of rules, 171-172
• • generally, 167-169
• • insolence, 173-176
• • insubordination, 173-176
• • neglect of duty, 170-171
• • refusal to perform duties, 170-171
• driving of company vehicle, 203
• employer's economic problems, 202-203
• groundless allegations
• • mental distress, and, 365
• • punitive damages, and, 369
• harassment, 110-111, 182-184
• improper use of information, 164-165
• intermediate status, 31
• loss of license, 203
• non-disclosure of information, 164-165
• non-employees, 31
• off-the-job conduct
• • criminal conduct, 201-202
• • general principles, 199-200
• • sexual conduct, 200-201
• onus of proof, 123-124
• personal appearance and habits, 185
• pleadings, 124
• probationary employment, 18-19
• redundancy, 202-203
• repeated minor misconduct, 122
• serious misconduct, requirement of, 122
• sexual harassment, 182-184, 201
• single incident of misconduct, 121-122
• substance abuse, 197-198

Just cause — *continued*
- summary dismissal
  - condonation of misconduct, 121
  - degree of misconduct required, 119-120
  - differing standards, 120
  - employer's remedies, 119
  - employment standards legislation, 121
  - entire context of employee's actions, 120
  - express agreement, 121
  - financial loss, no need for, 121
  - fundamental breach, 119, 120
  - just cause as exception, 119
  - narrow interpretation, 120
  - objective test, 120
  - onus, 120
  - right to dismiss *vs.* discipline, 120-121
- timing of misconduct, 123
- unacceptable performance
  - general principles, 139-140
- written rules, significance of, 122

L

Labour disputes
- frustration
  - shutdown due to strike, 62
- strikes
  - economic problems, 203
  - termination during, 49

Labourers
- reasonable notice charts, 493-497

Lapse of time, 240-241
Last employee, 262
Late career change, 277
Lateness, 195-197
Lateral transfers. *See* **Reassignment**
Layoffs
- constructive dismissal
  - return to work, and condonation, 114
  - term in contract permitting layoffs, 113
- effective date of termination, 49
- failure to return after layoff, 75
- frequent, and calculation of service length, 267
- onus on employer, 49
- pay changes during, 92
- permitted layoffs, 48
- re-employment offer, 49
- termination of employment, *vs.*, 48-49

Lease cancellation, 344
Leave of absence
- imposition of, 105-106
- notice of termination, effective date of, 47-48
- refusal of, 415
- right to, 105-106
- status as employee, 32

Legal advice, 374
Legal correspondence, exchange of, 235
Legal dispute with employer
- duty to bargain in good faith, 76
- refusal to sign release or agree to settlement, 76
- refusal to work through notice period, 76
- suing employer, 76-77

Length of service. *See* **Service length**
Letter of reference, 378
Letters to employees, 235
Liability
- directors and shareholders
  - other amounts, 36-37
  - other causes of action, 36
  - piercing the corporate veil, 36
  - statutory liability, 36
  - wages, 36
- employees
  - acting within authority, 38
  - bad faith, 38
  - denial of costs, 38
- government-funded training program, 39
- insurers, 39
- intentional interference with contractual relationships, 38
- partners, 37
- personal liability
  - directors and shareholders, 36-37
  - purpose of determining employer, 33
- priority of payment, 37
- receivers, 37-38
- related entities
  - absence of payroll practices, 36
  - employee's consent to change, 34
  - employer, identification of, 34
  - employment standards, 36
  - multiple possible employers, 35
  - payroll practices and common control, 35
  - rebuttal of presumption, 35
  - services provided to multiple entities, 35
- replacement employee, action against, 38-39
- sale or transfer of business, 33-34
  - both employers liable, 34
  - issues, 33-34
  - new employer, liability of, 34
  - old employer, liability of, 34
- trustees, 37-38
- unincorporated associations, 37
- unions, 37

Licence, loss of, 203
Lies, 151-152, 191
Life benefits, 328
Life insurance, 328-329
Limitation periods, 222
Limited experience, 274
Living allowances, 347-348
Living expenses, 372
Loan interest claims, 373
Loans, 434
Location changes, 107
Location supplements, 348

Long-distance relocation, 405
Long service, 265, 266
Long-term continuous employment, 13
Long-term employee, and unacceptable performance, 139
Long-term illness, 191
Long-term sales, 258
Loss of license, 203
Loss of reputation or opportunity, 366-367
Loss of seniority, 372-373
Losses in reliance on employment, 371-372
Lost opportunities, 373
Lower management
• reasonable notice charts, 458-462
Lower status jobs, 402-403
Lump sum, 292

M

Malice, 288
Malingering, 193
Managers
• duty re conflict of interest, 163
• employees *vs.* independent contractors, 25
• examples of, 26
• functions, and reasonable notice, 257
• outside business interests, 159
• reasonable notice charts
• • foremen, 463-467
• • lower management, 458-462
• • middle management, 450-458
• • sales/marketing managers, 477-484
• • senior executives, 443-446
• • supervisors, 463-467
• • upper management, 447-450
• workplace conflicts, and managerial standards, 181-182
Mandatory retirement age, 116
Manner of dismissal, 284-285
Marketing employees
• reasonable notice charts, 477-484
Maternity leave, 385
Maximum notice period, 252
Meal allowance, 347
Medical insurance, 327-328
Memoranda to employees, 235
Mental distress damages
• cause of distress, 364
• conduct justifying damages, 364-365
• conduct not justifying damages, 365-366
• degree of distress, 363-364
• failure to explain or give chance to respond, 365
• general principles, 363
• just cause allegations, 365
• tort, *vs.*, 363
Mental illness
• behaviour caused by, 193
• unacceptable performance, 139
Mental suffering, 433

Merits of employees, 289-290
Middle management
• reasonable notice charts, 450-458
Middle ranges of service length, 266
Minimum notice, 251
Ministers, 32
Minor illegalities, 4
Miscellaneous employees
• reasonable notice charts, 497-500
Misconduct of employee
• *see also* **Condonation; Just cause**
• costs to employer, 434
• warning letter
• • misconduct, final warning, 437-438
• • misconduct, first instance, 437
Misrepresentations during hiring, 206
Mitigation earnings
• different type of job, 421
• employee's own business
• • award during notice period, 422
• • business equity and income attribution, 423
• • business expenses, 423-424
• • business losses, 423
• • capital gain, 423
• • general principle, 421-422
• • pre-existing business, 422
• • proportionate calculation possible, 422
• • work in progress, 422
• generally
• • benefits in new job, 420
• • calculation of deductions, 420
• • constructive dismissal, 417-418
• • determination of amounts, 420
• • different currencies, 420
• • draw against future earnings, 419
• • earnings within notice period, 418
• • employment earnings, 418
• • failure to deduct, 417
• • general principle, 417
• • new job ending before notice period, 419
• • new job loss, 419
• • notice period not over, 419
• • overtime earnings, 419
• • sums not otherwise earned, 418
• higher-paying new job, 420-421
• mitigation expenses, deduction of, 424-425
Mitigation of damages
• career changes
• • retraining, 403-404
• • similar or dissimilar job, 401-403
• contractual notice periods, 391-392
• deduction of earnings in mitigation. *See* **Mitigation earnings**
• duty to mitigate
• • acceptable evidence, 390
• • benefits loss, 293-294
• • change of employers, 52
• • constructive dismissal situations, 85
• • continuing duty, 390

Mitigation of damages — *continued*
- death or disability during notice period, 390
- efforts and likely results, 390
- general principles, 389
- no duty to settle, 389
- onus to prove, 390
- reasonable steps only, 389
- statutory employment schemes, 389
- total lack of effort, 390
- failure to mitigate
 - confidential information, refusal to divulge, 411
 - conflict resolution, failure to participate in, 416
 - dismissing employer's offer, rejection of, 411-413
 - early retirement, refusal of, 415
 - Employment Insurance, no requirement to apply, 415
 - generally, 392-393
 - leave of absence, refusal, 415
 - new employer's offer, rejection of, 409-411
 - no duty to inquire, 415
 - professional help, failure to seek, 415
 - relocation counselling, refusal of, 414
 - return to bargaining unit, failure to, 415
 - salary continuation, refusal of, 414
 - working notice, refusal of, 413-414
- fixed-term contracts, 391-392
- geographical transfer, 115
- mitigation expenses
 - costs of new job, 358
 - generally, 358
 - mitigation earnings, deduction from, 424-425
 - new business expenses, 359
 - new business losses, 359
 - retraining costs, 358-359
- no condonation if mitigating, 86
- reasonable mitigation efforts
 - quality of job search efforts
  - consulting work, 400
  - general principles, 398
  - jobs with equal pay, 399
  - part-time work, 400
  - reasonable search efforts, 398
  - restricted efforts, 399
  - résumé distribution, 399
  - sufficient time, 399
  - unreasonable search efforts, 398
  - volunteer work, 399
 - refusal of assistance from employer, 400
 - standard of reasonableness, 395
 - timing of job search efforts, 395-398
- relocation
 - general principles, 404
 - industry custom, 405
 - long-distance relocation, 405
 - need to commute, 406
 - unnecessary relocation, 406
 - where not required, 405
 - where required, 405
 - starting a business, 406-407

Moonlighting, 158-159
Mortgage subsidy, 348
Moving expenses
- capital loss on resale, 357
- capital profit, 357
- dismissal must cause move, 355
- exceptions, 356
- house-related claims, 357-358
- moving or sale of specific items, 356
- no loss or avoidable loss, 355
- previous relocation costs, 357-358
- reasonableness of move, 355
- returning to original location, 356
- sale of home, 356-357
- types of costs awarded, 356

Multi-location employers, 115
Multiple possible employers, 33
Municipal employees
- abolition of position, 23
- at-will employment
 - presumption against, 21
 - rebuttals of, 22
- collective agreement coverage, 23
- discontinuance of position, 23
- exclusion, 3
- grievance schemes, 23
- narrow interpretation of statutes, 22
- notice of termination, statutory limit on, 22
- procedural fairness, right to, 23
- Saskatchewan statute, 22-23
- statutory dismissal procedure, 23
- statutory limitation, 21
- statutory protection of officers, 22

Mutual commitment, assumption of, 9

N

Natural justice, 129-130
Near cause, 289
Negative publicity, 285
Neglect of duty, 170-171
Negligence, 432
Negligent infliction of mental suffering, 433
Negligent misrepresentation, 432
New assignments, 100
New business expenses, 359
New business losses, 359
News release, 378
No service, 265
Non-cause explanation of dismissal, 137-138
Non-competition agreement, 250
Non-competition clause, 275
Non-disclosure of information, 164-165

Non-employees
- just cause, 31
- notice of termination and, 30-31

***Non est factum*, 224**
Non-management employees, 257
Non-unionized employees, 206-207, 269
Notice formulas, 252
Notice of resignation, 246, 248-249
Notice of termination
- *see also* **Reasonable notice**
- agents, 30
- assignment employees, 28-29
- casual employees, 28-29
- contractual notice provisions, 298
- delay in giving, 286
- effective date
  - changes during notice period, 47
  - constructive dismissal, 47
  - disability or other leave, 47-48
  - general principle, 46
  - working notice, 46, 47
- expiration of fixed-term contract, with continued employment, 239-240
- express termination
  - examples of effective notice, 45-46
  - form of notice, 43
  - generally, 42
  - notice must be received, 43
  - notice with indeterminate date, 45
- independent contractors, 30
- intermediates, 30
- no repudiation where notice given, 80
- part-time employees, 29
- precedents
  - just cause, 439
  - no just cause, 439-440
- probationary employment, 18
- project employees, 28-29
- refusal to work through notice period, 76
- resignation
  - improper notice given, 71
  - notice period, during, 70-71
- seasonal employees, 29
- statutory limit on
  - Crown employees, 22
  - municipal employees, 22
  - public employees, 22
- statutory termination notice provisions
  - group termination notice, 429
  - individual termination notice, 427-428
- temporary employees, 28-29

Notice period. *See* **Reasonable notice**
Novation
- factors to be considered, 53
- forced resignation, 53
- generally, 52-53
- time to decide on acceptance, 53

O

Objective standard
- dishonesty, 145
- downward change in status, 103
- unacceptable performance, 143

Objective test
- express termination at common law, 45
- frustration, 60
- humiliating treatment, 110
- reasonableness of continuing relationship, 413
- resignation, 63
- summary dismissal, 120

Off-the-job conduct
- criminal conduct, 201-202
- general principles
  - human rights, 200
  - objective view, 199
  - relationship to job, 199-200
- sexual conduct, 200-201

Off-the-job intoxication, 197
Offers of employment, 234-235
Office holders
- duty of fairness, 128-129
- office held at pleasure, and fairness, 129
- rights, 3, 31

Office reassignment, 101
Office space and equipment, 351
On-going negotiations, 44
One-industry town, 278
Onus to prove
- authenticity of contract, 225
- authorization for absence from work, 190
- condonation of misconduct, proof of, 134-135
- constructive dismissal, 83
- duty to warn, 125
- issue estoppel, 212
- just cause, 123-124
- layoffs, 49
- mitigation efforts, 390
- resignation, 64
- summary dismissal, 120

Oppression remedy, 25
Oral agreements, 223
Organizational documents, 235-236
Other jobs with same employer, 400
Other types of, 12-13
Out-of-town interviews, 354
Outplacement counselling, 400
Outside business interests, 159
Overpayments, 434
Overtime
- earnings in new job, 419
- elimination of, 91
- outstanding, claim for, 431
- pay, and damages, 303-304

P

Parental leave, 385, 396
Parol evidence rule
- defined, 224
- examples, 224-225
- exceptions, 224-225

Part-time employees
- change in status to, 268-269
- continuation of part-time work, 400
- generally, 29
- mitigation earnings and, 421
- reasonable notice, and, 256

Parties' conduct
- assurance of job security, 283-284
- manner of dismissal, 284-285

Partners
- employee capacity, in, 25
- employer, as, 37

Passive rebellion, 167
Patents, 375
Pay changes
- commissions
- • calculation method, change in, 95-96
- • changes in, 91
- • withholding commissions, 96
- overtime, 91
- pay
- • example where no constructive dismissal, 89
- • failure to hold annual review, 90
- • failure to increase, 90
- • failure to pay, 89
- • failure to renegotiate, 90
- • job reclassification, 90
- • layoffs, 92
- • limit on earnings, 89-90
- • minor changes in pay, 90
- • payment method, 92
- • red-circling, 90
- • reduction during probationary period, 91
- • reduction in pay, 89
- • salary freeze, 90-91
- • salary reduction when job changed, 90

Pay equity complaint, 215
Pay in lieu of notice
- deduction from damage award, 382
- employer's obligation, 245
- examples where constructive dismissal, 118
- general principle, 118
- termination date, and, 46, 47
- voluntary severance package, interest in, 118
- working notice, choice of, *vs.*, 245-246
- wrongful dismissal despite adequate notice, 118

Pay rate, 300-301
Payment in kind, 383
Payment method changes, 92
Payroll practices

- absence of, 36
- common control, and, 35

Pension Adjustment Factor, 337
Pension plans
- actuarial calculation, 337
- calculation of damages, 337-338
- commuted value, 337
- contractual entitlement, 335
- deductions from damage award, 383-384
- early retirement option, 338-339
- entitlement to damages, 335-336
- gratuitous pension benefits, 339
- indexing, 338
- method of paying damages, 339
- mistake, 339
- notice period contributions, 336
- Pension Adjustment Factor, 337
- pension payments, 219
- portability, 336
- post-retirement benefits, 339
- refund of pension contributions, 339
- retirement, effect of, 338-339
- specific performance orders, 378
- transfer of refund into RRSP, 339
- vesting, 265, 336, 337

Performance standards, 140-141
Performance warnings, 127
Permanence, intention of, 12
Permanently incapable, 191
Personal appearance and habits, 185
Personal characteristics
- accumulated sick leave, 276
- criminal charges, 277
- finances, 277
- health or disability, 276
- late career change, 277
- marital status, 275-276
- personality, 276
- pregnancy, 276
- racial origin, 276-277
- self-imposed limits, 277
- transience, 277

Personal interests, 159-160
Personal liability. *See* **Liability**
Personal services corporations, 32
Personal use of employer's tools, 160
Personality, 276
Personality conflicts, 137, 180
- *see also* Workplace conflicts

Personnel records, 164
Petition into bankruptcy, 56
Planning to compete, 158
Pleadings
- aggravated and punitive damages, 363
- just cause allegations, 124

Police officers, 3
- *see also* Office holders; Statute-governed employment

Poor performance. *See* **Unacceptable performance**

Poor performance allegations, 369
Post-dismissal financial decisions, 373
Post-retirement benefits, 339
Post-termination events, 247
Pre-employment contract, 206, 431
Precariousness of position, 260-261
Precedents
- release, 441
- termination notice
- • just cause, 439
- • no just cause, 439-440
- warning letter
- • misconduct, final warning, 437-438
- • misconduct, first instance, 437
- • poor performance, 438

Pregnancy, 184, 276, 396
Presumption of indefinite employment, 7
Previous civil action, 216
Principles of wrongful dismissal law
- common law principle, 1-2
- exclusions
- • described, 3
- • employees with limited rights, 3
- • office holders' rights, 3
- illegal contracts, 3-4
- Quebec principle, 2

Prisoners, 32
Private disagreements, 173
Private pension plans. *See* **Pension plans**
Probationary employees, 3, 206, 257
Probationary employment
- disciplinary probation
- • described, 15
- • full period to show improvement, 20
- • good faith and objectivity requirement, 20
- • imposition of, 20
- • timing of probation, 20
- • unacceptable performance, 143
- initial trial period, 15, 143
- probationary period
- • acquiescence, effect of, 17-18
- • agreement required before start of work, 15-16
- • assurances, effect of, 17
- • details in dispute, 17
- • expiration of, 18
- • express agreement required, 15
- • extension of probationary period, 17
- • extensions found, 18
- • specific terms required, 16
- • statutory probation, 16
- • when found, 16-17
- • when not found, 16
- termination
- • collective agreement, 20
- • conditions for reducing notice, 18
- • duty to warn, 19
- • employer's reliance on probation, 20
- • expected standard, employee's knowledge of, 19
- • failure to follow disciplinary procedure, 19
- • improper dismissal, 20
- • just cause and, 18-19
- • nonperformance-related reason, 19
- • notice, right to reduce, 18
- • objective assessment, requirement of, 19
- • performance-related reason, 19
- • principle of fairness, 18
- • proper training, requirement of, 19
- • timing of dismissal, 19
- types of, 15

Probationary period
- acquiescence, effect of, 17-18
- agreement required before start of work, 15-16
- assurances, effect of, 17
- details in dispute, 17
- expiration of, 18
- express agreement required, 15
- extension of probationary period, 17
- extensions found, 18
- implied, 85
- length of, and reasonable notice period, 249
- pay reduction during, 91
- specific terms required, 16
- statutory probation, 16
- unacceptable performance during, 143
- when found, 16-17
- when not found, 16

Procedural failures, 287
Procedural fairness
- examples where duty met, 130
- examples where duty not met, 130-131
- failure to comply with duty, 130-131
- lack of hearing not significant, 130-131
- natural justice, *vs.*, 129-130
- right to
- • Crown employees, 23
- • municipal employees, 23
- • public employees, 23
- right to be heard, 130
- third-party decision, 130-131

Profanity, 174
Professional advice, 374-375
Professional certification, 373
Professional education, 349
Professional fees, 349
Professional qualifications, 152-153
Professionals
- examples of, 26
- reasonable notice charts, 467-471

Profit sharing, changes in, 92-93
Profit-sharing plans, 319-320
Project employment
- expectations of project length, 10
- generally, 28-29
- special considerations, 10

Promotions, 240-241
Property orders, 379
Property sold after dismissal, 373
Proprietary information, 375
Public complaint, 173, 175-176
Public employees
- abolition of position, 23
- at-will employment
- • presumption against, 21
- • • rebuttals of, 22
- collective agreement coverage, 23
- discontinuance of position, 23
- grievance procedures, existence of, 208
- grievance schemes, 23
- narrow interpretation of statutes, 22
- notice of termination, statutory limit on, 22
- procedural fairness, right to, 23
- Saskatchewan statute, 22-23
- statutory dismissal procedure, 23
- statutory limitation, 21
- statutory protection of officers, 22

Public relations expenses, 375
Public servants. *See* **Public employees**
Public visibility, 259
Punitive damages
- *see also* **Aggravated damages**
- conduct following dismissal, 370
- conduct justifying damages, 368-369
- conduct not justifying damages, 368
- definition of terms, 362-363
- employee's conduct, 368
- general principles, 367-368
- harassment, 370
- poor performance allegations, 369
- post-dismissal conduct justifying damages, 370
- purpose of, 361
- relationship to other damages, 368
- retaliation, 370
- untrue cause allegations, 369
- use of, 361

Q

Qualifications, 273-274
Qualifications, professional, 152-153
Quantum meruit, 301
Quebec
- aggravated and punitive damages, 363
- reasonable notice, 2, 248
- similar considerations, 2

R

Racial origin, 276-277
Rate of pay, 300-301
Reasonable belief, 44
Reasonable mitigation efforts
- quality of job search efforts
- • consulting work, 400

- • general principles, 398
- • jobs with equal pay, 399
- • part-time work, 400
- • reasonable search efforts, 398
- • restricted efforts, 399
- • résumé distribution, 399
- • sufficient time, 399
- • unreasonable search efforts, 398
- • volunteer work, 399
- refusal of assistance from employer, 400
- standard of reasonableness, 395
- timing of job search efforts, 395-398

Reasonable notice
- age
- • employees in their 40s, 263-264
- • employees in their 50s and up, 263
- • employees over 65, 264
- • employees under 40, 264
- • general rule, 263
- • pension and benefits vesting, 265
- • planned retirement, 264-265
- • service length, and, 264
- • where age no hindrance to job search, 264
- ballpark approach, 252, 253
- character of employment
- • job status, 256-258
- • nature of industry and employer, 259-260
- • nature of job, 258-259
- • precariousness, 260-261
- • significance of job character, 255-256
- • specialization, degree of, 258
- • time of assessment of job status, 261-262
- court award, purpose of, 246
- deference on appeal, 253
- factors
- • individual decision, 247-248
- • other factors, 248
- • Quebec approach, 248
- job availability
- • economic climate, 278-279
- • employer's financial problems, 279-280
- • experience, 273-274
- • geographic location, 278
- • job characteristics, 274-275
- • personal characteristics, 275-277
- • proof of, 280-281
- • qualifications, 273-274
- • training, 273-274
- maximum notice, 252
- minimum notice, 251
- no deference on appeal, 253
- no deference to employer, 252-253
- notice formulas, 252
- notice period
- • aggravated and punitive damages, *vs.*, 362
- • based on estimate, 246
- • contractual, 391-392
- • cutting-off, 247
- • death or disability during, 390

Reasonable notice — *continued*
- • earnings within, 418
- • holidays during, 347
- • impending vesting of pension benefits, 339
- • new job ending before notice period, 419
- • pension plan contributions, 336
- • previous notice period, 249
- • purpose of, 246
- • raises during, 301-302
- • reduced, and failure to mitigate, 393
- • trial before expiry of, 419
- • vacation pay for, 345
- parties' conduct
- • assurance of job security, 283-284
- • employee's merits, 289-290
- • employee's near cause, 289
- • employer's bad faith, 286-289
- • manner of dismissal, 284-285
- parties' expectations
- • amount claimed by employee, 248
- • collective agreement, 249
- • contracts, 249
- • employer's other judgments, 250
- • employer's other settlements, 250
- • employer's policy, 250
- • industry custom, 250-251
- • non-competition agreement, 250
- • notice of resignation, 248-249
- • planned departure, 249
- • previous notice period, 249
- • probation, length of, 249
- • third-party notice, 249
- • weight given to, 248
- parties' obligations
- • choice of working notice or pay in lieu, 245-246
- • employee's notice, 246
- • pay in lieu of notice, 245
- • requirement of reasonable notice, 245
- Quebec, in, 2, 248
- service length
- • importance of, 265
- • interaction with character of job, 266
- • long service, 265, 266
- • middle ranges, 266
- • no service, 265
- • short service, 265, 266
- • total service, 266
- service length calculations
- • change in employer, 269-270
- • change of employment status
- • • business owner, change to, 269
- • • employee, change to, 268, 269
- • • exception, 268
- • • full-time, change to, 268
- • • non-union, change to, 269
- • • part-time, change to, 268-269
- • • parties' intentions, 268
- • enticement by employer, 270-271
- • interruption in service

- • • frequent layoffs, 267
- • • length of gap, 267-268
- • • parties' treatment, 267
- • • past service, no recognition of, 267
- • • rehiring with recognition, 267
- • relocation, 271
- statutory period, effect of, 251
- time for assessment
- • cutting-off notice period, 247
- • notice fixed on termination, 247
- • post-termination events, 247
- • views upon hiring, irrelevance of, 246
- • where re-employed before trial, 247

Reasonable notice charts
- administrators, 472-476
- clerical employees, 489-493
- foremen, 463-467
- labourers, 493-497
- lower management, 458-462
- marketing employees, 477-484
- middle management, 450-458
- miscellaneous employees, 497-500
- professionals, 467-471
- sales employees, 477-484
- sales/marketing managers, 477-484
- senior executives, 443-446
- skilled employees, 484-488
- supervisors, 463-467
- technical employees, 484-488
- upper management, 447-450

Reassignment
- where permitted in contract, 80
- without demotion
- • agreement to reassignment, 102
- • custom of the trade, 102
- • examples where constructive dismissal, 102-103
- • examples where no constructive dismissal, 103
- • express agreement, 102
- • general principles, 102
- • right *vs.* obligation, 102

Receivers
- appointment of, 56
- liability, 37-38

Rectification, 379
Red-circling, 90
Redundancy, 202-203
References, 289, 366, 433
Refusal of assistance from employer, 400
Refusal to perform duties, 170-171
Refusal to return to work. *See* **Work refusals**
Registered Retirement Savings Plans (RRSPs). *See* **RRSP**
Reinstatement, 24, 376-377
Related actions
- by employees
- • contract claims, 431-432
- • statutory claims, 431-432
- • tort claims, 432-434

Related entities
- absence of payroll practices, 36
- employee's consent to change, 34
- employer, identification of, 34
- employment standards, 36
- multiple possible employers, 35
- payroll practices and common control, 35
- rebuttal of presumption, 35
- services provided to multiple entities, 35

Releases
- consideration for, 221
- demand for, before payment, 221
- examples where release binding, 220
- examples where release not binding, 220-221
- general principle, 220
- human rights claim, effect on, 221
- precedent, 441
- refusal to sign, 76
- settlements, 217
- shareholder agreement, in, 323

Reliance on employment, losses in, 371-372

Religious ministers, 32

Relocation
- effect of, 55
- geographical transfers
- • constructive dismissal after move, 116
- • employer's financial situation, 115
- • examples where constructive dismissal, 115-116
- • examples where no constructive dismissal, 116
- • failure to mitigate, 115
- • implied terms, 114
- • multi-location employers, 115
- • multiple changes, 114
- • reasonableness, test of, 114-115
- mitigation of damages
- • general principles, 404
- • industry custom, 405
- • long-distance relocation, 405
- • need to commute, 406
- • unnecessary relocation, 406
- • where not required, 405
- • where required, 405

Relocation counselling
- payments, 382
- refusal of, 414

Remedies
- *see also* **Damages**
- employers
- • dismissal for cause, 119
- equitable remedies, 371
- failure to enter into written contract, 226-227
- reinstatement, 376-377
- specific performance, 377-379

Remuneration
- car allowances as, 341-342
- changes in
- • benefits, changes in, 93-94
- • bonuses, changes in, 92-93
- • computation methods, changes in
- • • accounts, change in, 96
- • • change of mix, 95
- • • general principles, 94-95
- • • manner of calculating commissions, 95-96
- • • reserve, imposition of, 96
- • • salary plus commission mix, 95
- • • salary to hourly rate or piecework, 95
- • • surcharge, imposition of, 96
- • • territory, change in, 96
- • • withholding commissions, 96
- • pay changes
- • • commissions, 91, 95-96
- • • overtime, 91
- • • pay, 89-92
- • profit sharing, changes in, 92-93
- damages for
- • advances, 304-305
- • bonuses. *See* **Bonuses**
- • commissions. *See* **Commissions**
- • directors' fees, 304-305
- • expenses, 304-305
- • extra fees for extra services, 304
- • general principles, 299-300
- • incentives, 304
- • overtime pay, 303-304
- • pay rate, 300-301
- • profit-sharing plans, 319-320
- • *quantum meruit*, 301
- • raises during notice period, 301-302
- • salary and wages, 300
- • share-purchase loan, 321
- • shift premiums, 304
- • stock options, 320-323
- • stock purchase plans, 321-322
- • tips or gratuities, 304
- dissimilar pay, 402

Renewal option, 297

Repeated minor misconduct, 122

Replacement employee, action against, 38-39

Reporting level changes, 103-104

Repossession of vehicle, 344

Repudiation
- *see also* **Constructive dismissal**
- absence from work
- • authorized absence, 75
- • failure to return after illness, 75
- • unauthorized absence, 75
- damages and, 296
- by employee
- • context, importance of, 74
- • described, 41, 73
- • general principles
- • • employer must act, 73
- • • examples of repudiation, 73

Index

Repudiation — *continued*
- • inability to attend work
- • • acceptance of constructive dismissal, 76
- • • conflicting work, acceptance of, 75
- • • failure to return after layoff, 75
- • • seeking new work, 76
- • legal dispute with employer
- • • duty to bargain in good faith, 76
- • • refusal to sign release or agree to settlement, 76
- • • refusal to work through notice period, 76
- • • suing employer, 76-77
- • reasonable excuse, 73
- • work refusals
- • • examples where no repudiation, 74-75
- • • refusal to accept work assignment, 74
- • • refusal to report to work, 74
- by employer
- • generally, 41
- factors to consider, 83
- no repudiation where notice given, 80
- resignation, *vs.*, 66
- without changing specific term, 81

Request to be let go, 64
Requisite mental capacity, lack of, 70
Reserve, 96
Resignation
- conduct amounting to resignation
- • examples of where resignation due to absence from work, 67-68
- • examples where no resignation based on conduct, 66-67
- • examples where resignation based on conduct, 66
- • examples where resignation by absence from work, 67
- • refusal to return to work, 67
- • resignation *vs.* repudiation, 66
- consequences
- • changes in employment after resignation, 71
- • disability payments, entitlement to, 71
- • employer not obligated to accept, 70
- • employer's options, 70
- • general principle, 70
- • improper notice given, 71
- • notice period, during, 70-71
- • return to work following resignation, 71
- • where employer misrepresentation, 71
- following constructive dismissal
- • allegations of constructive dismissal, 69
- • constructive dismissal must exist, 69
- • general principle, 69
- • hard bargaining, 69
- • right to sue, trigger of, 80
- dismissal before resignation, and vacation pay, 346
- forced resignation, 117
- general principles
- • clear and unequivocal, 63
- • indication of true intention, 64
- • objective test, 63
- • true reflection of employee's intention, 63-64
- • voluntary nature of resignation, 63
- involuntary resignation
- • duress, 68
- • examples of, 69
- • severance pay, acceptance of, 68
- • voluntary, *vs.*, 68
- notice of, 246, 248-249
- onus on employee, 64
- planned, and damages, 296
- requisite mental capacity, lack of
- • examples where resignation binding, 70
- • general principle, 70
- • threats to resign, 64
- voluntary resignation
- • examples of voluntary resignation, 68-69
- • involuntary resignation, *vs.*, 68
- words amounting to resignation
- • conditional resignation, 64-65
- • expressions of dissatisfaction, 65-66
- • expressions of opinion, 65
- • hypothetical statements, 65
- • request to be let go, 64
- wrongful resignation claim, 435

Restrictive covenants, 378
Résumé disclosure, 152-153
Résumé distribution, 399
Retaliation, 370
Retaliatory discharge, 433
Retirement
- damages, ending of, 296
- documents, 236-237
- early retirement
- • offer, 117
- • option of, and damages, 338-339
- • refusal of, 415
- forced retirement, 116, 117
- mandatory retirement age, imposition of, 116
- planned retirement, effect of, 264-265
- voluntary retirement agreement, 237

Retiring allowance, 352
Retraining, 358-359, 403-404, 425
Revival of past misconduct
- cumulative effect or pattern, 138
- new instance, 138

Room-and-board allowance, 347-348
RRSP
- contributions, 334-335
- transfer of contribution refund into, 339

S

Salary, 300
Salary continuation, 220, 292, 382
Salary freeze, 90-91

Salary level, 275
Sale of home, 356-357
Sale or transfer of business
- *see also* Change of employer
- general principles, 54-55
- liability
- • both employers liable, 34
- • issues, 33-34
- • new employer, liability of, 34
- • old employer, liability of, 34
- new employer's policies, 55

Sales documents, 236
Salespersons or sales agents
- commissioned, 274-275
- competing lines, 157
- employee *vs.* independent contractor, 27
- employees, examples of, 27
- general principle, 157
- independent contractors, examples of, 27-28
- intermediate status, examples of, 28
- long-term sales, 258
- non-competing lines, 157
- reasonable notice charts
- • sales employees, 477-484
- • sales/marketing managers, 477-484
- right of first refusal, 157
- sales documents, 236
- secret or unauthorized discounts, 157
- skills of, 274

Savings plan contributions, 352
Schedule changes, 106-107
Seasonal employment
- definite-term employment, and, 12
- dismissal during season, 29
- generally, 29
- notice period, 275
- reasonable notice, and, 258
- unstable job, 259

Secondment, 32
Secret discounts, 157
Self-induced frustration
- examples of self-induced frustration, 60
- examples where no self-induced frustration, 60
- generally, 60

Senior executives
- reasonable notice charts, 443-446

Seniority, loss of, 372-373
Service length
- age, and, 264
- agreement between employer, 54
- calculation of
- • change in employer, 269-270
- • change of employment status
- • • business owner, change to, 269
- • • employee, change to, 268, 269
- • • exception, 268
- • • full-time, change to, 268
- • • non-union, change to, 269
- • • part-time, change to, 268-269
- • • parties' intentions, 268
- • • enticement by employer, 270-271
- • • interruption in service
- • • • frequent layoffs, 267
- • • • length of gap, 267-268
- • • • parties' treatment, 267
- • • • past service, no recognition of, 267
- • • • rehiring with recognition, 267
- • • relocation, 271
- circumstances showing non-continuous service, 53-54
- importance of, 265
- interaction with character of job, 266
- long service, 265, 266
- middle ranges, 266
- no service, 265
- short service, 265, 266
- statutory service length, 54
- total service, 266
- vendor's promise to terminate employment relationships, 54
- where ownership changes, 53

Settlements
- accord and satisfaction, 218-220
- agreements in principle, 218
- breach of settlement, 218
- duty of disclosure, 218
- employer's other settlements, and notice period, 250
- general principle, 217
- independent legal advice, 218
- inequality of bargaining power, 217-218
- no duty to settle, 389
- oral acceptance, 218
- release, 217
- unaccepted offers, 218
- undue pressure, 217

Severance agreement. *See* **Termination agreements**
Severance clause
- express duty to mitigate, requirement of, 242
- termination clause, *vs.*, 241-242

Severance pay and arrangements
- accord and satisfaction, 218-220
- bad faith, 288
- cheque cashing, 219
- content of offer, 288
- deductions from damage award, 382
- discovery of misconduct after acceptance of, 123
- examples where granted, 242
- failure to promptly pay, 288-289
- involuntary resignation, and, 68
- timing and negotiations, 288
- undue pressure, 217
- voluntary severance package, interest in, 118

Sexual conduct, 200-201
Sexual harassment, 182-184, 201

Share-purchase loan, 321
Shareholder agreements, 236, 323
Shareholders
- dealings with, and cause for dismissal, 163-164
- employee rights, no impact on, 25
- personal liability
  - other amounts, 36-37
  - other causes of action, 36
  - piercing the corporate veil, 36
  - statutory liability, 36
  - wages, 36

Shift premiums, 304
Short service, 265, 266
Sick leave, 61, 329-330
Sick pay, 382-383
Similar job, 401-403
Single incidents
- disobedience, of, 167
- insolence or insubordination, 173-174
- misconduct, of, 121-122
- unacceptable performance, of, 141

Skilled employees
- reasonable notice charts, 484-488

Small industry, 259
Specialization, 258
Specialized job, 274
Specific performance
- definition, 377-378
- employers' policies, voiding of, 379
- employment record, deletions in, 378
- letter of reference, 378
- lifetime benefits, 378
- news release, 378
- payment of offer, 378
- pensions, 378
- property orders, 379
- rectification, 379
- reinstatement, 376-377
- restrictive covenants, 378

Spouses, 375-376
Standard form contracts, 229
Standard of conduct policies, 232
Starting a business
- mitigation earnings, and
  - award during notice period, 422
  - business equity and income attribution, 423
  - business expenses, 423-424
  - business losses, 423
  - capital gain, 423
  - general principle, 421-422
  - pre-existing business, 422
  - proportionate calculation possible, 422
  - work in progress, 422
- mitigation of damages, 406-407

Statute-governed employment
- *see also* **Office holders**
- affected employees, 23
- collective agreement, 24
- common statutory terms, 23-24
- duty to mitigate, 389
- exclusion, 3
- job abolishment by statute, 24
- judicial review, 24
- reinstatement *vs.* wrongful dismissal, 24
- statutory dismissal procedure, 24
- transfers, 23

Statute law
- change of employer, 51
- common law, effect on, 2
- economic problems or reorganization, 203
- statutory interpretation, 22

Statutory claims, 431-432
Statutory dismissal procedure
- Crown employees, 23
- duty of fairness, 24
- municipal employees, 23
- public employees, 23
- statute-governed employment, 24

Statutory holiday pay, 346-347
Statutory office holders, 3
Statutory probation, 16
Statutory termination and severance pay, 56
Statutory termination notice provisions
- group termination notice, 429
- individual termination notice, 427-428

Stock options, 320-323
Stock purchase plans, 321-322
Strategic litigation, 420-421
Strikes
- economic problems, 203
- frustration and shutdown due to strikes, 62
- termination during, 49

Subscriptions, 351
Substance abuse, 197-198
Suing employer, 76-77, 177
Summary dismissal
- condonation of misconduct, 121
- degree of misconduct required, 119-120
- differing standards, 120
- employer's remedies, 119
- employment standards legislation, 121
- entire context of employee's actions, 120
- express agreement, 121
- financial loss, no need for, 121
- fundamental breach, 119, 120
- just cause as exception, 119
- narrow interpretation, 120
- objective test, 120
- onus, 120
- right to dismiss *vs.* discipline, 120-121

Supervisors
- reasonable notice charts, 463-467
- supervisory duties, 257

Suppliers, personal dealings with, 162-163
Surcharge, 96

Suspension
- disciplinary suspensions, 113
- effect of, 49

Suspicion of dishonesty, 147

T

Tardiness, 195-197
Tax advice, 374
Teachers, 3
- *see also* **Statute-governed employment**

Teamwork skills, 273
Technical employees
- reasonable notice charts, 484-488

Technical mistakes, 43
Technological skills, 273
Temporary assignments, 100
Temporary employees
- change of status, 29
- generally, 28-29
- just cause, and, 31
- mitigation earnings and, 421

Temporary illness, 191
Termination agreements
- definition, 242
- duty to disclose job prospects, 243-244
- employment standards, 244
- examples where overturned, 243
- examples where upheld, 242-243
- payment issues, 244
- separate contract, 242

Termination clause
- duty to mitigate, 242
- fixed-term contract, 9
- severance clause, *vs.*, 241-242

Termination notice. *See* **Notice of termination**
Termination of employment
- constructive dismissal, *vs.*, 84
- express termination
- • common law, at, 42-46
- • under by-law, contract or statute, 42
- failure to explain, 287
- general principles
- • constructive dismissal, 42
- • question of fact, 42
- • repudiation by employee, 41
- • repudiation by employer, 41
- • termination of contract, 41
- • wrongful termination, 41
- layoff, *vs.*, 48-49
- non-cause explanation of dismissal, 137-138
- notice of termination. *See* **Notice of termination**
- strike, during, 49
- suspension, 49

Termination pay. *See* **Pay in lieu of notice**
Termination pay policies, 232
Territory changes, 96

Third-party notice, 249
Threats to resign, 64
Tickets, 351
Timing of dismissal, 275, 287
Timing of misconduct
- after-acquired knowledge, 123
- limits, 123
- misconduct after dismissal, 123
- settlement or offer of settlement, 123

Tips, 304
Tort claims
- damages, *vs.* mental distress damages, 363
- employees, by
- • abusive discharge, 433
- • bad faith, 433
- • breach of fiduciary duty, 434
- • conspiracy, 432
- • defamation, 433
- • harassment, 433-434
- • inducing breach of contract, 432
- • interference with contractual relations, 432
- • mental suffering, infliction of, 433
- • negligence, 432
- • negligent misrepresentation, 432
- • retaliatory discharge, 433
- • wrongful referencing, 433
- employers, by
- • breach of fiduciary duty, 434-435
- • employee misconduct, 434
- • overpayments and loans, 434
- • wrongful resignation, 435

Total service, 266
Training, 273-274
Training programs, 373
Transfer agreement, 236
Transfer of employment. *See* **Employee transfers**
Transferable skills, 260, 273-274
Transience, 277
Travel benefits, 351
Treatment costs, 375
Trustees, 37-38

U

Unacceptable performance
- assistance program, 143
- chronic performance problems, 142
- general principles
- • employee's own fault, 139
- • employer's knowledge, 139
- • employment standards legislation, 139
- • just cause, existence of, 139
- • labour relations standard, 139
- • long-term employee, 139
- • mental or other illness, 139
- • overall performance, 139
- • serious financial loss, 139
- • warning, 140

Unacceptable performance — *continued*
- performance standards, 140-141
- probationary periods, 143
- single incident, 141
- written contract
  - - agreed subjective standard, 143
  - - contractual standards, 143
  - - industry custom, 143
  - - objective standard implied, 143
  - - silent on issue, 143

Unaccepted settlement offers, 218
Unauthorized absence, 75
Unauthorized discounts, 157
Uncharacteristic act of dishonesty, 146
Unconscionability, 224
Unfair dealings by employer
- allegations of theft or fraud, 111
- examples where constructive dismissal, 111-112
- examples where no constructive dismissal, 112
- general principles, 111

Unfair evaluation, 286
Unfavourable references, 366
Unforeseen events, 59
Unincorporated associations, 37
Union job, 274
Unions
- bargaining unit
  - - failure to return to bargaining unit, 372-373, 415
  - - right to return to, on reassignment, 102
- employers, as, 37
- policies, 232
- switch from union, 261-262, 269

Unjust dismissal adjudication, 215
Unjustified discipline, 113
Unstable industry, 260
Unstable job, 259
Untrue allegations, 287
Untrustworthy character, 148-150
Upper management
- reasonable notice charts, 447-450

V

Vacation before job hunt, 396
Vacation pay
- deduction from damage award, 382-383
- for notice period, 345
- outstanding, claim for, 431

Vacations, 194-195, 344-346, 373
Valuation date, 322
Visible job, 274
Voluntary assignment in bankruptcy, 37
Voluntary resignation. *See* **Resignation**
Voluntary retirement agreement, 237
Volunteer work, 399
Vulgar language, 174

W

Wages, 300, 431
Warnings
- anticipatory breach, *vs.*, 82
- content
  - - clarity of, 127
  - - consequences, clarification of, 127
  - - language barrier, 127
  - - no condonation, 127
  - - performance warnings, 127
  - - reconciliation with company policy, 127-128
  - - seriousness of, 127
  - - specific nature of, 127
  - - unequivocal and unambiguous, 127
- customer relations, 186
- discipline, *vs.*, 135-136
- duty to warn
  - - drinking on duty, 197
  - - employee relation problems, 181
  - - employer policy, 126
  - - form of warning, 126
  - - general principle, 125
  - - good faith requirement, 128
  - - job insecurity, of, 284
  - - multiple warnings, need for, 126
  - - new warning, need for, 126
  - - no duty to warn of investigation, 125
  - - onus, 125
  - - oral warning, risks of, 126
  - - warning to refute condonation, 125-126
  - - where no warning required, 125
- effect of, on condonation, 135-136
- express termination at common law, and, 45
- neglect of duty, 170
- poor performance after, 142
- refusal to perform duties, 170
- sexual and other harassment, 183
- unacceptable performance, 140
- warning letter
  - - misconduct, final warning, 437-438
  - - misconduct, first instance, 437
  - - poor performance, 438
- where repeated minor misconduct, 122

Warranty, 431
Winding up of employer, 56
Work absences. *See* **Absence from work**
Work hours, changes in, 106-107
Work refusals
- refusal to return to work
  - - examples of no resignation due to absence from work, 67-68
  - - examples of resignation by absence from work, 67
  - - failure to return after illness, 75
  - - resignation, as, 67
- repudiation by employee
  - - examples where no repudiation, 74-75
  - - refusal to accept work assignment, 74
  - - refusal to report to work, 74

Workers' compensation
- benefits, and deduction from damage award, 384
- coverage, 331

Working conditions
- financial burden imposed on employee, 107
- general principle, 106
- job requirement changes, 107
- location changes, 107
- schedule changes, 106-107
- substantially different, 402
- work hours, changes in, 106-107

Working expenses, 387

Working notice
- deduction from damages award, 381
- pay, *vs.*, 292
- pay in lieu, choice of, *vs.*, 245-246
- refusal to work through, 413-414
- termination date, and, 46, 47

Working under protest, 86

Workplace conflicts
- behaviour justifying dismissal, 180
- contractual clause for incompatibility, 180
- disagreement, 180-181
- employer size, 180
- examples where just cause, 180-181
- examples where no just cause, 181
- fault, 180
- managerial standards, 181-182

Workplace safety issues, 194

Written contracts
- failure to enter into, 226-227
- form of contract, 225-226
- general principles
  - ambiguous terms, interpretation of, 224
  - consideration, 224
  - definite-term contracts, 223
  - duress, 224
  - express agreements, 223
  - express agreements strictly interpreted, 223-224
  - illegality, 224
  - inequality of bargaining power, 224
  - *non est factum*, 224
  - normal contract rules, application of, 224
  - offer and acceptance, 224
  - unconscionability, 224
  - written *vs.* oral agreements, 223
- parol evidence rule
  - defined, 224
  - examples, 224-225
  - exceptions, 224-225

Written rules, 122

Wrongful dismissal
- breach of contract action, 41-42
- dismissing employer's offer, effect of, 413
- duress, 68
- general principles, 41
- question of fact, 42
- related actions. *See* **Related actions**
- strikes, termination during, 49

Wrongful dismissal law
- application, 1-2
- essential components of, 1-2
- general principles of, 1-4

Wrongful referencing, 433

Wrongful resignation, 435